Studying the Media

AN INTRODUCTION

Studying the Media

AN INTRODUCTION

Tim O'Sullivan
Brian Dutton
Philip Rayner

A member of the Hodder Headline Group
LONDON • NEW YORK • SYDNEY • AUCKLAND

First published in Great Britain 1994 by Edward Arnold
Seventh impression 1997 by Arnold,
a member of the Hodder Headline Group,
338 Euston Road, London NW1 3BH
175 Fifth Avenue, New York, NY 10010

Distributed exclusively in the USA by
St Martin's Press Inc.
175 Fifth Avenue, New York, NY 10010

British Library Cataloguing in Publication Data
A catalogue record for this book is available from the British Library

Library of Congress Cataloging-in-Publication Data
O'Sullivan, Tim
Studying the media; an introduction/
Tim O'Sullivan, Brian Dutton, and Philip Rayner.
p.   cm.
Includes bibliographical references and index.
1. Mass media. I. Dutton, Brian, 1952–
II. Rayner, Philip, 1947–   , III. Title,
p90.084   1994
302.23—dc20   94–14195

ISBN 0 340 59828 X

Typeset in Bembo by Wearset, Boldon, Tyne and Wear
Printed and bound in Great Britain by The Bath Press, Bath

Contents

Acknowledgements   vii

Preface   ix

1   The Mass Media and Modern Culture   1

2   Histories   25

3   Forms and Analysis   76

4   Representations   113

5   Audiences   150

6   Institutions and Production   186

7   Media Practice   246

8   Changing Media Worlds   271

Bibliography   297

Index   304

Acknowledgements

We would like to thank the many people who have directly and indirectly helped with the production of this book. The process would have made an interesting case study in its own right. In addition to recognising the daily support from our immediate families and partners, we also wish to acknowledge the following:

Colleagues, students and friends, inside and outside our current institutions – De Montfort University, Palmers College and Newbury College.

Lesley Riddle and the team at Edward Arnold, who managed the project with enthusiasm and patience.

The British Film Institute and their continuing work in the field of Media Education.

Arthur Parker, Mike Edwards and Roberta Harries, Subject Officers at the W.J.E.C.

Jarrod Cripps, Michelle Frances and Gavin Wilkinson, for photographic work.

The *Newbury Weekly News*.

The authors and publishers would also like to acknowledge the following for permission to use copyright material in this book:

Gianpaolo Barbieri; BBC World Service, International Broadcasting Audience Research Library; BBC; Mike Beharell; Steve Bell; Blackwell Publishers; Bodleian Library; *Broadcast*; Broadcasters' Audience Research Board Ltd (BARB); Cadbury Ltd; Central Office of Information; Central Statistical Office; Collett, Dickenson, Pearch and

Partners Limited; Comedia; Commission for Racial Equality; *Daily Mail*; *Daily Mirror*; *Daily Racism*; E.P. Dutton & Co, Publishers; Faber and Faber Ltd; *Fiji Times*; *Financial Times*; Gallup; *Gamesmaster*; Guild Film Distribution Ltd; *Hammer* magazine; *Hello Albert* fanzine; HMSO; Hutchinson; Index on Censorship; ITN; John Brown Publishing Ltd/House of Viz; *Just Seventeen*; KATZ Pictures Ltd; London Institute; Longman Group UK; Matthew Clark plc; Richard McRoberts, Thomas Nelson publishers; National Dairy Council; National Readership Surveys Ltd; *New Statesman & Society*; Our Price Video; Pandora; Panos Pictures Ltd; Philips Electronics UK Limited; *Post-Courier*; Public Records Office; Radio Joint Audience Research Limited; *Radio Times*; Random House; Reckitt & Colman Products; Rex Features; Routledge; Sage Publications Ltd; Rosemary Sare; Richard Smith; *Spectrum*, Independent Television Commission; *The Sun*; *Sunderland Echo*; *Television Week*; *Ten 8 magazine*; The British Phonographic Industry; *The Guardian*; The Hampden Trust; The Macmillan Press Ltd; *The Mag*; *The Times*; *The Voice*; *TV Times*; Vodafone Group Services; Wendy Wallace; Carol White, Red Flannel Films.

Preface

In the last ten years, media studies has become a well-known established subject in many schools, colleges and universities. This development has been rapid, and, if somewhat against the grain of educational policy in the period, the subject has proved to be popular and worthwhile for many students and teachers.

> It may be mocked by Education Secretary John Patten as 'cultural Disneyland for the weaker minded' and regarded with suspicion even by journalists and broadcasters, but media studies is the boom subject of the nineties.
>
> *D. Macleod, The Guardian, 8 November 1993*

This book is the product of our combined experience of learning and teaching about the media in a variety of different contexts and syllabuses – GCSE, A-level, BTEC, GNVQ, undergraduate and postgraduate courses – over the last fifteen years. These diverse experiences, in secondary, further and higher educational settings, have provided the main impetus for the book and we hope that what has emerged has a wide application and will prove generally useful for a range of post-16 courses in media studies, including A-level, BTEC and GNVQ, as well as providing introductory reading for undergraduate courses.

As practised teachers, we recognised the need for a book addressed directly to students, which would provide an *accessible and stimulating introduction* to the systematic study of the media. The book covers key areas of study relevant to A-level students but will also be useful in a number of other courses of study and investigation. It provides a *foundation framework* to build upon, and a range of activities and suggestions for further reading is an important component of each chapter.

Media studies is a broad-ranging and fast-moving field of enquiry. This has forced us to be selective, and while we have tried to use relevant and current examples wherever possible, it is in the nature of the subject that these will become dated fairly quickly. There is no one right way to use or read the book, although we have organised what follows according to a particular sequence. This sequence may and should be varied, however, according to your specific interests and focus; each chapter provides a relatively self-contained discussion and analysis, but there are a number of key themes which recur throughout the book as a whole.

The first chapter begins by examining the presence of the media in our everyday lives. *Media saturation* is outlined and discussed, and this provides a central theme which is revisited regularly in later sections. The second chapter focuses on *media histories*, looking at the growth and development of key media institutions and audiences from the nineteenth century to the present day. Chapter 3 explores *forms of media output* and develops an analytical framework for studying media texts in detail. This emphasis is, in turn, extended in Chapter 4, which examines key questions surrounding debates over forms of *media representation*. Chapter 5 is devoted to the study of *media audiences*, and the relationships between audiences and media output. Chapter 6 discusses some of the central characteristics of *media institutions* in the current period, and, using case studies, focuses on some of the major determinants of media industries and organisations. Chapter 7 looks at forms of *media practice* and emphasises the value and importance of practical production work in the context of media studies as a whole. Finally, the concluding chapter addresses issues surrounding change in the current period, in particular examining key developments in *new media technologies* and the emergence of global or *world-wide media networks*.

Media studies in particular and media education more generally have now reached an important and critical stage of development. The momentum and dynamics of rapid growth are interwoven with some major issues; the precarious position of the subject within the National Curriculum and educational policy, debates over the most appropriate direction and rationale for the subject, and public perceptions of the subject area all contribute to this critical state. This book seeks to introduce some of the most important areas of study and the principal analytical approaches and questions which currently comprise the subject area. Between now and the end of the century, the significance of the systematic study of the media will not diminish, although its form and focus may have to change to keep up with changes within and across the media themselves. If this book enables you to ask the right kinds of question about the media and to keep pace with their relationships within modern social and cultural life, then it will have worked. However, the real test of the book lies in its use and application. We welcome any responses to or comments about the book, or any suggestions you might have for subsequent editions. Please write to us via the publishers.

Tim O'Sullivan
Brian Dutton
Philip Rayner

November 1993

The mass media and modern culture

MEDIA SATURATION

It is important to begin a book of this type by noting the commanding presence and power of the mass media in modern public and private life. Those of us who live in western and other highly industrialised and technologised societies inhabit cultures and worlds which have been described as *media saturated*. This fact of modern life provides the major rationale for media studies. This chapter aims to introduce and frame some of the key issues at stake in this idea and to provide you with a range of arguments and suggestions for developing relevant project work.

Initially, you should start your study of the mass media by systematically considering and taking stock of your own patterns and relations of media involvement and use. Throughout the chapter you will encounter a range of material which may help you to start to identify distinctive aspects of your own personal forms of media involvement. You will also find different forms of data presented, indexing larger-scale, social patterns of media involvement and use, which characterise current trends and dimensions. These will also enable you to locate and compare your own media-related experience in the current context.

activity **1.1**

Keep a diary for one week, noting your daily involvement with different media. Analyse the patterns and habits which emerge as a result. When do you tend to use different media and for what kinds of purpose? How do you use different media?

1.2, 1.3 Photographs: Jarrod Cripps

Tunstall (1983) makes a distinction between primary, secondary and tertiary forms of media consumption. *Primary* involvement occurs when the television programme, magazine, newspaper or radio broadcast is the exclusive and focused activity. *Secondary* types of involvement are those forms of media consumption and use which accompany other activities; for instance, listening to the radio or music while doing other forms of work at home. The *tertiary* category of use is in one sense the weakest and least intensive relationship, where, for example, the TV or radio set is on in the background, or in another room in the household. As Tunstall notes:

> Tertiary could literally mean that one listens to the sound through the wall, while awaiting the next item; or tertiary might refer to glancing back and forth at a newspaper, opened at the TV schedule or the sports fixtures ... one might be glancing at the television with its sound turned down, listening to radio news-on-the-hour, while inspecting the schedules in the newspaper.
>
> *Tunstall (1983), p. 135*

Using these distinctions, you should be able to arrive at a rough estimate of the number of hours in the week you spent in forms of media involvement and consumption. You may also want to consider use of video, visits to the cinema and other 'out-of-home' forms of media consumption.

The results of this type of activity generally provide evidence at the personal level for our extensive, patterned, everyday involvements with the mass media. In many ways we are reliant and dependent upon regular contact with the mass media for information, opinion, entertainment, ideas and a range of other resources, which are deeply bound up with our continuing attempts to maintain a coherent sense of 'who' and 'where' we think we are. We should begin by noting, then, that the nature of cultural experience in modern societies has been profoundly affected by the development of systems of mass communication. Indeed, many writers have argued that modern societies and cultures require such systems and that what we understand as modern life would be impossible without specialised institutions which are generically referred to as the *mass media*. Books, magazines, adverts, newspapers, radio and television programmes, films and videos, records, tapes or CDs occupy a central and pivotal role in our lives, providing a more-or-less continuous flow of information and leisure facilities.

All the Time in the World?

One of the primary ways in which we can start to get a grip on the notion of 'media saturation' is to consider the amounts of time that we spend in media-related activities, largely in forms and practices of media consumption – reading, watching or listening. At a general level, these activities account for considerable proportions of our non-sleep, discretionary time (Table 1.1). If we take, for example, that most domestic of media, television, recent measures of TV viewing in the UK

1.4 Spectrum 1993, ITC

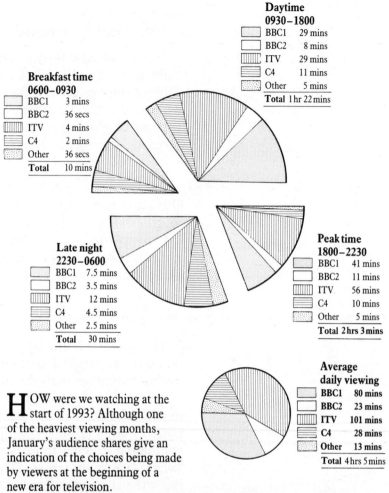

Breakfast time
0600–0930
	BBC1	3 mins
	BBC2	36 secs
	ITV	4 mins
	C4	2 mins
	Other	36 secs
Total		10 mins

Daytime
0930–1800
	BBC1	29 mins
	BBC2	8 mins
	ITV	29 mins
	C4	11 mins
	Other	5 mins
Total	1 hr 22 mins	

Late night
2230–0600
	BBC1	7.5 mins
	BBC2	3.5 mins
	ITV	12 mins
	C4	4.5 mins
	Other	2.5 mins
Total		30 mins

Peak time
1800–2230
	BBC1	41 mins
	BBC2	11 mins
	ITV	56 mins
	C4	10 mins
	Other	5 mins
Total 2 hrs 3 mins		

Average
daily viewing
	BBC1	**80 mins**
	BBC2	**23 mins**
	ITV	**101 mins**
	C4	**28 mins**
	Other	**13 mins**
Total 4 hrs 5 mins		

H OW were we watching at the start of 1993? Although one of the heaviest viewing months, January's audience shares give an indication of the choices being made by viewers at the beginning of a new era for television.

Figures given are average daily live viewing levels over four weeks ending 31 January 1993. 'Other' refers to the share taken by cable and satellite viewing across all individuals. Late night share reflects differing closedown times.

Source: AGB/BARB

point to a decrease in average amounts of time spent watching conventional, broadcast TV. In 1991, for instance, in spite of longer broadcasting hours and more choice of channels, viewers watched an average of just under 24 hours per week, compared to about 26 hours in the mid-1980s. This average decrease has been the source of not inconsiderable concern on the part of television companies in recent years. However, for our purposes here, we should note that it is 'normal' to spend about 3½ hours per day in the company of a television set which is switched on. To put it another way, we spend about one full 24-hour day per week continuously in the presence of TV. Commenting on the patterns of time spent with television in Britain and America, one recent study has extended this by suggesting:

If in such countries a typical viewer's total viewing during the year were laid end to end, it would fill two months, the whole of January and February say, for 24 hours each day! Although that may be hard to accept, it may be harder still to think of our imaginary television viewer having the set totally switched off throughout the other ten months of the year.

1.5 Spectrum 1991, ITC

Barwise and Ehrenberg (1988), p. 20

Children's Hours

% of viewers aged 4–9 years

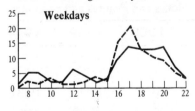

% of viewers aged 10–15 years

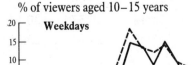

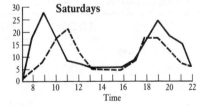

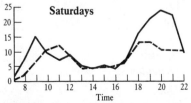

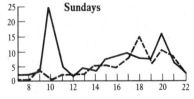

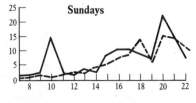

——ITV
– – –BBC

WHEN are they watching? The charts above show average sizes for ITV and BBC1 among children between 4 and 9 and those between 10 and 15 for a four-week period ending in early March. Weekday patterns are similar, dictated largely by availability for viewing. At weekends the two age groups clearly have different programme favourites.

1.6 Television viewing by type of
programme 1990, Social Trends,
1992, CSO

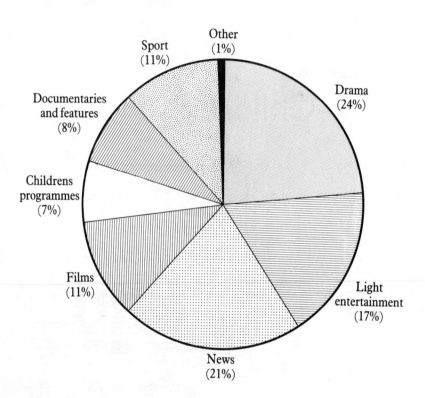

Percentages

Table 1.1 Television viewing[1]: by social class

United Kingdom			Hours and minutes and percentages		
	1986	**1987**	**1988**	**1989**	**1990**
Social class					
(hours:mins per week)					
ABC1	20:47	20:54	20:14	19:48	19:31
C2	25:18	24:40	25:25	25:00	24:13
DE	33:11	31:47	31:44	30:57	30:13
All persons	25:54	25:25	25:21	24:44	23:51
Reach[2]					
(percentages)					
Daily	*78*	*76*	*77*	*78*	*77*
Weekly	*94*	*93*	*94*	*94*	*94*

1. Viewing of live television broadcasts from the BBC, ITV and Channel Four
2. Percentage of UK population aged 4 and over who viewed TV for at
   least three consecutive minutes.
Source: HMSO 1992

Table 1.2 Radio listening: by age

United Kingdom				Hours and minutes and percentages	
	1986	**1987**	**1988**	**1989**	**1990**
Age group (hours:minutes per week)					
4–15 years	2:12	2:07	2:13	2:21	2:26
16–34 years	11:24	11:18	11:40	12:07	12:28
35–64 years	9:56	10:16	10:33	11:10	11:42
65 years and over	8:27	8:44	8:49	9:00	9:18
All aged 4 years and over	8:40	8:52	9:12	9:46	10:12
Reach[1] (percentages)					
Daily	*43*	*43*	*43*	*44*	*45*
Weekly	*75*	*74*	*73*	*74*	*74*

1 Percentage of UK population aged 4 and over who listened to radio for at least half a programme a day.
Source: HMSO 1992

Clearly, not all media demand and get the same kinds of time and attention as television. Listening to radio, for example, is estimated on average to account for about 10 additional hours per week (Table 1.2), and we make an average of 1½ visits per year to the cinema (Table 1.3). We should also note that this kind of data is based on averages, large-scale estimates of media consumption which on closer scrutiny vary considerably in the context of different lifestyles and their associated dimensions of age, gender, class, affluence and other significant factors. In addition, some of the key assumptions concerning the ability of this kind of data to 'measure' accu-

Table 1.3 Attendance at cinemas[1]: by age

United Kingdom					percentages
	1984	**1986**	**1988**	**1989**	**1990**
Aged					
7–14	73	87	84	85	85
15–24	59	82	81	86	87
25–34	49	65	64	72	79
35–44	45	60	61	67	70
45 and over	13	25	34	35	41
All persons aged 7 and over	38	53	56	60	64

1 Percentage attending at least once in any given year.
Source: HMSO 1992

rately what counts as average 'television viewing' or 'radio listening' have quite rightly been called into question in recent years. In spite of these important reservations, however, it remains the case that we continue to spend a large proportion of our time in a range of media-related activities.

Hardware and Commodities

In order to participate in these activities, we need access to certain media technologies or commodities (Table 1.4). You cannot watch TV if you do not have one available to you, cannot rent and view videos if you do not have a VCR, cannot read certain magazines if you do not buy them, and so on.

Table 1.4 Leisure-based consumer durables: by household type, 1989–90
Great Britain   Percentages

	1 adult aged 16–59	2 adults aged 16–59	Small family[1]	Large family[2]	Large adult house-hold[3]	2 adults 1 or both aged 60 and over	1 adult aged 60 and over	All house-holds
Percentage of households with								
Television	94	99	99	99	100	99	98	99
Video cassette recorder	48	78	81	82	84	39	11	60
Home computer	10	15	37	46	31	4	1	19
Compact disc player	15	21	17	21	28	7	2	15

1 One or 2 persons aged 16 and over and 1 or 2 persons aged under 16
2 One or more persons aged 16 and over and 3 or more persons aged under 16, or 3 or more persons aged 16 and over and 2 persons aged under 16
3 Three or more persons aged 16 and over, with or without 1 person aged under 16.
Source: HMSO 1992

Another way of indexing the 'media saturation' of contemporary culture, then, is to examine available evidence which charts either the diffusion or penetration of media hardware or the circulation of particular media products. Of all households in Britain, 99 per cent have at least one television and more than half of these are 'multiset' homes, with televisions in different locations. Statistically and culturally, it is abnormal to live without a TV. More than 60 per cent of households in Britain now have at least one video cassette recorder and about a quarter of these are used regularly each week to replay at least one rented video film (Table 1.5). Recent years have seen important changes in the patterns of musical consumption; compact discs, for example, have overtaken LPs, although cassettes continue to account for over a third of all items sold (Figure 1.8). Their continued success may partly be explained by the increase in ownership of personal stereos.

1.7 Photograph: Jarrod Cripps

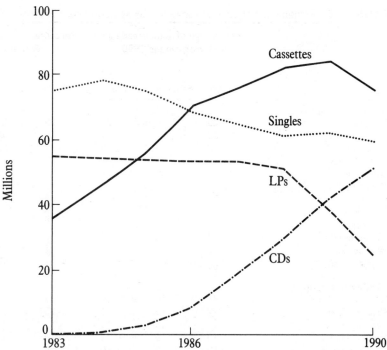

1 The figures include 7″ and 12″ vinyl singles as well as CD and cassette singles.

1.8 Social Trends, 1992, CSO

Table 1.5 Hiring of pre-recorded VCR tapes
United Kingdom

	1986	1988	1989	1990
Domestic video population[1] (millions)	9.66	12.20	13.80	14.80
Hiring of video tapes[2]?				
Percentage hiring tapes during previous 7 days	30	29	30	26
Average number of tapes per hiring	2.24	2.02	1.94	1.90
Number of tapes hired per week (millions)	6.5	7.2	8.0	7.3

1 Estimated number of households in possession of at least one video cassette recorder based on a survey of 13,000 households per quarter.
2 Figures refer to households in possession of a video cassette recorder.
Source: HMSO 1992

In 1990, the most widely read newspaper in Great Britain was *The Sun*, which was read regularly by one quarter of all men and one fifth of all women (Table 1.6, 1.7). The total readership of newspapers has declined in the post-war period,

Table 1.6 Reading of national newspapers: by sex and age, 1971 and 1990

	Percentage of adults reading each magazine in 1990			Percentage of each age group reading each magazine in 1990				Readership[1] (millions)	
	Males	Females	All adults	15–24	25–44	45–64	65 and over	1971	1990
Daily newspapers									
The Sun	25	20	23	29	24	21	16	8.5	10.2
Daily Mirror	22	17	19	20	18	21	18	13.8	8.7
Daily Mail	10	9	9	7	8	11	11	4.8	4.2
Daily Express	10	8	9	7	7	10	11	9.7	3.9
Daily Star	8	5	6	8	8	5	3		2.8
The Daily Telegraph	6	4	5	3	4	7	7	3.6	2.3
Today	5	3	4	5	5	3	1		1.7
The Guardian	4	2	3	3	4	3	1	1.1	1.3
The Times	3	2	3	2	3	3	2	1.1	1.2
The Independent	3	2	2	3	3	2	1		1.1
Financial Times	2	1	2	1	2	2	–	0.7	0.7
Any daily newspaper[2]	69	59	64	63	62	68	63		
Sunday newspapers									
News of the World	31	28	29	37	32	27	21	15.8	13.2
Sunday Mirror	22	19	21	23	21	21	17	13.5	9.3
The People	17	15	16	15	16	18	15	14.4	7.4
Mail on Sunday	13	11	12	14	14	13	7		5.6
Sunday Express	10	9	10	6	7	13	14	10.4	4.4
The Sunday Times	9	7	8	8	9	8	4	3.7	3.5
Sunday Telegraph	5	4	4	3	3	6	5	2.1	1.9
The Observer	5	4	4	4	5	4	3	2.4	1.8
The Independent on Sunday	3	2	3	3	3	2	1		1.2
Any Sunday newspaper[3]	74	69	71	73	70	75	67		

1. Defined as the average issue readership and represents the number of people who claim to have read or looked at one or more copies of a given publication during a period equal to the interval at which the publication appears.
2. Includes the above newspapers plus the *Daily Record*.
3. Includes the above newspapers plus the *Sunday Post*, *Sunday Mail*, *Scotland on Sunday* and *Sunday Sport*.
Source: HMSO 1992

as have magazine circulations (Table 1.8). However, in 1990 the *Radio Times* and *TV Times* had a combined average issue readership of one fifth of the adult population, over one third of whom regularly read a general monthly magazine. In 1990, one in eight women aged between 15 and 24 years old read *Bella* regularly.

These kinds of data, concerning either the time we spend with different media or the 'reach', frequency or diffusion of certain forms of media activity, offer important, if not altogether unproblematic, measures of the 'media saturation' of modern cultures. They indicate that some forms of media consumption are indeed widespread activities and they accord well with a predominant way of thinking about the mass media in terms of numbers – statistical profiles or percentages of readership, attendance, sales or ratings. These kinds of numerical expression are important, but they are always open to a range of interpretations and can be misleading. They are frequently used as historical evidence, to point to the growth,

Table 1.7 National newspaper circulation (*see also Table 6.2*)

	September 1993	August 1993	% change	Apr–Sept 1993	Apr–Sept 1992	% change
Dailies						
The Sun	3,838,000	3,832,397	0.15	3,633,539	3,556,557	2.16
Daily Mirror	2,630,061	2,694,256	-2.38	2,658,856	2,847,856	-6.64
Daily Record	761,526	749,721	1.57	751,349	755,406	-0.54
Daily Star	778,850	816,858	-4.65	775,093	812,124	-4.56
Daily Mail	1,693,107	1,709,402	-0.95	1,744,030	1,713,163	1.80
Daily Express	1,422,652	1,454,428	-2.18	1,470,594	1,545,580	-4.85
Today	559,014	570,274	-1.97	552,831	531,748	3.96
The Daily Telegraph	1,007,687	1,027,656	-1.94	1,017,291	1,036,029	-1.81
The Guardian	403,937	391,526	3.17	404,639	409,716	-1.24
The Times	440,291	354,280	24.28	375,496	362,793	-1.91
The Independent	332,435	325,856	2.02	336,004	377,175	-10.92
Financial Times	287,493	275,316	4.42	285,203	288,494	-1.14
Sundays						
News of the World	4,735,307	4,696,872	0.82	4,619,518	4,714,363	-2.01
Sunday Mirror	2,654,990	2,660,210	-0.20	2,645,738	2,737,253	-3.34
The People	1,994,985	2,016,732	-1.08	2,004,225	2,117,089	-5.33
Mail on Sunday	1,901,718	1,915,396	-0.71	1,951,743	1,929,773	1.14
Sunday Express	1,665,275	1,686,276	-1.25	1,694,770	1,765,135	-3.44
The Sunday Times	1,248,621	1,206,131	3.52	1,216,112	1,185,728	2.56
Sunday Telegraph	590,785	596,723	-1.00	594,625	567,394	3.04
The Observer	502,099	481,953	4.18	497,124	524,667	-5.25
The Sunday Independent	368,824	362,717	1.55	370,395	396,642	-6.62

Source: The Guardian, 1993

Table 1.8 Reading of the most popular magazines by sex and age, 1971 and 1990 (Great Britain)

	Percentage of adults reading each magazine in 1990			Percentage of each age group reading each magazine in 1990				Readership[1] (millions)		Readers per copy (numbers)
	Males	Females	All adults	15–24	25–44	45–64	65 and over	1971	1990	1990
General magazines										
Radio Times	18	19	19	20	20	18	17	9.5	8.5	2.9
TV Times	18	19	19	21	19	18	15	9.9	8.4	3.0
Reader's Digest	14	13	13	8	13	17	14	9.2	6.1	3.9
What Car	7	1	4	6	5	3	1		1.8	12.2
National Geographic	5	3	4	4	4	4	2	1.1	1.7	—
Exchange and Mart	5	2	3	5	4	3	1		1.5	8.2
Womens magazines[2]										
Women's Own	3	16	10	10	11	9	8	7.2	4.3	4.2
Bella	3	15	10	12	11	8	6		4.3	—
Woman's Weekly	2	11	7	4	5	9	10	4.7	3.1	2.6
Woman	2	11	7	6	8	6	5	8.0	3.0	3.2
Best	2	11	6	9	8	5	3		2.9	3.1
Prima	2	10	6	7	8	5	2		2.6	3.0

1 Defined as the average issue readership and represents the number of people who claim to have read, or looked at, one or more copies of a given publication during a period equal to the interval at which the publication appears.
2 The age analysis for women's magazines includes male readers.
Source: HMSO 1992

1.9 Photograph: Jarrod Cripps

for example of new media forms from the development of print media through to current shifts in broadcasting and other electronic media. Here, the data is often uncritically held to map or measure the declines or shifts in the 'popularity' of certain cultural forms and practices. These issues deserve further discussion and they are developed in the next chapter.

For now, a key point to note is that our own personal, private patterns of media consumption and use are parts of wider social and cultural relationships. Our individual media relations and choices are parts of a 'bigger picture', which operates outside of our own individual determination or control. The kinds of data considered here should most importantly suggest that the mass media are central social institutions in modern life. In order to develop further the theme of 'media saturation', we need to move on from asking questions about the basic scale and scope of media activities, to consider in more detail what is at stake in the time, money and attention we regularly and routinely give to the media.

Situation and Mediation

We all inhabit particular situations. These are defined not only in the geographical sense of specific place and location but also in terms of the patterns of culture and social relationships which characterise them. Our identities are fundamentally linked with this idea of personal place and biography. Much of the sense of identity and belonging is rooted in and derived from the immediate, familiar surroundings of place and from networks of regular, face-to-face contacts with family or friends in school, college, workplace, home and so on. Through these networks of direct interpersonal communication we participate in a *situated culture*. We may hear or relay news of recent events in the neighbourhood, likewise rumours, gossip, stories or jokes. We may attend and participate in local events, entertainments, family ceremonies or other rituals. These cultures of situation are primarily oral, by word-of-mouth relationships, and although they have historical and generational dimensions, they tend to be limited and defined in relation to a particular locale. In certain ways they embody elements of pre-industrial cultures, relatively small-scale forms of social interaction and groupings derived from the immediate, face-to-face environment and its daily experience.

We know these cultures to be distinctive, but they are also bound by a number of limiting factors. Of these, perhaps the most obvious is space. We do not know about events and issues occurring beyond the horizons of the situation or locale – that is, we do not know in the direct, experiential sense.

Since the mid-nineteenth century, however, we have increasingly learned to live not only in our situated culture, but also in a *culture of mediation*, whereby specialised social agencies – the press, film and cinema, radio and television broadcasting – developed to supply and cultivate larger-scale forms of communication; mediating news and other forms of culture into the situation. 'Our' immediate world co-exists with the mediated 'world out there'. The growth of these media were both a product of and a response to larger-scale social networks or collectivities. They also embodied certain applications of developing technologies and the growth of commercial economies in processes of social communication.

This juxtaposition and contrast of social formations without mass media and those with mass-mediated culture has been explored in a number of significant ways. Marshall McLuhan (1964), for example, writing of the ways in which modern media have 'shrunk' the world – by regularly 'transporting' us around the globe – talked of the potential for modern media technologies to establish what he called 'the global village', to connect the myriad of situated cultures into one, ideal, face-to-face planet-wide totality (for development of this idea, see discussion in Chapter 8). Another important way in which this distinction has been employed is in the definition of *mass communication*, which is held to be distinctively different from the direct and face-to-face forms and relations of interpersonal communication.

Characteristics of Mass Communication

In general terms, communication is understood, often somewhat mechanistically, as the transmission and reception of meaningful 'messages'. These are often expressed in language and speech but may be conveyed by means of other symbolic systems in accordance with shared rules or codes, signs or symbols, for example (see Chapter 3). Much communication in everyday life takes place in the situated context of direct face-to-face interaction, between people who are physically present and involved in a dialogue, more-or-less continuously reciprocating or providing 'feedback' for other participants. In the case of mass communication, the nature of the communicative relationship appears to be quite different and conventionally four main differences are identified (see Thompson, 1988, and McQuail, 1987, for further discussion).

First of all, there is an *institutional break* or *gap* between the participants in the communicative relationship. In crude terms, the 'senders' of mass-mediated messages do not have the same meaningful, tangible or direct forms of feedback relationship with the 'receivers' – the audiences. This is not to say that people do not regularly shout at their television screens or radios or disagree with the editor of their magazine or newspaper. It is, however, to say that such responses are rarely heard or received in such direct and unmediated ways by the producers. It is in the nature of the relationship that they cannot be. Admittedly, there are specialised systems for feedback – viewers' or readers' letters or phone calls, for example – but these differ in a number of ways from those which characterise face-to-face interaction.

Partly because of this, mass-mediated culture tends to be 'one-way': it is directed at either 'people out there', in general, or at specified 'target' groups. Not only are there issues here concerning the people who receive mass-mediated information and the position that this relationship places them in, but also this situation raises problems for those who 'send' or produce the programmes, films, newspapers and so on. *Whom* are they talking to? Or rather, whom do they think they are talking to? To overcome this problem of not knowing who their actual audiences or readers might be, media producers often have to work to imaginary, generalised constructs or stereotypes – the 'general public', the 'person (historically, usually a man) in the street', 'young people', the 'busy housewife' and the 'active career woman', are some conventional examples. These constructs allow media producers to select and 'shape' their products with the aim of establishing credible and engaging forms of communication with large numbers of people whom they cannot see or know and whose situation they do not share.

Part of this separation is the result of a related but second distinction. Most commonly, mass media or mass communications are defined in terms of *specialised technologies*, and indeed the technical means of exchange of direct, interpersonal forms of interaction and those characteristic of mass-mediated culture differ considerably. As noted above, media technologies have traditionally tended to reinforce a one-way system of communication *from* media producers *to* media audiences, giving rise to what one writer has described as an 'asymmetrical and unbalanced' relationship between participants (McQuail, 1975, p. 167).

There are other, additional issues worth considering here, however. These concern the ways in which mass communication is made available in material form. Unlike the transient, ephemeral nature of much face-to-face interaction – here, then gone, as with conversations, gestures etc. – mass communications tend to be inscribed or stored in physical and reproducible forms or texts: the book, the film, the video, the disc, the tape, the newspaper, the comic and so on. These material forms have consequences for the nature of the message itself, giving, for example, a permanency or reproducibility which is not conventionally found in everyday, direct, interpersonal interaction. This technical ability to record and reproduce messages and many varied forms of information results in a *historical permanence*. A good example here is to be found in the history of photography and film, where various writers have noted the impact that the technical ability to capture, hold and socially distribute visual records has had on our sense of 'history'. In this context, it has been argued that our sense of the 'modern world' is very much bound up with the period that saw the emergence of film and photographic records (Chanan, 1980).

A third distinctive feature of mass media or mass communication is implicit in this characteristic of technical reproducibility. Media messages differ from interpersonal forms of communication in that their potential *scale and availability* are greatly extended 'outwards', across space, time, population and culture. This means, for example, that events taking place in specific national or regional locations can receive 'worldwide' distribution and, with the intervention of satellite technologies, 'live' or simultaneous forms of global coverage or mediation. Audiences for major sporting spectaculars, such as the Olympic Games or other international 'mega' events – ecological disasters or political crises, for example – are frequently calculated in billions.

Having noted, however, that mass communications are potentially available across time, space and population, this does not mean that they are available in an unrestricted fashion – 'open to all'. On the contrary, access to such potential tends to be regulated in a number of important and decisive ways, notably by the operation of commercial markets and legal or statutory forms of control, which may differ significantly from one national or cultural context to another.

The fourth and final factor which is used to distinguish mass communication from interpersonal forms of direct, face-to-face interaction relates to this last point. In general it makes sense to understand media messages as particular forms of *commodity*. Despite the tendency to talk in terms of media 'messages', we need to bear in mind that mass communications are distributed as products or services, commodities which are developed and sold according to the logics of commercial markets. Profitability continues to be a decisive factor in shaping the available forms of mass communication. Indeed, at a basic level, we can understand mass media as specialised, industrialised agencies involved in the commercial supply of demands for diverse forms of information, communication and entertainment commodities.

Media Saturation: Dependency and Power

1.10 Photograph: Jarrod Cripps

While an index of media saturation is gained, as we have suggested, by examining the patterns of time, involvement and attention routinely accorded to varying forms of media, the kinds of data outlined in the introductory section are really only a starting point for further analysis. As the presence of successive mass media, from newspapers to film to radio and TV, have become accepted as everyday 'facts of life' and social existence, so, it is argued, we have become socially and culturally more *dependent* upon them. Limited, to an extent, by the particular confines of our respective situations, we have learned to rely on different media, in particular for news and information about the wider world and large-scale social processes. Around this increasingly private, domestic presence of forms of public, mediated culture, a series of central debates and arguments has been developed. These might be said to lie at the heart of media studies.

It has now become somewhat of a cliché to suggest that the media collectively act to provide their audiences with 'windows on the world' or 'definitions of social reality'. Implicit in this kind of claim is the idea that the media act as powerful agencies capable of shaping and directing public and private understanding of the world and its social, economic, moral, cultural, technological and political affairs. In this manner, the media have been termed 'consciousness industries'. That is, in providing images, interpretations and explanations of events occurring in the wider world, the modern media do not simply and neutrally provide information about that world but actively encourage us to see and understand it in particular ways and in certain terms. Rather than faithfully 'mirroring' the external world and its 'reality', it is argued that the media have come to play an increasingly central role in constructing and interpreting the nature of that world according to certain ideological frameworks and principles. For those engaged in the systematic study of the mass media, this recognition has resulted in a general and sustained focus upon questions of media representation – how and in what terms do the media re-present – aspects of society and social process to their audiences. This theme will be explored in more detail in Chapter 4.

For now, it is worth noting that questions of media saturation encompass some major issues which are bound up with arguments about the social and political consequences of our dependence upon mediated culture. There are key questions here which concern not only the nature of the images and versions of the world which are now, as one writer has noted 'as easily available as water, gas or electricity' (Hood, 1980). We also need to ask about the ways in which such images and accounts are produced, and under what kinds of conditions; controlled and formed in response to what kinds of social and political force. We need to analyse the relations between the controls on the mediation of information and entertainment to people and the dispositions of political power more generally. We also need to study in detail the diverse ways in which different everyday cultures respond to and interact with the presence of media saturation.

Many have argued that the case for this type of investigation has become more urgent, given the post-1950s growth in the management and manufacture of information, the development of new media and the increasing penetration of the media into both private and public spheres. It has been suggested, for example, that we now inhabit an *information* and *consumer* society, where the manufacture and dissemination of information have become a central facet of modern democratic and commercial processes. The media and cultural industries now encompass multinational corporations, government agencies and departments, political parties, advertisers, public relations and many other forms of corporate, private and public organisation. These are locked into increasingly sophisticated complexes of information gathering, management, manipulation and distribution. In the specific sphere of institutionalised politics, for example, elections have virtually ceased to have a social significance for the general public, outside of their construction and mediation as 'media events' (see Negrine, 1989; Seymour-Ure, 1991; Franklin, 1994).

Given these and related developments in the levels and dynamics of media saturation in the modern period, it is not surprising that the media have attracted considerable public debate and critique. We now briefly consider some of the dominant concerns that have accompanied the growth of media saturation.

MEDIATION AND SOCIAL CONCERN

As the mass media have developed, so have a number of competing claims about their social significance and impact. In historical terms, the various media have often operated both to condense and to relay anxieties and fears about the nature of change in a rapidly changing world. As such they have often been singled out as if they are the sole cause of particular tendencies in society and culture. This is a theme we shall return to in later chapters. For now, however, it is worth noting some of the predominant concerns which have regularly and recurrently structured public and private ideas and shaped thinking about the media. Such claims and concerns have, it is important to note, often formed the basis for advocating particular kinds of increased media regulation or control. Many of the concerns of the current period, dealing, for example, with the 'invasion' of privacy by the popular tabloid press, or the antisocial effects of video 'nasties' or computer games, have a lengthy heritage, stretching back in form at least to the nineteenth century. Three general themes and areas of concern have recurred, all focusing upon 'effects' that the media are claimed to have had on society.

The first of these concerns the political or persuasive powers of the mass media, particularly in terms of the supposed abilities of the press, film, radio or television to manipulate whole populations' attitudes. George Orwell's novel *1984*, first published in 1949, represents an interesting example of a 'dystopian' vision of a society where control over the masses is in part exerted through the incessant surveillance and propaganda of the 'telescreens'. In the context of the rise of fascism and dictators in a number of European states, and the widespread use of propaganda techniques to manipulate the minds of whole populations prior to and during the Second World War, the media appeared to have enormous political potential. The theme of mass persuasion was also foregrounded, although in slightly modified form, in consideration of the rise of advertising in the 1930s and in the period following the war. This theme of the 'mind-bending' powers of the media is one which still has considerable common currency.

A second recurrent theme can be traced back to the middle of the nineteenth century. This was rooted in a concern for conserving certain traditions, especially in aesthetic and cultural terms, and articulated a general opposition to the 'new' popular media and what was seen as their damaging impact upon long-established cultural values and practices. The popular press and publishing, followed by cinema and, later, radio and television, have all been accused of degrading or debasing cultural traditions and standards, eroding the authentic and replacing it with the 'trivial' and 'vulgar' substitutes of the modern age. Once again, this theme continues to exercise considerable influence in debates about the position and place of the media in the current period. A good example here is the series of debates and positions which have emerged in the context of the future of public service broadcasting in Britain in the 1990s.

The final theme has perhaps been the most influential. It concerns the arguments about the impact or 'effects' of the mass media on social behaviour – in fact, usually anti-social behaviour – and the moral contours of society. The most debated area in this context has been the issue of violence and delinquency, where the media have regularly been held to 'cause' outbreaks of violent or aggressive activity. These incidents have usually been part of wider and regular cycles of social concern, often referred to as 'moral panics', and they continue to make their presence felt in the 1990s.

CULTURE AND MASS COMMUNICATION

So far we have introduced a series of themes concerning the presence and the defining characteristics of mass communication in modern social life. We have also noted that the media have been a particularly powerful focus for a number of debates about the nature of modernity. In order to develop these themes further, it is important to consider briefly some general questions about the nature of the interrelations between culture and mass communication.

Culture, as we have suggested, first and foremost concerns the ways in which we understand and relate to social situations. We are socialised into a particular set of cultural orientations or ways of making sense of the world, and these encompass two particular dimensions. First of all, culture refers to the beliefs, values and frames of reference through which we learn to make sense of our experiences on a daily and ongoing basis. Secondly, any definition of culture must encompass the various means by which people communicate a sense of self and situation. This emphasis on communication is central because it highlights the view that:

cultures are not primarily collections of objects, but stocks of shared understandings and responses accumulated in the course of confronting a common set of social conditions. They provide a pool of available meanings and modes of expression which people can draw upon to describe and respond to their own particular experiences. Far from being separated from everyday life, therefore, involvement in culture is an integral part of people's continuing attempt to make sense of their situation and to find ways of coming to terms with it, or else of changing it.

Murdock (1974), p. 90

What we understand as the mass media are centrally involved and implicated in the production of modern culture. Most modern, technologically advanced societies now encompass a great diversity or plurality of cultures which correspond to the major and varied social groupings of class, gender, race, generation and so on. Since the mid-nineteenth century, the growth of the mass media has undoubtedly assisted in processes whereby certain forms of cultural differentiation have taken place – various media have responded to the particular needs or values of particular cultural groups. However, at the same time, the media have also been involved in the consolidation of forms of centralised, non-specific, 'public', national cultures which have purported to transcend particular sectional interests or differing points of view. In part, one's view of this dilemma is dependent upon the view or model of mass communication and its dynamics which one adopts.

Traditional perspectives on 'mass' communication have tended to emphasise a singular, mechanistic, process model. In these terms, 'messages' are sent to 'the mass'. At its crudest, this assumes a central, unitary 'sender', technically capable of transmitting a message to a large-scale 'mass' population, who reacted, as to a common stimulus, with virtually identical responses. The shortcomings of this notion are many, and we will suggest throughout this book that you consider viewing mass communication as part of a set of cultural 'circuits', composed of relations between forms of *media production*, *media texts* and *media reception*. In particular, it is important to avoid the tendency to cut the media off from their social, commercial and historical contexts. There are significant social and cultural conditions which surround both the composition of the screen, the page, the programme and so on, and their reception by diverse audiences.

1.11 Johnson, R. (1986): in Punter, D. (ed) *Introduction to Contemporary Cultural Studies*, p. 284. Longman

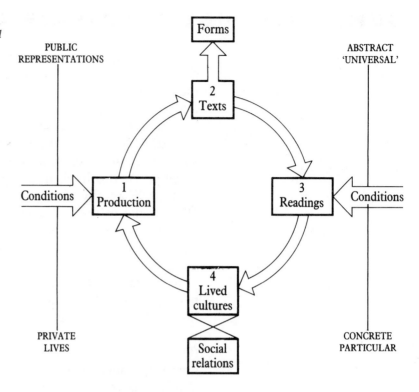

The 'map' of cultural circulation in Figure 1.11 usefully encapsulates the major relationships at stake in the study of the mass media. The diagram suggests a circuit or cycle in the production, circulation and reception of cultural products. For our purposes it can usefully be applied to virtually any form of media. Its strength lies in the manner in which it directs our attention to a 'holistic', encompassing mode of enquiry. You will note that the circuit links moments and conditions of production to the texts and forms so produced, to the readings or forms of reception they may activate, which link in turn to the contexts of lived or situated cultures and wider social relations, which are both directly and indirectly implicated in the circuit.

activity 1.2

This framework will be examined in more detail in the chapters that follow. As a way of opening up some of these issues initially, you will find it useful to note down some examples of contemporary media texts and output that you are familiar with. Work round the circuit noting some of the conditions which may shape or have consequences for your chosen cases.

SUMMARY: PUBLIC, PRIVATE AND POPULAR

In concluding this chapter, we want to suggest that you consider some of the ways in which the historical development of the media has been instrumental in the emergence of what we understand as modern social and cultural life. Three key aspects of their presence and operation should be noted.

First, they represent the emergence of large-scale systems of *public* communication, linked to what has been called the *public sphere*. At this level, newspapers and print media from the 1850s, followed by photography in the 1880s, cinema in the 1900s, radio in the 1920s and TV in the 1950s, all represent important developments of and extensions to public culture. Key themes here concern questions of power, access, representation and mediation.

At the same time, these developments have also had important implications for the *private* sphere and everyday life 'at home'. Radio and television, for example, have accompanied what one writer has called 'the withdrawal into inner space' (Donzelot, 1980), whereby leisure activities have become progressively concentrated in 'the home', the domestic sphere. While important changes might be said to be taking place inside households in the current phase, the private sphere is still 'connected' to the outside world in important and decisive ways via the media.

Finally, the media and mass communications have interacted with pre-existing cultures, forms and values in a number of significant ways. Of these, perhaps the most central has been in the development of *popular* culture, that 'site of struggle and contest' which, as Williams (1976) has noted, contains a number of contradictory ideas: from 'liked by many' to 'not elite or high culture'; from that of 'the common people' to 'mass-produced' culture.

These three themes – public, private and popular – will be explored in the chapters that follow. Before proceeding to the next chapter, however, here is an activity which draws together some of the major issues raised so far.

activity 1.3

Draw up two lists. On the first, list as many forms of *communication* as you can think of. On the second, list only forms of *mass communication* and *mass media*. When you have drawn up the lists, note down the key differences between them and the general features that distinguish them.

In List 1, you may expect all sorts of entries: speaking, writing, hieroglyphics, tom-toms, smoke signals, morse-code, music, art, theatre, gesture, mime, facial expression, body language, semaphore, walkie-talkies, CB radio, teaching, sermons, railways, roads, telephones, telex, satellite, letters, nudging, winking, the Post Office, war, photocopies, snapshots, architecture, clothes, hairstyles, handshakes, etc.

List 2 is likely to be much shorter, and no matter what else appears in it, you are likely to find that only a very few candidates get unanimous agreement about their status as mass media. These are: television, radio, cinema, newspapers. In addition, people may mention publishing, popular music, advertising, theatre, music, video, telephones, speech, photography, magazines, the music industry… Suggestions for important differences might include:

Those on List 2 all:

- reach large numbers of people;
- employ high technology;
- are modern;
- involve large-scale commercial corporations and finance;
- are state controlled or regulated;
- are centrally produced but privately consumed;
- are cooperative, not individual forms of communication;
- are popular (widespread and/or well-liked).

In fact, once such a set of characteristics has been found, it is quite easy to think of things that fulfil these criteria but are *not* mass media as commonly understood – religion and education being clear examples.

Further, there are things like music, photography, pictures, drama, speech and printing that appear in more than one of the mass media. Are these *forms* of communication, or *media* in their own right?

Working with lists generated in this way does serve one useful purpose, beyond showing that there's no *single* definition of the media.

That is, despite their plurality and the differences between them, the media are nevertheless *socially recognized*; everyone agrees that they include TV, radio, cinema, newspapers. After discussion, most will agree that music and publishing (magazines and fiction) should be included, as well as advertising. Usually, people will express their recognition of mass media most easily by reference to a *technological apparatus*, which explains why TV, radio, cinema and the press recur. But people are less used to thinking of the media as *social institutions* – although they can recognize one when they see it in the shape of the advertising and music industries, or popular magazines and fiction.

Hartley et al. *(1985), vol. 1, p. 12*

FURTHER READING

Burton, G. 1990: *More than Meets the Eye*. Edward Arnold.

Dutton, B. 1986: *The Media*. Longman.

Dutton, B. 1989: *Media Studies: An Introduction*. Longman.

McQuail, D. 1987: *Mass Communication Theory: An Introduction*. Sage.

Negrine, R. 1989: *Politics and the Mass Media in Britain*. Routledge.

O'Sullivan, T., Hartley, J., Saunders, D., Montgomery, M. and Fiske, J. 1994: *Key Concepts in Communication and Cultural Studies*. Routledge. '

Trowler, P. 1989: *Investigating the Media*. Tavistock.

Tunstall, J. 1983: *The Media in Britain*. Constable.

Watson, J. and Hill, A. 1993: *A Dictionary of Communication and Media Studies*. Edward Arnold.

Histories

2

The last chapter focused on the theme of media saturation and started with our own familiar and everyday relationships with the media in the present tense – in the here and now. This chapter aims to develop a range of issues about the *historical* development of the modern media and the conditions which have shaped their respective development. These themes should not, however, be confined to this chapter. Attention to the historical development of media institutions and organisations is an essential component of media studies. In short, studying the historical formation and evolution of the various media – how they have emerged and under what conditions – makes possible a more informed understanding of their present forms of operation, regulation, use, and likely patterns of development and change.

History, or rather the study of history, is often associated with lists of dates, successions of undeniable, historic events and 'facts'. For example:

1476   William Caxton prints the first English book.
1702   The *Daily Courant*, the first English daily newspaper, is published.
1785   The first issue of *The Times* is published (as the *Daily Universal Register*).
1896   The first moving picture show to a paying audience in London.
1922   The British Broadcasting Company (radio) is formed.
1927   The first full-length talking film is released.
1936   BBC Television starts broadcasting.
1946   Cinema attendance in Britain peaks at 1,635 million visits a year.

1962	The first communications satellite, Telstar, goes into orbit.
1969	Colour transmissions are introduced on BBC and ITV.
1973	The first independent local radio station opens (LBC).
1982	Channel Four is launched.

As Carr (1961) and other have argued, however, historians are involved in more than just the 'cult of facts', the uncritical compilation of lists of self-evidently important dates. Historical study always entails a sense of how certain events and processes, and their dates, are *selected* as significant, and how their significance should be *interpreted*. Common ideas of history, for example, tend to be deeply bound up with notions of 'progress' and 'development' and often hazy notions of 'industrialisation' or 'modernisation'.

A SENSE OF HISTORY

The development of organised systems of mass communication has had important consequences for both personal and public perceptions of history. Our own biographies are connected to 'media generations', bound up with remembered media events and shared experience of particular media at certain phases of their development. The pre-television era and experience, for instance, when viewed from the 1990s, seems a strange and rather alien bygone time. The ages before film or pre-photographic records appear even more 'historical' and 'out of sight':

> The modern world almost seems to have begun with the birth of film, at any rate in retrospect. Because we're used to seeing film images of the First World War, the First World War seems to be part of the modern period. But anything more than twenty years earlier than that belongs to an era which we easily feel to be lost.
>
> *Chanan (1980), p. 16*

activity 2.1

This quotation suggests that film and visual media have had an important impact on our sense of history.

List some of the most memorable media images associated with your own life. Conduct interviews or surveys among other members of your household or family, particularly from different generations, about their memories of earlier media and media coverage of significant events.

Think of other research you might do to explore this theme. You may find it useful to consider the impact of print media and the photograph as well, as extensions of this activity. Radio and television will also provide important topics for study.

As you work through the chapter you may find it useful to return to this activity.

THE BATTLE OF TRAFALGAR

When the Battle of Trafalgar reached its conclusion in favour of the British fleet on 21 October 1805, it was more than a fortnight before the news of the victory, and of the death of Admiral Lord Nelson, was published in Britain. The first account of the events reached *The Times* on 6 November (Figure 2.1). Admiral Collingwood's full despatch was published there on the morning of 7 November 1805 (Figure 2.2).

> The news, having travelled variously via the British Consul in Lisbon and overland by coach, did not reach London until early November... The story of Trafalgar was read in the newspapers of the day by at most a few thousand people.
>
> *Carter (1971), p. 9*

Needless to say, such events would not be covered in quite the same way in the late twentieth century. From the Falklands to the Gulf War, and in coverage of numerous other international conflicts and events, developments in the media have greatly increased the speed of transmission, the size of audiences and the amounts and types of information made available to them.

activity **2.2**

Compare the reporting of Trafalgar with that of any more contemporary international conflicts. What major differences would you identify in the patterns and forms of media coverage? How would the Battle of Trafalgar be covered by today's media?

For useful references see: Knightley (1978), Harris (1983), Taylor (1991) and Taylor (1992).

GLORIOUS AND DECISIVE
VICTORY
OVER THE
COMBINED FLEET,
AND
DEATH of LORD NELSON.

We know not whether we should mourn or rejoice. The country has gained the most splendid and decisive Victory that has ever graced the naval annals of England; but it has been dearly purchased. *The great and gallant* NELSON *is no more*: he was killed by almost the last shot that was fired by the enemy. The action took place off Cadiz, on the 21st ult.; the enemy were thirty-three sail of the line, Lord NELSON had only twenty-seven.

The following account we have received by **express; we** can pledge ourselves for its truth:

TIMES OFFICE, 11 o'Clock, A. M.

A Lieutenant of a man of war arrived this morning, with an account of a most glorious victory achieved by the British fleet, under the command of Lord NELSON.

The enemy's fleet consisted of THIRTY-THREE sail of the line, with frigates, &c. They came out of Cadiz on the 19th of October, and two days afterwards were encountered by the British fleet, consisting of only TWENTY-SEVEN sail of the line, (several having been detached under Rear-Admiral LOUIS) with some smaller ships. The battle continued during four hours, and ended in the capture of NINETEEN of the enemy's ships of the line, besides one which blew up in the action.

The *Victory* being closely engaged with several of the Enemy's Ships, a Musket-shot wounded Lord NELSON in the Shoulder, and thus terminated a Life of Glory.

A number of Prizes drifted on a lee-shore, in a gale of wind, a day or two afterwards, and probably many have been wrecked. Admiral COLLINGWOOD had ordered that every ship which could not be brought away should be destroyed. Two, however, effected their escape into Cadiz.

Admiral VILLENEUVE is a prisoner. On our side two Captains, we believe DUFF and COOKE, and three or four hundred men were killed. We have not lost a single ship.

2.1 *The Times*, 6 November 1805. ©
Times Newspapers Ltd. 1805

The Times.

6572.
LONDON, THURSDAY, NOVEMBER 7, 1805.
PRICE SIXPENCE

The LONDON GAZETTE EXTRAORDINARY.
WEDNESDAY, Nov. 6, 1805.

ADMIRALTY-OFFICE, Nov. 6.

Dispatches, of which the following are Copies, were received at the Admiralty this day, at one o'clock A. M. from Vice-Admiral Collingwood, Commander in Chief of his Majesty's ships and vessels off Cadiz :—

SIR,   Euryalus, off Cape Trafalgar, Oct. 22, 1805.

The ever-to-be-lamented death of Vice-Admiral Lord Viscount Nelson, who, in the late conflict with the enemy, fell in the hour of victory, leaves to me the duty of informing my Lords Commissioners of the Admiralty, that on the 19th instant, it was communicated to the Commander in Chief, from the ships watching the motions of the enemy in Cadiz, that the Combined Fleet had put to sea; as they sailed with light winds westerly, his Lordship concluded their destination was the Mediterranean, and immediately made all sail for the Streights' entrance, with the British Squadron, consisting of twenty-seven ships, three of them sixty-fours, where his Lordship was informed, by Captain Blackwood (whose vigilance in watching, and giving notice of the enemy's movements, has been highly meritorious), that they had not yet passed the Streights.

On Monday the 21st instant, at day-light, when Cape Trafalgar bore E. by S. about seven leagues, the enemy was discovered six or seven miles to the Eastward, the wind about West, and very light; the Commander in Chief immediately made the signal for the fleet to bear up in two columns, as they are formed in order of sailing; a mode of attack his Lordship had previously directed, to avoid the inconvenience and delay in forming a line of battle in the usual manner. The enemy's line consisted of thirty-three ships (of which eighteen were French, and fifteen Spanish), commanded in Chief by Admiral Villeneuve: the Spaniards, under the direction of Gravina, wore, with their heads to the Northward, and formed their line of battle with great closeness and correctness; but as the mode of attack was unusual, so the structure of their line was new; it formed a crescent, convexing to leeward, so that, in leading down to their centre, I had both their van and rear abaft the beam; before the fire opened, every alternate ship was about a cable's length to windward of her second a-head and a-stern, forming a kind of double line, and appeared, when on their beam, to leave a very little interval between them; and this without crowding their ships. Admiral Villeneuve was in the Bucentaure, in the centre, and the Prince of Asturias bore Gravina's flag in the rear, but the French and Spanish ships were mixed without any apparent regard to order of national squadron.

As the mode of our attack had been previously determined on, and communicated to the Flag-Officers, and Captains, few signals were necessary, and none were made, except to direct close order as the lines bore down.

The Commander in Chief, in the Victory, led the weather column, and the Royal Sovereign, which bore my flag, the lee.

The action began at twelve o'clock, by the leading ships of the columns breaking through the enemy's line, the Commander in Chief about the tenth ship from the van, the Second in Command about the twelfth from the rear, leaving the van of the enemy unoccupied; the succeeding ships breaking through, in all parts, astern of their leaders, and engaging the enemy at the muzzles of their guns; the conflict was severe; the enemy's ships were fought with a gallantry highly honourable to their Officers; but the attack on them was irresistible, and it pleased the Almighty Disposer of all events to grant his Majesty's arms a complete and glorious victory. About three P. M. many of the enemy's ships having struck their colours, their line gave way; Admiral Gravina, with ten ships joining their frigates to leeward, stood towards Cadiz. The five headmost ships in their van tacked, and standing to the Southward, to windward of the British line, were engaged, and the sternmost of them taken; the others went off, leaving to his Majesty's squadron nineteen ships of the line (of which two are first rates, the Santissima Trinidad and the Santa Anna,) with three Flag Officers, viz. Admiral Villeneuve, the Commander in Chief; Don Ignatio Maria D'Aliva, Vice Admiral; and the Spanish Rear-Admiral, Don Baltazar Hidalgo Cisneros.

After such a Victory, it may appear unnecessary to enter into encomiums on the particular parts taken by the several Commanders; the conclusion says more on the subject than I have language to express; the spirit which animated all was the same: when all exert themselves zealously in their country's service, all deserve that their high merits should stand recorded; and never was high merit more conspicuous than in the battle I have described.

The Achille (a French 74), after having surrendered, by some mismanagement of the Frenchman, took fire and blew up; two hundred of her men were saved by the Tenders.

A circumstance occurred during the action, which so strongly marks the invincible spirit of British seamen, when engaging the enemies of their country, that I cannot resist the pleasure I have in making it known to their Lordships; the Temeraire was boarded by accident, or design, by a French ship on one side, and a Spaniard on the other; the contest was vigorous, but, in the end, the Combined Ensigns were torn from the poop, and the British hoisted in their places.

Such a battle could not be fought without sustaining a great loss of men. I have not only to lament, in common with the British Navy, and the British Nation, in the Fall of the Commander in Chief, the loss of a Hero, whose name will be immortal, and his memory ever dear to his country; but my heart is rent with the most poignant grief for the death of a friend, to whom, by many years intimacy, and a perfect knowledge of the virtues of his mind, which inspired ideas superior to the common race of men, I was bound by the strongest ties of affection; a grief to which even the glorious occasion in which he fell, does not bring the consolation which, perhaps, it ought: his Lordship received a musket ball in his left breast, about the middle of the action, and sent an Officer to me immediately with his last farewell; and soon after expired.

I have also to lament the loss of those excellent Officers, Captains Duff, of the Mars, and Cooke, of the Bellerophon; I have yet heard of none others.

I fear the numbers that have fallen will be found very great, when the returns come to me; but it having blown a gale of wind ever since the action, I have not yet had it in my power to collect any reports from the ships.

The Royal Sovereign having lost her masts, except the tottering foremast, I called the Euryalus to me, while the action continued, which ship lying within hail, made my Signals—a service Captain Blackwood performed with great attention: after the action, I shifted my flag to her, that I might more easily communicate any orders to, and collect the ships, and towed the Royal Sovereign out to Seaward. The whole fleet were now in a very perilous situation, many dismasted, all shattered, in thirteen fathom water, off the shoals of Trafalgar; and when I made the signal to prepare to anchor, few of the ships had an anchor to let go, their cables being shot; but the same good Providence which aided us through such a day preserved us in the night, by the wind shifting a few points, and drifting the ships off the land, except four of the captured dismasted ships, which are now at anchor off Trafalgar, and I hope will ride safe until those gales are over.

Having thus detailed the proceedings of the fleet on this occasion, I beg to congratulate their Lordships on a victory which, I hope, will add a ray to the glory of his Majesty's crown, and be attended with public benefit to our country. I am, &c.

(Signed) C. COLLINGWOOD.

William Marsden, Esq.

The order in which the Ships of the British Squadron attacked the Combined Fleets, on the 21st of October, 1805.

VAN.	REAR
Victory,	Royal Sovereign,
Temeraire,	Mars,
Neptune,	Belleisle,
Conqueror,	Tonnant,
Leviathan,	Bellerophon,
Ajax,	Colossus,
Orion,	Achille,
Agamemnon,	Polyphemus,
Minotaur,	Revenge,
Spartiate,	Swiftsure,

Britannia,	Defence,
Africa,	Thunderer,
Euryalus,	Defence,
Sirius,	Prince,
Phœbe,	Dreadnought,
Naiad,	
Pickle Schooner,	
Entrepenaute Cutter.	

(Signed)   C. COLLINGWOOD.

2.2 *The Times*, 7 November 1805. © Times Newspapers Ltd. 1805

THE CONDITIONS OF MEDIA DEVELOPMENT: *DEMAND AND SUPPLY*

The growth of mass communications is a dual process. On the one hand it describes the development of an industry, on the other the evolution of an audience. The relationship between the two is one of supply and demand for two basic social commodities; leisure facilities and information.

Golding (1974), p. 14

Before proceeding to examine some detailed case studies of the historical development of particular media, it is useful to consider some general factors which have shaped and historically structured this relationship of supply and demand. In essence, this entails an analysis of certain general conditions which have had implications for media producers and processes of production (supply) and for media consumers and their access to reception of media output (demand).

Demand

The *demand* for information and entertainment has been influenced by a number of factors, three of which are of particular concern: the amounts of time available, the affluence or spending power of social groups, and a variety of other cultural factors.

Legal and technical changes in many forms of employment from the late nineteenth century onwards have resulted in decreased working hours, the widespread availability of statutory holidays, and more *time* being generally available for leisure or non-work activities. As noted in the first chapter, media consumption has grown as a significant component of this 'discretionary' time. In the 1990s there are important differences in the leisure time available to men and women, and to other groups in the population. Historically, the time available for media consumption has helped determine it and hence the media markets. One study of the press in the first half of the nineteenth century, for example, notes that:

> To say that conditions were against the growth of a working class reading public would be to put it mildly. In the towns, a fourteen-hour working day was commonplace: those in even the most favoured trades did not get home until 6 or 7 p.m.; not until the 1860s was the Saturday half-holiday introduced. Another major problem was the absence of light: the window tax was not abolished until 1851 ... and in most houses tallow dips or candles were the only source of illumination apart from the fireplace. So the worker confined reading to Sundays – hence, of course, the popularity of Sunday newspapers.
>
> *Cranfield (1978), pp. 120–1*

The *amounts of money* that different groups have been able to spend on media products has also been a key variable in determining the demand side of media markets. In short, if people and groups are not able to afford to invest in magazines, newspapers, films, videos, CDs or the licence fees for broadcast media, for example, this will have obvious consequences for the media organisations involved and their ability to operate viably or profitably. Consumer spending on entertainment and the media in Britain exceeded £10 billion in the late 1980s and this sector continues to represent a significant part of the UK economy overall.

There have been and continue to be important differences in media expenditure patterns – 'media spending power' – between low-income and high-income groups in British society. Actual expenditure on magazines and books, newspapers, cinema, video and computer-based software and hardware varies sharply with income. Different levels of income and resource are basic factors in wider social class differences and have had important consequences for the kinds of cultural demand that different audiences have been able to make on media markets historically.

Cultural factors are perhaps a final set of issues to be considered as historical determinants of the demand for various kinds of entertainment and information facility. These are often the product of larger divisions of social class, gender, age or occupation, and are examined in more depth in Chapter 5. For the purposes of the current discussion, however, it is important to note that these factors are to do with *differential* styles and patterns of media consumption and media use. Part of the history of the media in Britain from the late nineteenth century onwards concerns the emergence of more distinct and differentiated groups of consumers, increasingly privatised and mobile. The post-1950s period, for example, saw rapid growth in media forms and industries – music, fashion, films etc. – aimed at a range of youth audiences and subcultures. More recently, accelerating segmentation of demand has been claimed across gender ('new' men and women) and generation ('grey power'). Another important historical factor is literacy – the education and ability to read and write. While Britain is assumed to have near-universal literacy in the 1990s, this has not always been the case. For the development of print and publishing industries and the press, particularly popular newspapers and magazines, literacy was an important cultural precondition, especially in the nineteenth century.

activity **2.3**

Start to map the growth of local media histories for press, cinema, radio and TV in your own locality or region. Research the ways in which time, affluence and other cultural factors have shaped the historical demands for media consumption. What additional factors and issues need to be considered?

Supply

The historical growth and regulation of media industries and institutions have determined how the various demands for forms of mediated information, knowledge and entertainment have been met. The ability to *supply* forms of media output has at a general level been subject to three principal forms of constraint: commercial, legal and technological conditions. These forces are explored in contemporary detail in Chapter 6.

Commercial markets and their operation have been significant in a number of ways. First, some of the principal historical dynamics of media development have resulted from the motive of commercial investment for profit. This broad aim has structured the operations of media producers and the contours of media markets in important ways. Since the late nineteenth century, investment in media industries has often been a high-risk business, and commercial success has been described in terms of 'giving the public what it wants', supplying the 'mainstream' or popular, profitable forms of demand. In practice this is an oversimplistic view, which neglects the ways in which demands are structured by what is supplied. Although in the late twentieth century there are ways in which these blunt distinctions are held to be increasingly outmoded by the sophistication of 'deregulated' high-tech media, commercial logic remains an important and central historical determinant or condition of media production. An important, related issue here concerns commercial ownership and control. The history of media industries in Britain since the turn of the century involves studying the power of those who have owned them; from the press barons – Northcliffe or Beaverbrook – to modern-day media proprietors and owners, such as Rupert Murdoch. Media industries tend to have developed highly concentrated patterns of ownership, and questions of ownership and control have great significance for the historical analysis of the rise of commercial forms of broadcasting and other media (see Chapter 6 for related discussion).

Statutory and legal controls have also played an important part in determining how media institutions and industries have been able to develop and operate. Alongside commercial considerations, a significant dimension in the history of the media in Britain is that of their regulation by law, by government and by the state. Given the ability of the media to deal in information, opinion and imagery, it is no surprise that, from their earliest days, media producers have attracted the attentions of established authority and governments, which have sought to control, repress or regulate their output and operation. Early print systems, for example, in the sixteenth and seventeenth centuries were subject to very strict regimes of licensing and prepublication censorship – everything that was to be published was required to be vetted or censored first. As the final case study in this chapter will outline, the growth and development of broadcasting in Britain, first in radio and then in television, have been powerfully structured by the requirements of government policies and legal codes, which have conditioned and constrained broadcasters in a number of significant ways.

Technologies and inventions, whether in the form of the

development of the rotary, steam-powered printing press in the 1820s, the 'wireless' of the 1920s or the communications satellite in the 1960s, have rightly been regarded as key factors in the historical growth of media industries.

> Technological changes further complicate the pattern of media supply, based often in underlying industrial and economic developments. Necessity, in the form of wars, imperial expansion, and commerce, has mothered a large proportion of the inventions which punctuate the history of the mass media. The steam printing press, wireless telegraphy, the cathode ray tube, satellites have all in turn recast the supply of media material and thus the range of options within which audiences exert their demands.
>
> *Golding (1974), p. 18*

While the development of new media technologies has undoubtedly had important consequences for the overall historical growth of media industries and forms, it is important to recognise that the history of the media entails more than a linear account of 'great inventions'. As Williams (1990) has noted, accounts of the impact of modern technologies are often characterised by an overemphasis upon the technologies and inventions themselves. This stress on the inevitable power of technologies to cause widespread social change and effects is known as *technological determinism*:

> It is an immensely powerful and now largely orthodox view of the nature of social change. New technologies are discovered, by an essentially internal process of research and development, which then sets the conditions for social change and progress. Progress, in particular, is the history of these inventions, which 'created the modern world'. The effects of these technologies, whether direct or indirect, foreseen or unforeseen, are as it were the rest of history.
>
> *Williams (1990), p. 13*

To counter this view it is important to note several points. First, processes of invention are complex and interwoven and have been shaped in a number of ways by commercial or military factors (as in the case of wireless transmission or the cathode ray tube, for example). Secondly, once inventions have been made, there is a process whereby their social applications and uses are discovered. The potentials of inventions are realised in actual historical periods where social, economic and other forces operate to make them actual and regulate them in particular ways. The principal failing of accounts which adopt a technologically determinist view of media history is the tendency to cut the technology off from the many other forces and conditions which shape its invention and deployment. Some new technologies have not been taken up and have failed (such as the 8-track sound system), while others have taken off in unanticipated ways (such as the personal stereo). (See Chapter 8 for further discussion.)

activity **2.4**

Look back at the research on forms of local media production that you started in the last activity and consider the ways in which commercial, legal and technical factors have shaped their history.

Research the technical history of a selected medium. Compile a map of the key inventions which have been influential. How have these inventions subsequently been institutionalised and regulated by other historical forces?

The remainder of this chapter is devoted to three case studies. These are chronologically organised and begin with a study of aspects of the press and press development in the nineteenth century. This is followed by a study of the emergence of cinema in Britain from the 1890s to the 1920s. Both of these case studies are brief outlines which should provide opportunity for further research. Finally, there is a more fully developed account of the development of broadcasting in Britain, from the 1920s to the present day.

CASE STUDY: RADICAL AND POPULAR PRESS IN THE NINETEENTH CENTURY

The press in the nineteenth century was the most important single medium for the communication of ideas, opinion and knowledge, and the newspaper was the first recognisable modern mass medium. Newspapers were not a nineteenth-century invention, although their production, forms and readerships changed considerably during that period as they became industrialised. The first daily newspaper, the *Daily Courant*, was published early in the eighteenth century (1702), and before that there were pamphlets, '*Mercuries*' and '*Intelligencers*', which carried reports of international events, limited forms of opinion and propagandist argument. By the end of the eighteenth century, the press had been granted the right to report parliamentary proceedings, and in spite of the fact that newspapers were controlled by means of the stamp taxes – duties paid per copy which kept the prices high – the foundations for a national, commercial press had been established.

The Times, published first as the *Daily Universal Register* in 1785, epitomised the new, respectable middle-class commercial press. By 1803 it had turned away from direct government subsidy, developing a stance which was independent of the government but generally supportive of establishment interests. This idea of 'independence', partly based on the view that newspapers should play an important intermediary role between governments and the governed, represented a significant historical shift, congruent with the formation of the new industrial and professional middle classes and their authority. In 1800 some 2,000 copies of *The Times* were being produced daily. By 1817, with the installation of new technologies – the steam-driven press – production increased to over 7,000.

Between the late 1790s and about the middle of the nineteenth century, the ascendancy and authority of this new model for the newspaper was powerfully challenged by another kind of press which served to articulate the demands of a very different culture and class. In this period, the radical press, also referred to as the 'pauper' or 'unstamped' press, emerged to play a part in voicing popular, oppositional opinion. As many social historians have noted, these papers played an important role in radicalising working-class ideas and politics, acting as agents or catalysts in the broader context of the development and experience of an industrialising, capitalist system. The period between the 1790s and the 1830s was marked by political turbulence and instability. This accompanied rapid population growth centralised on cities, the growth of the factory system, economic depressions, poverty and disease. 'Revolutionary' ideas from the continent, calls for political agitation or industrial unrest, demands for voting rights, reform and the fundamental necessity for a free press, were all given voice and communicated by the radical press and its producers. For those in power, these publications were a subversive threat, often referred to as 'incendiary' or 'poisonous' elements requiring suppression.

The first wave of these papers broke the law by their existence and circulation. They were 'unstamped' – that is, they had not paid the required duties or taxes – and, furthermore, usually the products of unlicensed presses. Important writers in the medium in this period include Tom Paine and William Cobbett. Their works were usually in the form of a pamphlet, often the script of a speech (see, for example, Chapter 3, p. 78). Paine's *Rights of Man* sold 50,000 copies within a few

THE
POOR MAN'S GUARDIAN.
A Weekly Newspaper
FOR THE PEOPLE.

PUBLISHED, CONTRARY TO "LAW," TO TRY THE
POWER OF "MIGHT" AGAINST "RIGHT."

No. 3.   Saturday, July 23, 1831.   [Price 1*d.*]

Friends, Brethren, and Fellow-Countrymen,

OUR tyrants have summoned us to Bow-street, to act over again the farce of *the* "*Law,*" before "their worships" Birnie and Halls.

Our course is adopted, nor shall we waste any more of our valuable time in striving to *evade* the power of *tyranny*; we have raised our standard of *defiance*, and we will stand by it, or fall by it—if so it must be—if you desert us in the good fight which we undertake for your sakes,—but which you will not do; yes, we depend upon your support, and *fearless* and confident as the unarmed David, will we grapple with our giant foe!

So; our masters are not content with the convictions already obtained; they will not enforce *them*, but will obtain so many others, until they have sufficient to make our imprisonment perpetual, and beyond all ransom. Merciful masters!—Do you not see their policy—their deadly policy? all that they know of virtue, is the empty name; and they know no more of honesty or moral courage; they cannot imagine to themselves a man who could hold himself more happy and more free in the dungeon of a tyrant, and with the fetters of despotism around his limbs, than in the enjoyment of personal liberty and domestic luxury, purchased by the compromise of all his natural rights, and by tame submission to the will—or "THE LAW" —of a self-elected and arbitrary POWER:—but they shall find themselves mistaken; there are many such men, we trust, and of them, we equally trust, we are the very least determined and most unworthy. Are they not mistaken, fellow-countrymen? are there not among you thousands, and hundreds of thousands, who envy us the proud post which fortune has assigned to us; are there not millions among you ready to support us even to loss of liberty—to loss of life (if so it must be!) in our struggle for common *justice* against brute MIGHT? Need we ask you? OUR FULLEST TRUST IS IN YOU!—But—to return to whence we digressed —knowing no more of human nature than their own narrow and self-acquaintance teaches them, our tyrants *mercifully* restrain their present means of persecution, until they have completely hemmed us in on all sides, and shut out the possibility of escape: the humbuggery of "*the law*" is getting more and more into contempt, and requires some terrible proof

of its dangerous omnipotence; to enforce, therefore, two paltry convictions of five pounds each would, as they think, be a mere timely notice of which we should of course avail ourselves, nor continue our offending; but they require a victim—"*to guilty* minds a terrible example,"—and they, therefore, suspend their present powers, in order to lull us into indolent security, until their operations for our destruction are complete. Fools! they little think that we would resist the penalty of a single penny, as much as we would one of a million or tens of millions! the question with us is not one of pounds, shillings, and pence, but one of right--indisputable right--not "*legal*" right, but *moral* right—not of "law," but of justice—not of individual interest, but general principle,—and we cannot—will not—surrender one inch of ground! we may be vanquished—beaten down—enchained—imprisoned—murdered—but we shall be so overcome only by the no longer disguised "virtue" of BRUTE FORCE.

Again, let us firmly declare that we dispute the power of any one man, or any set of men, however small or however great their number, to make "laws" affecting life and liberty, without any other authority than their own pleasure: they make "law" for themselves, or for so many as please to sanction them, but though we were the only man in this kingdom who objects to their power, they can have no *moral right* to subject an unwilling and adverse party to rules which suit their own interests: we object to, and dispute all their "laws;" and we shall equally object and dispute the "laws" of any "*reformed*" legislature, which shall *not* be specially authorized by ourselves: what! do not they themselves declare by their own "laws," that nothing—no every day— trifling transaction, done on our behalf by any third party, is binding on us, without our specific warrant of attorney, or special appointment of agency? and must we then be bound against our will—against all principles of *right, morality,* and equity, in matters of life, and freedom, and happiness, by the independent "law" of perfect strangers? no, their own "laws" find them *guilty* of oppression and injustice —their own "laws" justify our resistance and defiance! numbers, either on one side or the other, cannot, in a moral point of view, alter the case: whether there be only one tyrant and millions of weeks in 1791; Cobbett's *Address to Journeymen and Labourers* sold 200,000 in 1826. Other radical publications, from the many titles in the period, include the *Black Dwarf* (1817), which specialised in sarcasm and attacks on government and royal personalities; the *Gorgon* (1818), which advocated practical reform of voting rights; and the *Penny Politician* (1818), which was published under the masthead 'Let's Die Like Men and Not Like Slaves' and attacked the whole system of industrial production and corrupt politics.

The high point of this early period was reached with the Peterloo Massacre (1819), when armed troops forcibly broke up a mass meeting about parliamentary reform held at St Peter's Fields, Manchester. Eleven people were killed as a result. During this period, the radical press faced the Gagging Bills (1819–20), laws which extended and increased the stamp taxes and strengthened the legal offence of seditious libel. Many of the writers and publishers of radical papers were arrested and served long periods in jail, in some cases continuing to write from prison. Against these odds, the papers had succeeded in establishing a radical reading public and unifying oppositional politics. The attempts at their suppression were an index of this success, as were the many counter-propaganda publications they gave rise to (the *White Dwarf*, for example).

By the 1830s, the early reformist types of argument became overlaid with a more radical critique of capitalism as a whole. The focus of attack for many radical publications switched from political oppression to the inequalities produced by the emergent economic and industrial order and the law. Increasingly, the papers called for mass agitation and the power of united combination of the working and labouring classes. Some of the most famous radical titles are associated with this period (Figures 2.3 and 2.4). The *Poor Man's Guardian* (1831), *Working Man's Friend* (1832), *Destructive* (1832), *Porcupine* (1833) and the *Gauntlet* (1833) all enjoyed high circulations by the standards of the day. In order to evade prosecution for not paying the stamp tax, some publications were printed either on cloth, like the *Political Handkerchief* (1831) or on a thin wooden veneer, like the *Political Touchwood* (1830).

Circulations for radical papers such as the *Poor Man's Guardian* are estimated to exceed 16,000 copies for some editions. To this figure, high by comparison with other publications of the age, it is important to add a multiple readership figure:

even if a cautious estimate of ten readers per copy is taken as the norm for radical papers such as the 'Northern Star' and its successor, 'Reynolds News', each reached at their peak, before the repeal of the stamp duty, half a million readers when the population of England and Wales over the age of 14 was little over 10 million.

Curran and Seaton (1991), p. 14

From the late 1840s onwards, however, the power of this type of newspaper began to decline. Some titles became affiliated to organised labour and union movements and, rather than advocating total change in society, they argued instead for practical reform. The decline in these publications is also explained in a number of other ways.

2.4 Source: The Bodleian Library. John Johnson Collection

WANTED
SOME HUNDREDS OF
POOR MEN

Out of employ, *who have* NOTHING TO RISK---some of those persons to whom DISTRESS, occasioned by *tyrannical government*, has made a PRISON a desirable HOME.

An honest, patriotic, and moral way of procuring *bread* and *shelter*, and moreover of earning the thanks of their fellow-countrymen, now presents itself to such patriotic Englishmen as will, in *defiance of the most* ODIOUS "LAWS" of a most *odious, self-elected Tyranny*, imposed upon an *Enslaved and Oppressed People*, sell to the poor and the ignorant The

"POOR MAN'S GUARDIAN" AND "REPUBLICAN,"

Weekly "Papers" for the People,

Published in defiance of "Law," to try the power of "*Might*" against "*Right*."

N. B. *A Subscription* is opened for the *relief, support, encouragement,* and *reward* of such persons as may be Imprisoned by the WHIG TYRANTS.

HETHERINGTON, Printer, 13, Kingate Street Holborn.

2.5 *(opposite) The Penny Magazine*, 27 October 1832. Source: The Bodleian Library. Johnson.d. 405–407

THE PENNY MAGAZINE

OF THE

Society for the Diffusion of Useful Knowledge.

36.]   PUBLISHED EVERY SATURDAY.   [OCTOBER 27, 1832.

THE BOA CONSTRICTOR.

[The Boa Constrictor about to strike a Rabbit.]

ONE of the most interesting objects in the fine collection of animals at the Surrey Zoological Gardens, is the Boa Constrictor. Curled up in a large box, through the upper grating of which it may be conveniently examined, this enormous reptile lies for weeks in a quiet and almost torpid state. The capacity which this class of animals possess of requiring food only at very long intervals, accounts for the inactive condition in which they principally live; but when the feeling of hunger becomes strong they rouse themselves from their long repose, and the voracity of their appetite is then as remarkable as their previous indifference. In a state of confinement the boa takes food at intervals of a month or six weeks; but he then swallows an entire rabbit or fowl, which is put in his cage. The artist who made the drawing for the above wood-cut, saw the boa at the Surrey Zoological Gardens precisely in the attitude which he has represented. The time having arrived when he was expected to require food, a live rabbit was put into his box. The poor little quadruped remained uninjured for several days, till he became familiar with his terrible enemy. On a sudden, while the artist was observing the ill-sorted pair, the reptile suddenly rose up, and, opening his fearful jaws, made a stroke at the rabbit, who was climbing up the end of the box; but, as if his appetite was not sufficiently eager, he suddenly drew back, when within an inch of his prey, and sunk into his wonted lethargy. The rabbit, unconscious of the danger which was passed for a short season, began to play about the scaly folds of his companion; but the keeper said that his respite would be brief, and that he would be swallowed the next day without any qualms.

All the tribe of serpents are sustained by animal food. The smaller species devour insects, lizards, frogs, and snails; but the larger species, and especially the boa, not unfrequently attack very large quadrupeds. In seizing upon so small a victim as a rabbit, the boa constrictor would swallow it without much difficulty; because the peculiar construction of the mouth and throat of this species enables them to expand, so as to receive within

JOHN BULL.

"FOR GOD, THE KING, AND THE PEOPLE!"

VOL. VIII.—No. 403. SUNDAY, AUGUST 31, 1828. Price 7*d.*

UNDER THE ESPECIAL PATRONAGE OF HIS MAJESTY,

ROYAL GARDENS, VAUXHALL.—OPEN A FEW NIGHTS LONGER.—The Proprietors respectfully acquaint the public, that in consequence of the decidedly favourable change in the weather, the Gardens will be open next MONDAY, WEDNESDAY, and FRIDAY, when the

UNION GALA

Will be Repeated, with, if possible, increased splendour and effect.

The whole of the ILLUMINATIONS, DECORATIONS, MOTTOS, &c. Which afforded so much delight last week, will be again exhibited, and a continual succession of Entertainments take place from the time the doors open, including the amusing

LOTTERY PRESENTS.

Doors open at Seven.—Admission, 4s.

THEATRE ROYAL, HAYMARKET.—To-morrow Evening, the Opera of CLARI, with The GREEN EYED MONSTER, and The TWO FRIENDS—Tuesday, Love in a Village, with The Green Eyed Monster, and Love, Law, and Physic—Wednesday, The Way to Keep Him, with The Green Eyed Monster, and The Sleeping Draught—Thursday, The Lord of the Manor, with The Green Eyed Monster, and The Two Friends—Friday, She Would and She Would Not, with 'Twixt the Cup and the Lip, and The Green Eyed Monster—Saturday, The Green Eyed Monster, with The Two Friends, and other Entertainments.

SURREY THEATRE.—Under the Direction of Mr. Elliston.—To-morrow, JANE SHORE, with POLICHINEL VAMPIRE, and The IRRESISTIBLES.—On Tuesday, a New Opera, entitled SYLVANA! (the first production of the late C. M. Von Weber), the principal characters by Miss Graddon, Mr. Philipps, Mr. Yardley, Mrs. Fitzwilliam, Mrs. Vale, Miss Helme, &c. &c. After which, The Irresistibles.—On Wednesday, Thursday, Friday, and Saturday Evenings, A favourite Opera, with The Irresistibles.—The Public will please to notice, that the doors of this Theatre will not in future be opened before Six o'clock,—the performance will commence as usual at half-past Six.

SADLER'S WELLS.—Under the Patronage of the Duke of Clarence.—To-morrow, and following Evenings, The FALSE MARRIAGE; or, Brother and Sister. After which, the new admired Ballet, by Mrs. Searle and Thirty of her Pupils, called the BRIDE and BRIDEGROOM. To which will be added the Melo-drama of The SWISS BOY; or, the Wanderers. The whole to conclude with, for this week only, the popular Comic Sketch, called JACK SHEPPARD, the Housebreaker.—In addition to the above performances, on Wednesday, Thursday, Friday, and Saturday, will be exhibited a Grand Display of FIRE WORKS.

ROYAL AMPHITHEATRE (ASTLEY'S).—Mr. WEST has the pleasure of announcing to the Public, that Mr. Price, Manager of the Theatre Royal, Drury-lane, having kindly granted permission to him to perform the magnificent Spectacle of BLUE BEARD; or, Female Curiosity, it will be produced (for the first time at this Theatre) TO-MORROW EVENING, Monday, Sept. 1, for the BENEFIT of Mrs. WEST; to commence at half-past six precisely. In the procession over the mountains, Blue Beard will appear on a real Elephant. After Blue Beard, the Elephant will go through his sagacious tricks in the Circle. First night of the Double Tight Rope, by Miss Woolford and Miss Cooke—Mr. Ducrow will appear three times in the Circle, and introduce his new Acts, and manage his beautiful Persian Horse—The Flying Indian on the Slack Rope. To conclude with "C'est l'Amour, l'Amour, l'Amour;" or, Who can Help it?—The whole of the Company will appear in the different performances of this evening, for particulars of which, see the bills of the day.

NOT FOR ME, OR THE APPLE OF DISCORD. The whole of the Music of the above Opera, composed by L. Maurer, and arranged by W. Hawes, as performed at the Theatre Royal, English Opera House, is now published, and may be had at No. 7, Adelphi Terrace, Strand, and at the principal Music-shops. Also, Mozart's Opera "Tit for Tat, or the Tables Turned," and Paer's Opera of "The Freebooters."

MUSICAL COMPOSITION.

Recently published, in folio, half-bound, price 21s.

A *TREATISE on the ART of MUSIC*; in which the Elements of Harmony and Air are practically considered, and illustrated by an Hundred and Fifty Examples, in Notes, many of them taken from the best Authors: the whole being intended as a course of Lectures preparatory to the Practice of THOROUGH-BASS and MUSICAL COMPOSITION. By the Rev. W. JONES, M.A. F.R.S., late of Nayland, Suffolk; Author of "Lectures on the Figurative Language of Scripture;" "The Catholic Doctrine of the Trinity Proved," &c. &c.

☞ The Musical Examples may be purchased separately, price 7s.

"Mr. Jones's Treatise may be studied with great advantage, and ought to be so, by those who have music (properly so called) in their souls."—Gent.'s Mag.

See also the Harmonicon for May, which contains Mr. Jones's admired Air, "Sweet, lovely, chaste."

Published by Longman and Co. London; and G. W. Fulcher, Sudbury.

HANDEL'S ORATORIOS.—Just published,

THE MESSIAH; a Sacred Oratorio, composed by G. F. Handel, with the additional Accompaniments by Mozart. Part One. The full Score, with a compressed Accompaniment for the Organ or Piano-forte; by J. Addison.

SAMSON, and JUDAS MACCABEUS: in full Score, with a compressed Accompaniment, by J. Addison.

☞ In this Edition of Handel's Oratorios, the Score is left for study, while the Accompaniment presents its essence, and offers every facility for the Amateur and the Student. The beauty of the compositions are too well known to require comment, and they are now presented in such a form as to render their addition to the library an acquisition which combines ornament and utility.

GOULDING and D'ALMAINE, 20, Soho-square.

Parts Two and Three of "The Messiah" will be ready in October.

Just published, price 3s.

THE HARMONICON, a Popular Journal of Music. In each Monthly Number of this elegant publication are given seven Pieces of Vocal and Instrumental music, arranged for the Piano forte and Harp, and occasionally with Accompaniments for the Flute and Violin. The original music is by some of the most celebrated composers of the present day, and the selections comprise the finest pieces of the great masters, modernized and newly arranged for private performance. The Magazine department of the Harmonicon consists of Essays on musical subjects, correspondence, and reports of the state of music in all parts of the world, together with elaborate criticisms, illustrated by extracts from new musical works. The various contents of this publication evidently render it an invaluable acquisition alike to musical families and societies, to the amateur and the professor. The Number just published for September, contains—Music: I. Arietta, by Carlo Delle Torre. II. Duet, George Haydn. III. Ballad, J. C. Taws, (of Philadelphia). IV. Rondoletto, for Piano-forte, F. Hünten. V. Introduction and Chorus, for Piano-forte, (from Jessonda,) Spohr. The Magazine Department contains the usual variety of essays, correspondence, criticism, and musical intelligence.—London: Published by Samuel Leigh, 18, Strand, and sold by all booksellers, musicsellers, and teachers in town & country

NEW MUSIC.—Published by MAYHEW and Co. 17, Old Bond-street.

BARNETT'S SONGS of the MINSTRELS, Price 15s.; dedicated by permission to her Royal Highness the Duchess of Kent; Containing—

Albert was the bravest Knight	Bohemian Minstrel.
Fair Christabel was a Lady bright	English Minstrel.
The Mountaineer's Return	Swiss Minstrel.
At a Moonlight hour a Lady listen'd	Venetian Minstrel.
A Highland Minstrel Boy	Scotch Minstrel.
Two Pages met in a Forest	French Minstrel.
Come strike the Harp in Woman's praise	Irish Minstrel.
I knew a Sicilian Maid	Sicilian Minstrel.
A Harper sat by a tranquil stream	Welsh Minstrel.
In earlier days I have often stray'd	Spanish Minstrel.
A Minstrel Savoyard	Savoyard Minstrel.
Merrily merrily sounds the Horn	German Minstrel.

The following are Harmonized:—

The Bohemian Minstrel	for Three Voices.
The Venetian Minstrel	for Two Voices.
The Spanish Minstrel	for ditto ditto.
The German Minstrel	as Glee and Chorus.

The whole of the above are arranged for the Spanish Guitar, in Four Books by Charles Eulenstein. Price 2s. 6d. each.

These compositions are entitled "Songs of the Minstrels," and do equal honour to the poet and the musician. They contain airs of twelve different nations, and very happily preserve the various characters of them all. Indeed, we may well pronounce them to form another of Mr. Barnett's truly characteristic works, adapted to words at the same time highly lyrical and expressive. The Scotch, Venetian, Savoyard, German and Spanish airs, are particularly attractive; and we are sure that when its merits are known, this series will find a place in every drawing-room.—Vide Literary Gazette.

HICKSON'S NEW GAME SAUCE, is particularly recommended to the notice of Sportsmen and Epicures as a Sauce differing from others, and peculiarly suited to impart a high-relish to Grouse, Game of all sorts, Wild Fowls, &c.—Hickson's, 72, Welbeck-street; and Milton and Co.'s, 171, Strand.

THE THIRD YORKSHIRE MUSICAL FESTIVAL for the BENEFIT of the York County Hospital, and the Infirmaries of Leeds, Hull, and Sheffield, by Permission, and with the Sanction, of the Very Rev. the Dean, and of the Venerable the Chapter of York, is appointed to be held in YORK MINSTER, on TUESDAY, SEPTEMBER 23, 1828, and the Three following Days. PATRON—The King's Most Excellent Majesty.

PRESIDENT—His Grace the Lord Archbishop of York.

And under the Patronage of the principal Nobility and Gentry of the County.

Chairman of the Committee of Management—Mr. W. H. Dixon.

On TUESDAY and WEDNESDAY, September 23 and 24, will be performed in the Minster, SELECTIONS of SACRED MUSIC.

On THURSDAY, September 25, The MESSIAH.

And on FRIDAY, Sept. 26, a THIRD SELECTION of SACRED MUSIC.

On TUESDAY EVENING, Sept. 23, and the Two following Evenings, will be GRAND CONCERTS, in the FESTIVAL CONCERT ROOM.

The following Performers are already engaged:

VOCAL.

Madame CATALANI, Madame CARADORI ALLAN, Miss STEPHENS, Mrs. W. KNYVETT, and Mrs. P. ATKINSON.

Mr. BRAHAM, Mr. VAUGHAN, Mr. PHILLIPS, Mr. W. KNYVETT, Mr. TERRAIL, Mr. E. TAYLOR, and Signor DE BEGNIS.

INSTUMENTAL.

Leaders of the Band—Morning, Mr. Cramer......Evening, Mr. Mori.

Other Principal Performers: Messrs. R. Ashley, Daniels, R. Lindley, W. Lindley, Moralt, Dragonetti, Anfossi, Nicholson, Card, Willman, Ling, Powell, Sharp, Witton, Tully, Addison, Gledhill, Lyon, J. Mackintosh, Harper, Wallis, A. Griesbach, Mariotti, Smithies, Schoengen, Chip, Wilcox, Fleischer, Eley, Brooks, Watkins, Bannister, Binfield, Ella, Reeve, Abbott, Dance, Taylor, Gattie, Jolly, Guynemer, Anderson, R. Mackintosh, Cole, Thomas, Pigott, Nicks, S. Calkin, J. Calkin, Platt, Rae, Cummins, Penson, &c. &c.

Conductor, Mr. Greatorex.—Assistant Conductors, Mr. Camidge, and Dr. Camidge, Organists of the Cathedral; Mr. White, and Mr. P. Knapton.

In addition to the names which have been particularized, the Orchestra will include many other eminent Performers. The Chorus will be complete and effective; and the entire Band will consist of SIX HUNDRED PERFORMERS.

On the EVENING of MONDAY, Sept. 22, there will be a BALL in the ASSEMBLY ROOMS; and on the EVENING of FRIDAY, Sept. 26, a GRAND FANCY DRESS BALL, in the Festival Concert Room and Assembly Rooms, for which Litolff's celebrated Quadrille band is engaged.

☞ The Committee are ready to afford assistance to strangers, in procuring LODGINGS and ACCOMMODATIONS. A List of Lodgings, with particulars and terms, is kept by Mr. Marsh, Bookseller, Minster-Gates.—Letters to be addressed to the Honorary Secretary of the Yorkshire Musical Festival, York.

PIANO-FORTES TUNED, by KIRKMAN, late Tuner at Broadwood's, (Son of Kirkman, Maker to his Majesty). N.B. Instruments within 10 miles of town attended on moderate terms. Address, (post paid), at 15, Mortimer street, Cavendish-square.

TO THE CLERGY.—A Beneficed Clergyman, having licence of non-residence, is anxious to obtain a CURACY or CHAPEL in a desirable sphere of usefulness. Full occupation being his principal object, stipend would not be particularly regarded. He would be willing to EXCHANGE his Village Living under value and with light duty, or the CURACY thereof, which might be accepted as a Title; for a more active scene of labour.—Letters with full particulars only, and real address, to be directed, post paid, to F. G., at Walsh and Son's, No. 2, Inner Temple-lane.

A LIVING.—WANTED to PURCHASE, the PERPETUAL ADVOWSON of a LIVING, within 100 miles of London, with prospect of very early possession.—Apply, if by letter, post paid, to A. B., Mr. James Darling's, Bookseller, 22, Little Queen-street, Lincoln's Inn-fields.

PRIVATE PUPIL.—A Married CLERGYMAN, for some years Tutor to a Nobleman, and subsequently receiving Six Pupils into his house, a moderate distance from London, would be glad to fill a VACANCY with a GENTLEMAN'S SON, whose education or health may require more than common attention.—Letters addressed to Rev. H. S., Messrs. Harding and Lepard's, Booksellers, 4, Pall-mall East, London, will be duly forwarded to him in the country.

ETON or HARROW SCHOOL.—A Private Tutor, whose chief employment is in preparing Young Gentlemen for the Public Schools, wishes to add to his number of Pupils. Parents who are under the necessity of keeping their children from school through illness, can engage the Advertiser for an indefinite period. References highly respectable will be adduced.—Direct, post paid, to B. A. at Mr. Creswell's, 121, Crawford-street, Portman-square.

ALL Persons having any Demands on the Estate of JOHN FOX, Esq. formerly of Kingston, Jamaica, and late of Loose Hill, near Maidstone, Kent, deceased, are requested to forward the particulars thereof forthwith to Messrs. Geo. and Park Nelson, Solicitors to the Executors, No. 11, Essex-street, Strand, London.

ONE HUNDRED POUND NOTE.—FIVE POUNDS REWARD.—LOST a £100 NOTE, No. 1760, and dated the 26th day of July, 1828; whoever has found the same, or will give information to Messrs. Bromley, Solicitors, 3, Gray's Inn-square, whereby the same may be recovered, shall receive the sum of 5l.—The note has been stopped at the Bank of England.

THEATRE OF ANATOMY, Great Windmill-street.—The following COURSES of LECTURES will be delivered during the ensuing Season:—

ANATOMY, PHYSIOLOGY, PATHOLOGY, and SURGERY, by Mr. Charles Bell, Mr. Herbert Mayo, and Mr. Cæsar Hawkins.

ANATOMICAL DEMONSTRATIONS, by Mr. Cæsar Hawkins.

THEORY and PRACTICE of PHYSIC, by Dr. Chambers and Dr. Macleod.

THEORY and PRACTICE of SURGERY, by Mr. Brodie.

PRINCIPLES and PRACTICE of MIDWIFERY, by Mr. Stone.

MATERIA MEDICA, by Dr. Macleod.

BOTANY, by Mr. Burnett.

For further particulars enquire at the Theatre; at the Hospitals or Dispensaries at the West End of London; or at the Residences of the different Lecturers.

TO BE LET.—BOARDING and DAY SCHOOL, which has been established more than 50 years, to be disposed of; the present owner and occupier is induced to relinquish it through the state of his health solely. The situation and adaptation of the premises are most eligible: the inhabitants of the place about forty thousand, the neighbourhood respectable and wealthy. Apply to A. T., at Combe and Son's, Booksellers, Leicester, if by letter, paid.

PURE WINE, free from Spirit, possessing a very agreeable flavour, at 26s. per dozen, 23l. per Hogshead, or 12l. per quarter pipe. A native of Spain has devoted a considerable time to the cultivation of the Sherry Grape, at the Cape of Good Hope, with such success, that the Governor and Inhabitants have declared his productions equal to the best Spanish Wine; which a single trial will prove, and remove the prejudices that exist against the wines of that Colony. Orders addressed to Signor Deroy, No. 3, Pall-Mall-place, Pall Mall, will meet due attention.

NATIONAL MEDAL.—To His Royal Highness PRINCE WILLIAM HENRY, DUKE OF CLARENCE, Lord High Admiral of Great Britain and Ireland.—THIS MEDAL, IN COMMEMORATION OF HIS ROYAL HIGHNESS'S ACCESSION TO THE ANCIENT AND IMPORTANT OFFICE OF LORD HIGH ADMIRAL, is, with permission, dedicated by the Subscribers.—The Portrait of His Royal Highness, expressly for this Medal, is modelled from the life, and executed in Steel by Mr. Henning. The Reverse, selected from the Drawings of eminent Artists, to be struck from the Press of Messrs. Rundell, Bridge, and Rundell. The MEDALS are of Silver Gilt, in purple cases, price Five Guineas; and of Copper, from His Majesty's Ships most distinguished in the late War, price One Guinea; STRUCK on the ANNIVERSARY of His Royal Highness the LORD HIGH ADMIRAL'S APPOINTMENT.

The following Bankers will receive Subscriptions:—Messrs. Coutts and Co. Strand; Messrs. Cockburn and Co., Treasurers, Whitehall; Sir W. Curtis, Bart. Robarts, and Curtis, Lombard-street; Messrs. Herries, Farquhar, and Co. St. James's-street; Bank of Ireland; Messrs. Ramsay & Co. Edinburgh; Messrs. Rothschild, Paris, Vienna, & Naples.

TWENTY-SIXTH LIST.

Names of Subscribers.	Medals.	Names of Subscribers.	Medals.
Capt. H. H. Christian	1 silver	Lieut. Robt. Wynyard	1 copper
Capt. Astley	1 silver	Lieut. E. B. Pim	1 copper
Capt. Hunn	1 silver	Lieut. A. Brooking	1 copper
Capt. Wm. Cook	1 copper	Lieut. J. N. Gladstone	1 copper
Capt. Robt. Maunsell	1 copper	Mr. Rich. Bullen, R.N.	1 copper
Capt. Thos. James	1 copper	Wm. Murray, Esq.	1 copper
Com: P. P. King	1 copper	Thomas Searle, Esq.	1 copper
Com. Rich. Devonshire	1 copper		

[List to be continued.]

The Subscribers, their Bankers, and Agents, are requested not to pay over any money, except to the Bankers above-named, nor receive any Medals except those issued through the medium of the Treasurers.

As the Dies will be destroyed so soon as the number of Medals commanded are struck, Persons wishing to subscribe are requested to send in their names without delay.

THEATRE of ANATOMY and MEDICINE, Webb-street, Maze Pond, Borough.

The WINTER COURSE of LECTURES delivered at this Theatre, will commence on WEDNESDAY, October 1st.

ANATOMY and PHYSIOLOGY, by Mr. Grainger and Mr. Pilcher.

DISSECTIONS as usual.

PRINCIPLES and PRACTICE of PHYSIC, by Dr. Armstrong.

MATERIA MEDICA and BOTANY, by Dr. Boott.

PRINCIPLES and PRACTICE of MIDWIFERY, and the Diseases of Women and Children, by Dr. Hopkins.

CHEMISTRY, by Mr. Cooper.

For particulars apply to Mr. Highley, Medical Bookseller, at the Theatre, or 174, Fleet-street.

☞ Mr. Highley is authorised to enter Gentlemen to the above Lectures.

GUY'S HOSPITAL.—The Autumnal COURSE of LECTURES will commence on WEDNESDAY, the 1st of October.

THEORY and PRACTICE of MEDICINE—Dr. Bright and Dr. Addison.

MATERIA MEDICA and THERAPEUTICS—Dr. Addison.

ANATOMY and OPERATIONS of SURGERY—Mr. Bransby Cooper.

PRINCIPLES and PRACTICE of SURGERY, (including Operations)—Mr. Key and Mr. Morgan.

MIDWIFERY, and Diseases of Women and Children—Dr. Blundell.

PHYSIOLOGY, or Laws of the Animal Œconomy—Dr. Blundell.

CHEMISTRY—Mr. A. Aikin and Mr. Barry.

STRUCTURE and DISEASES of the TEETH—Mr. Bell.

EXPERIMENTAL PHILOSOPHY—Professor Millington and Mr. Barry.

Clinical Lectures and Instructions, with Demonstrations in Morbid Anatomy, will be given during the Season.

For particulars apply to Mr. Stocker, Apothecary to the Hospital.

SCHOOL of ANATOMY, MEDICINE, SURGERY, and MIDWIFERY, Little Dean-street, Dean-street, Soho-square, London, (within a short distance of St. George's, St. Bartholomew's, the Middlesex, and Westminster Hospitals.)

The WINTER COURSES of LECTURES will be commenced on 2d of October.

ANATOMY and PHYSIOLOGY, with Demonstrations, Dissections and Examinations. By J. Smith, M.D. M.R.C.S.

PRINCIPLES and PRACTICE of MEDICINE, with Practical Instructions and Examinations. By Dr. Copland.

MATERIA MEDICA, PHARMACY, and MEDICAL BOTANY. By Dr. Wilmot.

PRINCIPLES and PRACTICE of SURGERY, with Practical Instructions and Examinations. By Mr. Alcock.

PRINCIPLES and PRACTICE of MIDWIFERY, with Cases and Clinical Instructions. By Dr. Hopkins.

MEDICAL JURISPRUDENCE, by Dr. Wilmot, (during the Summer.)

INFLUENCE of CLIMATE on HEALTH and DISEASE, embracing particularly the Disorders of Warm Countries, &c. [intended more especially for Gentlemen who purpose to enter the Public Services, or to proceed to the East or West Indies, or our other Colonies.] By Dr. Copland and Mr. Smith.

The Dissecting Rooms are very spacious, airy, and commodious; and the improved means of preventing putrefaction will be resorted to. Mr. Smith will personally superintend the Dissections.

. In addition to the usual Instructions, Students will have the advantage of observing, without expence, the Practice of the Lecturers at a dispensary attached to the School, where Practical Instructions on the Cases under treatment will be given. They will also have the benefit of attending the Medical Practice and Instructions of Dr. Copland, at the Royal Infirmary for Diseases of Children, and will have the use of a small but select Medical library at the School.

††† Prizes will be given, at the end of the Season, for Professional Attainments, to the most industrious and meritorious Students.

☞ For further Particulars apply at the School, or to Dr. Copland, 1, Bulstrode-street, Welbeck-street; to Mr. Smith, 16, Leicester-place, Leicester-square; to Dr. Wilmot, 3, Queen's-place, Kennington; to Mr. Alcock, 11, New Burlington-street; or to Dr. Hopkins, Queen-square, St. James's Park.

UNIVERSITY OF LONDON.

THE MEDICAL CLASSES will OPEN on WEDNESDAY, the 1st of October.

ANATOMY and OPERATIVE SURGERY—Granville S. Pattison, Esq., daily (except Saturday), from two to half-past three.

PHYSIOLOGY—Charles Bell, Esq., F.R.S. three times a week, 11 to 12.

NATURE and TREATMENT of DISEASES—John Conolly, M.D., daily (except Saturday), nine to ten A.M.

MIDWIFERY and DISEASES of WOMEN and CHILDREN—David D. Davis, M.D., four times a week, 10 to 11 A.M.

CLINICAL MEDICINE—Thomas Watson, M.D. Physician to the Middlesex Hospital, twice a week, six to seven P.M.

SURGERY and CLINICAL SURGERY—Charles Bell, Esq. Surgeon to the Middlesex Hopital, three times a week, six to seven P.M.

MATERIA MEDICA and PHARMACY—Anthony Todd Thomson, M.D. daily (except Saturday), eight to nine A.M.

CHEMISTRY—Edward Turner, M.D., daily, 10 to 11, commencing on the 3d November.

COMPARATIVE ANATOMY—Robert Grant, M.D., three times a week, from three to four P.M.

MEDICAL JURISPRUDENCE—John Gordon Smith, M.D. BOTANY—John Lindley, Esq. F.R.S., at the conclusion of the Winter and Spring Courses.

DISSECTIONS and DEMONSTRATIONS—James Bennett, Esq., daily.

HOSPITAL PRACTICE—Middlesex Hospital, daily, half-past twelve to half-past one.

DISPENSARY PRACTICE—University Dispensary, daily, from half-past twelve to half past one.

The MEDICAL CLASSES will close in May, but each Professor will give a Winter and Spring Course.

On WEDNESDAY, the 1st of October, at three o'clock, CHARLES BELL, Esq. will give the INTRODUCTORY LECTURE of his COURSE, and the other Professors will do the like at the same hour, on the succeeding days.—When all the Introductory Lectures of the several Medical Classes shall have been delivered, the Professors will commence their Courses at the hours above stated.

The Certificates of the Medical Professors will be received at the College of Surgeons and at Apothecaries Hall. The Lectures will be open to Students who may not desire certificates; or who wish merely to attend single Courses.

The classes for the other branches of education will open on the 3d of November, the particulars of which will be advertised hereafter.

Information respecting the system of education to be pursued at the University, with outlines of the Courses, tables of fees, &c., will be found in the "Second Statement by the Council," to be had of Longman's; Murray, Albemarle-street; and Taylor, 30, Upper Gower-street. Price 1s. 6d.

An abridgment of this Statement will be found in the chief periodical publications of June and July last.

The names of Students are entered at the University Chambers, 29, Percy-street; Bedford-square.—Letters requiring further information addressed to Mr. Thomas Coates as above, post paid, will be attended to, and all other particulars respecting the Medical School, may be obtained by application to any of the Medical Professors. By order of the Council,

University Chambers, Aug. 25. THOMAS COATES, Clerk.

TEN GUINEAS REWARD.—The following Persons having been indicted for ESCAPES out of the RULES of the KING'S BENCH PRISON, the above Reward will be paid by the Marshal, to any person or persons that will apprehend them, or any of them, or furnish the Marshal with such information as will enable him to apprehend them, or any of them, in this kingdom, viz.:—

SIR WALTER ROBERTS, Baronet. He was a banker at Cork, but is now in France, and comes over into this country occasionally to visit his estates in Devonshire.

HENRY WILLIAMS MACKRETH, Esq., lately a resident at Hammersmith.

NICHOLAS MILL, Esq. is supposed to be at Jersey or Guernsey, but occasionally comes to London.

FREDERICK CHARLES SPENCER PONSONBY, Esq. is well known in London.

WILLIAM KELLY, Esq. calling himself Captain Kelly, is well known in London and at Brighton.

CAPTAIN GEORGE FREDERICK ORD, a native of Cumberland.

Also, FIVE GUINEAS REWARD, for apprehending the following persons, viz.

RICHARD WILLIAM GLODE DOUGLAS, Esq. lately living at East Sheen, in the county of Surrey.

HAROLD STANLEY, an Attorney, well known.

EDWARD TIBBS, late a baker in the Borough.

There are many others who have committed escapes, whose names are intended to be laid before the public in a short time, with the sums which the Marshal has been obliged to pay for their BREACH OF HONOUR.

WM. JONES, Marshal.

King's Bench, 20th August, 1828

From the 1830s onwards, the radical press had to compete for sales with new publications which were stamped and legal and aimed at a more popular, educational or entertainment market. These appeared as weekly, instructive periodicals or as popular Sunday newspapers: *Lloyd's Weekly News*, the *Illustrated London News* and the *News of the World* all developed large, popular circulations during this period (Figures 2.5 and 2.6). The opposition to the stamp tax, or the 'tax on knowledge' as it was known, increased, and it became recognised that, contrary to its intended functions, it depressed the sales of the legal and respectable papers rather than those which continued unstamped. The solution to this paradox, for those in authority, lay in the reduction and then removal of the tax, which was finally repealed in 1855. As prices dropped and new technologies of production made possible cheaper, faster, more efficient processes, advertising came to play a central role in determining profitability, establishing what Curran and Seaton (1991) have called a new licensing system. Newspapers like *The Daily Telegraph* (1855) championed new forms of popular daily journalism developed first in the Sunday press, often illustrated, and featuring crime, sports stories and fashion reports, for instance. Newspapers came to depend upon large-scale investment, and became businesses. The latter half of the nineteenth century saw the continued expansion of this popular market, in part assisted by growing levels of literacy.

activity **2.5**

Choose one particular newspaper, local or national, and investigate its history. Research the key elements which have shaped its growth and development.

Using local library facilities, examine some of the different types of newspaper which were produced in your own locality or region during the nineteenth century. Visits to local newspaper archives can provide additional resources.

To what extent do radical publications exist today? In what ways do they differ from the earlier types of publication discussed above?

Choose some examples of popular papers from the late nineteenth century. How do they compare with the popular press of today?

2.6 *John Bull*, 31 August 1828

CASE STUDY: THE DEVELOPMENT OF BRITISH CINEMA FROM THE 1890S TO THE 1920S

> An historical survey needs to begin with the problem of how the cinema came into existence and to consider the reasons why certain potentials were realised and others ignored.
>
> *Armes (1978), p. 7*

There is considerable debate over the first cinematic performance in Britain. The first projected moving photographic picture show to a paying audience in Britain is generally recognised to have taken place at the London Polytechnic, Regent Street, in February 1896. This was a screening organised by the British representative of the French Lumière brothers, Louis and Auguste, who had staged what is generally regarded as the very first cinematic showing in the world, involving projection and audience payment, in Paris, December 1895. While this event is regarded as the forerunner of cinema, it is important to note that many other inventors and entrepreneurs across Europe and in the USA were on the brink of claiming to be the first to exhibit moving pictures. In 1894, the first English Kinetoscope Parlour had opened. This offered customers the chance to try Thomas Edison's patent kinetoscope, which was a coin-in-the-slot machine for viewing animated photographs.

The cinema is generally regarded as a means of modern mass communication which was invented. The technical development of *film* and the apparatus to project moving images were the result of processes of invention; however, the *cinema*, as a social institution, was discovered and evolved to realise the potentials of the technologies in particular ways. It did not emerge 'naturally' from the technologies. The principles underlying visual projection had been known and operated for centuries before the 1890s. The camera obscura, for example – a darkened room into which light passed through a small hole or lens, producing a projected picture on the wall opposite – had been used in Italy in the sixteenth century. Many inventions, including those central to the early development of cinematography, are best viewed as parts of complex and interwoven relationships:

> cinematography was usually the by-product of such various developments as the search for new types of explosives, the industrialisation of agriculture, and the invention of a new material for printers' rollers.
>
> *Chanan (1980), p. 10*

The formative influences on the emergence of moving picture technologies prior to this period include:

1 *Developments in photography* from the 1820s onwards. These include not only technical innovations but also consideration of the impact of photography on the visual arts and systems of representation.

2 *Developments in the 'science of perception'*. From the early nineteenth century some scientists had experimented with optical devices in the search for a more adequate understanding of how people 'saw' their environment. Several experiments were conducted which examined optical illusions, and the machines produced to test scientific hypotheses were later exploited in the Victorian, middle-class fascination for parlour spectacles and games. The bioscope and early animation machines were developed partly with this scientific impetus.

3 *Developments in the 'scientific study of motion'*. These were greatly assisted by, and in turn perfected, cameras and other photographic technologies. The work of some physiologists and photographers in Europe and the United States became concerned with capturing motion on film as realistically as possible.

4 *Pre-existing forms of exhibition and spectacle*, which included a diverse number of influences. Puppet shows and peep shows were popular much earlier than the nineteenth century. Theatrical traditions and devices, often using sophisticated lighting techniques, were also an important consideration. Of these precursors of the modern cinematic experience, one of the most important was the Magic Lantern, with which the principle of projection, albeit of still images, was firmly established. Throughout the nineteenth century they were developed to produce more and more sophisticated effects, some involving simple types of movement. The lantern developed, as Chanan has noted, somewhere 'between science and magic'. It was employed as a means of entertainment in music halls and fairgrounds, as a means of instruction, typically in the lecture hall, and as a domestic toy. Of these settings, the music hall and the travelling fairground became major exhibition centres for magic lantern shows, introducing the idea of frequent and reproducible visual performances; spectacles, often introduced by showmen, for which audiences paid money.

In the few years immediately before and after the Lumière brothers' invention in 1895, critics, journalists, and the pioneer cinematographers disagreed considerably among themselves as to the *social function* that they attributed to, or predicted, for the new machine; whether it was a means of preservation or of making archives, whether it was an auxiliary technology for research and teaching in sciences like botany or surgery; whether it was a new form of journalism, or an instrument of sentimental devotion, either private or public, which could perpetuate the living image of the dear departed one, and so on. That, over all these possibilities, the cinema could evolve into a machine for telling stories had never been considered.

Metz (1974), p. 93

It was, however, the ability to tell stories, recognised and developed by the traditions and expanding industry of popular entertainment, motivated by commercial gain and opportunity, which accounted for the very rapid take-off of cinema as a mass medium. By the end of 1896, only eight months after the initial public performance of film in Britain, moving pictures were part of many music hall shows up and down the country (Figures 2.7 and 2.8). The spectacle of moving pictures was augmented by music and often by live, spoken commentary or narrative to accompany the visual performance.

2.7 Wendon, D.J. (1974): *The Birth of the Movies*. E.P. Dutton & Co

This expansion in exhibition continued with accelerating speed and profitability into the 1900s. Renting and hiring circuits developed to supply and distribute films. Specialised premises and commercial interests pulled the exhibition of films out of music halls, first into vacant shops, known as 'shop shows' or 'penny gaffs', and after 1906 into custom-built premises – 'picture palaces', 'bijoux palaces' and 'majestics' (Figure 2.9). By 1909, largely to regulate the size, but also safety regulations concerning cinema assemblies, the First Cinematographic Act was passed in Parliament. In this year, estimates suggest that British production amounted to only about 20 per cent of films shown in British cinemas, and that

2.8 Wendon, D.J. (1974): *The Birth of the Movies*. E.P. Dutton & Co

2.9 Wendon, D.J. (1974): *The Birth of the Movies*. E.P. Dutton & Co

To-Night!   To-Night!

CALDER'S FAMOUS

CINEMATOGRAPH

AND

Popular Concert.

Don't miss seeing the Grand NEW PICTURES of

THE DREYFUS COURT MARTIAL.

The Prince of Wales in Edinburgh.
Sir Redvers Buller Embarking for Transvaal.
Scenes at the Highland Brigade Camp.
The Invercharron Gathering.
The Grand Fire Dance.
Barnum & Bailey's Procession.
The Mysterious Astrologer's Dream.
Spendid Train Scenes.
Grand Coloured Dances.
Comicalities and Burlesque Scenes, &c., &c.

Pictures of absorbing interest and Astounding Transformations.

SPLENDID • CONCERT

By First=Class Artistes.

DOORS OPEN AT 7.30.   CONCERT AT 8 P.M.
Popular Prices See Bills.

A BRIGHT UP TO DATE SPARKLING ENTERTAINMENT

2.10 Wendon, D.J. (1974): *The Birth of the Movies*. E.P. Dutton & Co

40 per cent were French, 30 per cent American and 10 per cent Italian.

By 1910, some 1,600 cinemas were in existence, and by the outbreak of the First World War in 1914, this figure had jumped to 4,000. The Cinema Commission of 1917 estimates annual weekly attendances at cinemas as 7–8 million pre-1914. It reported attendances of 20 million per week in 1917. By the end of the war, British cinema exhibition had developed into a major industry, based on a cinematic form inconceivable in the 1890s – the extended fictional feature film. This was reliant upon an increasingly complex product: melodramas, comedies, westerns, travelogues and superspectaculars were some of the early genres of popular 'silent' film (Figure 2.10). By the outbreak of war in 1914, however, Hollywood-produced American films accounted for over half of the domestic market: 'Ever since 1913 British audiences have seen more American than British films. Hollywood imagery, values and myths have for over sixty years been part of the imaginative and fantasy furniture of British minds' (Tunstall, 1983, p. 55). This trend – a domestic market dominated by overseas, mainly American productions – continued into the 1920s and, arguably, to the present day. Government legislation in 1927, the year of the first 'talkie', attempted to guarantee and preserve a quota of the home market for domestic production. Cinema attendances grew rapidly in the 1920s and throughout the inter-war period, becoming 'the essential social habit of the age' (Taylor, 1965).

activity **2.6**

Conduct some independent research on the early history of cinema in Britain. Oral history and local library and historical archives can be useful sources.

Research and build up a history of cinema from the earliest years onwards in your local town or area. Supplement this where possible with interviews and local newspaper archive research.

Investigate the reasons why the American Hollywood industry dominated British production and exhibition from the 1920s onwards.

CASE STUDY: BROADCASTING IN BRITAIN 1920-1994

The development of broadcasting from the 1920s to the present day covers a period of significant technological and cultural change, particularly in the areas of domestic affluence and lifestyle. The development of broadcasting can be seen as part of a relationship that also includes the state as regulator and the public as consumers. The dynamic nature of this relationship has meant that the means, structures and functions of broadcasting have had to evolve to meet the needs of new audiences and changing government legislation.

In the early stages of its history, broadcasting was shaped by government policy directed at establishing a national monopoly that was tied in with notions of offering a public service. This was an attempt to control both broadcasters and audiences. However, more recently, government legislation has been aimed at loosening some of these controls and 'deregulating' the duopoly of the BBC and IBA, in order to open up broadcasting and allow free-market commercialism to determine what is available to whom on what channels and at what cost.

BBC Radio: the 'Voice of the Nation'

From the beginning of broadcasting, various governments have tried to control its production. As early as 1904 the Postmaster General took responsibility for the allocation of broadcasting frequencies to avoid the 'chaos of the airwaves' that the introduction of commercial radio had created in America. During the First World War, radio transmissions were banned except for military use. In 1922 a group of radio equipment manufacturers, called the British Broadcasting Company, were given a licence to run a monopoly broadcasting service in London, Manchester and Birmingham.

The general manager of this new company was John Reith. The first programmes consisted mainly of news, political events and some music. All set owners were supposed to pay a fee of ten shillings (50p) which was collected by the Post Office, who then passed on half to the Company. As Scannell and Cardiff (1991) note, without any real discussion or ideological rationale two key ideas that were to shape broadcasting for the next seventy years had been established: the licence fee and the notion of a monopoly.

In 1923, when the *Radio Times* was first published (Figure 2.11), 80,000 licences had been issued. In 1924, King George V's opening of the Wembley Exhibition was broadcast live and heard by 10 million people; by 1925, the Company's

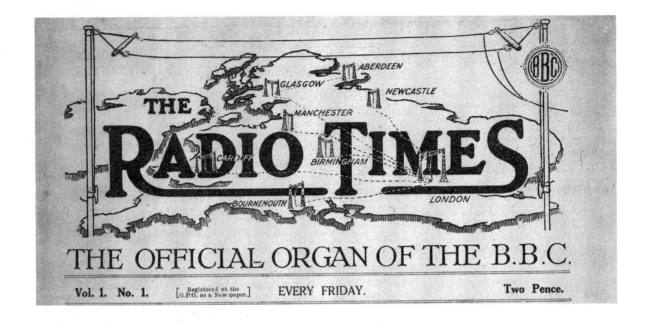

2.11 *Radio Times*, 13 January 1923

transmission covered 85 per cent of the United Kingdom. By 1927, the number of licences issued had increased to two million and there was concern from newspaper owners and producers that this new source of news and information might affect their profits from sales. As a result of their pressure the BBC was severely restricted, with a ban on news programmes before 7 p.m. and a clause that stipulated that the Company could not broadcast any news or information unless it had been obtained and paid for from the news agencies, which were controlled by the newspaper industry. Only in 1927, when the BBC became the state corporation, was it allowed to broadcast news bulletins earlier in the day.

In 1925 the government concluded that, although radio was too important to be left in the hands of a commercial company and that it was inappropriate in a democracy for broadcasting to be under direct state control, there was a need to maintain some kind of regulation on who provided what types of radio service. As a compromise, by Royal Charter, the British Broadcasting Company was changed from a public commercial company into an independent national organisation, the British Broadcasting Corporation, which would act as a monopoly and 'as a trustee for the national interest' (HMSO, 1966). The rationale was that the Corporation's political independence should be safeguarded by the fact that it would not be dependent upon the state for its finance but would be guaranteed an income through the licence fee, and would be spared the entertainment-led popularism of American radio or the British tabloid press.

The Royal Charter laid out the BBC's constitution: There would be twelve governors (the 'great and the good') appointed by the Privy Council for a five-year period and headed by a chairman. The governors would in turn appoint a Director-General who would be responsible for the day-to-day management of the BBC. This structure has continued into the 1990s with John Birt as the Director-General.

During the National Strike of 1926, when most newspapers were closed down by the strike action of the printing unions, the Company carried on broadcasting and provided the country with its only national source of news and information.

According to many commentators, including Garnham (1973), Hood (1980), Curran and Seaton (1991) and Scannell and Cardiff (1991), one of the strongest criticisms that can be and has been made of Reith was his apparent political naivety. Although he had a clear idea of what broadcasting should offer in cultural and moral terms, he never questioned its political role, perhaps assuming that independence guaranteed impartiality. Partly because of the limits the Charter placed upon the BBC's ability to deal with issues of 'controversy' and partly because of Reith's identification of a national culture that included the state, the church, the monarchy and his own 'élite' upper-middle-class Calvinist values, the BBC always seemed firmly to support the state and what was often identified as the 'national interest'. This resulted in Reith's inability to clarify the ambiguity that existed, and arguably still exists, in the relationship between the BBC and the government. Reith believed that the BBC should be above political fighting and he defended the use of the BBC by the government during the General Strike as an attempt to 'draw together the contending parties by creating an atmosphere of goodwill' (Curran and Seaton 1991). However, Reith also stated that 'Since the BBC was a national institution and since the Government in this crisis was acting for the people ... the BBC was for the Government in the crisis too' (Garnham, 1973, original reference).

As a result of this ambiguity there has continued to be tension between the BBC and the government of the day because of the expectations of governments, whether Conservative or Labour, that the BBC, as a national organisation, should support uncritically and without reservation the government's policies. This has often been in contrast to the BBC's belief that it is free to report in its own 'balanced' way about IRA supporters (*Real Lives*), military secrets (*Secret Society*), the wars in Suez, the Falklands and the Gulf, or the bombing of Libya by American planes. (See Chapter 4 for further discussion of these issues.)

By the time John Reith retired from the BBC in 1938, nearly 9 million radio licences were being issued annually (representing nearly three-quarters of all households in Britain). The radio had become the 'wireless', often combined with a record player to become a radiogram and given pride of place in the living room. The BBC was established as 'the voice of the nation' and was providing a service for people throughout Britain.

Reith's legacy

Any consideration of the development of broadcasting has to consider the influence of John Reith. Reith's philosophy is often summed up as simply being 'to educate, to inform and to entertain'. He believed that the BBC, through the new medium of radio, presented a great opportunity for helping the less educated (schools' broadcasts had been available since 1924) and the less informed, and for both 'bringing culture to the masses' and 'bringing the nation together'. Reith believed that the BBC had a responsibility to unify the whole nation with a public service where everyone had access to a wide range of high-quality programmes and reliable and objective news (Figure 2.12). The growth of radio had taken place at a time of great social change as a result of the aftermath of the First World War, partly because of increasing democratic emancipation as a result of the suffragette movement and partly because of wider educational opportunities. There were concerns in the government and upper classes about the Russian revolution and the social and political conflict of the General Strike and, later, the Depression. Reith saw the potential role of the BBC as a national service healing these wounds and promoting social unity, 'making the nation as one man' (Goodwin and Whannell, 1992).

The other main criticism of Reith's time as Director-General and of his legacy is the acceptance of the system of financing the BBC through the licence fee. As Garnham points out (1973), the BBC has never been financed independently by the licence fee but rather by the government deciding how much that licence fee should be. The BBC is therefore dependent upon the 'goodwill' of the government when its Charter comes up for renewal and, as a result of the tensions mentioned above, this goodwill is often absent. The BBC is also dependent upon the ideological imperatives of whatever political party is currently in power, and during the 1980s and 1990s, when the philosophy of 'deregulation' and 'market forces' have been paramount, the licence fee's increases have been limited and the BBC has been put under financial pressure (Figure 2.13).

PROGRAMMES for TUESDAY, January 10

2LO LONDON and 5XX DAVENTRY

10.30 a.m.	Time Signal; Weather forecast.
11.00	The Daventry Quartet with Frederick Allen (Daventry only).
12.00 p.m.	The Carlton Mason Sextet.
2.00	Interlude
3.00	The Daventry Quartet and Gerald Crofts, Anne Ballantyne.
4.00	William Hodgson's Marble Arch Pavilion Orchestra.
5.00	Miss Barbara Cartland: 'Settling into a House'.
5.15	The Children's Hour.
6.00	Gramophone Recital.
6.30	Time Signal; Weather Forecast; First General News Bulletin.
6.45	Gramophone Recital (continued).
7.00	Mr. J.W. Robertson Scott: 'The Month's Reviews'.
7.15	The Foundations of Music: Mozart's Violin Sonatas.
7.25	Topical talk.
7.45	A Light Operatic Programme.
9.00	Weather Forecast; Second General News Bulletin.
9.15	Prof. J. Arthur Thompson: 'Wonders of Deep Sea Life'.
9.30	Local Announcements (Daventry only).
9.35	Vaudeville.
10.30	Dance Music: Jay Whidden's Band.
12.00	Close Down.

2.12 Schedule taken from the *Radio Times*, 6 January 1923

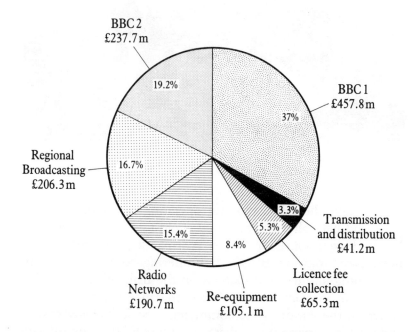

BBC 2
£237.7m — 19.2%

BBC 1
£457.8m — 37%

Regional Broadcasting
£206.3m — 16.7%

Radio Networks
£190.7m — 15.4%

Re-equipment
£105.1m — 8.4%

Licence fee collection
£65.3m — 5.3%

Transmission and distribution
£41.2m — 3.3%

Net other income: (£29.4m)   Deficit for year: £37.9m

2.13 How the licence income was spent in 1989/90

Broadcasting during the Second World Wars: BBC Radio as 'Voice of the People'

Up until the outbreak of the Second World War, the BBC tended to think of its audience as existing in a 'suburban utopia' – as a predominantly middle-class, discriminating, Home Counties audience whose interests were thought to include such 'high' cultural activities as poetry, drama, classical music and talks. This vision of the audience was largely based on the backgrounds and values of the people who worked in the BBC. According to Scannell (1987), the BBC under Reith promoted middle-class values of 'home life' and 'the family' as a comforting alternative to the cares and distractions of the world outside. In 1935 the *Radio Times* published a 'fireside edition' that espoused the virtues of the family sitting together around the fireside listening to the radio; just as the family came together to listen, so the nation came together through the radio (Figure 2.14). After John Reith's departure, some changes took place in this notion of who the BBC's audience was and what it wanted. The entertainment element was increased through the introduction of 'lighter' programmes like *Band Wagon*, with Arthur Askey, and the quiz show *Spelling Bees*, a genre imported from America that had been banned under Reith.

2.14 *Radio Times*, 15 April 1938

Although the BBC was still operating a monopoly, audiences did have alternatives. They could listen, for example, to Radio Luxembourg or Radio Normandie, commercial stations based outside Britain but offering some English-language programmes, and marked on the dials of most wireless sets. Their programmes were based on dance-band music from America; the stations were commercial and so had advertising, and some programmes were sponsored; the announcers sounded more casual and friendly; and the stations did not close down on Sundays on the assumption that listeners would all be at church.

2.15 *Radio Times*, Supplementary Issue, 4 September 1939

RADIO TIMES SUPPLEMENTARY ISSUE DATED 'SEPTEMBER 4, 1939   3

RADIO TIMES

Broadcasting Carries On !

With the crisis brought about by the outbreak of war in 1939, and particularly after Dunkirk in 1940, the BBC's role had to change (Figure 2.15). The audience could no longer be seen as the comfortable middle classes, actual or aspiring, but instead included workers in munitions factories, soldiers, sailors and airmen, as well as their wives, sisters and girl-friends, who were now being encouraged to move out of their domestic world and work in the factories or on the land. Instead of individual middle-class families sitting around the fireside, the audience had to be conceived of as a national, communal one in factory canteens or military camps. Under Reith the BBC had given the public not what it wanted but what the BBC (predominantly Reith) thought the public should have. In an attempt to address this 'new' audience, the newly formed Listener Research Unit actually asked people what they wanted and reported back on the popularity or otherwise of particular programmes.

The idea of 'segmenting' the BBC's provision to meet different audience requirements meant that the National Service was split into two: the Home Service, which continued to follow the style of the old National Service closely with its talks, plays and classical music, and the new, lighter, more popular Forces Programme, which was aimed specifically at this new working-class audience (Figures 2.16–2.18). The Forces Programme took on many of the populist styles and personalities of Radios Luxembourg and Normandie, including American shows by Bob Hope and Jack Benny. The station offered American dance-band music, revues and variety, and produced programmes like *Workers' Playtime*, *Music While You Work*, *Merry-Go-Round* and *Hi Gang*, a show made by Americans like B.B. Daniels and Ben Lyon who lived in Britain.

The style and content of the language became more popular and down to earth, with slang, humour, innuendo and

2.16 *Radio Times*, 16 February 1940

2.17 *Radio Times*, 16 February 1940

PROGRAMMES FOR
February 18—24

Radio Times, February 16, 1940. Vol. 66. No. 855. Registered at the G.P.O. as a Newspaper

PRICE TWOPENCE

RADIO TIMES
JOURNAL OF THE BRITISH BROADCASTING CORPORATION
(INCORPORATING WORLD-RADIO)

FOR THE FORCES

The twelve-hour daily
programmes start this week

The service of special programmes intended for men of the Navy, Army, and Air Force is being extended to twelve hours daily, from 11 a.m. to 11 p.m. Full details of all programmes are now given in the RADIO TIMES side by side with details of the Home Service programmes. Information about the new service will be found on page 3.

The Home Service

9.30 a.m.	Michaelmas Service.
10.15	Muriel Gale sings.
10.30	Interlude.
11.00	The Story of Russian Opera.
11.30	London Studio Players, music.
12.15 p.m.	The Diary of A Nobody, drama.
12.30	Plantation Echoes, folk-music.
12.50	Interlude.
1.25	Arthur Goldsbrough, organ music.
1.45	In Town Tonight.
2.15	In Your Garden.
2.30	Interlude.
4.30	Melody Mixture, light music.
5.00	Children's Hour including Prayers at 5.50.
6.00	Interlude.
6.25	National Savings Announcements.
6.30	Queen's Hall Light Orchestra.
7.00	Atlas of Snobbery, talk.
7.30	American Letter with Alistair Cooke.
7.45	Evening Service.
8.25	Interlude.
8.30	The Moonstone, drama.
9.00	Interlude.
10.38	Time For Verse.
11.00	Close Down.

2.18 Schedule taken from the *Radio Times*, 27 September 1946

---

11 a.m. to 7 p.m.	**FOR THE FORCES**	6 p.m. to 11 p.m.
804 kc/s 373.1 m.		877 kc/s 342.1 m.

3.30-4.0 *As Home Service*

4.0 ASSOCIATION FOOTBALL
The French Army *v.* The British Army
A commentary during the second half of the match, by Raymond Glendenning, from Lille

4.45 JAY WILBUR AND HIS BAND
in a special edition of
'Melody out of the Sky'
with star artists

5.15 W. H. SQUIRE
in a programme of popular cello pieces
Love, here is my heart
Silesu, arr. W. H. Squire
Gavotte in D..........................*Popper*
Träumerei (Dreaming)
Schumann, arr. Harold Samuel
Melody..............................*Rubinstein*

5.35 INVITATION TO THE DANCE
The first of a series of ballet music programmes
played by
The BBC Symphony Orchestra
Conducted by Clarence Raybould
Suite, The Nutcracker (Casse Noisette)
Tchaikovsky
1 Miniature Overture. 2 March. 3 Dance of the sugar-plum fairy. 4 Russian dance: Trepak. 5 Arabian dance. 6 Chinese dance. 7 Reed-pipe dance. 8 Flower waltz

On 804 kc/s 373.1 m.
and 877 kc/s 342.1 m.

6.0 CONCERT PARTY
from France
Part of a NAAFI entertainment given to the troops

6.30 DUDLEY BEAVEN
at the organ of the Granada, Welling, Kent
The oak and the rose...........*Hanmer*
In the waltz time
Around the British Isles } *arr. Beaven*
Songs, old and new

On 877 kc/s 342.1 m. only

7.0 A SHORT EVENING SERVICE
Order of Service
Hymn: Praise the Lord! ye heavens, adore him (A. and M. 292; Rv. C.H. 35)
Reading: Romans viii, 31-39
Psalm xxiii
Address by the Rev. J. W. Welch, Ph.D., Director of Religious Broadcasting
Prayer

FRENCH ARMY
v.
BRITISH ARMY

A commentary on the third of the series of matches will be broadcast from France this afternoon at 4.0.

Hymn: Soldiers of Christ, arise (A. and M. 270; Rv. C.II. 534; Army Prayer Book 101)
Blessing

7.20 'WEEKLY NEWS LETTER'

7.40 'ACCENT ON RHYTHM'
Presented by James Moody with Three in Harmony

8.0 'THESE YOU HAVE LOVED'
The songs you know so well and the tunes that you love to hear. Doris Arnold will play for you some more records she has chosen

8.40 A VARIETY CONCERT
with
Eric Barker
Rupert Hazell and Elsie Day
and
Jack Warner
Organised in aid of the Feltham War Relief Fund, from the Playhouse, Feltham, Middlesex

9.0-10.15 *As Home Service*

10.15 AL BOLLINGTON
at the theatre organ
with
Robert Wethmar (violin)
and
Sidney Burchall (baritone)

10.45-10.55 *As Home Service*

10.55 Summary of tomorrow's programmes

11.0 Close down

The Third Programme

6.00 p.m.	How to listen.
6.45	Bach.
7.30	Reflections on World Affaires.
8.00	Choral and Orchestral Concert, Part One.
9.00	The Third Programme, a talk by the BBC's Director-General.
9.15	Choral and Orchestral Concert, Part Two.
10.10	Living Opinion, discussion.
10.40	Madrigals by Montiverdi.
11.05	The Best of Yesterday.
11.30	Epilogue.
12.00	Close Down.

2.19 Schedule taken from the *Radio Times*, 27 September 1946

2.20 Schedule taken from the *Radio Times*, 27 September 1946

2.21 Philips Electronics UK Ltd.

occasionally some irreverence or vulgarity. Shows were often broadcast from factory canteens or barracks, and the 'live' audience was heard either through their laughter and applause or when 'ordinary' members of the public spoke directly into the microphone to make requests or to send messages. New programmes like *We Speak for Ourselves* allowed working–class people to be heard for the first time on radio, and fictional drama series like *The Plums* were based on a supposedly 'typical' working-class family and tried to reflect the realities of urban war-time life: bombings, rationing, shift work and members of the family fighting away from home.

The need for news and information during the war resulted in the rapid growth of the BBC's own news–gathering service. Topicality became an important news value; 'on-the-spot' reports from journalists accompanying troops in France and Germany towards the end of the war had a freshness and immediacy that would have been impossible pre-1938.

The Light Programme

8.00 a.m.	Breakfast Club, entertainment.
9.00	News.
9.10	Music in the Air, popular music.
10.15	Family Favourites, request show.
11.30	People's Service.
12.00 p.m.	Stand Easy with Charlie Chester, comedy.
12.30	Merry-Go-Round with Eric Barker, comedy.
1.30	Rocky Mountain Rhythm.
2.00	Armchair Melodies.
2.30	King Solomon's Mines.
3.00	Music Parade.
3.45	Radio Forfeits, a quiz with Michael Miles.
4.15	Just William.
4.45	Frances Day on gramophone records.
5.15	Nurse Dugdale has a Clue, spy drama with Arthur Marshall.
5.45	ITMA, comedy with Tommy Handley.
6.15	Variety Band Box.
7.00	News.
7.10	The Carroll Levis Show, happy-go-lucky, care-free entertainment.
8.15	Grand Hotel, music.
9.00	Sunday Half-Hour, community hymn singing.
9.30	At the Mulligan Inn.
10.00	News.
10.10	Talking with You.
10.15	The Twilight Hour, organ music.
10.45	Think on These Things, hymns.
11.00	Road to Dreamland, gramophone records.
11.50	News.
12.00	Close Down.

After the war this new philosophy remained; the Forces Programme was renamed the Light Programme and many of its shows carried on. The Home Service also continued and the Third Programme was introduced in 1946, most closely reflecting Reith's original aim of offering 'high cultural quality' (Figures 2.19 and 2.20). These three stations – the Light Programme, the Home Service and the Third Programme – continued the BBC's monopoly of national radio and remained unchanged until 1967.

Independent Television

The BBC had been broadcasting television regularly since 1936, although the broadcasts were stopped during the Second World War. After 1945 the BBC resumed its transmissions and until 1956 maintained a monopoly (Figure 2.21, 2.22).

One of the events that brought people into contact with television for the first time was the live coverage of the Coronation of Elizabeth II in 1953 (see Figure 4.2, **p. 117**). It was watched by 50 per cent of the population, about 25 million people – twice the radio audience. The transmission lasted all day and used twenty-one cameras spread around the centre of London and including, after some resistance, cameras in Westminster Abbey. The commentary was by Richard Dimbleby, who from that point on became a household name and the 'voice of the BBC'.

---

activity 2.7

Research what BBC television was like before the introduction of commercial television. Look in libraries to see what information is available; there may be old copies of the *Radio Times*, or old newspapers may have details of daily broadcasts. Interview someone who used to watch television in its early days.

Try to find out the types of programme being broadcast, the time slots or scheduling of these programmes (look particularly at Sundays), how people 'consumed' television in those days and how that is different to the way we use television today.

3.00 p.m.	Intimate Cabaret.
3.30	Cartoon film.
3.35	News Film.
3.45	In Our Gardens.
4.00	Interlude.
8.00	National programme (Sound only).
9.00	Sheppey, dramatic comedy.
10.30	Close Down.

2.22 Schedule taken from the *Radio Times*, 15 July 1939

In 1954 the Conservative government introduced a Television Act which proposed the setting up of an Independent Television Authority (ITA) which would oversee 'television broadcasting services additional to those of the BBC and of high quality ... which may include advertisements' (HMSO, 1966). The Television Act, partly in recognition of the role that the BBC was playing in the daily cultural lives of British people, included the remit that commercial television should also offer a 'public service' and strive to 'inform, educate and entertain'.

The ITA, like the BBC, was licensed by the Home Office. Like the BBC it had a governing body of twelve members (again the great and the good) with a chairman, all selected by the Privy Council. They oversaw the setting up of the regional 'networks' – the awarding of the franchises – that would provide a mixture of local and national television, and the leasing of the transmitters. ITA would also oversee the

2.23 *TV Times*, 21 October 1955

content of the programmes and advertising. The new television companies were to be 'independent', that, is, free of the licence fee. They received their income from the selling of advertising space and in return had to pay the ITA rental for the transmitters, plus a levy to the government based on each company's advertising revenue. Any money left over would be profit paid to the company shareholders (Figures 2.23 and 2.24).

One of ITV's most important early contributions to the development of television was its current affairs and news broadcasts, presented by ITN (see, for example, Curran and Seaton, 1991). They consisted of probing interviews and on-the-spot reports, which were very different to the BBC's deferring to politicians and allowing them to give their viewpoints unchallenged. Commentators like Robin Day were not so deferential in their questioning of politicians and the reporting of 'great' events like the state opening of Parliament. Through ITN, commercial television offered an alternative to the pomp of Richard Dimbleby's BBC commentaries. Compare, for example, these two commentaries by Richard Dimbleby and Robin Day, broadcast over the same pictures during the first live recording of the state opening of Parliament in 1958:

> Later today in the Commons the debate and doubtless the arguments over the Government's programme will begin, but for now as Her Majesty returns to the Robing Room, thence to Buckingham Palace she leaves behind in all of us a memory of a state occasion at its most magnificent and seen for the first time in our history by millions of people not only in our country but throughout the continent of Europe, from Sicily to Scandinavia.
>
> *Richard Dimbleby for BBC*

A new session of Parliament has been opened, the Queen will go back to Buckingham Palace, the Crown will go back to the Tower of London, all the scarlet and ermine robes will go back to wherever they came from and Parliament will go back to work, to pensions, education, unemployment, strikes, Cyprus, disarmament and all the rest of it. And the few moments of pageantry in the working life of Parliament are over, now comes the work, the questions, the arguments, the amendments which will be put down and the laws which will be made. From this afternoon onwards both houses will debate the policies set out in the speech from the throne to which they will all refer, with traditional politeness as 'the gracious speech'. As to what the Government has put in the gracious speech, comments from the opposition will be far from polite. In the speech today the Government has thrown down the gauntlet and the Opposition will take up the challenge, the party battle will be fought hard and long.

Robin Day for ITN

2.24 Schedule taken from the *TV Times*, 21 October 1955

SUNDAY OCT 23

TV TIMES

October 21, 1955.

AFTERNOON PROGRAMMES
Presented by Associated TeleVision, Ltd.

2.0 JACK JACKSON SHOW
Jack Jackson presents news and views, guests and music from the record world.
Produced by Peter Glover

2.30 FREE SPEECH
with
W. J. Brown
Randolph Churchill
Michael Foot
Alan Taylor
and in the chair
Kenneth Adam
Presented by John Irwin and Edgar Lustgarten

3.0 LIBERACE
America's No. 1 musical personality in his own inimitable show.

3.30 STAGE ONE

Your Anglo-American Theatre presents outstanding Stars from London and Hollywood.
CHARLES COBURN
in
THE WORLD IS MY OYSTER
with
Rosemarie Bowe, John Smith, Nana Bryant
Charles Coburn plays the rôle of a famous old Washington millionaire, and also that of a lovable old tramp. Because they are identical in feature, the millionaire arranges for the tramp to impersonate him. Then the plot develops.

4.0 SUNDAY AFTERNOON
A programme devised and presented by John Irwin. Based on the theme that "Nothing interests people so much as other people."

4.30 GOING SHOPPING WITH ELIZABETH ALLAN
Elizabeth Allan takes you on a visit to Harrods for the shopping news of the week.
Directed by Dicky Leeman
Produced by Advertising Features Ltd.

4.45 THE ADVENTURES OF NODDY
by
ENID BLYTON
No. 5. NODDY DOES SOME GARDENING
Enid Blyton's popular children's character seen on television in this new series of regular Sunday Afternoon adventures.
Puppetry by Peter Hayes ; directed by Quentin Lawrence : produced by A. D. Peters

5.0 ROY ROGERS
Each week a complete half-hour adventure with America's favourite cowboy star.
No. 5. THE TRAIN ROBBERY
Starring Roy Rogers and Dale Evans with Pat Brady, Bob Wilke, Michael Regan, Reed Howes, Charles M. Heard and William Fawcette.
Roy Rogers sees two desperadoes blow up a train and steal loot worth $50,000, but the culprits get away in the confusion that follows. Roy and Dale find evidence that leads them to the gunmen's hideout.
The robbers capture Roy's pal, Pat Brady, and then Roy and Trigger ride to the rescue in a gun-battle filled with thrills.

In Britain after the Second World War there seemed to be a mood of egalitarianism sustained by, among other things, the election of the Labour government, the establishment of the National Health Service, and the introduction in the 1944 Education Act of universal secondary education. This mood can in part be seen to echo the social crisis after the First World War and just as BBC Radio had played a role in creating a sense of national unity in the 1920s and 1930s, so did television in the 1950s and 1960s help reflect a 'popular' culture of equality and accessibility by bridging the gap between family and private life on the one hand and political, public life on the other.

Many writers have referred to the 1960s as the 'Golden Age' of television. BBC television in particular, under the Director-General Sir Hugh Greene, can be seen to have played a major role in confronting viewers with the social changes that had taken place during the previous decades. Just as radio had brought its version of the realities of unemployment in the north of England or slum conditions in the cities to the Home Counties in the 1930s, so *Cathy Come Home* exposed the plight of the homeless in what Harold Macmillan had called, in 1959, a 'never had it so good' society. It was possibly a version of Reith's 'public service' *par excellence*. As a result of *Cathy Come Home*, the Labour government introduced new policies, and organisations such as Shelter were set up to help the homeless.

Programmes like *That Was The Week That Was*, *Z Cars* and *Steptoe and Son* all provided entertainment but at the same time allowed 'ordinary domestic life' to be shown – what Richard Hoggart (1957) and Raymond Williams (1965) called the 'lived experience', the 'popular' culture, the everyday life of everyday people. Television could be seen to be discovering and disclosing information about other segments of society that had either been ignored or else only portrayed in the cosy images of *Dixon of Dock Green* or the Ealing comedies, or as second-best imitations of 'high culture'. This 'domestication' of television, Scannell (1987) suggests, reflects both the daily experiences of the majority of people and the method of their consumption of television: sitting at home in their living rooms, watching other people, real or fictitious, sitting in their homes, keeping each other company, helping to cope with life, and the next day sharing the experience with others, talking about what they had watched the night before.

Although television appeared to be operating under two different systems, many analysts have noted that the people who managed these systems still maintained a consensus. They appeared to be from the same social background, public-school educated, university-trained, and to have similar ideas about 'public service' and 'public interest'. Both systems had similar boards of management drawn from the same small and restricted social élite. Appointments to these boards were often given as the 'reward' for public service. The programme makers often changed between the two organisations and had been trained by the BBC, and so shared a common professional 'ethos'. Both organisations were dependent upon the goodwill of the government for their finances, the BBC through the increases of the licence fee and the ITA through the advertising levy that the companies had to pay to the government.

Independent Radio

During the 1950s and 1960s, a new, profitable, teenage audience had grown up who wanted radio that reflected their interests in pop music and 'youth' culture. The BBC's Light Programme had been offering programmes like *Saturday Club*, *East Beat* and *Pick of the Pops* as a concession to the new generation of bands like the Beatles and their fans, but still maintained its *Music While You Work*, *Uncle Mac* and other programmes developed during the Second World War.

In 1964 an alternative became available, as pirate radio stations started broadcasting from ships moored outside territorial waters. Stations like Radio Caroline and Radio London were based on the American format and broadcast, twenty-four hours a day, a continual flow of pop music interspersed with advertising, station identity jingles and the words of disc jockeys. These stations offered a new, popular way of using radio, based, like commercial television, on entertainment appealing to a mass local market and financed by advertising. At their peak about 20 million people listened to the pirate stations.

Eventually, in August 1967, the Labour government passed the Marine Broadcasting Offences Bill, which made it illegal for any British subject to supply or work on the pirate stations. In September 1967 the BBC, in acknowledgement of the demands of this new audience, changed the Light Programme into Radio 2, the Home Service into Radio 4, and the Third Programme into Radio 3, and created a new pop music service called Radio 1, which took many of the features and disc jockeys from the pirate stations (Figure 2.25).

Also in 1967 the BBC started to develop local radio. In 1971 the Conservative government gave the go-ahead for privately owned radio stations funded by advertising, although there was still a requirement to offer a 'truly public service'.

This new service was called Independent Local Radio (ILR). At the same time the ITA changed its name to the IBA (Independent Broadcasting Authority) to encompass radio.

2.25 *Radio Times*, September 1967

activity 2.8

Draw up a 'profile' of a local radio station. Find out who owns it and what competition (if any) it has. Establish what types of programming it offers, what type of audience it appeals to, and how that audience is 'targeted' (Figure 2.26).

2.26 Radio listeners (millions)

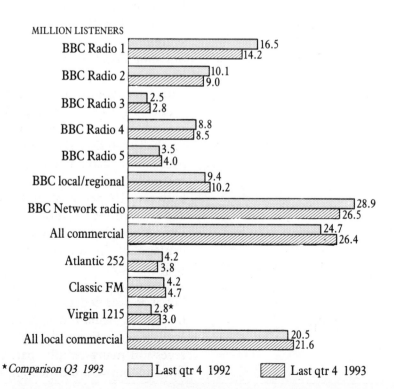

Satellite Television

British Satellite Broadcasting (BSB) was awarded the British satellite franchise in 1986. BSB was famous for its 'squarial' (a square aerial), and produced its own programmes aimed at a 'broadsheet', ABC1 audience. It launched its own Marco Polo satellite and as part of the franchise agreement had to develop a new, high-quality transmission system called D-MAC that would pioneer digital television in Britain. At the same time Murdoch's News International bought an ailing existing satellite station based in Luxembourg, called SKY. In 1989 Murdoch launched a service in Britain, a few months before BSB was to come into service. SKY used cheaper PAL hardware and offered a bought-in diet of American and Australian soaps and quizzes, with some of its own programmes aimed at a 'tabloid' C2DE market.

The two systems were in competition and both losing large amount of money – at one point News International was reputed to be losing £2 million per week. In 1991 the two systems merged and currently there is only one satellite service, BSkyB, owned by News International (50 per cent), Pearsons (17.5 per cent), Granada (13.5 per cent) and Amstrad. As it is based in Luxembourg it is not a British company, and so News International's majority ownership does not contravene the 'cross-media' limitations placed by the Broadcasting Act. News International also owns 64 per cent of Star TV, the satellite service for Asia. (See Chapter 6 for further discussion of News International.)

Since BSkyB became a monopoly it has been marketing aggressively to try and win subscribers. There have been various sports deals in cricket, boxing and football, where BSkyB has bought the exclusive rights to major events, trying to attract the young males who they hope will pay to see these events. In 1992 BSkyB paid £304 million, over a five-year period, for the exclusive right to show live Premier League football matches. By the summer of 1993 just over 2 million SKY dishes have been sold, and the service reaches another half million homes via cable. It is estimated to be available in between 10 per cent and 15 per cent of homes in Britain and to account for about 5–6 per cent of total television viewing, although in households with satellite or cable the percentage of 'non-terrestrial' viewing is considerably higher (Figure 2.27).

Estimates about the growth of satellite vary considerably, but it is assumed that by the year 2000 about 50 per cent of homes in Britain will have either satellite or cable services available (see Figure 8.3, **p. 274**). However, during a time of recession many people, particularly those on low earnings or fixed incomes, are unwilling to invest in new forms of entertainment. There is, however, a perceived need among many people for 'more choice' or something different to the terrestrial diet on offer, and BSkyB's twelve-channel package does seem to offer more variety. In Europe there are already over ninety satellite television channels available, and there is the technical potential for many more specialist satellite or cable channels that may create new audiences, but the advertising revenue available to television seems limited and therefore most of these new services are likely either to take existing advertising revenue away from existing channels or to be subscription-only.

The BBC is also becoming increasingly involved with satellite broadcasting. It shares two channels on Astra with Thames Television, UK Gold and UK Living, as well as sharing programmes such as *Breakfast with Frost* with SKY News and sporting events such as Wimbledon tennis with SKY Sports.

---

activity **2.9**   Investigate the costs of the various satellite packages that are on offer. Conduct a survey of the public to try and discover who watches satellite, how much they pay, and what they feel satellite offers that terrestrial channels do not.

Minority Broadcasting: BBC2 and Channel Four

When, in 1962, the Pilkington Committee investigated the service offered by the ITV companies, it concluded that they equated 'quality with box-office success' and 'failed to live up to [their] responsibilities as a public service' (Garnham, 1973). Because of this, according to Goodwin and Whannell (1992), ITV was not allowed to extend its services and the awarding of a third television channel was given to the BBC. BBC2 started transmission in 1964 and pioneered colour transmission in 1967 (Figure 2.28). ITV had to wait until the Annan Report on Broadcasting, which led to the 1981 Broadcasting Act that granted the fourth channel to ITV. Channel Four started broadcasting in 1982.

Both BBC2 and Channel Four (C4) were set up to provide an alternative to a mainstream station. C4 is specifically required to 'cater for tastes, interests and audiences not served by ITV (or other television channels), to innovate in the form and content of programmes and to devote a proportion of its airtime to educational programming' (Channel Four, 1991). In Wales, S4C has a remit to produce Welsh-language programmes. C4 is a 'publisher broadcaster': the only programme made by C4 is *Right to Reply*, and all others are commissioned

2.27 (a and b) BARB 1994

Share of total viewing

Homes with satellite

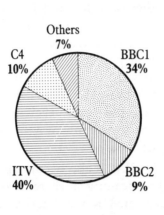

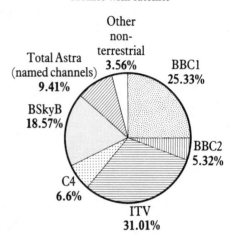

2.28 Schedule taken from the *Radio Times* April 23, 1964

BBC-2

7.20
LINE-UP
for Thursday
with John Stone, Denis Tuohy
and the latest news

7.30
JULIUS CAESAR
by WILLIAM SHAKESPEARE
To celebrate the 400th anniversary
of the author's birth, the exciting
modern-dress production of the
NATIONAL YOUTH THEATRE
with its original jazz score is seen
for the first time on television
Designer, Christopher Lawrence
Director, MICHAEL CROFT
Presented for television
from the Ashcroft Theatre, Croydon
by John Vernon
See page 51

10.0
THE SLEEPING BALLERINA
A film on the life of
Olga Spessivtzeva

Written and directed
by LUDOVIC KENNEDY
The tragic life story of the famous
Russian ballerina who spent twenty
years in an American mental hos-
pital, re-living the great roles of her
career.
*Spessivtzeva and Pavlova are the two
halves of an apple, and Spessivtzeva
is the half turned towards the sun.*
—SERGE DIAGHILEV
A Television Reporters
International Production
See page 53

10.25
NEWSROOM

10.50
CLOSEDOWN
and a look at tomorrow

and produced by independents, or other television companies, or imported from abroad.

C4 was funded by a levy on the ITV companies, which in return sold the advertising space. This guaranteed C4 an income and released it from direct commercial pressures. However, under the 1990 Broadcasting Act, C4 is now responsible for its own funding by selling it own airtime and will therefore be in competition with the other ITV compa-nies. Many commentators feel that this will result in C4 being less adventurous and point to the increasing numbers of early-evening American sitcoms like *My Two Dads*, *The Wonder Years*, *The Cosby Show* etc., as evidence of C4's more cautious and popularist scheduling.

During the early 1990s both BBC2 and C4 have each regu-larly averaged around 10 per cent of the viewing audience.

activity **2.10**

Look through past and present schedules for both BBC2 and C4 and try to assess to what extent these channels have fulfilled their remits.

Minority Broadcasting: Community radio

The Broadcasting Act of 1990 also set out to encourage com-munity radio, but its growth in Britain has been limited both by financial constraints and to some extent by consumer lack of interest. It was intended to offer specific groups, such as ethnic minorities, special interest groups, and communities based on location or language, their own service, but many of these groups are not attractive to advertisers or sponsors and so funding has always been difficult. Research by the Broadcasting Research Unit ('The Listener Speaks', Barnett, 1988) found only a very small interest among audiences for the idea of neighbourhood stations. Stations like For the People, in Bristol, have had considerable financial difficulties and have had to become much more mainstream and pop-music-based to win audiences and finance and so survive.

Market Forces and Deregulation: Competition, Choice and Quality

The White Paper 'Broadcasting in the 1990s', published in 1988, was underpinned by three key Conservative concepts: competition, choice and quality. The free market philosophy behind the White Paper suggested that if competition among broadcasters was increased then listeners and viewers would have more choice; this would in turn mean that only the successful stations would attract high enough ratings to survive and bring in the required advertising revenue. To attract the higher ratings broadcasters would have to raise standards, and so viewers would benefit.

The Act altered the regulatory bodies for commercial radio and television. The IBA and Cable Authority were replaced by the Independent Television Commission (ITC), which now has responsibility for terrestrial television (ITV's Channel Three, C4) as well as cable and satellite. Radio is controlled by the Radio Authority, which is responsible for independent radio, both local and national, and community radio.

Both of these new bodies have a 'light regulatory touch'. It is unclear what this means, but many commentators take it that these regulatory bodies will 'stand back' from the management of the new franchises. The IBA very rarely interfered with the running of television or radio companies, although it did criticise TV-AM after the company abandoned its 'mission to explain', sacked its original presenters (Anna Ford, Peter Jay, Michael Parkinson and Angela Rippon), reduced its news service and introduced Roland Rat. The IBA also intervened in 1988 when the government put pressure on Thames Television to withdraw its programme about the shooting of IRA terrorists in Gibraltar, *Death on the Rock*. This programme is considered by many people to be among the main causes for one of the central pieces of legislation in the Broadcasting Act, namely the 'auctioning' of the new ten-year franchises for Channel Three (C3) as from 1 January 1993. The new franchises were to be 'auctioned' and be awarded to the highest bidder after passing a 'quality' threshold. Only in 'exceptional circumstances' would the franchise not go to the highest bidder. New franchise holders could be 'publisher broadcasters' on the C4 model and some public service responsibilities were included.

Although C3 companies were commercial organisations, some people saw the old public service 'ethos' as still being strong at IBA. There was also pressure from Rupert Murdoch, a close ally of the Conservative government and, through the *Sunday Times*, a strong critic of Thames's *Death on the Rock*. At the 1989 Edinburgh International Television Festival, Murdoch described British television as 'no more than a reflection of the values of the narrow élite which controls it and has always thought that its tastes are synonymous with quality' (Figure 2.29). He went on to describe the 'old' Reithan notion of public service broadcasting as 'obsessed by an anachronistic fear of commercial interests'.

2.29 *Broadcast*, August 1989

Home truths

RUPERT MURDOCH set the agenda of the year's Edinburgh International TV Festival. His sneering indictment of British public service television obsessed by narrow class interests and immobilised by an anachronistic fear of commercial interests lingered uncomfortably throughout the weekend.

There was no logic to support his argument. But it was given impetus by the clarity of his sense of purpose. For Murdoch there is no precarious balancing act between commercial and creative interests. His targets were precise and his words hit home.

Sadly, the same could not be said of his audience. The response to Murdoch's speech was pathetic. There were familiar platitudes and feeble defences. John Birt, deputy director general of the BBC, said that Murdoch should not underestimate the popular appeal of British mainstream programming. The problem is that he doesn't. He is only too aware of what he is up against and he really wants to win.

"Much of what passes for quality on British television is no more than a reflection of the values of the narrow elite which controls it and has always thought that its tastes are synonymous with quality," Murdoch told squirming television mandarins.

Certainly Murdoch has an over-simplistic analysis of class and elites. Yet as Neal Ascherson said in a later session, broadcasters dismiss his text at their peril.

Murdoch's arguments are founded on the view that broadcasting is a business. It is a view which excludes the notion that television is also a cultural and political force. It is a perspective, which however limited, has shaped the new broadcasting policy.

Broadcasters should defend public service broadcasting. However, they should also be prepared to reassess exactly what it is. Without a proper understanding it can all too easily be dismissed as broadcasting by elites for elites.

Survival of television as a business has tended to preoccupy the industry. In one of Murdoch's most cutting statements, he accused broadcasters of trading their freedom in return for government protection of their monopoly. Every government would exact a price for that protection, he said.

The price they have paid has been a heavy one. Freedoms have been lost: the freedom to report on issues which challenge the government has become increasingly difficult to sustain; the freedom to allow viewers to hear the views of the Sinn Fein; the Broadcasting Standards Council now presides over taste and decency; the Offical Secrets Act limits television journalism and drama.

As television journalists still smart from the treatment they received from the Murdoch papers over *Death On The Rock*, it is a sad irony that he alone raised one of the gravest problems of this industry — its inability to fight for freedom of expression.

activity **2.11**

Read the article on the speech by Rupert Murdoch. Summarise the main points of his argument and consider why he is taking this point of view. What arguments could be used against it?

As a result of the auction process four new franchise holders became part of the C3 network: Carlton, which bid £43 million and replaced Thames in weekday London; Meridian, which bid £36.5 million and replaced TVS in the south of England (although TVS bid more, the ITC decided that TVS's bid was financially 'unrealistic' and threatened the quality of programming that they could offer); Westcountry Television, which bid £7.75 million and replaced TSW in Devon and Cornwall; and GMTV, which bid £34.5 million and replaced TV-AM. This was an ironic decision, as TV-AM under Bruce Gyngell, with its strong anti-union policy and cheap entertainment, in many ways epitomised the 'new' commercial ethos, and after the decision was announced there was considerable publicity when Gyngell received an apologetic letter from Margaret Thatcher saying how sorry she was that they had lost their franchise. The auction system was based on the 'value' of the potential advertising revenue in the different regions. Central Television, however, with one of the most lucrative areas, retained its franchise with a bid of only £2,000, as no other company bid against them (Figure 2.30).

The Broadcasting Act put a limit on 'cross-media' ownership. It originally specified that British newspaper companies could not own more than 20 per cent of British television or radio service, and vice versa, and that one television company could not own more than 20 per cent of another. Later this was amended to allow two television franchise companies to merge. Under pressure from leading press and other UK media groups, the National Heritage Secretary then agreed to look at wider issues of multimedia ownership to allow British companies to compete more successfully in the larger multi-national media market dominated by companies such as Time Warner, Bertelsmann, Sony and Matsushita. It also set out plans for a fifth, sixth or even seventh television channel as well as promoting the expansion of cable and local, small-scale microwave television. However, by the deadline of June 1992 the ITC had received only one application to run the Channel Five (C5) franchise. The ITC therefore decided to delay awarding it.

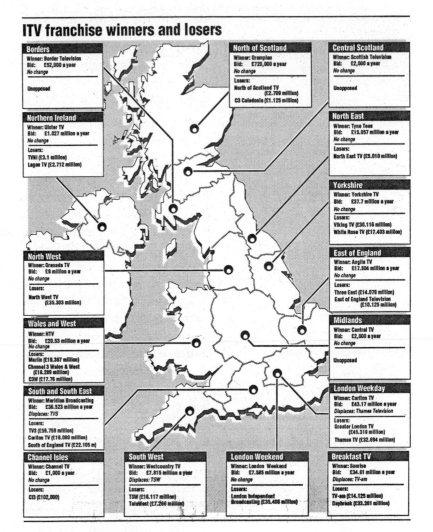

ITV franchise winners and losers

Borders
Winner: Border Television
Bid: £52,000 a year
No change

Unopposed

Northern Ireland
Winner: Ulster TV
Bid: £1.027 million a year
No change
Losers:
TVNI (£3.1 million)
Lagan TV (£2.712 million)

North West
Winner: Granada TV
Bid: £9 million a year
No change
Losers:
North West TV
(£35.303 million)

Wales and West
Winner: HTV
Bid: £20.53 million a year
No change
Losers:
Merlin (£19.367 million)
Channel 3 Wales & West
(£18.289 million)
C3W (£17.76 million)

South and South East
Winner: Meridian Broadcasting
Bid: £36.523 million a year
Displaces: TVS
Losers:
TVS (£59.758 million)
Carlton TV (£18.080 million)
South of England TV (£22.105 m)

Channel Isles
Winner: Channel TV
Bid: £1,000 a year
No change
Losers:
CI3 (£102,000)

North of Scotland
Winner: Grampian
Bid: £720,000 a year
No change
Losers:
North of Scotland TV
(£2.709 million)
C3 Caledonia (£1.125 million)

South West
Winner: Westcountry TV
Bid: £7.815 million a year
Displaces: TSW
Losers:
TSW (£16.117 million)
TeleWest (£7.266 million)

London Weekend
Winner: London Weekend
Bid: £7.585 million a year
No change
Losers:
London Independent
Broadcasting (£35.406 million)

Central Scotland
Winner: Scottish Television
Bid: £2,000 a year
No change

Unopposed

North East
Winner: Tyne Tees
Bid: £15.057 million a year
No change
Losers:
North East TV (£5.010 million)

Yorkshire
Winner: Yorkshire TV
Bid: £37.7 million a year
No change
Losers:
Viking TV (£30.116 million)
White Rose TV (£17.403 million)

East of England
Winner: Anglia TV
Bid: £17.804 million a year
No change
Losers:
Three East (£14.078 million)
East of England Television
(£10.125 million)

Midlands
Winner: Central TV
Bid: £2,000 a year
No change

Unopposed

London Weekday
Winner: Carlton TV
Bid: £43.17 million a year
Displaces: Thames Television
Losers:
Greater London TV
(£45.319 million)
Thames TV (£32.694 million)

Breakfast TV
Winner: Sunrise
Bid: £34.61 million a year
Displaces: TV-am
Losers:
TV-am (£14.125 million)
Daybreak (£33.261 million)

2.30 *The Guardian*, 1992

The Act also attempted to 'open up' radio by introducing three new national independent radio stations (INR) and encouraging the expansion of a new 'tier' of community radio. The first INR franchise offered was for a 'non-pop' station on the FM wavelength. Initially the franchise was offered to Showtime Radio, but as they could not secure funding the franchise then went to the runner up, Classic FM. The second franchise, on MW, went to Virgin 1215 (jointly owned by Virgin and TV-AM), although it was not the highest bidder.

The Radio Authority delayed advertising the third franchise, also on MW, and 'speech-based', because of the difficulty of starting up a new station in a period of economic recession.

Virgin 1215 bid £1,883,000 for its eight-year licence. As for the C3 companies, this sum will be paid annually to the Exchequer. Virgin will also have to pay 4 per cent of its advertising revenue, plus £645,000 per annum to the Radio Authority. In January 1994 London Country Radio started a London-based AM country music service and Sunrise Radio expanded its AM service for Asian listeners in London. In October 1994 LBC, the first commercial local radio station to go on the air, will be replaced by a 'rolling-news' service, London News Radio, on FM and London Forum Radio on AM. Also in 1994 two new London FM frequencies are being advertised as well as Capital Radio's licences.

As a result of pressure from organisations like the National Viewers' and Listeners' Association (NVLA), the Broadcasting Act also legislated on the content of programmes by setting up the Broadcasting Standards Council to work alongside the existing Broadcasting Complaints Commission. The NVLA had claimed for a long time that much of the television output contravened the guidelines, that the 9 o'clock watershed was not adhered to, and that 'self-regulation' by IBA and BBC was not sufficient. Broadcast material now comes under the Obscene Publications Act.

The government claims that the Act 'opens up' broadcasting; however, a look at the ownership of the C3 companies after January 1993 suggests that the opposite has occurred, and, particularly in television, ownership is limited to a small group of companies:

- Carlton has taken over Central Television (Central owns 20 per cent of Meridian) and has a 20 per cent interest in GMTV, the breakfast contractor. Carlton also owns 18 per cent of, and heads, the consortium that runs ITN. Carlton's head, Michael Green, is also on the board of Reuters, which, through Visnews, provides GMTV with its news service. Carlton shares its news facilities with LWT, the London weekend franchise holder, which also has a 20 per cent stake in GMTV.
- Meridian is owned by a consortium that includes MAI Broadcasting, Central Television and Select TV (makers of *Birds of a Feather*, among others) and is set to take over Anglia Television.
- Westcountry is 20 per cent owned by Associated Newspapers, publishers of the *Daily Mail*.
- GMTV is made up of a consortium that includes LWT

(20 per cent), Guardian newspapers (15 per cent), Scottish TV (20 per cent), Carlton (20 per cent) and the Walt Disney Company (15 per cent).

Since the new franchises came into operation, Yorkshire and Tyne Tees have merged and Yorkshire is sharing many of its services with Granada. Granada owns 20 per cent of LWT and would like to take it over completely. LWT owns 15 per cent of Yorkshire/Tyne Tees. Granada also owns 13.5 per cent of BSkyB. In 1993, Pearsons bought Thames Television for £99 million; it also owns 17.5 per cent of BSkyB and 15 per cent of Yorkshire/Tyne Tees. Thames owns 15 per cent of UK Gold, the 'golden oldie' satellite station run in conjunction with BBC. Thames and the BBC also share ownership of the Astra channel, UK Living, with two American companies.

Radio shows a similar concentration of ownership: Classic FM is owned by a consortium that includes Time Warner (35 per cent), GWR (17 per cent), Associated Newspapers (4 per cent) and Home Counties Newspapers (4 per cent). GWR also runs other 'local' stations in Reading, Swindon, Bristol, Bournemouth, Plymouth and Tavistock.

activity **2.12**

Try to assess the success or otherwise of the government's aim to increase competition, choice and quality. Has competition increased? Do viewers feel that they now have more choice? If so, in what ways? Are viewers aware of an increase or decrease in quality on C3? How does this manifest itself? Is there a difference between the ways the Broadcasting Act has affected television and radio?

The Future: The Renewal of the BBC's Charter in 1996

There are several issues that will have to be resolved, such as the question of a licence fee and an alternative method of paying for the various services that the BBC offers. For most of 1993 the Corporation's ratings were considerably lower than those of C3. In the early 1990s the BBC has had various public disasters, such as *Eldorado*, *Trainer* and *A Year in Provence*. Reith's notion of a common 'national culture' and 'national voice' are not as popular with today's politicians as they were in the 1930s, and with increased social diversification broadcasting seems to be moving away from the idea of a nation sitting together watching *The Morecambe and Wise Christmas Show* and towards a notion of 'narrowcasting' to specific targeted audiences. The BBC is again having difficulty in identifying who its audiences are and how to address them, as well as in justifying the universality of its licence fee.

Director-General of the BBC John Birt outlined plans for the future of the BBC in 'the new broadcasting age' in the 1992 document 'Extending Choice' (BBC, 1992). Birt talked of the BBC offering a service that was 'distinctive' and 'innovative' but at the same time providing 'more real choice' and 'something for everyone'. 'Extending Choice' also committed the BBC to providing a 'showcase for traditional and contemporary British culture', without clarifying what that means, as well as continuing to offer programmes that 'help to educate and inform'. Central to any debate about the future of the BBC is the future of public service broadcasting, with its ethos of free access for all and quality not quantity. Notions of 'quality' and 'success' are increasingly being seen as synonymous, and the test of quality and success is being judged more and more by high audience viewing figures.

Increasing Commercial Pressures

Many of the proposals outlined in the Broadcasting Act have been delayed due to economic recession in the early 1990s and the related lack of advertising revenue, but eventually new radio and television services will come on air, increasingly funded by either advertising, sponsorship or subscription. The new C3 franchise holders are committed to paying large sums of money to the government for the next ten years in an increasingly competitive market.

For the commercial sector, 'success' increasingly means attracting the younger ABC1 audiences that the advertisers want. These audiences have the money to pay for quality services. The danger is that other audiences, less desirable to advertisers or unable to pay for specialist, quality programmes, will be relegated to the margins of broadcasting. What is popular is sport, pop music and films; less popular are current affairs, documentaries and other minority programmes. This trend is already apparent with the move of *Highway* from the early evening 'god slot' on Sundays to make way for the 'family' films that are more attractive to younger audiences and advertisers. It is also the cause of the debate about the placing of *News at Ten*, which at present causes 'adult' films that have to start after the 9 o'clock watershed to have a half-hour break.

<table>
<tr><td>*activity* **2.13**</td><td>

1 Look at Chapter 5 and then design and conduct surveys into the viewing habits of audiences. Correlate types of service and programme with particular types of audience. Identify and explain any particular patterns or variations that occur.

2 Identify ways in which the analysis of the history of radio and/or television helps to explain the present organisation and/or output.

3 Look at Chapter 6 and choose one company to explore in more detail. List the particular media interests it has. Explain how this media interpenetration benefits the company. Consider whether it also benefits the consumer.

4 Look at Chapter 3 and try to illustrate the way changes in broadcasting organisation and legislation have affected the form and content of programmes.

5 Define what is meant by 'public service broadcasting' and consider its future role. Identify the parties involved in the debate about its future and list the arguments for and against the concept.

6 Summarise the debate surrounding the licence fee. Conduct research on attitudes to its continuation or replacement.
</td></tr>
</table>

FURTHER READING

General

Ward, K. 1989: *Mass Communications and the Modern World.* Macmillan.

Press History

Boyce, G. et al (Eds). 1978. *Newspaper History: From the 17th Century to the Present Day.* Constable.
Cranfield, G.A. 1978: *The Press and Society.* Longman.
Curran, J. and Seaton, J. 1991: *Power Without Responsibility.* Routledge.
Harrison, S. 1974: *Poor Men's Guardians.* Lawrence and Wishart.
Lee, A.J. 1976: *The Origins of the Popular Press 1855–1914.* Croom Helm.
McNair, B. 1993: *News and Journalism in the UK.* Routledge.
Seymour-Ure, C. 1991: *The Press and Broadcasting in Britain since 1945.* Blackwell.
Thompson, E.P. 1968: *The Making of the English Working Class.* Penguin

Cinema History

Armes, R. 1978: *A Critical History of British Cinema*. Oxford University Press.
Armes, R. 1988: *On Video*. Routledge.
Barnes, J. 1976: *The Beginnings of Cinema in Britain*. David and Charles.
Barr, C. 1986: *All Our Yesterdays*. BFI.
Chanan, M. 1980: *The Dream that Kicks: The Pre-History and Early Years of Cinema in Britain*. Routledge and Kegan Paul.
Curran, J. and Porter, V. (Eds). 1983: *British Cinema History*. Weidenfeld & Nicolson.
Robertson, J.C. 1989: *The Hidden Cinema: British Film Censorship 1913–1972*. Routledge.
Stead, P. 1989: *Film and the Working Class*. Routledge.
Walker, A. 1986: *Hollywood England*. Harrap.

Broadcasting History

Barnard, S. 1989: *On the Radio*. Open University Press.
Briggs, A. 1979: *The History of Broadcasting in the UK*. Vols. 1–4. Oxford University Press.
Corner, J. (Ed). 1991: *Popular Television in Britain*. BFI.
Goodwin, A. and Whannel, G. (Eds). 1992: *Understanding Television*. Methuen.
Lewis, P. and Booth, J. 1989: *The Invisible Medium*. Macmillan.
Madge, T. 1989: *Beyond the BBC*. Macmillan.
Sales, R. 1986: 'An Introduction to Broadcasting History' in D. Punter (Ed), *An Introduction to Contemporary Cultural Studies*. Longman.

3 | *Media Forms and Analysis*

As the previous chapter demonstrates, the form and content of the media change and develop as social, aesthetic, political and technical influences alter. This chapter will explore the relationship between the form that different media texts take and how meaning is 'created'. It will look at the encoding and decoding structure of media texts, visual and narrative codes, and the concepts of genre and realism.

ENCODING AND DECODING

Although, as mentioned in Chapter Two, the 'mass' media are generally assumed to date from the nineteenth century, it has been argued (Curran *et al*, 1977) that early religious ceremonies and rituals shared a similar function in trying to mediate, or act as a 'bridge', between a mythical or mystical, unknown 'other' world and the 'ordinary' world of daily experience. Like today's media, they addressed a 'mass' audience, not as a large number of individuals all listening/watching/reading the same programme, magazine or newspaper article, but rather as an audience made up of groups of people all in similar places at similar times, within earshot of the priests and all listening to similar messages.

As with modern media forms, the people who performed the 'bridging' role in these religious ceremonies often acquired power and status as a result of their specialised roles as mediators; that is, priests who interpreted the divine word either from a church pulpit or at the oracle in Delphi, as well as the elders from aboriginal tribes who interpreted the messages of nature and passed on the oral histories of their tribes or clans. The priests would 'package' their message in specialised language, using gestures and signs to emphasise points, dress in a particular way to reinforce their position of authority, and be physically raised above the congregation in a pulpit. All these elements would combine to help create the 'meaning' of the priest's sermon and the public place of worship. The audience, the members of the congregation, could interpret the message in a variety of ways that made sense to them individually. The 'meaning' that they constructed would partly depend upon how directly the priest's sermon related to their own daily lives, their position in the community, their degree of religious belief, their sense of guilt, or even the discomfort of the pews!

The modern equivalent might perhaps be the religious programmes on television, particularly *Songs of Praise* early on Sunday evening during the 'god slot'. The programme 'packages' a religious message that has been modified for the television audience. It is shorter than a 'typical' church service and consists mainly of familiar hymns sung by semi-professional choirs and congregations. The religious message is often broken up and interspersed with travelogue-type details about the community that is 'hosting' the week's programme, or by the intervention of a 'personality' who, acting as 'mediator', introduces the community and the hymns. To make the message more appealing, fiction and reality are sometimes entwined, as in an edition of *Songs of Praise* that featured the characters and 'pretend' settings from *The Archers*.

The 1990s' TV congregation will be sitting at home and will not have to worry about the hardness of the pews. They will interpret the programme and its message through its familiar time slot, title sequence and format. The presenter will help the audience through the programme, highlighting key moments. The meaning will have some religious significance, but of equal importance will be the form in which the message is transmitted; that is, as a familiar television programme on BBC TV on an early Sunday evening (Figure 3.1).

Although the church service is a fairly simple model it highlights the key stages in the process of communicating meaning, the way meanings are *encoded* or packaged by 'senders' and *decoded* or unpacked by audiences or 'receivers'. The steps and relations in this encoding and decoding process become apparent when the meaning of any item of media output is analysed. Although both priest and congregation may share some common code systems – of language, gesture and 'occasion' – it is probable that some of the priest's intended meanings were not shared by the listening congregation. Accordingly, to analyse the meanings of media output it is necessary not only to see how the producers encoded the

6.25pm
Songs of Praise

Thank You for the Music. Two thousand singers, the choirs of 150 churches and the New English Orchestra welcome the return of *Songs of Praise* with a musical feast. Shoppers and shop-workers join the congregation in the Meadowhall Oasis in Sheffield to raise the roof in joyful celebration. Pam Rhodes and Alan Titchmarsh look at the magic and majesty that music brings to worship, with the help of the Sheffield Celebration Choir, the Duke Street and Shi Loh Gospel Choirs and the award-winning Bolstertone Male Voice Choir.
Producer Diane Reid
Editor Helen Alexander   946909
(Repeated tomorrow 3.00pm on BBC2)

3.1 Extract of a BBC schedule taken from the *Radio Times*

message and the form it assumes but also how audiences have decoded it. The form of the text or message and the contexts in which it is produced or received should also be considered, because whether it is a church sermon, a television show or a tabloid newspaper, the routines and practices inherent in any particular form will affect both the encoding and decoding processes. These 'codes of production' can include the producers' sense of 'professional standards', institutional criteria or technical infrastructure. (This encoding and decoding model is discussed further in Chapter 5.)

Consider the message below, which is from an eighteenth-century pamphlet that, like the unstamped press (see Chapter 2), challenged the political and economic position of the government and was a 'radical' alternative to the establishment press.

> To all real lovers of Liberty, be assured that Liberty and Freedom will at last prevail. Tremble O thou the Oppressor of the people that reigneth upon the throne and ye Ministers of State, weep for ye shall fall. Weep ye who grind the face of the poor, oppress the People and starve the Industrious Mechanic. My friends, you are oppressed, you know it. Lord Buckingham who died the other day had thirty thousand pounds yearly for setting his arse in the House of Lords and doing nothing. Liberty calls aloud, ye who will hear her Voice, may you be free and happy. He who does not, let him starve and be DAMNED.
> N.B. Be resolute and you shall be happy. He who wishes well to the cause of Liberty let him repair to Chapel Field at Five O'clock this afternoon, to begin a Glorious Revolution.
>
> *Rosen and Widgery (1991)*

Written in 1793, the leaflet supports the ideals of the French Revolution and is aimed at a poorly educated, but literate, working-class audience. Part of the encoding process would include the tone and the religious nature of the language, which the audience would probably be familiar with. Words like 'Freedom', 'Liberty', 'tremble' and 'DAMNED' (in upper-case letters) would all suggest strong emotions, but with the vernacular 'arse' adding vulgarity and humour. Another consideration at the encoding stage would be the technical constraints of layout and printing, which would probably be done by hand. These, and the limitations of distribution, would probably influence the form the pamphlet would take, particularly affecting the size of the sheet of paper used, the number of copies printed and the area of circulation.

For the readers of this leaflet, part of the decoding would depend upon how and where they saw a copy or whether they knew who Lord Buckingham was. Many of the intended audience were probably illiterate and so would have had the message read out to them, perhaps aloud in some public place, or quietly in private. Different social groups would respond in differing ways to the leaflet's message depending to what extent they agreed with the political point of view being expressed. For a member of the House of Lords this might appear to be threatening and seditious, justifying its being made illegal and censored. For both author and reader part of the encoding and decoding process would include this notion of illegality and danger. There might be some kind of glamour or special value attached to receiving something illegal, or it might have gained extra value or status because the authorities were trying to suppress it.

activity **3.1**

In Chapter 2 there are examples of some media texts that have been declared illegal. Using these and any other examples that you may be able to think of, try to identify any common factors and consider why these texts were made illegal. Try to find out what happened to them.

3.2 Illustrated Mail, the weekly edition of the *Daily Mail*, 26 January 1901

As mentioned in Chapter Two, because of industrialisation during the nineteenth century, the most widely available media were mainly the popular press and cheap novels. By 1900, one adult in five or six read a daily newspaper and one adult in three read a Sunday newspaper. Figure 3.2 shows a special issue of the weekly edition of the *Daily Mail* with a photograph of the recently deceased Queen Victoria on the cover. Inside there were eight pages on the Queen's life and family, mainly illustrated with line drawings. Other pages included a 'Woman's Corner' and a sports report on the back page. Illustrated adverts were by this time common in British newspapers and magazines and were for many of these publications their main source of income (Figure 3.3).

These examples demonstrate how media forms have become increasingly dependent upon visual images. It is thus no longer sufficient merely to consider the written meaning; it is also necessary to explore the codes of the visual images.

3.3 *The Penny Illustrated Paper*, 24 September 1890

VISUAL CODES

We understand visual images and technical codes because we learn to read them in the same way as we do the codes of language: by learning the rules that affect how the components go together to make up recognisable units of meaning. To understand better how codes work we therefore have to examine sign systems and their conventions or rules. The study of signs and sign systems and their role in the construction and organisation of meaning is called *semiotics*, and it has been influential as one of the main methods for analysing media texts and output.

Semiotics has become an important part of media and cultural studies, due partly to Roland Barthes, who based his work on the linguistic models developed by Pierce and de Saussure. Barthes examined the idea of visual meanings; for example, the extent to which we 'read' a photograph by interpreting the various elements within it, rather than by simply reading a fixed and unitary message. A photograph, Barthes claimed, involves a mechanical process where the image – that which is denoted – is transferred onto photographic paper, but there is also an expressive, human process that involves the selection and interpretation of such elements as camera angles, framing, lighting techniques and focus. These extra connotations will provide different meanings depending upon the 'situated culture' (see Chapter 1, **p. 12**) of both the producer and the viewer of the photograph.

3.4 Photographs: Michelle Frances

In Figure 3.4 the denotative content – what the photographs actually show – is people of a certain ethnic background in front of buildings. These buildings are in a certain condition and the people's clothes and gestures could also be described. The connotative meaning is more difficult, more 'abstract' or subjective, more dependent upon the viewer and his or her point of view. We, as viewers, have to make different judgements about whether the people in the photographs look happy or contented with their situation, how the buildings in the background might affect our interpretation, and how easy or difficult it is to 'fix' or anchor a meaning without knowing more about the context in which the photographs were taken or displayed.

According to this view media texts always have a number of potential meanings; that is, they are *polysemic* – potentially open to many interpretations. An *open* text, for instance, can have many different meanings depending upon time, place, and the class or occupation of the 'reader'. Often a text is so constructed that the audience is directed into understanding one particular meaning. This is done through a process of *anchorage*, where words are used to direct the reader to a particular reading; for example, as part of an advertisement or by placing a caption next to an image. This dominant meaning is called the *preferred reading* and is discussed further in Chapter 5. Barthes called texts that have only one or a particularly dominant reading *closed* texts.

If we go back to Figure 3.4, does it help to 'explain' the meaning if we know that the photographs were part of an exhibition on apartheid? It may do, but until we can anchor the political stance of the exhibition it is difficult to fix an exact meaning to these photographs. In fact, the exhibition tried to be neutral and just report the scenes as impartially as possible. However, everyone who viewed the pictures added their own opinions and therefore interpreted the photographs as reinforcing their own particular views on apartheid.

Figure 3.5 demonstrates how the anchorage of an image can change its connotative reading. The photograph on its own could be rather ambiguous, but the headline and caption seem to anchor the connotative meaning of the photograph in a clear and explicit manner, one that might be considered to meet the expectations of many of the readers of the *Independent Magazine*. Yet the letter from the woman in the photograph reveals the 'true' meaning to be substantially different.

Figure 3.6 shows how the cropping of a photograph can also 'direct' the viewer towards a particular or preferred reading. Cropping is the process by which the 'superfluous' content of a photograph is removed, thereby highlighting only that which is essential to establish a particular meaning or focus. Here, one photograph can produce three different connotative meanings depending on how much denotative information is revealed to the viewer.

3.5 A West End shopper argues with a protester who is being taken away by the police.

Photograph: Richard Smith, Katz

THE MOB'S BRIEF RULE

EYE-WITNESS

Sir: In last week's article about the poll-tax riot in Trafalgar Square ("The Mob's Brief Rule", 7 April) there is a large photograph labelled "a West End shopper argues with a protester". The woman in the photograph is me, and I thought you might like to know the true story behind the picture.

I was on my way to the theatre, with my husband. As we walked down Regent Street at about 6.30pm, the windows were intact and there was a large, cheerful, noisy group of poll-tax protesters walking up from Piccadilly Circus. We saw ordinary uniformed police walking alongside, on the pavement, keeping a low profile. The atmosphere was changed dramatically in moments when a fast-walking, threatening group of riot-squad police appeared.

We walked on to the top of Haymarket, where the atmosphere was more tense and more protesters were streaming up Haymarket from the Trafalgar Square end. Suddenly, a group of mounted police charged at full gallop into the rear of the group of protesters, scattering them, passers-by and us and creating panic. People screamed and some fell. Next to me and my husband another group of riot-squad police appeared, in a most intimidating manner.

The next thing that happened is what horrified me most. Four of the riot-squad police grabbed a young girl of 18 or 19 for no reason and forced her in a brutal man-

ner on to the crowd-control railings, with her throat across the top of the railings. Her young male companion was frantically trying to reach her and was being held back by one riot-squad policeman. In your photograph I was urging the boy to calm down or he might be arrested; he was telling me that the person being held down across the railings was his girlfriend.

My husband remonstrated with the riot-squad policeman holding the boy, and I shouted at the four riot-squad men to let the girl go as they were obviously hurting her. To my surprise, they did let her go – it was almost as if they did not know what they were doing.

The riot-squad police involved in this incident were *not* wearing any form of identification. Their epaulettes were unbuttoned and flapping loose; I lifted them on two men and neither had any numbers on. There was a sergeant with them, who was numbered, and my husband asked why his men wore no identifying numbers. The sergeant replied that it did not matter as he knew who the men were.

We are a middle-aged, suburban couple who now feel more intimidated by the Metropolitan Police than by a mob. If we feel so angry, how on earth did the young hot-heads at the rally feel?

MRS R A SARE
Northwood, Middlesex

3.6 Photograph: Gavin Wilkinson

activity **3.2**

Using either your own photographs or the series in Figure 3.4 manipulate the 'meanings' of the photographs by cropping, or adding different captions or headlines. Then look at some newspaper photographs to see in what ways they too have been constructed to create particular meanings.

McMahon and Quinn (1988) provide a useful means of understanding or classifying codes as a means of structuring the analysis of visual images. They identify three types of code: technical, symbolic and written. For most written or printed texts these categories include:

Technical:	Symbolic:	Written:
Camera angle	Objects	Headlines
Lens choice	Setting	Captions
Framing	Body language	Speech bubbles
Shutter speed	Clothing	Style
Depth of field	Colour	
Lighting and exposure		
Juxtaposition		

As visual and linguistic codes are culturally defined and are therefore social constructs, they will change over time, reflecting change in, for example, social attitudes or opinion, the 'currency' or value of certain images, and the changing position of the intended audience. As the outside world changes so the manner in which the codes and texts 'bridge' or mediate that world will also change. Figure 3.7 is a poster produced in 1927 for the Empire Marketing Board as part of its brief to

3.7 Plate 17, *Buy & Build, The Advertising Posters of the Empire Marketing Board*, Stephen Constantine, PRO

'consolidate imperialist ideals and an imperial world view as part of the popular culture of the British people'. It can also be seen as a forerunner to the 'government public relations techniques and information services ... of the Ministry of Information in WW2 and of the later Central Office of Information'. The Board also helped to finance early documentary film makers. This poster, approximately 5 feet by 3 feet (1.5m by 1m), and others like it, would be placed on hoardings around British cities, in shop windows or in schools. The poster has a clear message about what it is to be 'British' and the relationship Britain has with its empire and the people that inhabit that empire. The land, the 'jungles', are 'ours' to develop (or exploit?) and to turn into the 'gold mines' of tomorrow. Although in 1927 this message may have been acceptable, in Britain in the 1990s these types of meaning and image look anachronistic and unacceptable both to people in Britain and to those living in the former colonies.

activity 3.3

Figure 3.8 shows two covers of the book *Young Renny* by Mazo de la Roche, one published in 1948 and the other in 1959. Decode the two covers using the headings of technical, symbolic and written codes. How can we tell which cover was published when? How have the covers changed over time? Why have the publishers felt the need to change the covers? What sort of cover illustration would be used today? Are these covers still aiming at the same audience?

3.8 *Young Renny*, by Mazo de la Roche, Pan Books Ltd

When using semiotics as a means of analysing media texts, the text is usually analysed in detail and broken down, or deconstructed, into smaller constituent parts or segments. The front page of the newspaper used in Figure 3.2 is a good example of a text that is made up of several different segments, all contributing to the 'whole' message.

In analysing newspapers, first look at the technical codes:

- How is the page laid out?
- What typefaces and fonts have been used? Why?
- What can be said about the size and quality of the photographs?
- Have they been cropped? If so, how and why? How do we know that cropping has taken place?
- How do the photographs relate to the rest of the stories and the front page?
- Why have these particular pictures been selected?

Secondly consider the written codes:

- How does the size of the headline(s) compare with the rest of the page?
- What are the key words and what do they signify?
- What conventions are being used?
- To what extent does the copy meet the expectations set up by the headline(s)?
- Is any information omitted from the copy?
- How does the headline influence the way the reader will approach the story?

- Does/do the caption(s) help anchor the meaning(s)?

Thirdly, look at the symbolic codes:

- What do the masthead and title of the newspaper signify? How do they achieve this signification?
- Why are particular graphics used and what do they signify?
- What colours are used and what do they signify?
- Are there any symbolic codes used in the pictures?

Fourthly, look at the front page as a whole:

- How does the overall layout help attract readers?
- Is any particular impression or message given out by the overall 'look' of the front page?
- How is it created?

3.9 *(and opposite)* Front covers of *The Sunderland Echo* from 26 April 1946 and 21 April 1986

activity **3.4**

Figure 3.9 shows two front pages, forty years apart, from the same newspaper. Compare and contrast these, pointing out how the front page has altered over the period from 1946 to 1986. Suggest reasons why these changes may have occurred.

CONVENTIONS

Codes or grammars, whether of language or signs, operate by means of conventions. These are the ways in which certain meanings can be shared and understood. They are often not written down but are hidden or unspoken rules that we learn to accept, apply and recognise. They are part of our culture and are therefore culturally specific, but as television particularly becomes more homogenised across the world, these conventions appear to become more 'global' or linked to a television culture dominated by America. (See Chapter 8.) They influence processes both of production and of reception and can eventually become so familiar that they appear to be the only, or 'natural', way of doing or understanding something. Those groups or individuals who, for a variety of reasons, want to appear different or challenge the established ways will often try to deliberately break or subvert these conventions.

Although various conventions are discussed separately in this chapter, it is important to understand that they are integrated and mixed together in the same way as different texts are integrated and mixed together in the media 'flow'. This mixing, or intertextuality, can create an extra layer of meaning, so that a text is often partly understood by what preceded it or what will follow it or even perhaps by references within the text to other media texts. In Chapter 5, the *Batman* films and image are given as an instance of intertextuality; the Carling Black Label television advert that referred to a previous Levi jeans advert that itself included a copy of a 1960s soul record and 1950s James Dean iconography is another good example.

Look at the Vodafone adverts in Figure 3.10. They are referring the reader back to a set of earlier images and 'adding' these to 'today's' message. In the 'October 1992' advert, the woman in the grey coat, the way she is standing and holding the telephone, the manifesto with its 'declaration of rights' and 'people's charter' are all signs associated with the codes of revolutionary posters of communist Russia. These associations are trying to create a sense of revolution, of a 'new dawn breaking'. These associations can only work if the reader can recognise the sources. The advertisers therefore have to place the adverts where they think an 'informed' reader will recognise and understand these 'quotations', in this case *The Independent* or *The Sunday Times*. A bonus for the advertiser may be that if the reader does recognise the references to the earlier texts, he or she may then feel 'informed' or 'special' in some way because of having 'understood' the story, and that goodwill may then be associated with the product itself.

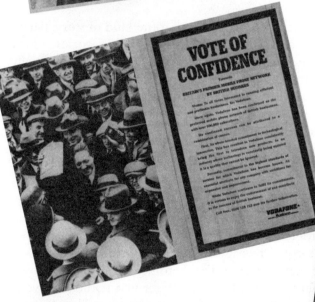

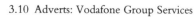

These methods have also been used as a basis for analysing films. This has meant not just focusing on the 'meaning' of films but also looking at how images or sets of images are 'read' by the viewer. Emphasis is placed less on the technical production of the images than on the viewer's interpretation, based partly upon his or her position in the social and cultural system. Some writers (Fiske, 1987) have taken this semiotic methodology and used it in the study of television, in particular as a basis for analysing how television texts create meaning through the encoding and decoding of a common, easily accessible shorthand of codes of 'meaning' that both producer and receiver understand.

NARRATIVE CODES

If we assume that all media texts tell some kind of story, narrative is a way of analysing this process of telling stories – how these stories are organised, structured and then potentially decoded and understood.

Analysing narrative structure follows from the idea that most narratives have a common structure, starting with the establishing of a plot or theme or problem; for instance, the murder by an unknown person at the beginning of a detective series. This is then followed by the development or elaboration of the problem, perhaps with the main suspect being murdered or new characters or 'twists' being introduced. Finally comes the resolution of the plot, theme or situation, in which the problems are solved. This resolution may happen when the detective 'reveals all' and the murderer is exposed, or when the hero marries the heroine. Other well-known forms of resolution include the gunfight in a traditional western or the 'big bang' endings of action adventure films like the James Bond, _Die Hard_ or _Rambo_ series.

These narratives can be unambiguous and linear, as in traditional story telling ('Once upon a time . . . and they all lived happily ever after') or factual, as in the news ('These are today's main stories'). Sometimes the narrative structure is altered or manipulated and the narrative can begin at the end and be a recapitulation or series of flashbacks (as in _D.O.A._, _Bad Timing_ or _Citizen Kane_). Occasionally the narrative is structured as a combination of both 'real time' and flashback, as in a live sports broadcast, where key moments in the development of the narrative are highlighted as action replays or edited highlights.

In advertising there is often a simple before-and-after narrative that says: 'Before it/I was like this, after using product X, it is/I am like this.' Sometimes the narrative structure is obscure and the key elements of character, time and narrator deliberately ambiguous or surreal, so that audiences are asked to create their own meanings. This was a characteristic of the Chanel Egoiste aftershave adverts on television in the late 1980s and early 1990s.

Narrator

The meaning of a narrative is often encoded through the use of a narrator who establishes the relationship between the narrative and the audience and tells the story; for example, 'It was a dark and stormy night and the captain gathered his men together one by one ... "Tell us a story, Captain", they said, and so he began ... "It was a dark and stormy night".'

If the narrative is told in the first person, with 'I' as participant, the audience is drawn into the story, the relationship between text and audience can become more subjective, and the audience identifies with a particular character. Examples include the Raymond Chandler books and films, such as *The Big Sleep* or *Farewell My Lovely*: 'I got up at nine, drank three cups of black coffee, bathed the back of my head with ice-water and read the two morning papers that had been thrown against the apartment door.' On the other hand, if the narrator is spoken of as 'He/she/it' as reported by an observer or witness, the relationship between text and audience is more detached and objective and, as in news bulletins or documentaries, 'we' the audience are positioned as interested but impartial observers: 'Protesters took to the streets of Moscow again today as ...'. Sometimes, however, the story is told by a silent, 'invisible' or detached third party represented by just the camera lens as observer. In this case the relationship between text and audience is less clear and each individual has to construct his or her own position or point of view. (There is more detailed discussion on mode of address and point of view in Chapter 5.)

Narration

Narration is the act of telling the 'story', and the form which it takes will affect how the narrative is told. One of the main differences between these forms is how *time* is handled; for instance, a 500-page novel can deal with a time span of many years (*War and Peace*) or a few hours (*Ulysses*), and equally the time taken to read the novel can also vary widely. A thirty-minute radio or television programme can attempt to cover a similar time period but has to do so in a finite, or fixed, time slot. Consumption by the audience is also much more limited, although the video recorder does offer some degree of control and choice. To bridge this difference between the audience's 'real time' and the narrative's 'story time', various conventions are used. One of the most common devices for showing the passing of time used to be the speeding up of the hands of a clock or the leaves of a calendar flying away; today these are both rather clichéd or heavy-handed, and as audiences we accept and understand more sophisticated technical conventions, such as the use of fade-outs or slow mixes from one shot to another, or even a single caption that may say 'two years later'.

3.11 National Dairy Council TV commercial

NEW 60 SECOND DOORSTEP TV COMMERCIAL

MUSIC: Builds Slowly.

MILKMAN: Attention!

Two semi-skimmed ...

One silver top ... No. 18 ... Ah! Rice pudding tonight.

Lads ... Lads ...

What are you playing at! They're away for a fortnight.

Ah! Next door want two extra.

ANNOUNCER: Whatever your order ...

Your milkman can deliver ...

All the fresh milk you'll ever need.

<table>
<tr><td>

activity **3.5**

</td><td>

Look at the storyboard in Figure 3.11 and note how by cutting from the fourth shot to the fifth we understand that the milkman has 'ordered' two pints of milk to move onto the door step. Consider also the use of the announcer in the twelfth shot: how does this alter our point of view?

</td></tr>
</table>

Soap operas often try to blur the gap between real time and story time; for instance, a *Brookside* episode may start in the morning with families meeting over breakfast, follow characters through the day and end with the families meeting again over dinner. By the evening the events being shown on the screen may be happening at the same time as the audience is watching them happen. Events in soap operas may parallel 'real' events and seasons; for instance, Christmas editions of popular soaps often show the characters themselves celebrating Christmas.

3.12 Family holiday album: Bournemouth, 1923

Sontag (1977) focuses on the family photograph album as a good illustration of the stories families tell about themselves and how their history is a social construct (Figure 3.12). The contents of a family photograph album can cover several generations but will tend to highlight the positive, the great occasions: marriages, holidays, births, anniversaries. Like soap operas, family photograph albums attempt to represent life 'with the boring [or unhappy?] bits left out'.

---

activity **3.6**

Either use the examples in Figure 3.12 or look through your own family photograph albums. How is the family portrayed? What narratives are being told? How do they relate to our own personal experiences of the family?

We often create the story ourselves by decoding the clues that we are given and then filling in the gaps to create the story. Adverts and title sequences are particularly successful at giving just enough information for us to do this. Television title sequences can be seen as mini-narratives that act as trailers for the coming programme and mark the end of the previous segment, perhaps a commercial break. The use of certain types of image and the importance of music prepare us for the next narrative segment by introducing the character and signposting the type or genre of programme. Title sequences can be seen as a familiar and reassuring element of a programme's popularity which each week repeat the broader narrative of a series. In the television series *Quantum Leap*, each week viewers see the hero suffer again the nuclear accident that now allows him to travel through time. These title sequences are an important part of attracting and maintaining the interest of the audience and can last for several minutes. In *Star Trek* the title sequence has developed its own catch phrase, 'to boldly go where no man has gone before', which has become part of the series' mythology. In America the first commercial break, the next narrative segment, comes directly after this title sequence.

Even the most 'open' of narratives, however, usually has a clear start and finish point, even if the structure within the narrative itself is unclear. A detective or police story that starts with a murder and then recaps the events leading up to it will often start with a title sequence and end with credits. In newspapers the headlines can be seen to mark the start of a particular narrative. The audience is being given a clear marker as to when each narrative is beginning or ending. However, because of the changing social contexts in which we consume media texts it may be that we are increasingly creating our own narratives, stopping or starting part way through a radio or TV programme, film or magazine or, through the use of the remote control, 'zapping' from one narrative segment to another, heightening the intertexuality and creating our own 'synthesis' of narrative structures.

Codes of Enigma and Action

There are two key codes involved in the sequencing of narrative, the action code and the enigma code. Action codes are often used as a shorthand for advancing the narrative; Tilley (1991) cites as an example the buckling of a gun-belt in the western as a prelude to the gunfight, or the packing of a suitcase which 'signals' confrontation, panic or escape. Others can include the starting of a car engine or the whistle of an approaching train.

The enigma code 'explains' the narrative by controlling what, and how much, information is given to the audience. This code is intended to capture the audience's interest and attention by setting up an enigma (Who was the murderer whose hand we saw in the opening sequence? What does 'Rosebud' mean in *Citizen Kane*? Why was the phrase 'In space no one can hear you scream' used to promote the film *Alien*?) that is then resolved during the course of the narrative. Headlines in a newspaper serve the same function of summarising the key elements ('Killer dogs foil cops acid party raid') and making a direct appeal to readers, as do the 'trailers' for films and new television or radio programmes: 'Another chance to catch up with *The Old Devils* on BBC1 tonight at 10.15' or 'Taggart is back in a new and exciting series.'

Advertisements are particularly good at using and compressing these enigma codes. They try to raise the audience's interest but at the same time want to contain and limit what we know. Look at Figure 3.13 with its narrative enigma. The advert shows someone being 'saved', but what actually is being saved? The owner of the legs by an unseen (male?) rescuer? Or the hairiness of the model's legs by the use of Immac? Or 'our' legs? The advert tries to create an enigma that aims to attract the reader's attention while at the same time suggesting some kind of parody or joke: 'wherever you are' – even when shipwrecked?

In analysing advertisements, technical codes include:

- quality of the image;
- colour or black and white;
- cropping;
- composition;
- lighting;
- juxtaposition;
- camera angle;
- focus.

3.13 Immac: Reckitt & Colman
Products

SALON SMOOTH
LEGS
WITHOUT THE
SALON.

Immac

IMMAC'S IMPROVED WAX STRIPS, COMPLETE WITH A UNIQUE VIAL OF SKIN CONDITIONING OIL,

GIVE YOU SALON SMOOTH RESULTS, WHEREVER YOU ARE.

Immac

Written codes include:

● slogan;
● copy;
● typeface(s);
● use of graphics.

Symbolic codes include:

● people – age, gender, race and class;
● clothing;
● non-verbal communication – expression, eyes, gesture, touch;
● objects – props, setting, product, background, colour.

Overall, consider:

- function;
- narrative;
- identification;
- promise;
- values;
- aspirations;
- power;
- money.

activity **3.7**	Select your own range of adverts or else use the ones in this chapter (Figures 3.3, 3.10 and 3.13) and analyse them using the checklists above.

As audiences become more sophisticated and adept at recognising these codes of enigma and action, we begin to perceive patterns and anticipate developments. There is then a 'pleasure of the text', recognising what is going to happen, the feeling of being 'in the know' that the promise of familiarity brings. It is this familiarity and continuity that for many of us make the narrative likeable, predictable and understandable. We know what is going to happen because it is the convention of this type of narrative or programme to be resolved in a certain way (the policeman gets his man, the hero and heroine live happily ever after), but we will watch anyway, wanting to confirm our knowingness, our familiarity and understanding of the narrative structure: 'Ah yes! I was right, he is the secret father of her child.'

Part of this pleasure in predicting and recognising what is going to happen lies in an overlap between these fictional narratives and the 'real' narratives of our own lives. In the same way as we recognise our own lives as stories, so we recognise that these fictional stories reflect our own lives (or our projected desires and fantasies), the social world we inhabit and our place in it. The real and the fictional often have common values and attitudes, and perhaps the members of the audience can rewrite their own personal narratives to produce different meanings or different endings.

Many writers have suggested that narratives generate a dynamic of equilibrium and disequilibrium. This suggests a model of narrative which starts with equilibrium or 'harmony', a state where all is well, which is then disrupted, often by an outside influence which causes a disequilibrium or tension. For instance, a peaceful American surburban family or community is threatened from outside in many of Steven Spielberg's films (*Close Encounters, E.T., Gremlins, Back to the Future* etc.) or in David Lynch's *Blue Velvet,* before finally the threat is resolved and replaced by a new equilibrium. In other narratives the disruption may be violent as in *Alien* or some of the spaghetti westerns.

The notion of equilibrium highlights questions on the way narratives can speak ideologically about how social order is represented and how equilibrium functions to effect closure within narratives: 'At the end of *The Outlaw Josey Wales* a new community has been created – a sharing and stable community of male and female, young and old, white and red' (Tilley, 1991).

activity **3.8**	Choose three films that you know well and analyse the ways in which disequilibrium occurs. Compare the two states of equilibrium, the first at the beginning and the second at the end of the film. How has the equilibrium changed? In what ways has it remained the same? Have the characters' positions, status or relationships to each other altered in any significant way?

Character Functions

In 1928, in a famous analysis of narratives, Propp used fairy tales as a basis for his model of over thirty character types, all of whom perform some kind of function in the way narrative is organised and developed. Some of these key character functions include:

- the *hero*, who seeks something;
- the *villain*, who hinders or is in competition with the hero;
- the *donor*, who provides some kind of magic talisman that helps the hero;
- the *helper*, who aids the hero and his or her quest;
- the *heroine*, who acts as a reward for the hero and is the object of the villain's schemes.

activity **3.9**	Consider these categories and how they apply to various films that you are familiar with; for example, Harrison Ford as the hero in the Indiana Jones films, or SMERSH, Dr No or Blofeld as the villains in the James Bond films, where perhaps the character of Q could be the donor. In what ways do these character types help 'advance' the narrative?

The importance of these characters is less to do with who they are or what they are like than with the part they play in the development of the narrative and our recognition of their general function. We recognise the hero and heroine and identify with the (usually male) hero – 'us' – and the resolution that should bring them together. We are encouraged to take sides and oppose the villain – 'them' – and occasionally even boo when they appear on the screen, the stage or wherever the narrative is being played out.

Propp's character functions allow for individual changes in attitudes and/or beliefs – for instance, the main character's coming to the view that war is useless or corrupting in *Born on the Fourth of July* or *Apocalypse Now* – for undertaking a mythic 'quest' or search, perhaps for some personal justice as in *The Searchers* or *Mona Lisa*; and for conflict between hierarchies or within subcultures, in films like *Rebel Without a Cause*, *My Beautiful Laundrette* or *The Godfather* series.

Different types of narrative may be identified by their gender characteristics. Clarke (1987) suggests that male narratives tend to be clearly resolved at the end of each segment, with the 'hero' overcoming the problem, and the status quo being re-established. These fictional narratives are found particularly in police or adventure series and can be seen as integral to news bulletins, where order and equilibrium is restored at the end of every programme. Film narratives tend to have a more distinct closure whereas television often tries to create some sense of narrative continuity. Female narratives, Geraghty (1992) suggests, tend to be more open-ended, ongoing and not so clearly resolved. These types of narrative can often be found in soap operas and are one possible reason why this genre tends to be popular with female audiences. (See the section on gender preferences in Chapter 5.)

GENRE

Repetition is a key element in the way audiences understand and relate to narratives:

> Repetition in the t.v. narrative occurs at the level of the series: formats are repeated, situations return week after week. Each time there is novelty. The characters of the situation comedy encounter a new dilemma; the documentary reveals a new problem; the news gives us a fresh strike, a new government, another earthquake, the first panda born in captivity... The series is composed of segments. The recognition of the series format tends to hold segments together and to provide them with an

element of continuity and narrative progression from one to the next.

Ellis (1982)

The concept of genre, developed particularly through the study of film, is a way of classifying particular styles or types of media text by identifying common elements that are repeated again and again, or associated with certain types of text. Originally these common elements related to narrative or story types; for instance, Hollywood westerns tended to have not only common ingredients (horses, guns, ranchers, 'Indians' and cavalry) but also common narratives ('Indian' uprisings, people being cheated out of their land, prospecting for gold, family feuds). As the concept has become more sophisticated it is possible to identify other components that are common to certain types of genre: in the Hollywood western there are particular directors (John Ford), actors (John Wayne or Clint Eastwood), particular types of character (the loner or outsider, as in *The Searchers*), sets (Monument Valley) and even theme music (*The Good, the Bad and the Ugly*).

The concept of genre is becoming more detailed in the way it is used. For a long time television comedy was considered to be a genre, which perhaps it still is, but the generic term is now too broad to cover the wide and varied output of comedy that appears on television. It is now possible to identify a set of subgenres of television comedy: alternative comedy, sitcom, American comedy, stand-up comedy. Different production locations may also produce specific characteristics; for instance, British soap operas tend to be described as 'realistic or gritty', whereas American ones are more escapist and Australian ones seem more idealistic.

Once a genre has proved successful it is often repeated again and again (the *Rocky* or *Superman* series, *Police Academy*, *Star Trek*, *Nightmare on Elm Street*, etc.). In films some of these genres move in and out of fashion; for instance, some years ago disaster movies were popular, and in the late 1980s and early 1990s there was a fad for 'baby' movies like *Three Men and a Baby*, *Look Who's Talking* and *Baby Boom*.

activity **3.10**

Look at some recent films and try to categorise them into genres by looking for certain common basic ingredients. What story types do these films have? What sorts of character do they have? What actors and actresses are particularly associated with them? Are there particularly distinctive sets, lighting or other 'production values' associated with them?

It should be noted that this is not just a way of categorising 'types' of film but that the notion of genre is important to both audience and producer. Audiences are said to like the idea of genre (although they may not identify it by that term) because of its reassuring and familiar promise of patterns of repetition and variation. They know what they are getting: if they enjoyed *Back to the Future 1* they will most probably enjoy *Back to the Future 2*. Producers are said to like genres because they can exploit a winning formula and minimise taking risks. The concept of genre also helps institutions budget and plan their finances more accurately. It is important to note, however, that the formula approach does not always work; for example, *Crocodile Dundee 2* was not as successful as *Crocodile Dundee 1*.

This concept of genre is now widely used as a way both of categorising media production and output, whether it be from women's magazines or television quiz shows, and of explaining how we, the audience, make sense of the 'flow' of media output by identifying and 'organising' certain types of television programme within an evening's viewing, or certain features within a daily newspaper or weekly magazine. The concept of genre allows us to name the process by which we identify certain landmarks on the map of the media's 'flow' in the same way as we go to different sections in a library or record shop.

Quiz or game shows are a particular genre of radio and television, and their common components are likely to include, to a greater or lesser degree, the following:

- a personality who hosts the show, often an ex-comedian;
- prizes;
- women as decoration and/or assistants;
- live audiences;
- 'real' people – members of the general public;
- a sense of competition;
- excitement;
- glamour;
- catch phrases.

activity **3.11**

Watch several quiz shows on television and decide whether you agree with the list of components. Are there other ingredients that should be included? How do 'serious' quiz shows like *Mastermind* fit the list? To what extent do radio quiz shows fit it? You can also identify other genres of popular television and compare their common characteristics.

It has been suggested that this dominance of genre, particularly in television, has several consequences, one of which is to marginalise those programmes that do not fit into generic conventions because audiences will not recognise or accept them. Although this is true to some extent, there are instances where the notion of genre has been specifically challenged; for instance, in television series such as *Police Story* and *Twin Peaks* or the films *Blazing Saddles* and *The Rocky Horror Picture Show*, where the genre characteristics have been deliberately usurped or parodied.

The other consequence relates to the power of the generic structure, which can be ideologically limiting and in which the form can dominate over content. In police series such as *The Bill* or *Inspector Morse* we are placed on the side of the police, who are the familiar characters that we are asked to identify with. In sitcom there is a need to maintain the status quo so that the original situation can be used again. This may mean that although an interesting problem might be set up, such as those of the mother's personal fulfilment and satisfaction in *2.4 Children* or of changing the way the old people's home is run in *Waiting For God*, it can never actually be answered and allowed any progression, because that would destroy the generic formula that has made the programmes successful.

REALISM

Part of the process of creating meaning is the degree to which we, the audience, can recognise and identify with what is being portrayed – the text's credibility or realism. We expect what we see, listen to or read to have some connection with our own lives and experiences and the world we inhabit, or to appear to be based upon some sort of recognisable reality. This then helps us to identify and understand the text and its meaning. We often judge how successful this illusion or story is by measuring the text against our own experiences, our own 'situated culture' and biography. What is 'real' therefore can become a subjective and controversial concept, where a text that one person perhaps considers to be realistic may not be considered so by someone else with another perspective. A programme that describes all football fans as 'hooligans' may appear convincing to someone who knows nothing about football fans except what they read or see in the media, but to someone who has been supporting a football club for many years this may seem to be a very unfair and one-sided portrayal.

There are, however, certain types of text that we all generally accept as more 'realistic' than others; for example, we accept something labelled 'documentary' as real but probably not something called 'science fiction'. Some soaps are called realistic (particularly *Brookside* or *EastEnders*) whereas others are seen to be more fictionalised and artificial (*Neighbours* or *Home and Away*) or even fantasy (*Dallas*). Some sitcoms are seen as being realistically based (*Bread*) whereas others are deliberately surreal (*The Young Ones*).

Four particular criteria are usually needed for a text to become accepted by audiences as realistic. One is the surface realism or 'getting the details right'; for example, making sure that no characters are wearing wristwatches in a nineteenth-century play. A popular genre on British television has been the 'period drama', where production values seem to concentrate on using vintage cars from the correct period or shots of steam trains puffing in and out of small country stations in an attempt to create both 'atmosphere' and 'period charm', both of which are very saleable in the foreign television sales market.

The second criterion refers to the 'inner' or emotional realism of the characters and their motivation. This allows the audience to identify with the situation and characters portrayed and in particular 'feel' or 'share' the emotions that are an essential part of the story-telling process; for instance, the sadness in tear-jerkers like *Love Story* or the fear and suspense in films like *Jaws* or *Jurassic Park*.

The third criterion is less to do with how a text looks than with the overall message that is transmitted; for example, not to challenge taken-for-granted notions, or upsetting a consensus of opinion as to what the 'truth' or 'reality' is. In fictional work there has to be a logic or plausibility of the plot or characters that appears appropriate to the text's particular terms of reference; the situation in a science fiction film might not appear 'realistic' if used in a period drama but may seem plausible in the context of a film set in the future. This consensus on what 'truth' is is more problematic in documentary work or in the more ambiguous 'docudrama' or 'faction' programmes like *Threads* or *Who Bombed Birmingham* which are produced in a realistic style. Especially controversial are programmes like *Tumbledown*, which criticises Britain's war in the Falklands Islands, or the Ken Loach film *Hidden Agenda*, which is set in Northern Ireland. The question of how 'realistic' the text is then becomes more contentious and perhaps part of a wider political debate. (See Chapter 4.)

The fourth criterion refers to the employment of technical and symbolic codes of realism that correspond with the audience's notion of what 'realistic' is. As the newspaper front pages used earlier in the chapter illustrate, codes and conventions can change over time. Originally 'silent' films had a live piano player who musically 'signalled' the climax of a scene or speech, or the development of the narrative was indicated by captions. We have learnt to accept the use of music in the background as a 'mood enhancer', but only as long as it is discreet. In *Dallas*, music, as well as a slow zoom in, is used to 'warn' viewers of an impending climax as well as being a 'bridge' into the next scene, yet many viewers will not be aware that music is used in the series.

Even in documentaries we often accept apparent contradictions in how realism is presented. For instance, we may accept the unrealistic convention of someone apparently alone talking to the camera; we ignore the fact that behind that camera will be several crew members and a large amount of equipment. We suspend disbelief and accept the illusion that the person is alone and that it is normal to talk aloud.

A good example to look at when considering how 'truthful' or 'real' media can be is to look at television news bulletins. These, according to Fiske (1987), are high-status texts due to their agenda-setting role in the political and social life of our culture. This importance is highlighted by the statutory obligations that television news programmes have to be objective and independent, and their obligation to be 'balanced' and 'impartial'. The status that broadcasters attach to news bulletins is also reflected in their position as fixed points' in the schedules. News bulletins, however, are also part of the 'entertainment' function of television and therefore have to be popular and produce good ratings. In the early 1990s there have been calls by newscasters like Martyn Lewis for 'good news' to be reported, as well as a debate over whether *News At Ten* should be moved to allow more popular programmes to run uninterrupted across ITV's peak-time slot. News bulletins are the subject of complex and often competing claims that, along with their crucial informative and ideological role, make them important texts to analyse.

In analysing a news bulletin, consider how it is introduced:

- What type of music is used? What does it signify?
- What pictures are shown as the bulletin is introduced?
- How do these pictures and music set the tone of the programme?
- What are they suggesting about the content and presentation of the bulletin?
- How is the name of the programme presented? Could it have been presented in a different way? If it were, how would the meaning change?

Consider how it is presented:

- Who is presenting the news?
- What sort of people are they?
- What sort of accent and appearance do they have?
- Who do they represent?
- Could different people present the news in the same way, or would it change?
- Is one gender more prominent than another?
- How many stories are contained in the bulletin?
- What types of story come first? Why?
- What types of story come towards the end of the bulletin? Why?

Choose one particular story:

- Whose viewpoint is presented?
- Who appears in the bulletin?
- Who else could have been included?
- How is balance attempted?
- How are we, the audience, addressed?

The 'truth' is often considered to be most apparent in documentary, particularly when the conventions of *cinema verité* (a 'live', hand-held camera) are used. Known as fly-on-the-wall, this approach presents the subject apparently unmediated by a film crew, a presenter or reshooting. Those participating in this type of documentary tend to speak for themselves, and their words or actions are apparently merely recorded and observed, not reflected upon or mediated by a presenter.

One of the earliest British examples of documentary realism was the film *Night Mail*, made by John Grierson's GPO Film Unit in 1936, which recorded the work of the post office on the night train from London to Glasgow. The first part of the film was recorded in the cramped conditions of the carriage sorting office, recording the 'real' actions of the postmen and allowing them to speak for themselves. It was an unromantic but accurate portrayal of their work. Towards the end of the film, however, the mood changes and Grierson uses a score by Benjamin Britten as background to the poem *Night Mail* especially commissioned and read by W.H. Auden. What had started as a documentary record finishes as what Grierson called 'the creative interpretation of reality' (Goodwin and Whannel, 1990).

Much more recent and developed examples include *The Police* (1982), made for the BBC by Graef and Stewart, and Paul Watson's *The Family* (1974) and *Sylvania Waters* (1993). This type of programme has increased in popularity, perhaps partly because of the reduction in the size of recording equipment that now allows film crews to be much more 'discreet', and partly because of the humour that can result from 'real people' not modifying their language or actions for the camera. These programmes also tend to be relatively cheap to produce, as they rely upon 'real' people, not actors, and 'real' environments, not constructed sets.

While seeming more 'natural' and unmediated, these fly-on-the-wall documentaries are subject to considerable editorial control during post-production. With a shooting ratio of up to fifty hours of recorded video to one hour broadcast, the onus is on the editor to generate as much dramatic interest and entertainment as possible.

The term reality television has been increasingly applied to all those programmes which seemingly allow ordinary people access to appear as themselves, utilising actual or sometimes reconstructed scenes, often made possible by the growth in availability and technical sophistication of the video camcorder. In practice, the label embraces a wide variety of programmes which feature ordinary people in a range of different roles:

- as subjects in dramatised reconstructions of real events (*999* or *True Crimes*);
- as subjects of entertainment or humour in spontaneous or contrived situations (*You've Been Framed* or *Candid Camera*);
- as subjects within a professionally produced fly-on-the-wall or *verité* documentary (*Culloden: A Year in the Life of a Primary School*);
- as amateur directors offering a personalised documentary of an event or way of life (*Videodiaries*).

Only in the last example could it be claimed that professional mediation has been largely bypassed, permitting a more genuine and authentic expression of 'ordinary people'.

activity **3.12**

Using one particular programme as an example, consider the main issues and principles involved in fly-on-the-wall documentaries.

Content Analysis

The focus of this chapter has been on methods of analysis based on the semiotic/literary tradition, where the emphasis is placed upon the text's meaning and how it may be 'read' or decoded. It is important to note, however, that there is an alternative approach called *content analysis*. This is a method of analysing media texts by 'quantitative' research based on breaking them down into different components or categories, whose frequency can then be measured. Meaning is inferred from the number of times a particular feature occurs; for example, a study carried out by the Commission for Racial

Table 3.1 Total number of appearances of actors in BBC programmes monitored by ethnic origin

Ethnic Origin	BBC1					BBC2			
	Week 1	Week 2	Week 3	Total no. of actors	% of total no. of actors	Week 1	Week 2	Total no. of actors	% of total no. of actors
White* (British)	176	133	157	466	92.6	18	32	50	100
West Indian	1	—	1	2	0.4	—	—	—	—
Black (African)	—	1	1	2	0.4	—	—	—	—
Indian	1	1	5	7	1.4	—	—	—	—
White (except British)	8	2	5	15	3.0	—	—	—	—
Middle Eastern	—	—	5	5	1.0	—	—	—	—
Chinese	1	1	2	4	0.8	—	—	—	—
Japanese	1	1	—	2	0.4	—	—	—	—
Black (USA)	—	—	—	—	—	—	—	—	—
Totals	188	139	176	503	100	18	32	50	100

*Includes Eire/N. Ireland

Source: Commission for Racial Equality (1982): *Television in a multi-racial society*

Table 3.2 Total number of appearances of actors in ITV programmes monitored by ethnic origin

Ethnic Origin	London					Granada			
	Week 1	Week 2	Week 3	Total no. of actors	% of total no. of actors	Week 1	Week 2	Total no. of actors	% of total no. actors
White* (British)	273	314	337	924	95.8	298	300	598	96.0
West Indian	6	4	10	20	2.1	6	4	10	1.6
Black (African)	1	1	—	2	0.2	1	1	2	0.3
Indian	1	—	—	1	0.1	1	1	2	0.3
White (except British)	4	6	2	12	1.2	4	6	10	1.6
Middle Eastern	—	—	—	—	—	—	—	—	—
Chinese	—	—	—	—	—	—	—	—	—
Japanese	—	1	—	1	0.1	—	1	1	0.2
Black (USA)	—	—	5	5	0.5	—	—	—	—
Totals	285	326	354	965	100	310	313	623	100

*Includes Eire/N. Ireland

NB Each programme monitored was taken as a separate entity so that certain series shown more than once a week would have each part considered as separate programmes.

Source: Commission for Racial Equality (1982): *Television in a multi-racial society*

Equality in 1982 attempted to examine the number of appearances by actors of different ethnic origins (Tables 3.1 and 3.2). A similar study could be made of the number of times positive images of ethnic minorities appear in advertisements during peak-time television. One of the problems with this type of exercise is that there are already uncertainties about how the categories are defined; for instance, what constitutes a 'positive' image? Even if this is clearly defined from the outset, the content analysis exercise focuses purely on the output of the media and ignores much of what the reader or viewer contributes to the creating of a text's 'meaning'. Content analysis, however, does have a useful purpose in identifying broad pat-

Table 3.3 Dominant themes, all subjects[a], all titles, 1979–80 (%)

	1979–80			
	W	**WO**	**WW**	**Total**
Self-help: overcoming misfortune	35	32	40	36
Getting and keeping your man	11	10	15	12
Self-help: achieving perfection	13	14	6	11
The happy family	9	12	12	11
Heart versus head	12	8	12	10
The working wife is a good wife	9	13	7	10
Success equals happiness	11	8	8	9
Female state mysterious	—	—	—	—
Gilded youth	—	—	—	—
Other	—	3	—	1
n	24	24	24	72

[a] Excluding beauty
n = 1 per item, 3 items per issue, 4 issues per year;
W = Woman; WO = Woman's Own; WW = Woman's Weekly
Source: Ferguson (1983): *Forever Feminine: Womens Magazines and the Cult of Feminity*. Heinemann.

Table 3.4 Sub-themes, all subjects, all titles, 1979-80 (%)

	1979–80			
	W	**WO**	**WW**	**Total**
Getting and keeping your man	35	24	31	30
Self-help: overcoming misfortune	7	24	17	16
Heart versus head	26	8	14	16
The working wife is a good wife	18	15	15	16
The happy family	—	11	23	12
Self-help: acheiving perfection	14	18	—	11
Female state mysterious	—	—	—	—
Gilded youth	—	—	—	—
Success equals happiness	—	—	—	—
Other	—	—	—	—
n	14	17	12	43

n = open-ended
W = Woman; WO = Woman's Own; WW = Woman's Weekly
Source: Ferguson (1983): *Forever Feminine: Womens Magazines and the Cult of Feminity*. Heinemann.

terns and has been used particularly by the Glasgow Media Group (see the section on broadcasting and political bias in Chapter 4) and by Ferguson (1983) in her study of the dominant and sub-themes that appeared in women's magazines between 1979 and 1980 (Tables 3.3 and 3.4). (For further discussion of Ferguson's work see chapter four, page 137–8.)

activity 3.13

It may be useful to look at one particular type of programme as a way of identifying how all the different codes and conventions discussed in this chapter work together.

Consider several episodes of a particular genre of television programming, such as soap operas. To what extent are they a genre? Some of the key components that might be looked at could include the types of setting, types of character and issue found in them, as well as the story types and their narrative structures.

- Are there any other common characteristics?
- Are there different types of sub-genres of soaps? Try to explain what the differences are.
- Are there certain types of narrative that commonly appear in soaps? List the most common stories in recent episodes.
- Chronicle the time scale represented in one particular episode.
- Identify the stories in one particular episode, for instance – which stories are being established, which are in the process of elaboration and which are close to resolution.
- Choose a particular story. Try to decide what will happen next.
- Who informs us about soaps and what to expect in different episodes?
- What are the most common types of character found in soaps? Why?
- What musical codes are used?
- What types of setting are used? (Street, Close, etc.)
- How is a sense of realism created?

activity **3.14**	**1** What conclusions can be drawn from the information contained in Tables 3.1–3.4? Are there any criticisms that can be made of this data? Now plan your own contents analysis exercise, choosing a particular area and categories to study.
	2 Using the checklist for analysing newspaper front pages, analyse the front page of your choice. It is useful to compare broadsheet and tabloid newspapers to highlight the conventions that are used to make tabloids more popular.
	3 Select a television or film genre, such as film noir, and list its distinctive characteristics. Choose one particular film and analyse it in detail.
	4 Consider the extent to which the concept of 'genre' is useful in analysing and categorising media texts.

FURTHER READING

Berger, J. 1972: *Ways of Seeing*. Penguin.

Ellis, J. 1992: *Visible Fictions*. Routledge.

Goodwin, A. and Whannel, G. (Eds) 1990: *Understanding Television*. Routledge.

Izod, J. 1989: *Reading the Screen*. Longman.

McMahon, B. and Quinn, R. 1986: *Real Images*. Macmillan.

Monaco, J. 1977: *How to Read a Film: The Art, Technology, Language, History and Theory of Film and Media*. Oxford University Press.

Morgan, J. and Welton, P. 1992: *See What I Mean*. Edward Arnold.

Williamson, J. 1978: *Decoding Advertisements: Ideology and Meaning in Advertising*. Marion Boyars.

Representation

4

The concept of representation embodies the theme that the media construct meanings about the world – they *repre-*sent it, and in doing so, help audiences to make sense of it. For representation to be meaningful to audiences, there needs to be a shared recognition of people situations, ideas, etc. What require closer examination are the ideas and meanings produced by those representations. There may be shared recognition of the world as represented through familiar or *dominant* images and ideas, but there is little social consensus about how to interpret those representations, and always the possibility of *alternative* representations.

This chapter is concerned with what kinds of media representation are more typical, and what explanations might be made to account for such patterns. Given that society is increasingly pluralistic in terms of variety of social groups, interests and perspective, emphasis will be given to key social identities such as gender and ethnicity, and also to problems of achieving political unity.

WHOSE REPRESENTATIONS?

Before considering what kinds of representation appear in the media, it needs to be made clear that any examination cannot be entirely innocent. Academic approaches to the study of human culture either start or end with broad explanatory models, or theories, which are used to make sense of all the information gathered in the course of research. Media studies embraces a number of such theoretical frameworks which have been applied over the years, not least in the analysis of media content. This chapter will begin with a brief outline of two alternative models which have been influential in their analysis of media content. There is a fuller discussion of the key determinants of media output in Chapter 6.

THE HEGEMONIC MODEL

The underlying assumption of those subscribing to a hegemonic view of society is that there are fundamental inequalities in power between social groups. Those groups with most power are in the main able to exercise their influence *culturally* rather than by force. The concept has its origins in Marxist theory, where writers have attempted to explain how the ruling capitalist class have been able to protect their economic interests. Hegemony refers to the winning of popular consent through everyday cultural life, including media representations of the world as well as other social institutions, such as education and the family. To understand how hegemony may be achieved, it is necessary to consider the concept of ideology.

Ideology

Ideology is a complex concept, but broadly speaking refers to a set of ideas which produces a partial and selective view of reality. This in turn serves the interests of those with power in society. It has its roots in the writings of Karl Marx in the nineteenth century, arguing that the property-owning classes were able to rule by ideas which represented as natural the class relationships of production, therefore justifying their own wealth and privilege. These ideas could be found in all areas of social knowledge, such as religion; for example, the notion that it is 'God's will' that some are born rich and that the poor will be rewarded in the next life. Thus the notion of ideology entails widely held ideas or beliefs, which may often be seen as 'common sense', *legitimising* or making widely acceptable certain forms of social inequality. In so doing, ideologies are able to disguise or suppress the real structure of domination and exploitation which exists in society.

Modern writers (Marxist and others) have adapted and developed this idea so that all belief systems or world views are thought to be ideological. Although some ideas and beliefs seem more 'natural' or 'truthful', there is no absolute truth with which to measure the accuracy of representations. What interests those who analyse media representations is whose ideological perspective is privileged. This raises the issue of power inequalities. While Marxists have emphasised social class differences, others have increasingly pointed to gender and racial inequalities. What is agreed is that popular culture, especially media output, is the site of a constant struggle over the production of meaning. The media's role may be seen as:

- circulating and reinforcing dominant ideologies;
- or (less frequently), undermining and challenging such ideologies.

What is important to note is that the media and the audience are both part of the process of producing ideological meaning (where the balance of power lies is addressed in the next chapter).

Myth

Ideologies 'work' through symbolic codes (see Chapter 3), which represent and explain cultural phenomena. Barthes (1973) labels this symbolic representation as mythic, not in the traditional sense of being false (as in fairy tales), but in the sense of having the appearance of being 'natural' or 'common sense', so that it is not questioned. Advertising draws heavily on myth, using cultural signifiers to represent qualities which can be realised through consumption of the advertised product. Williamson (1978) has identified some of the value systems which are represented in the language of advertising. Particularly prominent in her analysis are adverts which she claims invite us to reunite ourselves with nature (even more relevant in the 'green' 1990s), and those which attribute the power of science and technology to products. In nearly all adverts, she sees two processes at work: first, an appeal to our belief in the 'magical' powers of products to solve our problems, and second, the divorce of production from consumption. Hidden from our view are the capitalist conditions from which advertised products originate (conditions which Marxist writers see as alienating and exploitative of workers). See Figure 4.1.

The British Nation: An Ideological Construction

What does is mean to be British? The extent to which the people of Britain can be considered a nation is problematic. A shared sense of belonging and identity is certainly a real sentiment for many people living in Britain. However, closer scrutiny raises questions concerning divisions between various groups comprising the British population, not least nationalism within Scotland and Wales. Even if England is taken as the national 'core', further divisions can be identified along ethnic, religious, regional and class lines. If there are so many alternative sources of identity, how has the national sense of identity achieved such a strong hold? While there is not the space here to address this question adequately, we can examine how the media may contribute towards the symbolic representation of what it means to be British.

4.1 Hovis, Collett, Dickenson, Pearce and Partners Limited

How does this advert work as a myth?

It is in the context of 'us' and 'them' that a sense of national identity may be articulated. International competition or conflict provides a good opportunity for 'British values' to be asserted in contrast to an enemy, real or imagined. The Second World War inspired countless stories celebrating the triumphant British spirit in the face of overwhelming odds, including many films like *Battle of Britain* and *The Dam Busters* still regularly recycled on television. Such transparent patriotism was invoked in 1982 by the popular press during the Falklands War (most notoriously with *The Sun*'s headline 'Gotcha!', in reference to the sinking of the Argentinian ship the *General Belgrano*), and also in 1991 during the Gulf War (Figures 4.2 and 4.3).

I've a theory. The older we get, the more we relive childhood.

Myself, I love to recall those old memories..

Walking back from church, with the smell of fresh baked bread to guide us home.

Father switching on ITMA on the wireless, mother fussing out her best teapot.

Toasting bread over the coals on a long fork - that was my job.

There was a real art to getting it evenly brown.

Old memories, stirred up by the taste of a country white loaf from Hovis.

A sturdy white slice that tastes like real bread used to.

Anyway, that's why I'm here with my old toasting fork crouched over a fire in a grate that hadn't been lit for years.

As good today as it's always been.

At the heart of the sense of being British is the idea of tradition, and this is most strongly personified by the monarchy. The Queen, as head of state, symbolises national unity as well as being a historical point of reference, reminding us of our 'great' history. Rising above day-to-day politics, she is often seen as epitomising what is good about Britain. Her ritualistic role is strongly supported by a largely deferential media. Within broadcasting she is exempt from the critical scrutiny normally applied to anyone with her power and status. The annual Christmas address to the nation, broadcast on all national television and radio channels, is supplemented by frequent documentary features which celebrate her role.

4.2 *Radio Times*, 29 May–4 June 1993. Photograph: Cecil Beaton, by permission of Camera Press

4.3 *Radio Times*, 29 May–4 June 1993

How does the Radio Times cover and feature represent the relationship between the royal family, history and the nation?

Contrast this treatment of the royal family with that of the *Daily Mirror* in Figure 4.4

The Prince and Princess of Wales lead the 50th anniversary tribute to the heroes of the Battle of the Atlantic

ATLANTIC TRIBUTE

The Prince and Princess of Wales make a rare public appearance together on Sunday at the Anglican Cathedral in Liverpool to commemorate the 50th anniversary of the Battle of the Atlantic.

Attended by more than 1,000 international veterans, the service (live coverage on Sunday's edition of *Morning Worship* 10.15am BBC1) is the culmination of a five-day series of events around Liverpool and the Mersey – site of the Second World War HQ of Western Approaches Command and the convoy system.

In *The Battle of the Atlantic – 50 Years On* (Spring Bank Holiday 4.25pm BBC1) Brian Redhead presents a round-up of the events, for which there's a full royal turn-out.

Included is a Fleet Review by the Duke of Edinburgh of 40 warships from 16 nations, a Gala Concert by massed army, navy and airforce bands at Goodison Park, to be attended by the Prince of Wales, and a visit to Liverpool by the Queen to meet Battle of the Atlantic veterans and to open the Maritime Museum.

May 1993 was chosen as a fitting date for the commemorations because it was 50 years ago, in May 1943, that Germany withdrew its U-boats from the Atlantic and lost the initiative in the struggle for good. But the battle itself began when the first ship was sunk 12 hours after the declaration of war in 1939 and it continued until 1944.

The documentary *For Those in Peril* (Sunday 11.10pm BBC1) talks to people who fought in the battle, in which 73,600 Royal Navy personnel, 30,000 merchant seamen and 29,000 servicemen in enemy submarines perished. Lord Callaghan and Jon Pertwee are among the veterans interviewed.

NICKI HOUSEHOLD

An alternative perspective is voiced by writers like Rosalind Brunt, who perceive the monarch to be a barrier to real democratic freedom and self-determination:

> In so far as ideologies are never simply ideas in people's heads but are indeed the myths we live by and which contribute to our sense of self and self-worth, then I think it actually matters that the British have no real identity as 'we the people' but continue to consign ourselves to a subordinated position as 'subjects' of the Queen. Not that we see it that way; the commonsense view is that the British are freer than their monarch; we can go anywhere we please without a police escort and 'I wouldn't have her job for the world!' In this way we happily consent to the monarch's continuing to act on our behalf. But the very popularity of present day monarchy is also how we, the British, tell ourselves that we're not quite ready for self-government yet.

Brunt (1992)

How can the Queen be seen as an ideological force? As she is the country's richest landowner and a member of a privileged élite, the Queen's status as unifying the nation is seen as mythic. The media, not least television, appears to have conspired in perpetuating this myth by acting as public relations agent on behalf of the royal family.

THE PLURALIST MODEL

4.4 *Daily Mirror*, 2 June 1993

Instead of seeing media content as narrowly ideological, pluralists argue that there is diversity and choice. Just as society comprises a range of interest groups and points of view, so does the media. If and when certain values and beliefs predominate in media output, then it is due to their being shared by most of society. This is because media production is essentially based on the need to please the audience. If audience needs are ignored then the likely outcome is commercial failure.

In the case of the monarchy, pluralists would argue that the media's endorsement of the Queen simply reflects genuine popular support. Furthermore, not all media coverage is necessarily sympathetic. The tabloid newspapers have been sharply critical of members of the royal family, exposing adultery and deceit within the royal marriages, as well as questioning the Queen's right to tax exemption (Figure 4.4). Even television has ridiculed the royal family in programmes like *Spitting Image* and *Pallas* (a spoof soap opera employing voiceovers dubbed on to news footage of the royals).

POLITICAL REPRESENTATIONS

It is when the media represent political issues that the hegemonic and pluralist perspectives can be clearly contrasted. The question of political bias has been the focus of much academic debate.

Propaganda

There is general consensus that some political content in the media qualifies as *propaganda*. In broad terms, the conscious manipulation of information in order to gain political advantage is propaganda. Historically, it has been most evident during times of war or national crisis, when the need for national unity has led governments to seek control over the media. In such situations, dissenting or alternative views are usually suppressed or marginalised.

Two fairly recent examples in Britain provoking much controversy were the Falklands War of 1982 and the Gulf War of 1991. In both cases there was strict external control (mainly by the Ministry of Defence) of how the wars were reported. Ostensibly, this was for reasons of military security. However, it could also be argued that the aim was to ensure public support was not undermined by information (especially pictures) revealing the less attractive aspects of the wars, such as military and civilian casualties. American support for the Vietnam War in the late 1960s had been eroded by the media's close

4.5 *The Guardian, 23 January 1991*

MAD DOGS AND ENGLISHMEN

We have	They have
Army, Navy and Air Force	A war machine
Reporting guidelines	Censorship
Press briefings	Propaganda

We	They
Take out	Destroy
Suppress	Destroy
Eliminate	Kill
Neutralise or decapitate	Kill
Decapitate	Kill
Dig in	Cower in their foxholes

We launch	They launch
First strikes	Sneak missile attacks
Pre-emptively	Without provocation

Our men are ...	Their men are ...
Boys	Troops
Lads	Hordes

Our boys are ...	Theirs are ...
Professional	Brainwashed
Lion-hearts	Paper tigers
Cautious	Cowardly
Confident	Desperate
Heroes	Cornered
Dare-devils	Cannon fodder
Young knights of the skies	Bastards of Baghdad
Loyal	Blindly obedient
Desert rats	Mad dogs
Resolute	Ruthless
Brave	Fanatical

Our boys are motivated by	Their boys are motivated by
An old fashioned sense of duty	Fear of Saddam

Our boys	Their boys
Fly into the jaws of hell	Cower in concrete bunkers

Our ships are ...	Iraq ships are ...
An armada	A navy

Israeli non-retaliation is	Iraqi non-retaliation is
An act of great statesmanship	Blundering/Cowardly

The Belgians are ...	The Belgians are also ...
Yellow	Two-faced

Our missiles are ...	Their missiles are ...
Like Luke Skywalker zapping Darth Vader	Ageing duds *(rhymes with Scuds)*

Our missiles cause ...	Their missiles cause ...
Collateral damage	Civilian casualties

We ...	They ...
Precision bomb	Fire wildly at anything in the skies

Our PoWs are ...	Their PoWs are ...
Gallant boys	Overgrown schoolchildren

George Bush is ...	Saddam Hussein is ...
At peace with himself	Demented
Resolute	Defiant
Statesmanlike	An evil tyrant
Assured	A crackpot monster

Our planes ...	Their planes ...
Suffer a high rate of attrition	Are shot out of the sky
Fail to return from missions	Are Zapped

• *All the expressions above have been used by the British press in the past week* scrutiny and questioning of American aims and methods, contributing towards its eventual withdrawal from Vietnam.

External censorship was reinforced by media self-censorship and propagandistic reporting. Tabloid newspapers like *The Sun* were vociferous in support for 'our lads' against 'the Argies' in the Falklands War and 'the evil dictator' (Saddam Hussein) in the Gulf War (Figure 4.5). The BBC even went to the extreme of banning certain records from being played on its radio stations during the Gulf War. The list included Abba's *Waterloo*, The Bangles' *Walk Like an Egyptian*, and Elton John's *Saturday Night's Alright for Fighting*! Nevertheless, it was still possible to find some media coverage which allowed space for alternative or oppositional views to be expressed. Channel Four broadcast *The Gulf Between Us* just prior to the Gulf War, presenting an Arab perspective on the conflict. In the build-up to the Falklands War, the BBC's current affairs programme, *Panorama*, contained criticism of the decision to send the task force. Consequently, the BBC was accused of treachery by both the government and newspapers promoting military action.

Other than during wartime, media propaganda is largely confined to either political advertising, such as party election

Contrast these front pages as examples of political propaganda.

4.6 Front covers of the *Daily Mirror* and *The Sun*, 9 April 1992. © Rex Features

broadcasts, or politically partisan newspapers and magazines seeking to persuade audiences to support a particular political party (Figure 4.6). However, there is no clear demarcation between propaganda and the ideological bias that could be said to characterise much political representation in the media. If a distinction can be made, it concerns the question of how conscious media professionals are of any bias in their coverage. While some newspaper journalists would admit to being selective in their political reporting (especially in the tabloid newspapers), many would claim to apply rigorous but fair standards of news journalism, especially in broadcasting.

Broadcasting and Political Bias

Television and radio are required by law to be politically impartial. Audiences support this perception, as reflected in surveys which show that a large majority of the population regard television as their most trusted source of information. Furthermore, when it comes to accusing broadcasters of political bias, the attacks have come from all positions in the political spectrum.

Consider the following extracts:

Contrary to the claims, conventions, and culture of television journalism, the news is not a neutral product. For television news is a cultural artefact; it is a sequence of socially manufactured messages, which carry many of the culturally dominant assumptions of our society. From the accents of the newscasters to the vocabulary of camera angles; from who gets on and what questions they are asked, via selection of stories to presentation of bulletins, the news is a highly mediated product.

Glasgow University Media Group (1976)

The proposition that emerges is this: that the main television news channels have done their best to present a fair, balanced and accurate account; that there were occasional mistakes, misjudgements and inadequacies; but that, in the face of real difficulties, they offered their audiences a generally reliable and dispassionate news service.

Hetherington (1985)

In our third report, which covered the period April to December 1988, *World in Action* featured one-sided programmes on a whole range of issues, including the Neighbourhood Watch scheme, the 'discovery' that 'unemployment can damage your health', the Rowntree takeover, the so-called 'safer' cigarette, the dangers of roll-on-roll-off ferries, reform of the Official Secrets Act, and environmental pollution. Each programme shared a common theme: an overwhelming desire to embarrass the present Conservative Government and/or 'capitalist' multi-nationals whose desire for profit allegedly ignores the interests and safety of their customers.

Media Monitoring Unit (1990)

The Glasgow Media Group have been the most consistent critics of what they see as the inbuilt bias in television news coverage. Beginning with *Bad News* in 1976, the research team have produced a series of case studies in which they have subjected television news to a form of content analysis (see Chapter 3). In each case, hundreds of hours of news broadcasts are recorded and analysed for the explanations of certain events they offer. The group have particularly focused on industrial relations, and their main conclusion is that strike coverage is biased against workers and trades unions and in favour of management and the government. This is because, first, journalists share certain 'consensual assumptions' about the world which are rarely questioned. In relation to industrial relations, these include: strikes are harmful and disruptive, whereas uninterrupted production is a 'good thing'; management exercises control as of right, whereas workers' industrial actions are often illegitimate; etc.

The second main explanation for biased reporting is that those in power have privileged access when it comes to setting the agenda for reporting news stories. In the case of the 1984–1985 miners' strike, this meant that the dominant framework for reporting strike developments centred on two issues: the 'return to work' of those giving up the strike, and the violence used by pickets in confrontations with both police and non-striking miners. Such an emphasis served to undermine the strikers' solidarity as well as public sympathy, according to the Glasgow Media Group, who largely attributed it to the skilful news management employed by the Coal Board and the government. Alternative frameworks for understanding the dynamics of the strike, such as the plan to close pits, and Coal Board and police provocation, were notable by their absence from the main news bulletins.

The findings of the Glasgow Media Group have been challenged, not least by the broadcasters themselves. Hetherington (1985), for example, did research into the coverage of the miners' strike that suggests both the BBC and ITN provided a fair account of events. Any inaccuracy, he feels, is due to the practical constraints under which journalists work, especially having to distinguish facts from opinion within a tight time schedule. Even the Glasgow Media Group acknowledges that current affairs programmes such as *World in Action,* or, in the case of the miners' strike, *Brass Tacks,* do supply the kinds of interpretation for controversial issues which may be absent in news bulletins.

Hetherington is not the only critic who has reached different conclusions to the Glasgow Media Group when studying the same event as covered on television. This could imply that content analysis as a method is not as scientific as it may appear. There are questions not only of how systematic or comprehensive the monitoring of television output is, but also of which criteria are applied to the recorded material. The many possible strategies for interrogating the recordings include investigating the following:

- Which sources are given priority (for example, who is interviewed and where)?
- Which explanations are given priority (such as headlines)?
- Does the story sequence produce certain meanings?
- What terms of reference (language) are used to describe or label the participants and their actions?
- What point of view is produced by the camera shots?

activity **4.1**

Record a television news broadcast and choose a news story which involves a degree of political controversy. Find a second treatment of the same story in either radio or the press and subject both to the criteria listed above (substituting photographic images or sound effects, if relevant, for television camera shots).

The dispute between those like the Glasgow Media Group, who assert that all news is constructed and by implication cannot be value free, and those like Hetherington, who claim that some news is neutral and detached, is tied to how the term *impartiality* is interpreted. As stated in law, it means broadcasters are not allowed to express a point of view on matters of public policy. This was reinforced by the 1990 Broadcasting Act, so that broadcasters can now be prosecuted if they do not preserve due impartiality on 'major matters' such as political and industrial controversies. In practice, this has come to mean that there should be balanced reporting.

This does not necessarily mean equal coverage for all points of view, but those which are thought to reflect existing public opinion.

Hetherington concludes that news broadcasters are mostly fair because he sees them as 'socio-centralist', or positioned

within the political and social middle ground,
by a majority of the population. However, wh
whether or which 'minority' points of view should
access to a debate? In the Gulf War, should President
views have been balanced with those of Saddam Huss
Should the government's views on the need for the poll tax
have been balanced by those advocating (illegal) non-payment
of the tax? Besides the issue of which views should be legitimately represented, there is the problem of adjudicating on
when broadcasts have been imbalanced in their coverage.
Academic differences of opinion point to some of the difficulties involved, and what is more, there is the question of how
audiences interpret such coverage.

Many of the issues raised in the debate about impartiality
are pertinent to the discussion of how the conflict in
Northern Ireland has been covered. One critic, Liz Curtis
(1984), feels that broadcasters operate a policy of 'hidden censorship'. While stories are not often overtly censored, there is
a system of 'checks and balances', which in effect means key
positions and points of view, largely Republican, are not represented. One procedure in the BBC is for all Northern
Ireland stories to be referred upwards for managerial approval.
Consequently, according to Curtis, between 1970 and 1983,
as many as forty-four programmes or items were 'banned,
censored or delayed', including a video, *Invisible Sun*, being
banned from *Top of the Pops*!

A prime source of information for stories in Northern
Ireland is the army, who are accepted by most of the news
media as pursuing a legitimate objective. The accepted
'enemy' is the 'terrorists'. This raises questions about how the
political motivations of those using violence can be explained
to audiences. Terrorism has connotations of being irrational,
criminal and lacking any legitimacy whatsoever. Attempts
made to investigate either the philosophy of members of terrorist organisations like the IRA (as in *Real Lives*, 1985) or
whether the security forces have acted illegally (as in *Death on
the Rock*, 1988) have met with strong official resistance. *Real
Lives* was temporarily banned by the BBC governors, and
only shown after re-editing; *Death on the Rock*, about the
killing of three IRA members in Gibraltar by British agents,
was subject to an enquiry (which subsequently cleared
Thames TV, the programme makers).

In 1988, control of broadcasters' coverage of Northern
Ireland was extended with a ban on interviews with members
of terrorist groups to prevent them being given what Margaret
Thatcher called 'the oxygen of publicity'. The interviews
could be shown if the subjects' voices were removed and

replaced by dubbing or subtitles. It appears the ban has had the desired effect: terrorist group members, especially the IRA, are rarely now interviewed or quoted. Opponents of the ban claim that this has meant denying a voice to those people whom the censored groups represent – often legitimately as in the case of Sinn Fein MPs, elected by their constituencies. A further concern is that such a ban could in future be extended to other 'illegitimate' groups whom the government dislikes, whatever the opinions of the broadcasters.

STEREOTYPES

A stereotype is a label which involves a process of categorisation and evaluation. Although it may refer to situations or places, it is most often used in conjunction with representations of social groups. In its simplest terms, an easily grasped characteristic (usually negative) is presumed to belong to a whole group, e.g. estate agents are insincere, devious and smooth talking (Figure 4.7).

4.7 © John Brown Publishing Ltd./House of Viz

Viz, edition 35

Terrace trendies

A new breed of soccer hooligan — dressed in £800 suits and drinking bubbly at fifty quid a bottle — is replacing the traditional soccer thug.

And you won't catch them wearing scarves, hats or Doctor Marten boots. Instead the new yuppie yobs sport dapper suits by Giorgio Armani. Lager is out too. The new generation of louts quaff Dom Perignon champagne by the crate full. No expense is spared. Unlike their predecessors the terrace trouble makers of today hold down highly paid jobs in the City.

FLICK KNIVES

Flick knives are replaced by filofaxes. The new breed of thug is highly organised. And tattoos are frowned upon. A diamond encrusted Cartier wristwatch is more in keeping with the new image.

Football thugs who dress to kill

MACHETE

With their £250 hand stitched Jermyn Street silk shirts, you won't catch these thugs 'putting the boot in'. They wouldn't want to risk chaffing their made-to-order Italian pig skin brogues, at £300 a pair.

SAMURAI SWORD

And it isn't their style to look for trouble. Indeed with their £500 leather Gucci ties, they

don't go to football matches at all. Instead they go out, in their solid gold Dunhill cufflinks and Chinchilla socks at £900 a pair, and eat nouvelle cuisine in fasionable restaurants, or just stay at home in their £2 million converted dockland warehouses, relaxing and listening to their £3000 top-of-the-range Nakamichi CD players, with quadraphonic sound.

In ideological terms, stereotyping is a means by which support is provided for one group's differential (often discriminatory) treatment of another. If black Africans could be represented as uncivilised and savage in the nineteenth century, then slavery and exploitation of blacks by their white rulers could be justified. In contemporary society, old people are frequently portrayed as physically and mentally infirm, asexual and unable to adapt to social change. Such 'ageist' sentiments contribute to a lowering of the social status of the aged, including a lowering of their own self-esteem.

However, stereotyping is not a simple process. Tessa Perkins (1979) has identified many shortcomings in the way that stereotyping is normally assumed to operate.

- Stereotypes are not always negative (e.g. 'The French are good cooks').
- They are not always about minority groups or the less powerful (e.g. 'upper-class twits').
- They can be held about one's own group.
- They are not rigid or unchanging (e.g. the 'cloth-cap worker' of the 1950s became the 1980s 'consumerist home-owner who holidays in Spain').
- They are not always false, but can be supported by empirical evidence (e.g. 'Media studies teachers tend to be liberal/left-wing in their politics').

activity **4.2**

Compile a list of ten stereotypes from media material, identifying examples which might be considered to be stereotypical representations. Examine where each of the stereotypes fits the points made by Perkins.

Indeed, Perkins argues that stereotypes would not work culturally if they were so simple and erroneous.

Martin Barker (1989) goes further, to the extent of dismissing the concept of the stereotype as a 'useless tool for investigating media texts'. His first objection is that stereotypes are condemned for both misrepresenting the 'real world', e.g. for reinforcing the (false) stereotype that women are available for sex at any time, and for being too close to the 'real world', e.g. for showing women mainly in the home and servicing men – which many in fact do. This latter example bears out Perkins' point that for stereotypes to work they need audience recognition, i.e. to appear 'natural' and everyday. The ideological process, though, reinforces that 'naturalness' by failing to reveal any contradictions or inequalities in the representation, e.g. that women may feel trapped, undervalued and lacking economic independence in their domestic role. Barker's second main objection is that the concept of stereotyping implies that it is wrong to see people in categories. Yet within social psychology, it has long been recognised that categorisation is a fundamental cognitive process necessary to make sense of the world. Humans constantly impose structure on events, experiences and people, particularly when faced with only limited information. Thus stereotypical judgements are made by everyone as part of creating order out of everyday life, as well as providing a sense of group identity.

Media representation may serve to inform, reinforce or challenge such stereotypes. This is partly for reasons of pure economy. Constraints of time and space, plus the desire to achieve rapid audience recognition, mean that stereotypical representations are constructed rather than fully fledged characters with individual identities. This is articulated effectively by Trevor Griffiths in the play *Comedians*, which is about a night school for budding comedians led by an experienced comedian, Eddie Waters, who rails against the easy laugh achieved at the expense of minority groups.

> WATERS (Driving home) If I've told you once I've told you a thousand times. We work through laughter, not for it. If all you're about is raising a laugh, OK, get on with it, good luck to you, but don't waste my time. There's plenty others as'll tek your money and do the necessary. Not Eddie Waters.
>
> MCBRAIN (conciliatory, apologetic): So, a few crappy jokes, Mr Waters . . .
>
> WATERS: It's not the jokes. It's not the jokes. It's what lies behind 'em. It's the attitude. A real comedian – that's a daring man. He dares to see what his listeners shy away from, fear to express. And what he sees is a sort of truth, about people, about their situation, about what hurts or terrifies them, about what's hard, above all, about what they want. A joke releases the tension, says the unsayable, any joke pretty well. But a true joke, a comedian's joke, has to do more than release tension, it has to liberate the will and the desire, it has to change the situation. (Pause). There's very little won't take a joke. But when a joke bases itself upon a distortion – (At PRICE, deliberately) – a 'stereotype' perhaps – and gives the lie to the truth so as to win a laugh and stay in favour, we've moved away from a comic art and into the world of 'entertainment' and slick success. (Pause). You're better than that, damn you. And even if you're not, you should bloody well want to be.

Griffiths (1976)

The Dumb Blonde

Some of the complexities of utilising stereotyped labels in analysis of media representations can be seen through a consideration of one example: the dumb blonde. A list of the main ingredients for a dumb blonde stereotype might include: blondeness, seductive body language, strong make-up, innocence or naivety, childlike voice, humour and wit, illogical thinking etc.

The first problem is that not all of these ingredients are consistent: childlike *and* seductive; witty *and* simple and empty headed. In terms of whether the label is descriptive or evaluative, much depends on social perceptions of what kind of female image and behaviour is desirable. To be blonde is often defined as more attractive ('blondes have more fun'), while to be 'dumb' may be seen as both (sexually) appealing (to many men) and undesirable – being considered of low intelligence.

Dumb Blonde Characteristics
Childlike

High or breathy voice, rounded face, wide eyes; deliberate, self-conscious or awkward movements; naive responses, lack of concentration, an emphasis on 'fun' and 'play'; irresponsibility and emotional indulgence.

Inappropriate

Behaviour or appearance showing 'inability' to grasp (or refusal to obey?) rules of conventional (particularly middle-class) social contact. Includes over-dressing, unrestrained voice (volume/pitch) or especially 'excessive' laughter.

Unconventional

Unusual forms of logic, exaggerated gestures, unexpected responses; characteristics, behaviour and desires which do not concur with feminine roles; emphasizing a unique individuality.

G. Swanson (Chapter 6 – Representations) in D. Lusted ed.
The Media Studies Book, *Routledge 1991*

What kinds of judgement may be made about women possessing the above characteristics, individually or in combination?

An examination of specific examples of dumb blonde types quickly reveals variations, which reflect both changes in the way the dumb blonde has been perceived over time and personal qualities brought to the role by individual performers. Marilyn Monroe is often considered to epitomise the dumb blonde, yet her own performances in the 1950s (both off and on screen) clearly accentuated sexuality and seduction (e.g. in the film *The Seven Year Itch*). In contrast, Goldie Hawn's film and television performances in the 1970s emphasised the giggly or kooky facets of her personality. In the 1990s, the dumb blonde is as likely to be the source of parody (e.g. within adverts) as to be represented seriously (although Marilyn in *Home and Away*, the Australian television soap opera, could be said to maintain the essence of the type).

GENDER AND IDEOLOGY

Before considering media representations of gender, it is necessary to establish what is meant by the term. To be male or female can be defined biologically, but masculinity and femininity are socially constructed. This can be demonstrated by both cultural and historical comparison: ideas about what it means to be masculine or feminine vary between societies and change over time, even though there may be some aspects of gender difference which are found virtually universally, e.g. the mother–child bond, and hence are closely linked to biology.

Ideas about gender difference are produced and reflected within language. Both objects and abstract concepts can be seen as gendered. While this applies systematically in other languages like French, in English it is quite selective. Modes of transport are given feminine labels – car, ships, steam engines etc. – as if to signify something possessed and controlled by men. Likewise, countries, nations and nature itself are ascribed a female status as representing caring, home and a sense of belonging. In contrast, ultimate power rests with a masculine God, and the word 'man' has been used to represent all humans, as in 'mankind', 'man in the street' or 'man-made'.

Feminism is a label that refers to a broad range of views containing one shared assumption – that there are profound gender inequalities in society, and that historically masculine power (patriarchy) has been exercised at the expense of women's interests and rights. This power may be expressed physically, but is more generally reproduced ideologically. Language is seen to be a form of social control in so far as the terms 'masculine' and 'feminine' carry very strong connotations of what is 'natural' for each sex, whether that refers to personal traits (like rationality or emotionalism) or to social roles (like businessman or housewife).

Appearance

One of the strongest cultural values concerning gender difference is that women are judged by their looks more than men. In the world of popular culture this is especially noticeable. When comparing the social attributes of male and female

Hollywood film stars between 1932 and 1984, Emanuel Levy (1990) concluded that physical looks and youth were far more important for the female stars (the list of stars being based on box-office appeal). For men, attractive looks were a weak basis for longevity of appeal – indeed, many of the most successful men were anything but handsome, e.g. Humphrey Bogart, Jerry Lewis and Dustin Hoffman.

Associated with appearance was age. The median age for female stars was 27, compared to 36 for men; and many men only achieve stardom after 40, e.g. John Wayne (at 42) and Charles Bronson (at 52). Given the ephemeral nature of youthful attractiveness, it is not surprising that few women stars have been able to sustain their box-office appeal over many years. Those that have lasted longer have tended to possess 'something else' beyond glamour and beauty, e.g. Barbra Streisand's singing plus the ability to play career women.

America's most durable film stars (over four years on the poll)

Men				*Women*	
John Wayne	25	James Cagney	6	Betty Grable	10
Gary Cooper	18	Mickey Rooney	6	Doris Day	10
Clint Eastwood	18	William Holden	6	Barbra Streisand	10
Clark Gable	16	Frank Sinatra	6	Elizabeth Taylor	9
Bing Crosby	14	Sylvester Stallone	6	Shirley Temple	6
Bob Hope	13	Wallace Beery	5	Joan Crawford	5
Paul Newman	13	Marlon Brando	5	Greer Garson	5
Jerry Lewis	12	Lee Marvin	5	Jane Fonda	5
Burt Reynolds	12	Woody Allen	5	Bette Davis	4
Cary Grant	12	Harrison Ford	5	Sandra Dee	4
Spencer Tracy	10	Will Rogers	4	Julie Andrews	4
James Stewart	10	Randolph Scott	4		
Steve McQueen	9	Richard Burton	4		
Dean Martin	8	Sean Connery	4		
Abbott and Costello	8	Charles Bronson	4		
Humphrey Bogart	8	Al Pacino	4		
Rock Hudson	8	John Travolta	4		
Jack Lemmon	8				
Elvis Presley	7				
Dustin Hoffman	7				
Robert Redford	7				

Levy (1990)

activity **4.3** Select two male and female stars from the above list, and, with the help of background research, try and identify what individual qualities may have contributed to their box-office appeal. You will need to consider the kind of image and appeal produced by a combination of personal characteristics, on-screen performances and general publicity.

What is clearly apparent from this research is the sheer inequality in number of male and female stars, a pattern that shows no sign of changing, and that also applies to other areas of the media like television, where it has been estimated that men outnumber women by two to one within programmes as a whole.

TELEVISION ADVERTISING AND SEX ROLE STEREOTYPING

1 **Overview**

Men outnumbered women by a ratio of nearly 2:1. The vast majority of adverts had a male voice-over (89%).

2 **Physical attributes**

Overall, one half of women were judged to be between 21 and 30 years old, compared with less than one-third (30%) of males. Among those judged over 30 years old, men outnumbered women by a ratio of 3:1 (men 75%, women 25%).

In terms of body type, most people were characterised as 'ordinary'. The slim, model or 'ideal' category was applied to only one in ten (11%) men compared with more than one in three (35%) women.

One-third (34%) of women were blonde compared with only one in ten (11%) males.

Being 'attractive' (defined as the kind of person who might appear in a clothes magazine) fitted the description for nearly two-thirds (64%) of females but under one-quarter (22%) of males. One in five (21%) females were judged 'beautiful' (for example, the Cadbury's Flake model) compared with only 4% of males.

The conclusion is that women occupy a decorative role far more commonly than men. In the few examples of women characters predominating, they were almost all for 'personal maintenance' products.

3 **Activities and roles**

Occupation, when given or implied, revealed that men were almost twice as likely as women to be represented in some kind of paid employment (30% of men, 16% of women).

In only 7% of cases was housework shown as the dominant activity for women. However, women were more than twice as likely to engage in household labour as were men (45% of women, 21% of men). Cooking was performed by a greater proportion of men (32%) than women (24%), but when men cook, it is portrayed as a special and skilled activity.

4 Relationships

In terms of marital status, most men could not be coded. Although women were more likely than men to be single (19% female, 11% male), they were much more likely to be married (27% female, 18% male). This would explain why their social integration was twice as likely to be with a partner (female 24%, male 10%) as with members of the same sex (11% females, 26% males). Same-sex adverts were most common in adverts for alcohol.

Women were twice as likely both to attract (25% females, 13% males) and to show they were attracted (26% females, 12% males). Moreover, while only 9% of men received some sort of sexual advance, nearly twice as many women (17%) did so. In categorising the gain achieved by characters from the product being advertised, implied sexual success was almost twice as common for women (18%) as for men (10%).

Conclusion

The patterns that emerge lend strong support to the concern that women exist in what is essentially a man's world.

Adapted from Cumberbatch et al. *(1990)*

---

activity **4.4**

Conduct a similar content analysis by recording thirty television adverts from different times of the day and coding the content according to the criteria employed in Cumberbatch et al.'s research. Compare your findings to those of Cumberbatch et al.

What do you think are the shortcomings of using this method to analyse gender representations in television adverts?

Looking at Women

The objectification of women's bodies in the media has been a consistent theme in analyses of women's representation. Laura Mulvey (1975) argues that the dominant point of view within cinema is masculine, especially where a woman is concerned. The female body is displayed for the male gaze in order to provide erotic pleasure (voyeurism), and ultimately a sense of control over her. She is rendered a passive object. This tendency is carried to the extreme in pornography, where erotic pleasure from looking is the sole motivation for the production. This issue has spilled over into newspapers in recent years with the growth of the 'pin-up', most notably in *The Sun* on page three. Some feminists feel that these images reinforce a 'fantasy of willingness: the page three girl is waiting "to kiss the next man she sees"' (Joan Smith, 1990).

There is little doubt that sexual behaviour has considerable news value, especially stories involving sexual crime like rape. A survey by Channel Four's *Hard News* research team in the first six months of 1990 found more than 600 articles in the ten major national daily newspapers, an average of more than four a day. (*The Sun* topped the league, followed by *The Daily Telegraph*.) What concerned the researchers was the way in which rape tended to be misrepresented. Rape victims were stereotyped as either 'good' women who had been violated or 'bad' women who had led men on. Rapists were overwhelmingly portrayed as strangers in the guise of a 'sex fiend' or 'beast', despite the fact that in two out of three rapes the rapist is known intimately by the victim. Regarding the crime itself, many newspaper reports dwelt on the details provided by the victim of the attack under courtroom cross-examination to the exclusion of other details, such as forensic or medical evidence.

The difficulties of dealing effectively with rape in the context of fictional 'entertainment' are very well illustrated by the controversy surrounding *The Accused* (a film based on a real court case) in which the actual rape itself is left to the climax of the film. Some concern was expressed that the prelude to the rape and some of the camera shots included in the attack might offer some members of the male audience voyeuristic pleasure, even though the film was praised for its overall treatment of the case. (For a discussion of women's responses to *The Accused* see Schlesinger *et al.*, 1992.)

activity **4.5**

1 From a popular tabloid paper, analyse how women are represented in terms of:
   a the number of stories featuring women as the main subject;
   b the approximate proportion of the overall editorial content (excluding adverts).
2 Identify the main categories of story within which women appear in order of frequency, e.g. borrowed status, sportswomen etc.
3 Are there any distinctive differences in the photographic images of female and male subjects?
4 Choose one story featuring a female subject and one story featuring a male subject, and examine whether there are any differences in the language used and details provided for each story.

Physical attacks on women have also been the subject of numerous films, often containing a combination of voyeurism, female fear and extreme violence. Notable examples include *Psycho*, *Dressed to Kill* and *Peeping Tom*. In the last example, the voyeurism of the male killer is itself subject to scrutiny, and he is eventually challenged by a woman who refuses to be intimidated. Indeed, it is not clear that masculine control over women is always a product of the camera's gaze at women. Women playing lead roles in film noir in the 1940s often projected power and mystery as well as sexuality, and in the role of 'femme fatale' were able to exercise control over men. In a pop video by Madonna for her song '*Open Your Heart*', she performs in a 'peep show' for a variety of male voyeurs, but the gaze is reversed so that the men are seen through Madonna's eyes – as pathetic and frustrated. Madonna is an example of a growing self-consciousness among female performers who are able to exercise greater control over their look and image.

Looking at Men

Conventional approaches to looking at male subjects within the media tend to be limited to acceptable contexts in which traditional masculinity is not threatened. Television sports coverage provides numerous moments of close-ups of male bodies, but this is not given any sexual legitimacy by the camerawork or commentary, despite the fact that there is evidence that female viewers may gain pleasure from such images. Dorothy Hobson (1985) suggests that the strong appeal of television snooker for women is that the players exude a masculinity stripped of unattractive aggression and competitiveness.

Until recently, it was only in gay culture that an open display and objectification of the male body for sexual pleasure was able to flourish. This has become less true in recent years, particularly as more women assert their own sexual desires and men have become more sensitive to how they look. This is most noticeable in women's magazines targeting young single women, such as *Cosmopolitan* and *Company*, which have been challenged by new titles like *Bite* and *For Women* focusing almost exclusively on sexuality (Figure 4.8).

Pop music has had many male singers willing to submit themselves to the female gaze, whether in girls' magazines or more recently, in pop videos. Some have consciously feminised their appearance so as to create considerable ambiguity

How equivalent is this coverage of male sexual appeal to tabloid newspapers' representation of females as objects of sexual appeal?

4.8 *The Sun*, 10 January 1991. © Rex Features

4.9 Kouros, Yves Saint Laurent

To what extent do these images challenge traditional ideas of masculinity?

4.10 Photograph: Gianpaolo Barbieri

about their sexual identity, e.g. David Bowie, Boy George and Michael Jackson. Growing consciousness of the masculine body has also been reflected in advertising, whether it be for aftershave or clothes, and in the rise of men's magazines such as *GQ* and *Arena*. The question that arises is to what extent these images are for the male and/or female gaze (Figures 4.9 and 4.10). Audience identification and pleasure are discussed in the next chapter.

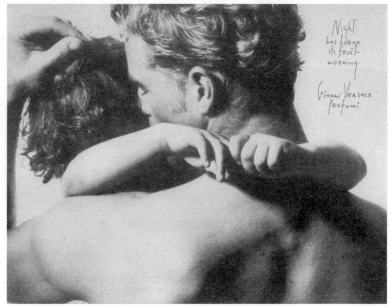

Gender Roles

In so far as the classical narrative structure in cinema involves a drive towards resolving a problem or disruption posed early on in a story, it could be said that it is the male hero who usually makes things happen and moves the narrative along. More often than not, the female serves either as the reward for the hero's action or as the target of that action, e.g. 'the damsel in distress'. This masculine form of narrative is not confined to cinema, but has been a dominant feature of most areas of popular culture. Meanwhile, women's 'action' is more likely to be confined to the domestic domain, revolving around the search for a man or the care of the family. The contrast is very evident in adolescent magazines - compare the focus on learning to succeed with boys in *Mizz* and *Just Seventeen* with that on learning to succeed against the enemy in *2000 AD* and *Gamesmaster* (Figures 4.11 and 4.12).

I have argued that women's magazines collectively comprise a social institution which serves to foster and maintain a

4.11 *Just Seventeen*, 14 July 1993

4.12 *Games Master*, August 1993

cult of femininity. This cult is manifested both as a social group to which all those born female can belong, and as a set of practices and beliefs: rites and rituals, sacrifices and ceremonies, whose periodic performance re-affirms a common femininity. These journals are not merely reflecting the female role in society; they are also supplying one source of definitions of, and socialisation into, that role.

Ferguson (1983)

Women's magazines could be seen as providing step-by-step instructions into how to achieve womanhood, with two roles being central to that status: 'wife' and 'mother'. Marjorie Ferguson (1983), surveying changes in women's magazines in post-war Britain, identifies two main changes. First, there has been a shift from 'getting and keeping your man' to 'self-help'. This involves 'achieving perfection' (being a better mother, lover, worker, cook and staying slim) and 'overcoming misfortune' (such as physical or emotional crises). Second, the role of paid worker or 'independent woman' has emerged from the mid-1970s in magazines like *Cosmopolitan*. Despite these changes, Ferguson feels the basic message has still prevailed – that women should identify with a femininity which 'focuses on Him, Home and Looking Good'. She only considers one mainstream women's magazine as challenging this orthodoxy, *MS*, an American production recently made available in Britain. (See also Ferguson's data, Tables 3.3 and 3.4.)

Not everyone accepts Ferguson's emphasis on the narrow agenda constructed by women's magazines. Janice Winship (1987) stresses the supporting role the magazines play, which is important given women's exclusion from the masculine world of work and leisure, and the lack of similar editorial content (in any depth) in other areas of the media. Even in teenage magazines, readers are being supplied with a broader range of options than before. For example, *Just Seventeen*, the market leader at the beginning of the 1990s, tackles problems such as domestic violence and sexual abuse, as well as offering advice on how to pursue an independent lifestyle. Judging from the significant number of male readers of women's magazines, there seems to be a latent demand for information and advice on how to succeed in personal relationships and other subjects which are not given space anywhere else in the media.

Strong, independent women are not just a recent phenomenon in the media. In the 1930s, actresses like Bette Davis and Katherine Hepburn specialised in playing tough women who fought to gain acceptance in male-dominated worlds. What is new is the emergence of female lead characters in masculine-dominated genres, such as science fiction and police detective stories. *The Terminator*, *Alien* and *The Abyss* are three examples of action-adventure films with a woman as the 'hero', yet surrounded by males in supporting roles (Figure 4.13). In television, the last decade has seen numerous examples of women starring as detectives. *Cagney and Lacey* provided an alternative to the male 'buddy' police action series of the 1970s, such as *Starsky and Hutch*, and in Britain, Helen Mirren played a strong female detective succeeding in spite of male chauvinism in *Prime Suspect*. Moreover, for the last thirty years, there has been a series of independent and assertive female characters in television soap opera. *Coronation Street* has had a succession of such characters, from Elsie Tanner to Bet Lynch. In contrast, strong and sympathetic male characters are notable by their absence in British soaps. Rather the opposite is the case, with most men being exposed for their weaknesses, whether they be emotional instability, vanity or just plain incompetence.

The man within the domestic sphere (or 'woman's world') has been an increasing issue of late, fatherhood being one prominent theme. *Kramer vs Kramer* in 1979 made the case for men being capable of taking responsibility for children. In this case, the man (Dustin Hoffman) was successful in breaking away from the traditional masculine role, and indeed there is now an increasing range of roles and identities for men represented in the media. The Gillette advertising campaign of the

4.13 Linda Hamilton in *Terminator 2*

late 1980s/early 1990s displayed a full spectrum of masculine images: father, lover, companion, sportsman, businessman etc.

Meanwhile, for women it is less clear that seeking independence is the 'right' path. Women seen as turning their back on the family have long been represented as unfulfilled or even punished in Hollywood cinema. Examples of this in recent popular films include *Fatal Attraction* (a neurotically obsessed single woman eventually suffers death), *The Hand that Rocks the Cradle* (a career woman nearly loses her husband and children to the nanny) and *A Stranger Among Us* (a female detective realises motherhood is superior to having a career). Another trend has been the re-emergence of the 'femme fatale', a seductive but dangerous woman, who manipulates men for her own ends. The detective writer played by Sharon Stone in the 1992 thriller, *Basic Instinct*, is just such a character, with the added twist that she is bisexual with psychopathic tendencies!

Basic Instinct also highlights the homophobic tendency to render homosexual characters as a 'problem' or 'maladjusted'. Lesbians, in the few cases where they appear on the screen, are inclined to be represented as neurotic or childlike, while gay men are invariably seen as camp or butch. There are notable exceptions, e.g. *Desert Hearts* and *Another Country* in the cinema, and increasingly both television and radio have been prepared to include gay and lesbian characters in leading roles as well as providing space for specialist programmes focusing on gay and lesbian issues and lifestyle, e.g. *Out* on Channel Four.

In conclusion, it has to be said that much of the above discussion has dwelt on the more dominant patterns of gender representation in the media. These are only patterns, and the more closely media texts are analysed, the more evident the variety of gender representation becomes, particularly once it is recognised that many texts are capable of more than one audience reading. Outside the mainstream, production also flourishes at the margins, which may challenge the dominant ideologies, whether this production be feminist magazines like *Everywoman* or independent films like *I've Heard the Mermaids Singing*.

RACE AND IDEOLOGY

Racial difference is based on biologically determined human variations which have long ceased to exist in the world. Colonisation and interracial mixing mean that there are no simple racially distinctive groups left. However, perceived physical and culture difference is the basis for social definitions of racial or, more specifically, ethnic difference (an ethnic group having a shared culture usually linked to national and religious identity). The belief that other racial/ethnic groups are inferior is at the root of racism/ethnocentrism, and such ideologies can usually be traced back to imperialism and colonialism as a means of justifying the colonial conquest and exploitation of other social groups.

Most western societies today are multicultural, largely as a result of immigration from ex-colonies linked to the demand for cheap labour. How far this multiculturalism is adequately reflected in the media is questionable. Since many of the ethnic minorities in countries like Britain and the USA are not white, the extent to which racism is prevalent in media representations needs to be examined.

Race and Entertainment

Having dark skin has long been thought to signify difference not just of colour but also of 'nature' from a white perspective. The idea that black people are more physically expressive than whites is deep-rooted in western culture. Blacks have been able to achieve most visibility in the media via music and sport, both of which reinforce the notion of 'natural rhythm'. The fact that their disproportionate achievements in such areas may be a product of poverty and the lack of alternative avenues to gain success is rarely considered. In such roles, black people remain unthreatening and only reinforce existing stereotypes of their rhythmic nature. Indeed, early performances by blacks in Hollywood cinema consciously played up to white prejudices – e.g. the eyeball-rolling servant and 'mammy' stereotypes in films like *Gone With The Wind*.

Within both pop and jazz music, much of the creative drive and inspiration has been provided by Afro-American musical culture. Yet most black musicians have been marginalised. More often than not, white versions of black music have predominated, frequently watering down the emotive and sexual power of the music in the process. For example, rock and roll, the new 'youth rebellion' music of the 1950s, was simply black rhythm and blues sung by white performers like Bill Haley and Elvis Presley. This was seen by many American whites as an unwelcome infiltration of their culture by the back door, as they tried (unsuccessfully) to suppress the 'nigger music'.

It is not only in pre-war Hollywood that patronising and demeaning images of blacks were produced. The tradition of 'blacking up' by white singers such as Al Jolson in *The Jazz Singer* was sustained on British television up to 1976 with *The*

Black and White Minstrel Show. Likewise, the 'simple' and 'quaint' delivery of English by ethnic minorities has been a constant source or ridicule, as in *It Ain't Half Hot Mum* (Indians living under colonial rule), *Fawlty Towers* (Manuel, the half-witted Spanish waiter) and *Mind Your Language* (a foreign student class containing several crude stereotypes). All of these are 1970s British television sitcoms, frequently repeated since.

Much racism in comedy is unconscious, and is rarely perceived as racism by the white audience – 'It's only a laugh.' Indeed, the pleasures of comedy are complex and the reasons for laughing not easily explained by either audiences or comedians. One function served would seem to be the sense of collective identity produced by laughing at 'others' – those who are perceived as different and possibly a threat. Too often, when blacks appear alongside whites in comedies, racial issues become a main focus for the humour, e.g. *Rising Damp* and *In Sickness and In Health*, rather than these being comic characters who just happen to be black and white. Furthermore, the audience may well end up laughing *with* rather than *at* the racial bigotry expressed by characters such as Alf Garnett.

Race and Social Problems

Portraying black people as problems

The main way in which black people are treated in newspapers is as a social problem. Black people are portrayed as constituting a threat to white British society, first through their immigration to this country and then, when settled here, as posing a law and order problem. This is done in a number of ways: through dramatic presentation of stories involving banner headlines and prominent positioning, provocative or damning quotations and statements from people portrayed as authoritative figures, popular stereotypes, repetition of unreliable stories, and the creation and manipulation of popular fears.

Gordon and Rosenberg (1989)

Given that 'bad news is good news' when it comes to choosing stories in the press and broadcasting, it is not surprising that incidents involving violence and crime and ethnic minorities are given prominence. What matters is the explanatory framework offered to enable the audience to understand such stories.

All journalists in the media are bound by a professional code of conduct which forbids racist reporting, and most would claim they simply report the facts without prejudice. However, unconscious or inferential racism may be detected in the language used to tell a story: 'Riots' imply rampaging mobs who need to be controlled; 'uprisings' imply rebellion against injustice. The desire for simple stories with single causes and themes of 'good' and 'bad' often means that long-term causes and morally ambiguous actions may be overlooked or not understood by the journalists themselves (Figure 4.14).

4.14 © Rex Features

The Los Angeles riots of 1992 were widely seen as a rerun of previous examples in inner city black 'ghettoes' (except this time the initial outcry was based on the broadcast of an amateur home video showing white police beating a defenceless black man). What was not revealed was the fact that blacks were now a minority in the inner city of Los Angeles (Hispanics and Latinos were by far the majority), and much of the violence and looting was directed against Korean immigrants who owned most of the stores in the 'ghetto'. Meanwhile, the amateur video images of the police beating have become an icon for racial inequality in the USA and elsewhere, being incorporated into Spike Lee's 1993 film of *Malcolm X*. The broadcast of the video on television helped to transform the incident itself into a criminal trial, whose verdict led to the riots. Another example of television images providing a strong public response can be found in the dramatic television news pictures of famine in Ethiopia during 1984, which stimulated the subsequent 'media event' Live Aid the following summer (Figure 4.15).

What are the problems in using images of starving children to highlight famine in Africa and other parts of the world?

What alternative images might be used to represent problems of poverty and exploitation in Third World countries?

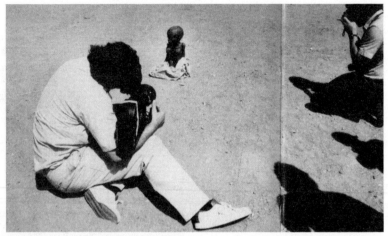

4.15 British media at work in a relief camp at Haiya in the Red Sea Hills, Eastern Sudan, December 1984. People in the camp put the child on the ground for display, aware that publicity for their plight might eventually bring some help. Photo: Wendy Wallace

Third World Images

Black and white inequalities within western societies are reproduced on a global scale when the inequalities between the affluent minority of modern industrialised countries like the USA and the poor majority of the Third World are examined. As with the reporting of racial problems within western countries, the causes of problems like famine are grossly simplified for audience consumption, the one difference being that sympathy and pity are offered. Yet the emphasis on aid as a solution only serves to reinforce the sense that Third World countries (especially in Africa) are largely helpless, and depend for their survival on 'our' help; it also obscures the colonial exploitation and subsequent economic dependency which have played a significant role in the failure of Third World economies to become self-sufficient (Figure 4.17).

An alternative to the image of poverty or war is that of the 'exotic' and 'colourful'. Television holiday programmes are inclined to dwell on these qualities when featuring long-distance tourist packages, complete with a backdrop of the locals' friendly smiling faces and atmospheric native music. An exception to this is BBC2's *Rough Guide* series, which attempted to provide a social and political context within which tourist attractions could be experienced. The 'Singapore Girl' of the airline advert is a reassuring and (sexually) seductive image promising the western male 'service with a smile', effectively effacing the widespread hardship and sometimes sexual exploitation faced by many young women in South East Asian countries like Thailand and the Philippines.

Changing Representations: the American Cinema

As society changes, so do the media. The shifts in how black people in the USA have been represented in Hollywood films reflects wider social changes in American society. In their own way, the films themselves will have contributed to the changing perceptions of black and white identities in the USA.

The pre-war period was characterised by the use of black characters as light relief – as song-and-dance acts or eye-rolling simpletons. These patronising images drew heavily from white perceptions of black life in the southern plantations. In the post-war period, a growing number of films reflected the growing consciousness of racial injustice, particularly the segregation policies of the south. In *The Defiant Ones* (1958), a black and a white escaped convict are symbolically chained together and forced into co-operating in their bid to stay free. The film starred Sidney Poitier, who later appeared in numerous films in which he challenged, and usually overcame, white prejudices, e.g. *In the Heat of the Night* (1967) as a black detective working with a white police force in the southern states of the USA.

It was not until the 1970s that films began to feature predominantly black casts and thus move closer to capturing black American culture. However, the emphasis was on large doses of violence and sex, in a bid to be commercial. The cycle which began with *Shaft* (1971) came to be known as 'blaxploitation' films. While containing some ethnic authenticity (e.g. the argot), and often reflecting a sense of black pride, the films also could be said to reinforce white perceptions of the black man as aggressive gangster or drug dealer.

A few black actors became 'stars' in the 1980s, e.g. Eddie Murphy and Richard Pryor. Nevertheless, most of their roles could be seen as 'safe' for white audiences in the sense that they could be said to be 'deracinated'. This means that they tended to play isolated black characters whose black culture is used only as an entertaining decoration, e.g. Eddie Murphy's street-talking, wisecracking detective in *Beverly Hills Cop*, *Beverly Hills Cop II*, *24 Hours* etc.

At the start of the 1990s there was a surge in American films made by and starring blacks. This was precipitated by the commercial success of *Do the Right Thing* and *House Party* in 1989 (both made over $26 million profit), and the growth in young (mostly male) black film makers eager to represent the

High tea in Sri Lanka

Amid relics of the colonial past, MATTHEW GWYTHER is reminded of Sri Lanka's strife-torn present

What do Tigger Stack Ramsay-Brown MC, Bo Derek, Yuri Gagarin, Noël Coward and Emperor Hirohito of Japan have in common? Answer: they have all stayed at the Galle Face Hotel in Colombo, lucky people.

Sitting with a sundowner on the 128-year-old veranda bar, surrounded by colonnades of white-washed columns and acres of marble floor, watched over by attentive staff in spotless white sarongs and pressed linen tunics with gold epaulettes as the sun descends into the Indian Ocean – what better way to come to one's senses after being canned up for the 5,500 mile long haul from London?

Sri Lanka has a growing supply of modern beach hotels, particularly down the coast to the south of Colombo, but it is the older establishments dating from colonial times, such as the Galle Face, that offer something truly out of the ordinary. If you would rather have a fan and a mosquito net than an air-conditioner, birds flying around the lobby rather than piped music, mild eccentricity rather than smooth, five-star efficiency, then the Galle Face is your kind of place.

In fact the Galle Face does have air-conditioners, but they are of the old fashioned free-standing variety rather than the noisy through-the-window type. The chairman of the Galle Face, Cyril Gardiner, ensures that nothing disturbs the GFH's unique combination of 'Yesterday's charm and Tomorrow's Comfort'. The King Emperor Suite has a living room in which, once you had put the antique furniture to one side, a five-a-side football match could be conducted. The suite is thought to be one of the largest in the world but can be yours for the absurdly low price of £100 per night. (The rate is actually £200 but all the GFH's rooms are currently at a long-term 50 per cent discount.)

Dotted all over the GFH are maxims and polite entreaties on plaques: 'Please don't smoke in bed because the ashes we find may be yours' and next to the lift, 'Please walk down. It's good for you. Two flights only.' The Thoughts of Chairman Cyril are even carried over to the hotel's headed notepaper, which proclaims, 'Share wealth, grow food, conserve water, keep fit, don't gamble.' The effect is to envelop guests in a kindly paternalism which is highly seductive. The maître d' wears an oversized pair of Chaplinesque shoes without socks as he bounces over the teak floor-boards to take your order – Scotch broth or brown Windsor soup to kick off. The GFH is one of the few establishments left in the world where you will find a menu section headed 'Farinaceous Dishes'. ▷

Main photograph: lotus carriers personify Sri Lanka's lush beauty. Right: ancient sites abound, such as Polonnaruwa's rock temple. Centre: K.C. Kuttan began working at the Galle Face Hotel (far right) in 1942

62

How does this travel feature represent Sri Lanka to the potential western tourist?

many facets of black culture largely ignored by white-dominated Hollywood. Some of the films contained a political agenda and ethnic assertiveness derived from hip-hop and rap-music culture. However, the freedom for such film makers as Spike Lee to pursue these themes is contingent, as always, on continued success at the box office.

Growth in Visibility on Television

In both American and British television, there has been a steady growth in the number and range of ethnic representations on the screen, e.g. news readers (Trevor McDonald), chat-show hosts (Oprah Winfrey) and police series (*Hill Street Blues*). One development has been the emergence of the ethnic minority sitcom. In the 1970s, early examples were *The Jeffersons* (USA) and *The Fosters* (UK). Beginning in 1984, *The Cosby Show* has been the most successful, but not without some controversy. In many respects, it represents a recoding of some of the traditional black stereotypes shared by white Americans. The family is a strong and cohesive unit with the perfect father figure. Both parents are successful professional workers (doctor and lawyer) who, although affluent, are not frivolous in their consumption. There is a strong emphasis on the value of education (particularly in the spin-off series *A Different World*, set in a black college). From time to time, the theme of racial pride is foregrounded with references to black history and culture, and yet the family is clearly well integrated into a multiracial America.

Critics of *The Cosby Show* argue that it fails to address questions of racial or class conflict, and that its representation of black culture and lifestyle is very superficial and idealised. The series is seen as reassuring white American audiences that the American Dream is alive and well, and that black people can be successful through hard work and discipline. (See pp. 177–8 for audience responses.) On British television, ethnic minority representations in soap opera has been a contentious issue. *Coronation Street*, Britain's most successful soap opera, has failed to feature a black character in a prominent role throughout its history (beginning in 1960), despite being set in an area which would in reality be multicultural. In contrast, *EastEnders* has included a range of ethnic minorities (Bengali, Turkish, West Indian etc.) and tackled the issue of racism, albeit as a transient 'story'. Christine Geraghty (1991) proposes that there have been three strategies adopted by soaps in handling black characters. First, there is 'the exotic' – the one-off character who is used to add drama to a story, but whose blackness does not become an issue itself. For 'the singleton', Geraghty's second category, being black means being used as a vehicle for stories about racial issues, which tends to produce a separate and marginalised status for the characters. Finally, there is 'incorporation', where blacks share similar problems to those of other members of the community, and clearly belong to that community as insiders. This allows the characters to be much more varied in their representation, and to be active in developing the narrative.

Ethnic Minority Media Production

With the mainstream media failing to represent ethnic minorities adequately, such groups have found their interests more effectively served by independent media production.

The growth of incremental and community radio stations has included ethnically based services such as Sunrise Radio (for Asians in west London) and WNK (for the Afro-Caribbean community in North London). Sunrise can also be received on satellite television, as well as being responsible for the weekly newspaper, *Asian Leader*. Newspapers for Britain's black population include *The Voice* and *The Weekly Journal* (Figure 4.17). Independent black media production in the USA has been gaining strength, particularly in response to a growing black middle class. An early success story was the Tamla Motown record label headed by Berry Gordy, which provided strong support for artists such as Stevie Wonder and Diana Ross. More recently, labels like Def Jam have helped rap and hip-hop acts to flourish. This is in stark contrast to the British music industry, where record companies (almost exclusively controlled by whites) have been accused of failing to develop black talent (with the possible exception of Island Records, for whom Bob Marley recorded).

Independent television producers catering for ethnic minority audiences in Britain do have two channels (BBC2 and Channel Four) that are committed to creating space in their schedules for such groups. Consequently, there has been a variety of programmes targeting Afro-Caribbean and Asian audiences, including an Asian soap, *Family Pride*, a sitcom, *Desmond's*, a black music magazine, *Behind the Beat*, and a number of current affairs series like *The Bandung File*.

FURTHER READING

Baehr, H. and Dyer, G. (Eds) 1987: *Boxed In: Women and Television*. Pandora.

Daniels, T. and Gerson, J. 1990: *The Colour Black*. BFI.

Dyer, G. 1982: *Advertising as Communication*. Methuen.

Geraghty, C. 1991: *Women and Soap Opera*. Polity Press.

Glasgow University Media Group. 1985: *War and Peace News*. Open University Press.

Goodwin, A. and Whannel, G. (Eds) 1990: *Understanding Television*. Routledge.

Pines, J. (Ed) 1992: *Black and White in Colour*. BFI.

Stead, P. 1989: *Film and the Working Class*. Routledge.

Strinati, D and Wagg, S. (Eds) 1992: *Come on Down: Popular Media Culture in Post War Britain*. Routledge.

Tasker, Y. 1993: *Spectacular Bodies: Gender, Genre and the Action Cinema*. Routledge.

Winship, J. 1987: *Inside Women's Magazines*. Pandora.

5

Audiences

In Chapter 1, it was emphasised that the media play a prominent part in the everyday lives of the population. Given the time spent by audiences consuming the media, it is hardly surprising that much speculation and debate has focused on the exact nature of the relationship between audiences and media output. In reviewing the progress of this debate, it is possible to identify distinct phases of audience analysis. What makes these phases distinct is the degree to which the balance of power and influence is attributed to the media, in terms of production and content, or to the audience, as receiver of that production.

5.1 © Steve Bell

PHASE 1: FROM MASS MANIPULATION TO USES AND GRATIFICATION

Mass Manipulation Model

Concern about media 'effects' on audiences, especially harmful influences, has been expressed almost continuously since the turn of the century. The idea that the media are a powerful social and political force gathered momentum in the 1920s and 1930s, when the political propaganda of first Soviet Russia and then Nazi Germany seemed capable of seducing and persuading ordinary citizens in ways not thought possible prior to an age of mass media.

Audiences came to be seen as comprising a mass of isolated individuals vulnerable to the influence of the powerful new media such as cinema and radio – hence the label *mass manipulation*. Propaganda of a different sort, advertising, was later perceived in the same way by writers such as Vance Packard. His best-selling book, *The Hidden Persuaders* (1957), claimed to expose some of the ways advertisers were manipulating ordinary people to consume goods without being conscious of the persuasive techniques in question.

Children and teenagers have consistently been considered susceptible to the harmful influence of popular entertainment. From time to time, moral panics have been generated, often orchestrated via the media, especially tabloid newspapers. Each medium in turn has been accused of corrupting young people, whether it be Hollywood crime films in the 1920s, pop music in the 1950s or 'video nasties' in the 1980s. The heightened social concern and anxiety associated with moral panics often stimulates more stringent controls of the media to protect 'the innocent' from any damage. In the case of video nasties, the 1983 Video Recordings Act was passed. This introduced strict regulation of videos via the British Board of Film Classification. However, concern over young people's access to violent videos rose again in the early 1990s. A number of highly publicised crimes of aggression in which a violent film was implicated (most notably the linking of the James Bulger murder with a video, *Child's Play 3*) resulted in further restrictions being enacted in 1994. The British Board of Film Classification now has to take into account the psychological impact of videos on children, and the possibility they will present inappropriate role models.

Television has been particularly singled out by many critics as being responsible for antisocial and psychologically injurious outcomes. Marie Winn's *The Plug-in Drug* (1977) is typical in its claim that children watch television in a 'trance', their eyes having a 'glazed vacuous look'. Using the drug analogy, with its notions of addiction and passivity, is a familiar ploy, most recently employed in the context of video games. Consequently the mass manipulation model is sometimes referred to as the *hypodermic needle* effect.

Effects Research

The last sixty years have seen a mountain of academic research investigating the potential links between media content and audience thinking and behaviour. As early as the 1930s, the Payne studies in the USA assessed the effects of cinema on audiences, and concluded that films did in fact cause harm to children by disrupting sleep, encouraging delinquency and crime through imitation etc. (Peterson and Thurstone, 1933).

One media production alone, Orson Welles' *War of the Worlds* broadcast on radio in 1938, seemed to demonstrate the power of the media. As many as one million Americans believed their country was being invaded by Martians, as a result of the play being produced in the form of a spoof 'live' news report with eye witnesses, sound effects etc. Such trust in radio 'news' caused considerable panic and hysteria. Although contemporary audiences might be considered more sophisticated and sceptical, spoof productions continue to fool large numbers of people, a recent example being *Ghostwatch*, broadcast during Halloween night on BBC in 1992 (Figure 5.2). To pursue the issue of media effects, two areas of considerable debate will be discussed: children and political persuasion.

Most of the research claiming proof of direct effects, especially on young audiences, is rooted in behaviourist psychology or social learning theory. The assumption is that children learn through conditioning. 'Good' behaviour is rewarded, and this is reinforced by seeing positive adult role models. Supporting evidence cited frequently centres on experiments in which children are exposed to a media stimulus and their response is then measured. An example is Bandura and Walters' 'Bobo Doll' experiment of 1963, in which children were shown films of adults acting aggressively towards the doll, behaviour later imitated by the children when left alone with the dolls. Such experiments have been criticised for failing to reflect normal viewing conditions under which the media are con-sumed. Children do not usually encounter such a strictly con-trolled media diet, and the aggression shown may well result from a desire to please the experimenter. Furthermore, chil-dren can distinguish between real and simulated violence both in media content and in their own play.

Other psychologists, drawing on developmental psychology, have instead emphasised how the media, particularly televi-sion, affects cognitive development. While this is a complex and multifaceted subject, much of the work stresses the active

Halloween spoof riles BBC viewers

THE BBC yesterday refused to disclose how many calls had been received from angry viewers after a spoof Halloween-night TV documentary proved too realistic.

But a spokesman conceded there had been a "substantial reaction", with many people convinced the gory scenes in Saturday night's Screen One special, Ghosts, were real.

Most callers simply rang to ask if the 90-minute show — starring Michael Parkinson, Sarah Greene and Mike Smith, all playing themselves — was a genuine documentary.

But BBC staff said many others were angry at realistic scenes including an interview with a young girl apparently possessed by spirits and with blood dripping down her face.

"People thought it was real," said one.

"We've had anything from being sworn at to people who say they are going to write to the director-general."

Last night the BBC insisted the programme had been clearly billed as a drama in the Radio Times and other listings magazines, and in an on-air announcement before the start.

In the show, Michael Parkinson played the anchorman of a Watchdog-style current affairs programme and Mike Smith hosted a spoof phone-in on ghostly manifestations. Meanwhile, a mock outside broadcast team investigated "Britain's most haunted house" — a council house in Northolt, west London — where the fictional Early family had complained of paranormal experiences.

These included objects flying around rooms, dark figures and mysterious puddles — all owing a great deal to the BBC's special effects department.

5.2 *The Guardian*, 2 November 1992.
© The Guardian

learning which accompanies media consumption. Marie Messenger Davies' book, *Television is Good for Kids* (1989), describes many positive learning outcomes which have been identified in various academic studies. These include: the development of television literary skills, such as understanding visual narrative, editing conventions etc.; improved memory of events due to visual aids, which also stimulate imagination; being able to differentiate different degrees of realism (so-called 'modality judgements') across narrative forms; the acquisition of knowledge, understanding and practical skills; and not least the play value, usually involving social games in which favourite television programmes are 'remade' or re-enacted.

These claims need to be qualified on the grounds that a psychological framework of research, whether it be behaviourist or developmental, often lacks an adequate social context. Children's response to the media will vary according to social group membership such as family, class and gender. Television viewing needs to be seen as only one form of social learning alongside the immediate cultural environment, including other forms of media. Little empirical work has been undertaken on the ideological 'effects' of media representation, such as gender or ethnic stereotypes, on children.

One of the most influential studies of media effects on audiences was *The People's Choice* in 1944, which highlighted political persuasion. Lazarsfeld, Berelson and Gaudet set out to discover what influence the media exerted over voters during the American presidential campaign. Using a panel sample over a period of six months, they concluded that voting intentions were very resistant to media influence. This was due to a combination of individual cognitive and wider social processes.

A majority of the sample already had well-formed political attitudes, and this predisposition was reinforced through selective exposure, whereby newspapers were read which were likely to support existing views. Even when confronted with politically challenging ideas, these could be resisted via selective perception – filtering the message to fit existing attitudes, or interpersonal discussion. Opinion leaders – people whose political views were trusted – were a much more significant influence than the media, whose information the sample could mediate via a process the authors called the *two-step flow*. The overall conclusion was that the media's 'effect' on the audience was one of reinforcement rather than change.

Although subsequent research in Britain supported these findings, the potential for media influence on political behaviour seems to have increased in recent years as the strength of voters' loyalty to one party has declined. At the same time the British tabloid newspapers have become more politically partisan (especially in support of the Conservatives). W. Miller's research (1992) into the last two British elections identifies a disproportionate swing towards the Conservatives during the campaign among readers of the Conservative tabloids (see *The Sun*'s front cover on p. 121, and Table 5.1).

Nevertheless, it seems clear that as an agent of direct social and political influence, the media's power is quite modest. Persuading consumers which brand of jeans or breakfast cereal

Table 5.1 Newspaper readership and voting intentions, UK 1992
(percentages)

	Con	Lab	Lib		Con	Lab	Lib
The Daily Telegraph	71	13	15	*The Sun*	39	48	10
Daily Mail	66	17	15	*The Independent*	31	40	26
Daily Express	66	19	13	*The Star*	23	64	9
The Times	61	18	17	*Daily Mirror*	19	59	10
Financial Times	50	27	18	*The Guardian*	12	59	22
Today	48	35	14				

Source: The Sunday Times, 2 February 1992

What does this table reveal about the power of newspapers over their readers' political judgement? (Remember these findings were published two months before the 1992 general election)

SKIN CARE BY HEROIN.

At first you think you can control heroin.
But before long you'll start looking ill, losing weight and feeling like death.
Then one day you'll wake up knowing that, instead of you controlling heroin, it now controls you.
So, if a friend offers you heroin, you know what to say.

HEROIN SCREWS YOU UP

5.3 Central Office of Information

This 1987 anti-heroin poster failed because the boy proved too appealing to some girls, who wrote in for the poster.

to buy is a plausible objective, but advertising which attempts to alter more deep-rooted and complex forms of behaviour, such as drug taking or sexual relationships, has been found to have minimal impact (Figure 5.3).

In summary, instead of the media being seen as an all-powerful force working on the audience, there emerged the view that:

● audiences are active in interpreting media content;
● audiences comprise individuals whose membership of social groups should not be ignored.

Therefore, the concept of 'effect' has come to be seen as problematic within media studies because:

● it implies some degree of audience passivity;
● there can be confusion between short-term effects, such as during elections, and long-term *ideological* effects of a much more subtle but profound nature, e.g. on gender identities;
● it is virtually impossible to measure media effects – the media cannot be isolated from all the other potential influences at work within society.

Consequently, there was a shift in perspective within audience research, represented by James Halloran's (1970) much-repeated phrase: 'We must get away from the habit of thinking in terms of what the media do to people and substitute for it the idea of what people do with the media.'

The basic tenet underlying this approach to studying audiences is that individuals actively consume the media in order to meet certain needs. Blumler and Katz (1974) listed four broad needs fulfilled by viewers' watching of television, following group discussions they undertook in which subjects' statements were listed and categorised:

1 *Diversion* – a form of escape or emotional release from everyday pressures.
2 *Personal relationships* – companionship via television personalities and characters, and sociability through discussion about television with other people.
3 *Personal identity* – the ability to compare one's life with the characters and situations within programmes, and hence explore personal problems and perspectives.
4 *Surveillance* – a supply of information about 'what's going on' in the world.

---

activity 5.1

Undertake a uses and gratifications survey by:

1 taping informal conversations about specific programmes or genres with a sample of television viewers;
2 listing the most common motives mentioned for viewing such programmes;
3 clustering together similar statements under a collective heading (e.g. for quiz shows: excitement appeal, basis for social interaction etc.);
4 presenting the list of headings to a further sample as a self-report survey allowing for a graduated response to each heading (e.g. from 'very much' to 'not at all' or 1 to 5).

The notion of the media providing needs and pleasures continues to inform much contemporary audience research. Blumler and Katz's concept of 'diversion' or 'escape' was developed by Richard Dyer (1977) in relation to cinema and television entertainment. In trying to answer the question of how 'escapism' works, he offers three suggestions of how real life is suspended or temporarily erased. First, it may be obliterated in so far as the content completely ignores reality, as within dance, music, magic, slapstick comedy etc. Secondly, it may work via contrast. Here, the reality provides a pleasing positive alternative for the audience, e.g. within soap operas like *Coronation Street* which supplies a sense of close community. Finally, Dyer identifies incorporation, where reality is shown to be better than imagined, thus creating a sense of optimism. An example of this might be the television telethon promoting a sense of a caring and altruistic society. (For a further discussion of Dyer's scheme see p. 174.)

Nevertheless, 'uses and gratifications' as an analytical model for understanding audiences does have its limitations. At its crudest, it implies audiences comprise individuals whose conscious search for gratification elicits a media response which supplies their needs. This laissez-faire market concept overlooks the extent to which audience needs are partly a product of media supply (learning to enjoy what is available), and the social context from which the audience originates, e.g. class and ethnic subcultures.

Another criticism is that of the tendency to concentrate solely on *why* audiences consume the media rather than extending the investigation to discover what meanings and interpretations are produced and in what circumstances, i.e. *how* the media are received. These issues form the focus of reception theory, discussed below.

PHASE 2: TEXTUAL DETERMINATION TO AUDIENCE RECEPTION

Audience Positioning

During the 1970s, a new theoretical framework emerged which could be applied to analysing the relationship between media content and audiences. Drawing heavily on semiology and structuralism, media texts were seen as structured according to well-defined codes and conventions (see Chapter 3 for a fuller discussion). Rather than recognising the polysemic nature of such texts, some writers chose to emphasise how audiences (or subjects) were positioned by the text.

Much of this theory was applied to film, and in Britain was articulated most strongly in the academic journal *Screen*. The main thrust of the argument is that the structure of film language produces a perspective or point of view for the audience. The spectator is drawn into the flow of the narrative through various strategies of camera work. One example is the shot/reverse shot, where the perspectives of two characters are interchanged so we as an audience are able to 'stand in' for each subject and identify with their view. Another example is the glance/object shot. Here we are shown a close-up of a character as he or she looks off screen. A second shot reveals what the character can see and thus simultaneously situates us in his or her position. Through the editing of camera shots and perspectives the spectator is able to gain a privileged view of events, and yet unconsciously has been 'sewn in' to the narration, a process referred to as *suture*. It is as if we are invisible onlookers, an effect most films never deny, in order to produce a sense of witnessing objective reality.

As noted on p. 134, it has been argued by writers such as Laura Mulvey that the spectator perspective achieved by dominant Hollywood cinema is masculine. The camera shots and editing conventionally reproduce a male gaze or subject position, with the woman as object. Given strong characterisation in association with this process of spectator suture, the sharing of the character's experiences and emotions will lead to effective audience identification. This works powerfully when identification and attraction are combined in a sexual or romantic context.

Mode of Address

This refers to how a media text 'speaks to' its audience. It thus helps to establish a relationship between media producer and audience. It implies a less determinate outcome than audience positioning and identification. To quote Martin Barker (1989), ' "Identification" suggests that we are spoken for. "Dialogue" suggests we are spoken to.'

To look first at cinema: spectators are rarely acknowledged within Hollywood films. The dominant mode of address is impersonal. There is little sense of an author or identifiable source beyond the film credits. That does not mean there are no points of view supplied; indeed, some films contain a first-person voice-over to guide us through the story. Nevertheless, there is normally a sense of reality being pre-existent, 'out there', waiting to unfold before us.

A kind of variety of address may be achieved through differing narrative viewpoints. It is possible for the audience to know more than the characters, the dominant perspective of popular cinema. Sometimes audiences know only as much as one or more of the characters, e.g. in many detective films, and finally, some films deny audiences as much knowledge as the characters.

Occasionally, the impersonal mode of address is broken when characters look into the camera to speak to the audience, thereby undermining the illusion of transparent 'reality'. This is most common in comedy, where the audience is invited to share a character's feelings towards events. An early example is that of Laurel and Hardy, where Hardy's looks of exasperation with Laurel are frequently directed to the camera. Recent examples from Hollywood include *Kuffs* and *Ferris Bueller's Day Off*.

Robert Allen (1987) has characterised television viewing as centrifugal, in contrast to cinema, where watching a film is centripetal. By this he means that whereas the cinema screen draws in the audience to witness another world, television's programmes are directed outwards to viewers:

> In those instances in which contestants are selected from the studio audience, they are plucked from among 'us'.
>
> By splitting off one or more characterized viewers from the rest of the studio audience, the game show sets up a circuit of viewer involvement. When Bob Barker asks the contestant to guess how much the travel trailer costs, we almost automatically slip into the role of contestant, guessing along with him or her. If we guess correctly along with the contestant, the bells and whistles go off for us as well as for him or her. But we can also distance ourselves from the contestants and take up the position of the studio audience as they encourage the contestants and, on *The Price Is Right*, at least, shout out what they believe to be the correct guess. As we watch a game show, we constantly shift from one viewer position to another, collapsing the distance between contestants and ourselves as we answer along with them, falling back into the role of studio audience as we assess contestant prowess and luck (or lack thereof), assuming a position superior to both when we know more than they. The viewer-positioning strategy of the game show encourages us to mimic the responses of the characterized viewer in the text.
>
> *Allen (1987)*

Two factors help to explain this situation. First, television texts tend to refuse resolution – the news, soap opera, sitcoms etc. are continuous, daily or weekly. In conjunction with this, viewing is intermittent or casual, and thus television needs to 'work' to attract our attention.

Apart from obvious strategies like strong music, studio applause and laughter etc., one prominent feature is the use of direct address. The viewer is openly acknowledged. Allen considers this to be a rhetorical mode of address in that television is 'pretending' to speak on behalf of the viewer. Presenters, reporters, comedians etc. look directly into the camera as if in a face-to-face conversation, yet of course it is only one-way communication. Hence the use of phrases like 'we', 'you the viewer', 'what the viewer at home wants to know'.

It is usually assumed the audience comprises members of a family situated within the living room as part of a wider community or nation of viewers. This is underlined by the family viewing policy which regulates against explicit language or controversial 'adult' material being represented before nine o'clock in the evening. The sense of a national audience tends to be inscribed within representations of certain annual rituals, such as the Queen's Christmas address to the nation or sporting occasions like the FA Cup Final. Moreover, in international competitions, like the World Cup or Olympic Games, British commentators and presenters shift from a detached and neutral form of address to a more partisan and emotional delivery when describing British participants.

As television audiences become more fragmentary it seems likely that different types of viewer will be more specifically addressed. Already, there is clear variance in the modes of address contained in breakfast television, late-afternoon children's television and late-night weekend programmes. Furthermore, differing channels may adopt distinctive styles of delivery in accordance with both their perceived audience and the organisation's sense of its own identity, e.g. Channel Four. This latter point is particularly pertinent when considering radio.

When the BBC maintained a monopolistic situation as Britain's only national radio service, it adopted a mode of address which was designed to reflect its public service ideals – to be authoritative and set high standards. This meant speaking a form of English which used correct standard grammar, had no regional accent and was delivered in a formal tone – what came to be called 'BBC English' or, (more technically accurate) *received pronunciation*. Only gradually in the post-war period did this verbal style decline and leave space for more varied forms of address, e.g. on Radio 1.

With the shift away from national to local and regional radio services, and the conscious targeting of distinctive audiences, there is a greater need for radio's mode of address to fit its perceived audience identity. The use of accent and vernacular language, the tone and pace of delivery and the structuring of a dialogue with the audience (e.g. via the phone-in programme) are all differing ways by which the listener is addressed. One telling clue to a station's sense of identity and consequent mode of address is its choice of signature jingle, which is repetitively broadcast between programmes or segments within programmes. These jingles are often given as much thought and attention as the rest of the station's schedule.

activity 5.2

Compare the mode of address adopted in the following:

1 the different breakfast television services offered on BBC, ITV and Channel Four;
2 the different news programmes broadcast on BBC Radios 1–5 and your local ILR station(s);
3 quiz/game shows on radio and television.

The front page or cover of newspapers and magazines is the key to creating both a sense of identity and a point of contact with the potential reader:

> On any magazine stand each women's magazine attempts to differentiate itself from others also vying for attention. Each does so by a variety of means: the title and its print type, size and texture of paper, design and lay-out of image and sell-lines (the term the magazine trade aptly uses for the cover captions), and the style of model image – but without paying much attention to *how* a regular reader will quickly be able to pick out her favourite from others nestling competitively by it. Cover images and sell-lines, however, also reveal a wealth of knowledge about the cultural place of women's magazines. The woman's face which is their hallmark is usually white, usually young, usually smoothly attractive and immaculately groomed, and usually smiling or seductive. The various magazines inflect the image to convey their respective styles – domestic or girl-about-town, cheeky or staid, upmarket or downmarket – by subtle changes of hairstyle, neckline and facial pose. . . .
>
> There is one other important and defining characteristic of this cover image: the woman's gaze. It intimately holds the attention of 'you', the reader and viewer... The gaze is not simply a *sexual* look between woman and man, it is the steady, self-contained, calm look of unruffled temper. She is the woman who can manage her emotions and her life. She is the woman whom 'you' as reader can trust as friend; she looks as one woman to another speaking about what women share: the intimate knowledge of being a woman. Thus the focus on the face and the eyes – aspects which most obviously characterise the person, the woman – suggests that inside the magazine is a world of personal life, of emotions and relationships, clearly involving men and heterosexuality, but a world largely shunned by men. This is all women's territory.
>
> *Winship (1987)*

activity **5.3**

With reference to Janice Winship's analysis of how women's magazine covers vie for readers' attention, compare the mode of address employed by three different women's magazine covers.

You might also compare the masculine versus feminine mode of address of the teenage magazines featured on p. 138, as well as contrasting adult male magazines such as *Arena* and *GQ* with their female equivalents, e.g. *Cosmopolitan* and *She*.

Broadsheet newspapers can be distinguished from tabloids in Britain by their more impersonal, formal and detached mode of address. The tone is subdued and measured, in contrast to that of the emotive 'loudness' of papers like *The Sun* and the *Daily Mirror*. Even here there are important differences. As described by Peter Chippendale and Chris Horrie (1990), *The Sun* under Rupert Murdoch cultivated a sense of the 'cheeky cockney' who, while happy to stick two fingers up at the establishment, was keen to show it was speaking on behalf of its readers. It continues to hail its readers whenever possible through encouraging participatory action or gestures, including various xenophobic stances towards foreign 'enemies' like Argentina or the EC.

As with radio, the more specialised the target audience, the more distinctive will be the mode of address. Some magazines, like those representing computer interests, will incorporate a style and argot which exclude access to those without the necessary knowledge and expertise.

Encoding–Decoding

Parallel to the work of those privileging the ways in which media texts position audiences was the contribution made by members of the Centre for Contemporary Cultural Studies in Birmingham under the leadership of Stuart Hall. His own encoding–decoding model, discussed below, was very influential in examining the relationship between text and audience (Figure 5.4).

To some extent, the encoding process tends to contain a sense of textual power at work. Using a hegemonic theoretical framework, Hall argues that media texts such as television programmes contain dominant ideological discourses. This is due to the fact that media producers' own professional routines and practice contain certain assumptions and ideas about how programmes should be made (the 'relations of production'). They draw agendas and meanings – 'definitions of the situation' – from the wider society, which are ideological in

5.4 S. Hall (ed.), 1980: *Culture, Media, Languages*, Hutchinson

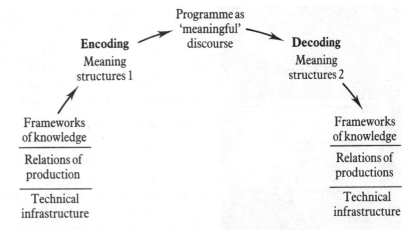

nature (the 'framework of knowledge'). Finally, television's own codes and conventions are employed to complete the encoding process, whose effect is to *naturalise* or make transparent the meaning of the programme for the audience (to deny its own ideological construction).

However, because the communication is achieved in a coded form – i.e. it is polysemic – there is no guarantee the audience's decoding will 'fit' or be consistent with the encoded meaning. Despite this possibility, polysemy does not equate with there being a plurality of possible interpretations. Instead, Hall argues that texts are structured in such a way that they contain a dominant or *preferred meaning* which limits the scope for different audience interpretations. The more closed the text, the more obvious is the preferred meaning. Thus an advert whose images are heavily anchored by rhetorical language will be 'read' with considerable consistency by audiences, whereas the relative openness of a television soap opera may make the preferred meaning more problematic.

The concept of preferred meaning has been subject to some criticism. The main objections raised are as follows:

- Preferred meanings are more applicable when analysing factually based texts like news reports or television documentaries. Fictional narrative is more likely to contain competing perspectives and values.
- It is not clear whether preferred meanings are a property of the text (they are there whether we see them or not), something identified by 'expert' analysis, or that which is agreed by most members of the audience. Ultimately, who decides what is the preferred meaning?
- Are hegemonic values so dominant that professional practice within the media cannot undermine and challenge such ideologies through producing a 'progressive' or radi͡c text?

5.5 Jill Posener, *Spray it Loud*, Pandora

Jill Posener's book features the work of graffiti artists who specialise in producing political messages, especially on advertising billboards.

Despite these problems in acknowledging that the audience plays a key role in producing the meaning of media texts, Hall's encoding–decoding model is a significant shift away from the overdetermined subject as represented in some of the theory found in *Screen* magazine, discussed above. Hall's model identifies three types of audience decoding:

1 A *dominant hegemonic position* is established when the audience takes the full preferred meaning offered by the text.
2 A *negotiated position* is established when there is a mixture of adaptation and opposition to the dominant codes.
3 An *oppositional position* is established when the preferred reading is understood but reconstructed drawing on alternative values and attitudes (Figure 5.5).

It is possible to include a fourth audience response – that of aberrant decoding, where the text is read in a deviant and largely unanticipated manner, the preferred reading not being recognised.

Hall's encoding–decoding model is essentially a theoretical construction, but it helped in redirecting attention as to how audiences interpret media texts.

Doing Audience Research

How can information about audiences be discovered? Much depends on the *type* of information required. There is a constant production of audience data gathered by market research organisations primarily for commercial purposes. This data is essentially quantitative in nature.

Tables like those reproduced on p. 11 reveal the broad patterns of media consumption. National totals for television programmes watched (the ratings), newspaper circulation figures etc. help to inform those working in the various media industries about the relative success of their products in a competitive market situation. Although these figures are quite crude in nature, they are still an important barometer of cultural consumption. The fact that one in four people in Britain read *The Sun* each day means it merits much more attention as a media text than, say, *The Times* with an average circulation of about 350,000.

One of the key motivations in the media industry to research audiences is to supply data to potential advertisers who are looking to reach their target audiences in the most effective way. Therefore there is an increasing trend towards monitoring the social profiles of media audiences. Such demographic data reveal how audiences are composed in terms of variables like social class, age and gender. Again, this is valuable as a preliminary point of reference for audience research which seeks to investigate how and why social groups respond differently to the media (Tables 5.2–5.5).

Table 5.2 Top Ten Quiz Shows – Adults

	Programme (day)	Channel	Production company	Audience share (%)	Audience (millions)
			Week Ending 21 June		
1	Through The Keyhole (Fri)	ITV	Yorkshire	56	9.23
2	Every Second Counts (Thurs)	BBC1	BBC Light Ent	42	7.69
3	That's Showbusiness (Sat)	BBC1	BBC North	44	5.43
4	Joker in The Pack (Fri)	BBC1	Action Time	29	5.17
5	Have I Got News for You? (Fri)	BBC2	Hat Trick	16	3.02
5	Fifteen–To–One (Tues)	C4	Regent Television	43	3.02
7	Fifteen–To–One (Weds)	C4	Regent Television	42	2.59
8	Crosswits (Weds)	ITV	Tyne Tees	77	2.55
8	Crosswits (Fri)	ITV	Tyne Tees	78	2.55
10	Fifteen-to-One (Fri)	C4	Regent Television	34	2.51

Table 5.3 Quiz Shows* – Gender

Programme	Day/Time	Men	Women
	Week Ending 21 June		(millions)
Through The Keyhole	Fri (7pm)	3.32	5.91
Every Second Counts	Thurs (8pm)	2.56	5.13
That's Showbusiness	Sat (6.35pm)	2.49	2.95
Joker in The Pack	Fri (8.30pm)	2.13	3.05
Have I Got News For You?	Fri (10pm)	1.53	1.48
Fifteen–To–One	Wed (4.30pm)	1.31	1.71
Crosswits	Mon (9.26am)	0.72	1.84
The Crystal Maze	Thurs (8.30pm)	0.78	1.41
The Music Game	Fri (8.30pm)	0.61	0.94
Treasure Hunt	Tues (6pm)	0.46	0.54

Table 5.4 Quiz Shows* – Age Groups

Programme	18-24	25-34	35-44	45-54	55-64	65+yrs
	Week Ending 21 June					
			Audience (millions)			
Through The Keyhole	0.78	1.22	1.24	1.18	1.39	3.42
Every Second Counts	0.87	1.27	1.15	1.05	1.13	2.22
That's Showbusiness	0.69	0.94	0.96	0.68	0.80	1.36
Joker in The Pack	0.57	1.06	0.94	0.65	0.66	1.30
Have I Got News For You?	0.32	0.57	0.73	0.44	0.42	0.53
Fifteen–To–One	0.15	0.18	0.19	0.32	0.56	1.62
Crosswits	0.20	0.35	0.36	0.37	0.36	0.92
The Crystal Maze	0.37	0.45	0.51	0.24	0.26	0.36
The Music Game	0.30	0.35	0.21	0.16	0.15	0.38
Treasure Hunt	0.16	0.20	0.19	0.12	0.08	0.25

*Where programme is stripped, table shows highest rating single show in the week.

Table 5.5 Quiz Shows* – Social Class Groups

Programme	Week Ending 21 June AB	C1	C2	DE
		Audience (millions)		
Through The Keyhole	1.21	2.07	2.10	3.85
Every Second Counts	0.85	1.81	2.09	2.95
That's Showbusiness	0.77	1.40	1.40	1.87
Joker in The Pack	0.56	1.04	1.44	2.13
Have I Got News For You?	0.94	0.89	0.73	0.46
Fifteen-To-One	0.32	0.55	0.76	1.40
Crosswits	0.18	0.51	0.59	1.27
The Crystal Maze	0.33	0.58	0.60	0.68
The Music Game	0.25	0.38	0.36	0.57
Treasure Hunt	0.08	0.22	0.31	0.38

*Where programme is stripped, table shows highest rating single show in the week
What explanations could be offered to account for the patterns revealed in these tables?
Source: Television week (July 1992)

Some audience research has relied almost exclusively on quantitative data. The correlation of television viewing figures and attitudinal surveys according to sociodemographic variables like age and family membership has been used in *cultivation analysis*. This is designed to test whether television viewing could be said to influence general attitudes to the world. For example, Gerbner and Gross (1976) argue that the more television you watch, the more likely you are to have a fearful or distrustful attitude to the world outside.

However, quantitative data does have serious limitations for media studies. In short, it reveals little about the meanings audiences produce from media texts and the context in which such texts are received. An example to illustrate this point is the television ratings figures compiled by the Broadcasters Audience Research Board (BARB). These measure the audience size via a sample of 4,500 computer-linked homes in which meters are installed. When members of the household select a programme to view, the meter records their presence and which channel is chosen. What is not measured, though, is whether the set is actually being watched, the motivation for watching, how much social interaction is happening within the room, and the kind of meaningful response produced by the programme. Currently, the only supplementary information systematically gathered is audience appreciation statistics – an index of how interesting and/or enjoyable viewers found a particular programme.

Qualitative data seeks to uncover audience interpretations and observations via in-depth personal interviews and discussions with individuals or small groups. At its best, it should allow subjects to express their responses freely in as natural a setting as possible. Such an approach is sometimes dubbed ethnographic or even anthropological, in that the researcher fits in with, and is accepted by, the people being studied. It has been the basis of much recent audience research, especially with respect to television viewing. Nevertheless, ethnography and qualitative approaches in general are not without their problems. Reliance on subjects' own perceptions assumes they are fully conscious of how they are responding to a media text. Thus, there is a need for skilful interviewing to probe beyond glib or surface comments, while avoiding putting words in people's mouths:

> Eighteen families were interviewed in their own homes during the spring of 1985. Initially the two parents were interviewed, then later in each interview their children were invited to take part in the discussion along with their parents. The interviews, which lasted between one and two hours, were tape-recorded and then transcribed in full for analysis.
>
> The fact that the interviews were conducted *en famille* doubtless means that respondents felt a certain need to play out accepted roles, and doubtless interviews with family members separately would bring out other responses. However, I was precisely interested in how they functioned *as families*, within (and against) their roles.
>
> Moreover, the interviewing method (unstructured discussion for a period between one and two hours) was designed to allow a fair degree of probing. Thus on points of significance I returned the discussion to the same theme at different stages in the interview, from different angles. This means that anyone 'putting me on' (consciously or unconsciously) by representing themselves through an artificial/stereotyped *persona* which has no bearing on their 'real' activities would have to be able to sustain their adopted *persona* through what could be seen as quite a complex form of interrogation!
>
> *Morley (1986)*

Once a collection of interviews has been gathered, how can the material be organised? Where possible, common themes and patterns should be identified, so-called 'meaning structures'. Even so, there is still the problem of explaining their wider origins. In our media-saturated society (see Chapter 1), responses to any single media text are bound to be influenced by exposure to previous related texts − what has been called intertextuality. For example, filmgoers viewing *Batman* may be influenced by having read the comic as children, seen the television series, been exposed to the publicity, had preconceptions about star performers like Jack Nicholson etc. Furthermore, individuals' frameworks of interpretation can always be seen as being partly a product of social determinants such as class, gender, nationality etc., a key theme of much ethnographic audience research.

Reception Theory

'The unity of a text lies in its destination not its origin' (Eco, 1981). Eco's famous quotation is a recognition of the fact that whatever an author may intend when writing a text, it is the reader's interpretation which really matters in terms of the end result. During the past ten to fifteen years, considerable research, largely of an ethnographic nature, has gone into uncovering what meanings audiences produce from media texts and under what conditions.

The Active Reader

The concept of audience identification has been reviewed as a result of some of these audience studies. Total audience identification rarely occurs while audiences are engaged with media narrative. Instead, there is likely to be a constant shift between *implication* – when the audience imagines how they would behave in the situation represented – and *extrication* – the release from that involvement. What helps to prevent over-involvement is a sense of critical distance brought to the proceedings, e.g. judgements made about how 'real' the story is, or the quality of acting.

In writing about children's responses to *EastEnders*, David Buckingham (1987) concluded that they were 'by turns deeply involved, amused, bored, mocking and irreverent', and regularly moved between these positions. This is expressed in another way by Ien Ang (1985), in writing about women's pleasure in watching *Dallas*: 'The "flight" into a fictional fantasy world is not so much a denial of reality as playing with it.' This 'playing' with reality in soap operas may include direct responses to the characters and episodes (e.g. sending letters) not because reality is confused with fiction, but because the audience has chosen to treat the serial as 'real' in order to gain more pleasure.

Cultural Competence

In 1978, David Morley investigated how different audience groups (largely based on economic class) decoded or made sense of a television current affairs magazine programme, *Nationwide* (Morley, 1980). While he found differences that in part fitted Hall's encoding–decoding model – of dominant, negotiated and oppositional readings – much of the response failed to fit. This was, first, because additional social variables like gender and ethnicity were at work, and, second, because for many of the sample the programme either was irrelevant or failed to make much sense. Morley later reflected that it is more appropriate for audience research to recognise the knowledge, experiences and taste which different people bring to their media usage: what has been called *cultural competence* or *cultural capital*. It is a key concept, as it helps to explain varying audience preferences and pleasures. As Richard Dyer (1977) has argued, this means that the decoding model based on agreement or opposition to encoded ideologies needs to be replaced by one that recognises audience enjoyment or boredom. This in turn opens up space for audience readings of texts which are unanticipated or alternative to any presumed preferred reading, as will be seen in some of the research reported below.

Gender Preferences

In an important contribution to understanding patterns of media preference according to gender within households, Ann Gray (1992) arrived at a typology of preferred texts in relation

Table 5.6 Group 1: A, B (Social classes)

Context	Film	Television
Family together	*Superman*; *Gremlins*	*EastEnders*; nature; Rolf Harris cartoons; *Great Languages of the World*; *Shakespeare*; *Dallas*; *Dynasty*
Children only	*Mary Poppins*; *Star Wars*; *Bed Knobs and Broomsticks*	*EastEnders*; children's TV; *Dallas*; *Dynasty*; *Top of the Pops*; *The Young Ones*; *Spitting Image*; *Grange Hill*
Male and female together	*Local Hero*; 'quality' films; Burt Reynolds; *Casablanca*; *Inherit the Wind*; *Company of Wolves*	*Paradise Postponed*; *First Among Equals*; *Minder*; *Hill Street Blues*; *Jewel in the Crown*; *Edge of Darkness*; *Fawlty Towers*; *Alias Smith and Jones*; *MASH*; *Star Trek*; news; *Juliet Bravo*; *The Bill*; *Coronation Street*; documentaries
Male only	*Brazil*; horror; cowboys; science fiction; war; spy films	'trash' to relax; news; sport; nature; *Question Time*; elections; *Tomorrow's World*; *Monty Python*; *Fawlty Towers*
Female only	*Woodstock*; *Slipper and Rose*; love stories weepies; comedy	*EastEnders*; *Dallas*; *Dynasty*; *Princess Daisy*; 'quality' plays; *Coronation Street*; *Brookside*; *A Woman of Substance*

Source: Gray (1992)

Table 5.7 Group 2: C1, C2 (Social classes)

Context	Film	Television
Family together	*Star Wars*; James Bond; *Superman*; comedy *Stir Crazy**; *Animal House**; *10**; *Chitty, Chitty, Bang Bang*; *Jaws*; *Blazing Saddles*; Walt Disney; *ET*; *Close Encounters*	*Countdown*; *Soap*; *Auf Wiedersehen Pet*; *Boys from the Blackstuff*; *Shogun*; *EastEnders*; *Blockbusters***; quiz shows; *Dallas***; *Dynasty*
Children only	*Star Wars*; *Flash Gordon*; *Raiders of the Lost Ark*; *High Society*	children's TV; *Top of the Pops*; *EastEnders*; cartoons
Male and female together	*Trading Places*; *An Officer and a Gentleman*; *Deer Hunter*; Clint Eastwood; *Being There*; *Educating Rita*; *The Champ*; *Kramer vs Kramer*; comedy; adult comedy; *Lemon Popsicle*; *Blade Runner*	*Fawlty Towers*; *Open All Hours Fresh Fields*; news; *Minder*; *Wogan*; *Duty Free*; *Face the Music*; *Call My Bluff*; *The Boat*; *Brookside*; *EastEnders*; *Butterflies*; *The Gentle Touch*; *32 Magnum*; *Crossroads*; *Coronation Street*; *Crimewatch*; documentaries; *Dallas*; *Dynasty*; *Cagney and Lacey*; *Starsky and Hutch*; *The Brief*; *Travelling Man*; *The Bill*
Male only	action adventure; science fiction; war; boxing films; Stallone; *Rocky*; horror; space; Charles Bronson; cowboys; *Close Encounters*	*The Young Ones*; *Benny Hill*; *Monty Python*; *The Two Ronnies*; *Tomorrows World*; space astronomy; American football; sport; business programmes; news; *A Team*; boxing; doucumentaries
Female only	*Evergreen*; *The Jazz Singer*; *My Fair Lady*; *Ellis Island*; *Mistral's Daughter*; *Sarah Dane*; *Princess Daisy*; *Tootsie*; *Hollywood Wives*; romance; tear jerkers; *Who Will Love My Children?*; horror; *Reds*; *Tess*	*Mapp and Lucia*; *The Thornbirds*; *Far Pavillions*; *Dallas*; *Dynasty*; *Falcon Crest*; local news; chat shows; cookery; medical programmes; *Return to Eden*; *Butterflies*; *Lace*; *Master of the Game*; Al Jolson; *Sons and Daughters*; *Emmerdale Farm*; *Take the High Road*; *Gems*; *Coronation Street*; *Where There's Life*; *Quincy*; *General Hospital*; *A Woman of Substance*

*families with older children
**women watching with their children
Source: Gray (1992)

to differing contexts of household composition (Tables 5.6–5.8). Although her research was based on a relatively small sample of thirty women contacted via a video library in Yorkshire, she found that social class was an additional variable affecting choice (Figures 5.6–5.7).

Table 5.8 Group 3: D, E (Social classes)

Context	Film	Television
Family together	*Kramer vs Kramer; The Champ; Porkys; Police Academy; Rocky; Dirty Harry;* Clint Eastwood; comedy; Walt Disney	*EastEnders; Coronation Street; Dallas; Dynasty*
Children only	Musicals; children's films; Walt Disney	*EastEnders; Coronation Street; Dallas; Auf Wiedersehen Pet; Top of the Pops; The Young Ones*
Male and female together	*Aliens; Who Will Love my Children?; The Champ;* horror	Bestsellers; *Sherlock Holmes; Travelling Man;* snooker; Olympics; World Cup; cricket; boxing; *Fawlty Towers*
Male only	Cowboys; war; *Rocky;* boxing films	*Cannon and Ball;* motor cycle racing; car racing; snooker; football
Female only	Weepies; Richard Gere; romance; horror	*Falcon Crest; Sons and Daughters; Dallas;* bestsellers; *Coronation Street;* local news; medical programmes; *Lace*

Source: Gray (1992)

What qualities characterise:
1 male preferences for viewing?
2 female preferences for viewing?
3 joint preferences for viewing?
How does social class affect choice of viewing?

A further distinction Gray made was that of education. She found that women with a minimum experience of education (i.e. leaving school between ages 14 and 16) were much more likely to be critical of their own tastes, using phrases like 'soppy' or 'silly', whereas those women with experience of higher education were more inclined to retain a critical distance from what were perceived as more 'trashy' or 'trivial' media texts. Despite these differences, *all* women took pleasure in texts which focused on personal relationships, believable characters and a strong story. Men were perceived as disliking texts in which emotions were openly displayed:

Love Story . . . I've seen that about half a dozen times, I think it's just as good, no matter how many times you watch it – it can still make you cry. Men find them soppy, don't they? I think probably because they're frightened that

the might actually feel some little bit of sympathy or feeling
... men don't like to show their emotions very much do
they? (Barbara).

Gray (1992)

These findings are echoed by other studies into how gender
affects choice of media text (Table 5.9).

5.6 Our Price Video

What criteria have Our Price employed
in their selection of videos for feminine
and masculine audiences?

1.   Winning
A racing car spectacular which
explores the relationships surrounding
the drivers. Starring Paul Newman,
Joanna Woodward and Robert
Wagner. Includes film footage from
the Indianapolis 500, and the pile-up at
the starting line which actually
happened in 1968.
Cert PG

**2.   Kevin Turvey - The Man
       Behind The Green Door**
Kevin Turvey is an anorak clad hack!
He is also an investigative reporter -
or so he claims. Hilarious comedy
starring Rik Mayall with Robbie
Coltrane, Ade Edmondson
and others.
Cert PG

3.   Jim Bowen
Recently recorded in Blackpool, this
video features a side of Jim Bowen
that you certainly won't see on TV.
Jim as stand-up comedian. Guaranteed
to hit the bull's-eye every time!
Super, smashin', great!
Cert 15

4.   Churchill
This four-hour, two tape package
presents an extensive profile of
Winston Churchill, including unique
archive footage from the vaults of the
BBC of Churchill's wartime speeches.
Cert E

5.   Man In A Suitcase
McGill is a discredited CIA Agent
turned international bounty hunter
and spy. Two tapes are now available,
each containing two classic episodes.
Cert PG

**6.   Jason King - Chapter One:
       The Company I Keep**
Heart-throb Peter Wyngarde takes
the title role in this series, a sequel
to "Department S", about the
globe trotting adventures of a
playboy author.
Cert PG

7.   Billy Connolly - 25 Years
Join Billy in this special video
celebration of his twenty-five years as
a comedian, including classic routines
and chatshow appearances.
Cert 18

**8.   Vulcan - A Farewell
       To Arms**
Historic footage featuring the XH558,
the last flying Vulcan. It also charts the
history of the plane, from its early
days at Farnborough in the 1950's to
its last flight in 1992.
Cert E

**9.   The Double Life
       Of Veronique**
A haunting romantic mystery, starring
Irene Jacob, winner of the Cannes
1991 Best Actress award, for her
performance. Explores the love,
grief and loss of two identical women,
born 20 years ago in Poland and
France.
Cert 15

10.   The Last Boy Scout
Bruce Willis stars as a private
investigator in this action-packed film
from the director of "Top Gun" and
the writer of "Lethal Weapon". The
P.I. investigates a dancer's murder,
helped and hindered by her boyfriend,
("In Living Color's" wise-cracking
Daymon Wayans).
Cert 18

11.   Lover's Guide 3
The best selling sex education tape
aims to enhance sexual performance
within a loving relationship.
Cert 18

5.7 Our Price Video

1. Black Robe
Bruce Beresford's stunning film about one man's mission to help save a tribe living in the hostile wilderness of seventeenth century North America.
Cert 15

2. Annie Hall
Woody Allen's autobiographical "nervous romance", which has won four Oscars, including Best Picture. An intelligent adult comedy which incisively comments on contemporary social issues. Starring Woody Allen and Diane Keaton.
Cert 15

3. The Accidental Tourist
Based on Anne Tyler's novel, with a challenging script. Stars William Hurt, Kathleen Turner and an Oscar-Winning performance by Geena Davis.
Cert PG

4. The Darling Buds Of May
Comedy from the series adapted from H.E. Bates' popular stories, featuring television's favourite family, the Larkins. Stars David Jason and Catherine Zeta Jones.
Cert PG

5. The Shape Challenge
A unique programme, containing both a diet and exercise plan, to help you shape up and lose inches. Devised by RSA qualified Libby Roberts.
Cert E

6. The Man Who Cried
Catherine Cookson's romance set against the background of the Depression. Abel Mason conducts a desperate search for love and happiness in relationships with four women.
Cert PG

7. Jennie Garth's Body In Progress
The star of "Beverly Hills 90210" introduces her personal fitness plan, using low-impact body toning, and a careful diet.
Cert E

8. French And Saunders 3
The first three episodes from the comedy duo's third series, with over twenty-five sketches, including the terrific "Star Test" sketches with Sonia and Bros.
Cert PG

9. Egypt - Land Of Ancient Wonder
Visit Cairo, travel along Egypt's lifeblood the Nile, and see the monumental pyramids of Giza and the mighty Sphinx. All this and more in the comfort of your own home.
Cert E

10. Sting - Ten Summoner's Tales
The eleven songs in this new video, performed at Sting's home in Wiltshire, make up his new album. The video includes the latest single, "It's Probably Me".
Cert E

11. So You Want To Be A Model?
A step by step guide to modelling, made in association with Elite Premier, one of the world's top model agencies. This will show you what it takes, but more importantly how you can get started.
Cert E

12. Ballroom Dancing For Absolute Beginners
Learn the basics of ballroom dancing in your own home with acknowledged expert Peggy Spencer. Dances include the Tango and the Waltz.
Cert E

Christine Geraghty (1991) argues that there are four elements which explain the appeal of so-called 'women's fiction' – a label embracing soap opera, romance and melodrama:

1 an emphasis on a central woman whom the audience is invited to support;
2 a division between the public and private sphere, with women understanding and controlling the private space;
3 an emphasis on building and maintaining relationships;
4 an element of fantasy in which values linked to the personal private sphere are privileged.

Table 5.9 China: family members' favourite programme types*

Programme type	Female percentage of mentions	Male percentage of mentions
Drama	67	31
Drama series/specials	32	14
Chinese opera	26	8
Foreign drama	2	4
Movies	3	2
War dramas	1	3
Foreign movies	1	0
Historical drama	1	0
Sports	4	35
Sports (all)	2	27
Kung-fu	2	8
Information	10	25
News	5	16
Educational/TVU	3	3
Travel	1	3
Documentaries	1	1
Language	1	1
Political	0	0
Light entertainment	19	9
Variety	11	5
Children/cartoon	2	1
Animal shows	2	1
Crosstalk	1	1
Game shows	1	0
Music shows	1	1
Comedy	1	0
Totals	100	100

*Excludes children 11 years old and younger
Source: Lull 1988

As a case study in a television genre with strong female appeal, soap opera research illustrates much of Geraghty's case. Dorothy Hobson's (1982) pioneering study into the unfashionable *Crossroads* revealed how many women saw it as 'their' programme – a kind of cultural space or even resistance to masculine control. Hobson describes how outraged the women were when the lead character, Noele Gordon, was written out of the serial, as if a close relative or friend had been murdered (by male producers).

In seeking to explain the pleasures of soap opera for women, Christine Geraghty has applied Richard Dyer's categories of 'utopian solutions'. These refer to compensations offered by popular entertainment in relation to specific inadequacies in society experienced by people. Energy contrasts a Bood.

with the exhaustion of daily life; abundance with scarcity a.
deprivation; intensity with dreariness and monotony; trans-
parency with manipulation and dishonesty; and community
with isolation and transience:

Utopian possibilities in women's fiction

	Energy	Abundance	Intensity	Transparency	Community
British soaps	strong women characters, quick repartee, pace of plot		emotions strongly expressed at key moments, Angie/Den Sheila/Bobby	*sincerity of key characters;* Deirdre Barlow, Kathy Beale, Sheila Grant, *True Love:* Deirdre/Ken Chris/Frank	characters offer support, friendship, gossip outside programme
US soaps	strong male characters, business activity, pace of plot	glamorous settings clothes, luxurious objects food etc.	emotions strongly expressed at key moments, Sue Ellens's madness	*sincerity of key characters:* Bobby, Pamela, Miss Ellie, Krystle *True Love* Blake/Krystle Bobby/Pamela	asserted within family, rarely achieved, relationship with audience

Source: Geraghty (1991)

---

activity **5.4**

1 Choose an example of British and American soap opera, and examine the extent to which it seems to reflect the patterns described by Geraghty.
2 Where would an Australian soap opera like *Neighbours* fit in the table?

Various studies have confirmed that males generally prefer factual programmes (news, current affairs and documentaries),
sport, action-based narrative where there is a minimum of
dialogue and emotion (for a discussion of 'masculine' versus
'feminine' narrative see pp. 137–40), and realist fiction. David
Morley (1986) found that men often disapproved of watching
fiction on the grounds it was not 'real life' or sufficiently serious. They were consequently inclined to define their own
preferences as more important. It is clear that large numbers of
males do watch 'feminine' programmes such as soap opera,
but to admit as much seems to present a threat to their sense
of masculinity.

Polysemy and Subcultural Readings

Much of the above discussion on gender preferences assumes a heterosexual audience. Given the paucity of explicit gay and lesbian media representation, it is not surprising that such groups have tended to find pleasures in those texts perceived as providing an alternative gay or lesbian reading to the dominant heterosexual discourse. An example of this is *Dynasty*, which in the 1980s became a cult serial among gays in America. They took pleasure in its camp discourse as personified by the 'masculine' Joan Collins character, Alexis, and the programme's emphasis on high fashion and personal rivalry. *Prisoner in Cell Block H*, an Australian drama serial based on a women's prison, has a lesbian following in Britain, while in Australia research by Hodge and Tripp (1986) discovered a strong empathy among children with the situation of the prisoners. They compared the prison to their school, and the warders to their own teachers. Particularly appealing were the prisoners' attempts to oppose and subvert official authority. For girls, the relatively rare sight of strong, active women fighting the system was a source of support for their own identity and self-esteem.

A similar kind of subversive reading has been identified by Martin Barker (1989) in his analysis of how comics in Britain give pleasure to children. Characters like Dennis the Menace and the Bash Street Kids in *The Beano* guarantee adult power will be constantly challenged in a way which is likely to undermine adults' image as sensible figures of respect for children. Barker argues that adult 'policing' of many comics and their general denigration by parents and teachers serves to enhance their appeal to children. It might be argued that computer video games are beginning to take over this role in the 1990s.

The most popular forms of media text seem to succeed because they contain a degree of openness and ambiguity which allows very different groups in society to decode them in a pleasurable way. In the pop world during the late 1980s the two most successful artists, Michael Jackson and Madonna, not only created music with 'crossover' appeal, focusing on dance, but also contrived images of gender and race which were polysemic to say the least! Madonna's performances provided sufficient support for a view of her as a strong, liberated woman or a sexual plaything:

> 'She's sexy and she doesn't need men . . . she's kind of there all by herself'.
> or
> 'She gives us ideas. It's really women's lib, not being afraid of what guys think.' (quoted in *Time*, May 27 1985)

'Best of all, her onstage contortions and Boy Toy voice have put sopping sex where it belongs – front and centre in the limelight.' (quoted in *Playboy*, September 1985)

Fiske (1987)

Michael Jackson's physical appearance has generated considerable controversy – has he attempted to dilute or deracinate his blackness? Like Madonna, he has consciously played with his image, not least in his video, *Thriller*, where he calls his own identity into question via a blend of generic codes – horror, musical, pop video and 'teen pic movie'. *Thriller* is a classic example of intertextuality at work.

The only black performers in America to rival Michael Jackson in black/white crossover appeal in the late 1980s were Bill Cosby and Eddie Murphy. *The Cosby Show* regularly topped the television ratings and attracted much academic speculation as to its racial message (see p. 147). In an attempt to discover how black and white audiences in America responded to it as a *black* situation comedy, Justin Lewis (1991) conducted interviews with fifty black and white viewers of the show of mixed social class origins. Most of the subjects' reading of the specific episode watched were consistent with that of the programme's 'preferred reading' (a gently progressive feminist narrative in which women proved they could outperform men in the mechanics of fixing a car). However, Lewis found significant racial differences in their perceptions of the Huxtables as a black family. The dominant white perspective was one of colour blindness. Cliff Huxtable (Cosby) was seen as 'typical' or 'everyday', an observation reinforced by his upper-middle-class status and home (like those of many white families on American sitcoms). The show was thought to be different from other black television sitcoms in its absence of 'black humour' and style – defined as being loud and slapstick in nature. Lewis concluded that for most of the white audience *The Cosby Show* served to sustain the ideal of the 'American Dream', i.e. that colour is not a barrier to upward mobility.

In contrast, black interviewees were very sensitive to the show's reference to black culture, e.g. anti-apartheid posters on the wall. Lewis comments that this is indicative of how the show treads a thin racial dividing line: 'The symbols of black culture are strong enough to incorporate a black audience and weak enough to entice a white audience.' Moreover, blacks approved of the show because of their awareness of how few positive black representations appear on American television. That is not to say they were not also conscious of absences in the form of social realism. The lack of struggle and racism was regretted by many blacks, but this reservation was largely suppressed by the desire to have positive black representations made available.

As an example of an internationally consumed media text, *Dallas* has been subject to considerable academic analysis involving a number of audience studies in different countries. Far from *Dallas* being a case of 'cultural imperialism' (see pp. 289–296), whereby American capitalist values are spread throughout the world, the audience research makes clear that *Dallas* is made sense of via the local cultural framework of interpretation people bring to the programme. In Israel, Katz and Liebes (1986) discussed a *Dallas* episode with several ethnic groups including Israeli Arabs, Moroccans and Russian Jews. The more traditional ethnic groups, e.g. Israeli Arabs, tended to see *Dallas*'s 'message' as being that wealth cannot bring happiness and that rich Americans are immoral. Meanwhile, in Holland, Ien Ang (1985) found some female viewers enjoyed the programme through adopting an ironic attitude, treating it as 'trashy' and inferior. Some even applied a Marxist/feminist perspective and enjoyed it for its excess of sexism and capitalism, which could be viewed as evidence to support their own criticisms of American cultural values.

Clearly, much of the audience research summarised above has provided important insights into the limits of power media texts may exert over their audiences. Furthermore, it is now accepted that the meanings audiences produce will to some extent be shaped by their own cultural competences and social origins.

However, there is a danger that the pendulum swings too far the other way and audience power over the text is exaggerated. As with uses and gratifications, there may be a tendency to attribute consumer sovereignty to the audience and hence ignore the wider constraints which determined the production, circulation and reception of media texts. In the context of the hegemony–pluralism debate, this is a case of veering towards a pluralistic position.

Likewise, in celebrating the ability of the audience to resist dominant ideologies, there is frequently a conflation of alternative with oppositional readings. The fact that the polysemy or ambiguity of texts allows a variety of meanings to be produced is not the same thing as the text being actively challenged for its ideological content. As Justin Lewis points out with *The Cosby Show*, its hegemonic or ideological power actually depends upon its ability to strike a chord with different audiences in different ways.

The Context of Reception

Much of the academic controversy surrounding the encoding and decoding of media texts has had to be significantly qualified in the light of recent research into how audiences receive the media. The assumption that full attention is given when listening to the radio, reading magazines etc. has been discarded in favour of schemes which differentiate between levels of attention. One example is Jeremy Tunstall's (1983) definitions of levels as *primary* (close attention), *secondary* (the medium in question is relegated to the background) and *tertiary* (although the medium is present, no conscious monitoring of it is taking place). These varying levels of attention are in turn influenced by the specific nature of the media in terms of technology, audiovisual codes etc., and the social context in which it is received.

Andrew Crisell (1986) argues that the defining characteristic of radio as a medium of communication is 'flow' (a term borrowed from Raymond Williams, 1974 – see below), analogous to water pouring from a tap when switched on. There is a lack of clear programme boundaries, because listeners tend to dip in and out as it suits them. More often than not this sporadic listening is accompanied by other activities such as driving the car, making the breakfast etc., and so radio seems to be clearly a secondary medium. It is used in conjunction with the routines of daily life in a way in which no other media can achieve. This is because it does not require visual concentration and is extremely portable.

This quality of mobility has led some people to claim that radio is capable of considerable intimacy, since it can function as a 'personal companion' accompanying us into very private situations, not least in bed! The walkman, or 'personal stereo', delivering radio and music, has been criticised on the grounds that its wearers retreat behind the headphones into their personal space, which excludes everybody else.

activity 5.5

Ask a sample of radio listeners to keep a diary of their daily listening including details of:
1 what radio programmes are listened to;
2 for how long (on average);
3 under what conditions, e.g. alone, in the car, at work etc.

In contrast to radio, cinema requires an audience commitment in every sense of the word. A deliberate decision to visit a cinema, and the cinematic environment itself, contribute to the sense of seeing a film as being a special occasion. The viewing conditions deny almost all alternative activities apart from watching the screen. These conditions include the large screen size, the powerful sound system, the darkness and collective audience concentration; all of which make cinema a primary medium. What is to some extent ambiguous is the degree to which the conditions privilege a private/personal or collective response to the film. The audience usually comprises a large public gathering, but the opportunities for social interaction are minimal.

Print media by their nature require some degree of close attention, if only to read the words! Nevertheless, reading newspapers and magazines is qualitatively different to reading a book. Selectivity, skimming and scanning all reflect the sense of leisurely engagement which characterises much newspaper and magazine reading. Having said that, there is little in the way of contemporary research into this area.

It was Raymond Williams (1974) who first described television programming as a 'flow'. Unlike the singular text foregrounded at the cinema, television emits a constant fragmentary stream, including adverts, trailers, continuity announcements etc. An excellent example of this pattern can be found on MTV, where the core form of the pop video informs the style of the accompanying adverts, title sequences and features. John Ellis (1982) has refined the notion of flow to one of *segments*: relatively self-contained scenes conveying an incident, mood or particular meaning. He argues that these segments, which rarely last more than five minutes and usually contain a kind of climax, link closely to the context of television viewing.

Television is above all a domestic medium. It is watched in the home and consequently is part of the domestic atmosphere, providing mood and comfort. The flickering set in the the corner is almost equivalent to the 'warmth' of a fire, and, from the 1950s, replaced the radio as the focus of the living room. Given that a large variety of social activity takes place in the home it is not surprising that much television viewing is intermittent in nature.

This is borne out by the results of Peter Collett's research (1986), which involved installing a specially designed television cabinet that contained a video camera directed at those watching television. From the resulting 350 hours of videotape he concluded that people only have their eyes on the screen for about 65 per cent of the time they are in the room. For the rest of the time, they are engaged in eating, sleeping, talking, ironing etc. It also confirmed the social nature of much viewing: 'Even the more popular programmes like soap operas and the news are punctuated with conversation and idle chatter. People exchange views on the plot, complain about the mismanagement of the weather, or comment on the newscaster's hairdo.'

Family Viewing

One trend that television has contributed towards is that of families staying at home for their evening entertainment – part of the privatisation of family life. The specific dynamics of how television interacts with family relationships and domestic life is a subject of much recent research. Utilising crosscultural evidence, the following extract indicates how domestic time usage is affected both by general cultural values and the nature of television itself as a structuring social activity:

> Cultures also have their own general sense of time, and there are tendencies to regulate social activity accordingly. Let me illustrate how cultural orientations toward time can influence family television viewing: time means something very different in Denmark compared to Pakistan. In Denmark, nearly all families eat the evening meal at almost precisely the same time – 6:00 p.m. The evening television news is broadcast at 7:30, so that it won't interfere with dinner. The systematic, predictable pattern of the Danish orientation toward time, including the scheduling and viewing of television shows, is an extension of this very orderly culture. In Pakistan, on the other hand, television programs often appear on the state system at times that differ from the published schedules, or fail to appear at all. Audiences generally are not surprised or angered by these irregularities . . .
>
> But in the long run television also influences perceptions and uses of time within cultures that are very different. Mealtimes, bedtimes, chore-times, periods for doing school homework, and patterns of verbal interaction, among other activities, are influenced by the scheduling of television shows. Television is transforming the lives of some rural Indian families by changing their routines away from regulation by nature to regulation by the clock and by television. As Behl reported in her article, Sunday has become a 'TV holiday' and 'TV time' in the evening has replaced time that was previously used for transacting business and 'integrating thought' in rural Indian culture. The reports from India and China demonstrate another phenomenon that has occurred in all cultures with television – the speeding up of home activity, especially the preparation and consumption of the evening meal. Parts of the day become redefined and structured around the

scheduling of TV shows, and certain behaviors (such as differing meal times for men and women in rural India) are consolidated in the interest of preserving time for viewing.

Lull (1988)

---

activity **5.6**

Investigate how family routines are related to television by asking each member of the family sampled to keep a daily diary for a week, with all television viewing recorded along with accompanying activities (if any) and other subjects with whom the viewing is shared.

As to whether television integrates or divides families, there is no single pattern. In some families, television acts as a point of common reference and discussion, whereas in other families, it offers a means of avoiding social contact or even potential conflict.

A growing pattern which seems likely to mean a decline in family viewing of television is that of the multiset home. It is not unusual for homes to contain three or four television sets, and, with the growth in choice of channels, it seems inevitable that individual viewing will increase. The only countervailing influence to this trend is the fact that video rental has a special status which often makes the event more social.

Gender and Television Viewing

In what David Morley (1986) calls the 'politics of the living room', the question of who exercises the most power and control over programme choice is firmly linked to gender. His own research, based on eighteen families in south London, confirmed that where men are in paid employment, they have the most control over what is watched. This was symbolised by their domination over the use of the remote control handset. (Peter Collett (1986) recorded one instance where the man carried the remote control with him even when he left the room to make coffee!)

Another difference Morley discovered was that men preferred to watch television attentively, in silence and without interruption, whereas women were more inclined to engage in conversation or perform other domestic activities while viewing. Men's approach to viewing was generally more deliberately planned, closely scrutinising the evening's schedule. These differences reflect more general distinctions in gender roles and identities, particularly in relation to work and leisure. Men make quite a sharp demarcation between work outside the home and leisure within it. Women, however, are more inclined to define home as a site of labour, and therefore watch television more distractedly and with a sense of guilt (hence their greater enjoyment of viewing when the rest of the family is absent). Finally, as the main 'breadwinners' in most families, men see it as their 'right' to exercise first choice, and in the event of any dispute may invoke this as a justification for prevailing over what is watched.

Such patriarchal patterns are not necessarily universal. James Lull (1988) reports that in China there is no dominance of night-time viewing by males, and that in Venezuela it is women who control viewing (based largely on the *telenovellas* – Latin American soap operas) as a reflection of their greater control of domestic space. Finally, in India, television viewing has actually helped to increase democracy in the household at the expense of traditional patriarchy.

Gender and Media Technology

The main theme of Ann Gray's research into women's response to video in the household is that gender is a key determinant in the use of, and expertise in, specific domestic technologies. In the case of the video cassette recorder (VCR), men's influence prevailed in a number of ways, ranging across the initial decision to purchase or rent a VCR, the mastery and control of the timer programming and the ownership of videotapes (men being more inclined to develop their own personal archive). When it came to time-shifting, many of the women failed to operate the timer with any confidence. This was partly due to lack of motivation and a sense that it was masculine terrain.

The gendering of video technology as masculine is a key issue emphasised by Gray and others and recognisable in some of the commercial advertising stressing the 'high-tech' nature of VCRs. This is in contrast to 'feminine' technology like microwave ovens, dishwashers and washing machines, which are no less technically demanding. Apart from VCRs, other new technology defined as masculine includes computers and video games.

Sherry Turkle (1984) has argued that computer culture appeals to masculine pleasures because of its abstract formal systems and its ability to offer a safe and protective retreat from personal relationships. 'Hackers' are preoccupied with winning and take risks, qualities traditionally perceived by women as 'non-feminine'. Meanwhile, video-games software seems to emphasise masculinised images of action-adventure scenarios in which a single male hero tackles overwhelming odds. The games focus on a quest which is attained via technological intervention.

Comparison of two households: a student case study

James Family: Mother (36) manager of accountants, father (43) gas service engineer, son (18) trainee apprentice, daughter (17) student.
All share a three-bedroomed bungalow. Daughter is currently studying A-levels and mother has a degree in business management.
Social class: lower middle class.

ICT [information and communications technology] owned

Father: television and double-decker video situated in the front room as well as separates including multiplay CD, tuner, tape deck and amplifier. Clock/TV/radio alarm situated in bedroom as well as radio in the en suite bathroom and walkman for personal use.

Mother: washing machine, tumble dryer (gas)

Son: television, video, CD player, amplifier, radio alarm, car radio

Daughter: TV, video, CD player, amplifier, radio alarm, radio (portable), walkman.

General (shared by everyone): dishwasher, oven, microwave, sandwich toaster, chip-fryer.

The television, although bought by the father, is situated in the living room, a place where the family congregate. It is the meeting place of the family. Therefore the television is watched by all members, yet only the father and daughter know how to fully operate the video recorder. This also applies to the stereo equipment situated in this room. All things technical are usually used and operated by the father and daughter. The son has too many other outside interests and a car which he is more interested in than the father's latest addition to the stereo system. The mother will only watch *Coronation Street* and has no idea how to work the video, 'It fazes me'. The remote control passes to and from father to daughter with the father's position as head of family taking precedence should he want to watch *Top Gear* whilst the daughter would prefer a new sitcom.

The stereo is used by the father but more often by the daughter, as it is she who buys the CDs and she who prefers the loudness of her father's stereo to her own.

General ICTs which include the dishwasher and oven are not referred to as 'mum's' because mum works full time and all housework and cooking is shared equally. The washing machine, however, belongs to the mother, as it is she who knows when it is about to fill up too much on certain programmes.

Both son and daughter's ICTs are similar and are mostly used in the morning (radio alarm) and in the evening, when they escape to their own private domain to relax, do homework or have friends round.

Most items owned by the father tend to be situated in the front room and are considered as being for use by the whole family, yet the son and daughter's stereos and televisions are their own personal property and any using of the other's equipment without permission is seen as an 'invasion of privacy'.

The mother's lack of items draws attention to the fact that she rarely watches television and is too busy studying, besides the fact that she would prefer to read a book than listen to loud music.

Pacey family: Mother (42), father (42), eldest son (20) works as a bank clerk, son (10) at school, eldest daughter (19) currently at university, youngest daughter (17) A-level student. Father is a painter/decorator who is currently out of work. Mother works part-time as a sales assistant in a department store.
Social class: working class

ICT owned

Father: television (situated in front room), record player

Mother: fridge/freezer, washing machine, dryer, cooker, toaster

Eldest son: walkman, car stereo, cassette deck

Son: Sega games console, walkman

Eldest daughter: CD stack system

Daughter: cassette deck, walkman

General: a TV and video which is rotated: one month in the girls' room and the next in the boys'. A share scheme.

The television in this household is on for many hours in the day due to the fact that it is one of only two in a six-person household. It is the focus of the living room and even more so for the youngest son, who spends at least three hours a day using it in conjunction with his Sega games console.

The mother has full dominance over the kitchen. She may work part time but the kitchen is regarded as her territory; it is she who cooks the meals and washes the clothes and cleans the house. The technology involved in working the cooker is virtually unknown to the father and each child (yes, even the girls). This is in stark contrast to the James family, who share the chores and are all quite capable of distinguishing between the oven and the kettle.

What the father says, in regard to the remote control and choice of channels, goes. He has dominance over this as do most men over the television. Yet when the father is out the remote is held by the eldest son, standing in for the father: the girls do not get a look in.

The stereo is the least used equipment in the house, because of the fact that it only plays records while the majority of the children prefer the latest technology of their CDs and non-scratch cassettes. The record player, however, is not replaced as it belongs to the father, and it plays all his old 78s and is handy for those family parties.

The sharing of the TV is biased as well as that of the video, male dominance being shown in the fact that the 'boys' month share usually turns into six weeks. The daughter much prefers to listen to her music and often lets the extra two weeks pass; after all, the 'family' TV downstairs is available and she has no idea how to work the video properly anyway.

The major differences between the two households is the male dominance over all things 'technical' (but not involved in cooking) in the Pacey household. The James family tend to share all technical items, with the daughter interested in the latest technology as much as the next man.

activity 5.7

Compare two households, as in the case study opposite, in terms of information and communications technology (ICT) in the home.

1 Profile each household in terms of occupation, housing, age and education where possible.
2 List the ICT owned and its physical distribution in the house (see list below).
3 How is ICT viewed in general by each member of the household?
4 Identify which member(s) of the household 'own' and control which items of ICT (e.g. use of remote control). Include the number of each possessed or rented.

ICT:
Television (teletext?)
Video recorder
Satellite dish
Camcorder
Video-game console
Computer
Radio (walkman?)
Music centre/hi-fi (CD?)

FURTHER READING

Buckingham, D. 1987: *Public Secrets: EastEnders and its Audience*. BFI.
Geraghty, C. 1991: *Women and Soap Opera*. Polity Press.
Gray, A. 1992: *Video Playtime*. Routledge.
Lewis, J. 1991: *The Ideological Octopus*. Routledge.
Lull, J. (Ed) 1988: *World Families Watch Television*. Sage.
Morley, D. 1992: *Television Audiences and Cultural Studies*. Routledge.
Peterson, R.C. and Thurstone, L. 1933: *Motion Pictures and Social Attitudes*. Macmillan.
Schlesinger, P., Dobash, R.E., Dobash, R.P. and Weaver, C. 1992: *Women Viewing Violence*. BFI.

Media Institutions and Production

In this chapter we will examine the media as a contemporary social institution with specific determinants and processes of production (whose historical antecedents are discussed in Chapter 2). After providing an overview of institutional determinants, the analysis will focus on two case studies of media production, pop music and local newspapers.

THE MEDIA AS INSTITUTION

The media form a significant part of the everyday cultural life of modern industrial societies. As audiences, our routines are often structured around viewing, reading and listening to media output, and we regularly refer to specific media texts in social encounters. There is then a sense in which the media are part of the social fabric. When certain social practices take on a regularity and structure which are apparent to ordinary people, then they may be called an *institution*. This is not to be confused with the more common usage of the term as referring to a specific organisation or building (e.g. a prison).

A helpful framework for examining the constituent elements of institutions is provided below:

> It may be useful to think of all social institutions in terms of the varying degrees to which they represent historical and continuing social responses to conflicts at the level of:
>
> 1 *Economy*, concerned with the production and distribution of materials goods and wealth.
> 2 *Politics*, concerned with the exercise of power and processes of social regulation.

3 *Culture*, concerned with the production, exchange and reproduction of meaning.

O'Sullivan (1994)

The emphasis in previous chapters, especially Chapters 4 and 5, has been on the third element in the list, the making of cultural meaning. While this is a critical ingredient in the analysis of institutional processes, the intention here is to focus on the economic and political dimensions and how these shape media production, distribution and consumption.

INSTITUTIONAL DETERMINANTS: *ECONOMIC*

Despite the fact that media texts are an important source of cultural meaning, they also share many of the characteristics of industrial commodities like motor cars or washing powder. Assembly line production, marketing, research and development etc. can all be found in media industries. The capital investment for a typical Hollywood feature film in the 1990s is likely to be over $25 million. *Terminator 2*, for example, cost $80 million to produce in 1991, and that did not include the marketing budget. For Hollywood studios, such costs can only be justified by success at the box office, manifested as profit in the form of revenue from admissions, video rights etc.

With such high financial stakes, it is not surprising that companies make every effort to minimise their risks in what is at times a very uncertain market. For Hollywood, this has meant the increasing tendency to produce sequels for successful films like *Batman*, *Alien*, *Nightmare on Elm Street* etc. until public interest declines. A further strategy is to rely more on research-based marketing from the initial packaging of a film (title, synopsis, stars etc.) to the selection of the final cut on the basis of test screenings of alternative climaxes. For example, *Fatal Attraction*'s ending was eventually chosen (against the director's wishes) by a vote of preview audiences. The simplest way of maximising your chances of profit in media production is by extending your control of the market.

Concentration of Ownership

In all industrial markets there is a tendency for the bigger, more successful companies to take over smaller companies in a search for even greater growth. When the takeover involves a direct competitor in the same sector then the process is referred to as *horizontal integration*, e.g. a newspaper publisher buying out a rival publisher. *Vertical integration* is when a company takes over another company which is responsible for one stage of the production cycle, e.g. a newspaper company buying out a newsagents' chain or a paper manufacturer. Such processes of integration are occurring almost daily in the media, as can be detected by a quick survey of the industry's trade magazines. What they mean in practice is that mainstream media production is characterised by a growing concentration of ownership. In all the media industries, a few (between three and five) large companies control a sizeable share of the market (Table 6.1).

Table 6.1 Concentration of media ownership

Market share of top five companies in selected media sectors

	%
ITV Programmes (Transmissions)	45.5
National dailies (circulation)	95
National Sundays (circulation)	92
National & Regional dailies (circulation)	75
Books (sales)	40
Single records (sales)	58
LPs, cassettes, and compact discs	60
Video rentals	66

Sources IBA Annual Report and Accounts (1985-6); 32nd Annual Report of the Press Council 1985 (1986); Jordan's Review of Marketing and Publishing Data (1984); British Phonograph Yearbook (1986); British Videogram Association ★Gallup, (1986).
Source: Curran and Seaton 1991

Often these companies own shares in several media sectors and on an international scale, in which case they are referred to as media conglomerates. A prime example is Rupert Murdoch's News Corporation (Figure 6.1).

The most recent development has been the vertical integration of Japanese hardware electronics companies (manufacturers of CD players, televisions, computers etc.) and American 'software' entertainment companies (producers of films, television programmes, music etc.) Two examples are Sony's takeover of Columbia and Matsushita's takeover of MCA/Universal.

These media conglomerates are in a much stronger position to take advantage of the growing international media markets (see Chapter 8 for a discussion of globalisation) as well as exploiting opportunities to sell their own products across the various sectors of the corporation. Such multimarketing is a growing media phenomenon. Of *Batman*'s estimated $500 million revenue, between a third and a half came from licensed merchandising, such as T-shirts and toys. More

6.1 *The Guardian*, 2 August 1993. © The Guardian

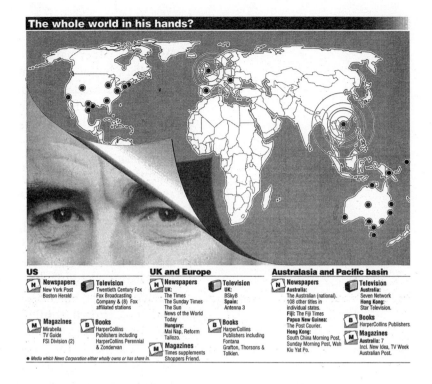

specifically within the media, the profits to be made from a film's release may be multiplied through sales of accompanying music soundtrack, video sell through, paperback novel, television spin-off rights etc.

JURASSIC SCHLOCK

Next Friday, Universal Pictures will release *Jurassic Park* in Britain, directed by Steven Spielberg and starring Jeff Goldblum and Laura Dern. Noteworthy for its $60m price tag, *Jurassic Park* is also the centrepiece of one of the most wide-ranging merchandising efforts in film history. In addition to multimillion-dollar tie-ins with McDonald's and Choice Hotels, Universal and Spielberg have, in their words, 'carefully selected' a 'family of licensees', which will turn out more than a thousand trademarked products carrying the *Jurassic Park* name. The items below are from the list of products for which companies have acquired UK licences.

Jurassic Park holographic watches
Jurassic Park plush 'fun' slippers
Jurassic Park vinyl model dinosaur kits
Jurassic Park flasks with integrated straws
Jurassic Park party crackers
Jurassic Park chocolate eggs

Jurassic Park fantasy balls
Jurassic Park video game gloves
Jurassic Park paper napkins
Jurassic Park balloons attached to sticks
Jurassic Park arcade-style pinball machines
Jurassic Park swivel office chairs
Jurassic Park children's socks (4–12 years)
Jurassic Park hair care bags
Jurassic Park boys' briefs
Jurassic Park imitation credit cards
Jurassic Park 'glow in the dark' stickers
Jurassic Park sweet popcorn
Jurassic Park bed headboards
Jurassic Park Christmas cards
Jurassic Park nylon flight jackets with reversible linings
Jurassic Park Celebration Novelty Boxed Cakes (Marks and
      Spencer only)
Jurassic Park fruit-flavoured moulded ice lollies
Jurassic Park toothbrush and toothbrush holders
Jurassic Park metal TV trays with plastic folding legs
Jurassic Park building bricks with electronic micro-chips
      creating dinosaur sound-effects

                                    The Independent on Sunday, *11 July 1993*

---

activity **6.1**   Undertake your own research into the multimarketing of a
well-publicised (or hyped) new media product. Try in particular to identify the various media spin-offs such as supporting
books, music and videos.

A similar example of media secondary marketing is integral to
the concept of synergy – the selling of two or more compati-
ble products simultaneously. In the late 1980s, a series of 'classic' pop songs from the past were used to create the desired
atmosphere and mood for the advertising of Levi 501 jeans on
television. Apart from the massive boost to sales of 501 jeans,
the revived songs invariably recharted, often reaching number
1. This pattern has been repeated with recent films such as
Robin Hood, Prince of Thieves (Bryan Adams, *Everything I Do*,
topping the singles chart for nine weeks) and *The Bodyguard*
(Whitney Houston's *I Will Always Love You* also reaching
number 1).

Finally, media conglomerates are also able to take advantage
of their crossmedia ownership to promote products within the

company. For example, Rupert Murdoch's British newspapers have been consistent supporters of his satellite station, BSkyB. Indeed, at one time the chief executive of BSkyB, Andrew Neil, was also editor of *The Sunday Times*.

Ownership and Power

What has concerned many people about the trend towards concentration of ownership and the rise of international conglomerates is the potential for using media outlets to exercise potential power and influence. Marxist writers have particularly emphasised how, under capitalism, the property-owning class promote and defend their own interests at the expense of the rest of society – the thesis of political economy. The search for profit is seen as the key arbiter of what is produced in the media, first in the economic sense of achieving surplus revenue and secondly in the ideological sense of those values and beliefs which support capitalism. (This echoes the hegemonic model outlined in Chapter 4.)

There is little doubt that the major companies do exercise their economic muscles in squeezing, or taking over, new competition. This might involve, for example, undercutting the competitor's prices and advertising rates, or increasing the marketing budget. When the *Daily Star* was launched in 1978, *The Sun* implemented all these strategies and almost managed to deliver its new rival a fatal blow. From the consumer's point of view, the net result is less choice and diversity.

As to the ideological effect of concentrated ownership, it is difficult to arrive at a conclusive judgement. Curran and Seaton (1991) argue that with respect to the press, owners have sought to promote business interests in general, usually by ensuring their newspaper supported the Conservative party. In return, newspaper editors and proprietors have been given honorary titles (e.g. Sir Larry Lamb, ex-editor of *The Sun*, and Sir David English, ex-editor of the *Daily Mail*).

The proprietor most notorious in recent times for his interventionism is Rupert Murdoch. His admiration for Margaret Thatcher was strongly echoed in *The Sun* despite the fact that the majority of its readers were not Conservative voters. On acquiring *The Times* and *The Sunday Times* in 1981, the editors of both titles came under strong pressure to endorse Thatcherite policies, and duly obliged or resigned (e.g. Harold Evans from *The Times* in 1983).

Even so-called 'independent' newspapers do not seem to be immune from such pressures. While *The Observer* was owned by Lonrho, its editor, Donald Trelford, often allowed the paper to carry stories favourable to the activities of Tiny Rowland, Lonrho's chairman (e.g. his attempt to take over the Fraser Group, owner of Harrods department store). See Figure 6.2.

6.2 The *Daily Mirror*, 6 November 1991

Within days the *Daily Mirror* was savagely criticising its former 'saviour' owner in the light of revelations about his corrupt misuse of *Daily Mirror* pension funds (the paper had suppressed all criticism of Maxwell while he was its owner).

The Limits of Ownership Power

The profit drive in media industries is not always consistent with upholding dominant ideologies. Rupert Murdoch, famous for shifting his publications towards the political right, has allowed some of his titles to advocate minority or ideologically ambiguous views. In 1991, the Scottish edition of *The Sun*, anxious to boost its relatively poor sales north of the border, switched its political support to the Scottish Nationalists. Meanwhile, in 1993, *Today* newspaper, still in search of a clear identity, moved leftwards towards the Labour Party. In the music industry, few companies have hesitated to release and promote songs containing politically radical or unorthodox ideas if there was a reasonable chance of such songs being commercially successful. In the late 1960s, CBS records in the

USA had a large roster of 'countercultural' artists, many of whose music expressed anti-Vietnam war sentiments, and yet CBS itself was part of a corporation with investments in military expenditure.

Unlike the other consumer commodities, media products can never be uniformly standardised. This makes control of the market virtually impossible to attain. Nowhere is this more apparent than in the film industry, where the size of the budget, the casting of stars and the intensity of publicity cannot guarantee a profitable outcome, such is the unpredictability of the audience response. Contrast the fate of *Ishtar*, a comedy film starring Dustin Hoffman and Warren Beatty which lost $37 million in 1987, with *Rocky*, which starred the then unknown Sylvester Stallone in 1976 and made $56 million, having cost only $1.5 million to make. There are numerous similar instances from across the media of audiences supporting or rejecting media products in a seemingly capricious manner. Prominent recent examples include *Viz* (comic), *The Darling Buds of May* (television) and Classic FM (radio), all of whose popular appeal took most people by surprise.

It is far easier for major companies to dominate the market when the capital costs of investment (especially in technology) are high. The potential for would-be rivals to BSkyB is modest, given the hundreds of millions of pounds necessary for starting up a satellite service. In contrast, making a pop record or launching a fanzine is within the means of most people who might wish to take a small step into such media markets.

Given the size and complexity of much media production today, the actual *control* of such production usually lies with the professional who has the requisite technical expertise. Such professional autonomy is discussed below.

Market freedoms are not unfettered. Not only are there monopoly controls to prevent a single company exercising complete control in the market, but all the media are subject to regulatory frameworks often backed up by legal sanctions. These are discussed below.

While acknowledging the variety of institutional determinants of media production, most commentators would probably stress the economic forces as being of greatest significance. However, the phenomenon can be interpreted in different ways. As we have seen, hegemonic theorists would relate it to the structure of economic inequality in society and the perpetuation of powerful group interests, particularly via the direct or indirect influence of owners. Pluralist thinkers would rather wish to emphasise the sovereignty of the audience, with media production acting as a barometer of changing tastes and preferences. Diverse audience interests are reflected in a diversity of media choice.

But how effective are the media in fulfilling the 'demands of the market' (if these can ever be known)? As stated above, the larger media conglomerates have the power to squeeze the new competition and thus keep control of the market. Furthermore, audiences are not of equal commercial interest to media producers.

Advertising Revenue

Apart from revenue gained from sales of newspapers, magazines, videos etc., the other main source of revenue for the media is advertising. For commercial television and radio, advertising is the lifeblood of the industry. What concerns advertisers using the media is reaching the target audience, i.e. those people most likely to buy the product in question. Consequently, there is little point advertising Armani clothes in *The Sun* or MFI furniture in the *Financial Times*. The size of audience is obviously of interest, especially on television, where advertising rates are in direct proportion to numbers of viewers as revealed in the ratings. As a consequence, the profitability of ITV and Channel Four, as well as independent local radio (ILR), is dependent on the ability to achieve good viewing and listening figures. This in turn has implications for the type of programming scheduled. Those programmes which have a broad popular appeal, e.g. soap opera, films, sitcoms etc., invariably predominate over programmes which are seen as attracting minority audiences.

The second criterion for advertisers is the social profile (or demographics) of the audience in terms of social class, gender and age. Of least interest to most advertisers are older working-class people, who have the lowest disposable income. This is particularly significant for those media productions with a well-defined audience profile. The more 'upmarket' the audience, the easier it is to attract advertisers and hence achieve profitability. Consequently, there is a greater choice for younger, more middle-class audiences (Table 6.2).

activity 6.2

From listing the adverts which appear within different television programmes (at varying times of day) on ITV and Channel Four, see if there is any pattern which indicates a target audience for that programme (age, gender, class etc.).

A similar exercise can be undertaken with newspapers and magazines, whose readership is usually more well-defined in terms of social profile.

Table 6.2 Readership of national daily newspapers by sex, social class and age, 1993

	Sex			Social grade		Age		Readership	Circulation
	Total	Men	Women	ABC1	C2DE	15–44	45+	(millions)	(millions)
				(percentage of adults)					
Daily newspapers									
The Sun	21.4	24.6	18.5	12.7	28.6	24.9	17.6	9.72	3.52
Daily Mirror	16.9	19.4	14.6	10.5	22.2	16.4	17.5	7.67	2.68
Daily Record	4.3	4.6	4.0	2.9	5.5	4.7	3.9	1.96	0.75
Daily Mail	10.4	10.9	10.0	13.9	7.5	9.2	11.7	4.72	1.77
Daily Express	8.5	9.1	7.9	10.8	6.6	7.2	10.0	3.85	1.50
The Daily Telegraph	6.1	7.0	5.3	11.4	1.7	4.3	8.1	2.77	1.02
Daily Star	5.3	7.1	3.7	2.6	7.6	7.0	3.4	2.42	0.77
Today	3.9	5.0	2.9	3.5	4.3	4.6	3.2	1.78	0.54
The Guardian	3.3	3.7	2.9	5.7	1.4	4.0	2.6	1.51	0.42
The Independent	2.7	3.2	2.1	4.9	0.8	3.3	1.9	1.21	0.35
The Times	2.6	3.0	2.3	5.1	0.6	2.9	2.4	1.19	0.37
Financial Times	1.7	2.4	1.1	3.3	0.4	1.9	1.5	0.78	0.29
Any daily newspaper	61.8	66.6	57.5	61.5	62.1	59.5	64.5	28.01	13.97

Source: National Readership Survey, Jan – June 1993, Audit Bureau of Circulation, Jan – June 1993

This distribution of revenue from advertising also has implications for the political bias of national newspapers. Because newspapers like the *Daily Mirror* need a large circulation to flourish, they tend to ignore hard political news and focus on entertainment values. More in-depth political coverage is left to the more upmarket tabloids (like the *Daily Mail*) or the broadsheets, whose more affluent middle-class readership prefers conservative political values. In the past, this has meant the closure of a Labour supporting paper like the *Daily Herald* (which folded in 1964 with a circulation five times that of *The Times*) and the Liberal *News Chronicle* (whose circulation equalled that of *The Daily Telegraph* when it closed in 1960). Even the *Daily Mirror's* commitment to the Labour Party seems threatened following the death of Robert Maxwell in 1991, and the attempt to make the paper an attractive, commercial proposition to new owners in the face of intense competition from *The Sun*.

There is every danger that, in the future, the more advertisers are keen to pinpoint their target audiences via the media, the more those audiences unattractive to advertisers will tend to be ignored. This is because the trend is towards *narrowcasting* (or niche targeting) in the media – i.e. supplying customised services to specialist audience groups: as with other market-based services, those with most disposable income exercise greatest choice.

INSTITUTIONAL DETERMINANTS: *PROFESSIONAL AUTONOMY*

Although ownership of media companies makes possible power over production from the point of view of allocating resources (capital investment, budgets etc.), the day-to-day management of media organisations in the operational sense lies with media professionals. Of course, in small-scale enterprises the owners and controllers of production may well be the same people, but most organisations require a division of labour based on specialised areas of skill and technical expertise.

Such skills and expertise are often elevated to an occupational ideal, making it possible to lay claim to professionalism. Most media organisations require new recruits to undertake considerable in-house training on top of any formal qualifications already obtained. The ethos of the organisation – what it stands for and how it goes about things, together with the 'house style' of production – are central to the process of occupational socialisation. The ensuing collective thinking and practice provide a degree of solidarity from which external threats (owners, the government, the public etc.) can be resisted. This also has implications for the boundaries of creative freedom within media production. The 'correct' or conventional way of doing something becomes enshrined in professional practice until, and if, someone is bold or strong enough to break or question the 'rules'.

The freedom to deviate from the accepted codes and conventions will very much depend on a previous hierarchical position. In cinema and television, producers and directors exercise the greatest control over the content and style of films and programmes. Some film directors have been seen as 'auteurs' or artistic authors, able to imbue their films with a personal vision or look, e.g. Orson Welles, Alfred Hitchcock, David Lynch etc. However, media production, not least film, is essentially a co-operative venture, necessitating considerable mutual assistance and interdependence (Figure 6.3).

In newspapers and magazines, editors are in the strongest position to influence the shape and direction of the publication. Some individual editors have made a recognisable impression on their newspaper or magazine's identity, e.g. *The Sun* under the editorship of Kelvin MacKenzie:

> But it was in the afternoon, as the paper built up to its creative climax of going to press, that the real performance would begin. MacKenzie would burst through the door after lunch with his cry of 'Whaddya got for me?' and the

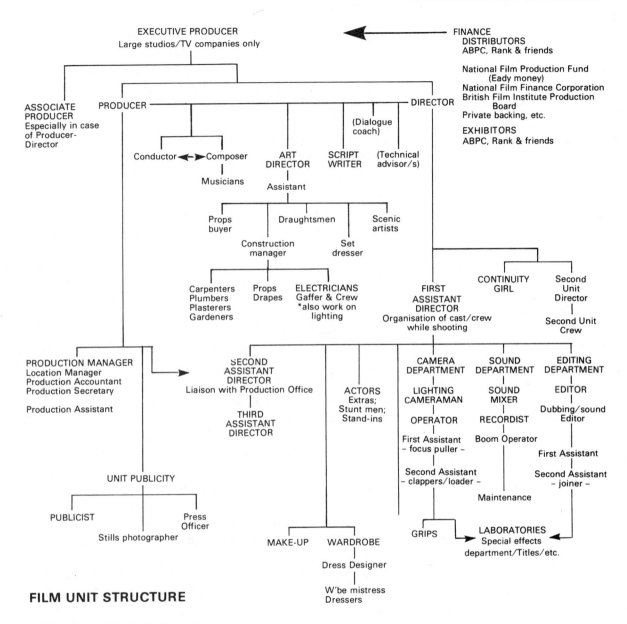

FILM UNIT STRUCTURE

6.3 *Making Sense of the Media*, Comedia
1985

heat would be on. He had total control – not just over the
front page, but over every page lead going right through
the paper. Shrimsley was remembered as a fast and furious
corrector of proofs, but MacKenzie was even faster,
drawing up layouts, plucking headline after headline out of
the air, and all the time driving towards the motto he
hammered into them all: 'SHOCK AND AMAZE ON EVERY
PAGE.' . . .

True to the code of sarff London MacKenzie also wanted
to be surrounded by 'made men', who had proved
themselves by pulling off some outrageous stunt at the

expense of the opposition. One way of becoming a made man was to phone the *Mirror* and ask for the 'stone' where the final versions of pages were assembled for the presses. The trick was to imitate another member of the *Mirror* staff to fool the stone sub into revealing the front-page splash. One features exec became a made man by walking across Fleet Street into the *Express* and stealing some crucial pictures from the library. Hacks refusing to get involved in this sort of behaviour were suspect – falling into the category of those who were not fully with him, and could therefore be presumed to be against him.

Chippendale and Horrie (1990)

The Limits of Freedom

The ability of media professionals to achieve autonomy is subject to two key constraints:

1 *Profitability*. Few owners of the media are content to maintain a 'hands-off' policy if there is not a healthy flow of profit or at least the prospect of one. 'Creative' film directors are only indulged by Hollywood studios if their last film was a blockbuster. Virtually no part of the media is now immune from economic pressures. The BBC's decision to axe *Eldorado*, their expensive soap opera, in 1993 was largely due to a need to bolster their falling share of the ratings (and thus strengthen their case for the continuation of the licence fee).

Equally, media professionals may be trapped by success. Productions with popular appeal become formularised, with writers, editors, actors etc. working in assembly-line 'factory' conditions, allowing little scope for experimentation or risk taking (e.g. television soap operas).

When it comes to a showdown between proprietor and professional, the former nearly always prevails. Even the ebullient Kelvin MacKenzie of *The Sun* is known for his subservience to Rupert Murdoch, and prior to his death Robert Maxwell was intolerant of any dissidence within his corporation. Curran and Seaton (1991) can only find one occasion when journalists actually succeeded in decisively defeating their proprietor (when *The Observer*'s staff resisted Lonrho's boss, Tiny Rowland, who tried to change the newspaper's liberal stance towards South African politics).

2 *Regulation*. On the one hand professional independence is actually bolstered by self-regulation. Like doctors and lawyers, media professionals operate within codes of practice designed to prevent unacceptable standards of production or irresponsible behaviour. If members adhere to such codes, then there are less likely to be attempts made to

Which of these clauses seems to have been most ignored by newspapers (especially tabloid) in recent years?

Why should clause 18, 'the public interest', be the subject of so much controversy?

impose conditions from outside the industry (e.g. by the government).

However, not surprisingly, there is limited state or public faith in any organisation's or industry's attempts to police itself, and all the media are subject to a variety of external controls either enshrined in the law and/or administered by external, independent bodies (Figure 6.4).

Code of Practice

The Press Complaints Commission are charged with enforcing the following Code of Practice which was framed by the newspaper and periodical industry and ratified by the Press Complaints Commission on 30 June 1993.

All members of the press have a duty to maintain the highest professional and ethical standards. In doing so, they should have regard to the provisions of this Code of Practice

1 Accuracy

i) Newspapers and periodicals should take care not to publish inaccurate, misleading or distorted material.
ii) Whenever it is recognised that a significant inaccuracy, misleading statement or distorted report has been published, it should be corrected promptly and with due prominence.
iii) An apology should be published whenever appropriate.
iv) A newspaper or periodical should always report fairly and accurately the outcome of an action for defamation to which it has been a party.

2 Opportunity to reply

A fair opportunity for reply to inaccuracies should be given to individuals or organisations when reasonably called for.

and to safeguarding the public's right to know.

Editors are responsible for the actions of journalists employed by their publications. They should also satisfy themselves as far as possible that material accepted from non-staff members was obtained in accordance with this Code.

While recognising that this involves a substantial element of self-restraint by editors and journalists, it is

3 Comment, conjecture and fact

Newspapers, whilst free to be partisan, should distinguish clearly between comment, conjecture and fact.

4 Privacy

Intrusions and enquiries into an individual's private life without his or her consent including the use of long-lens photography to take pictures of people on private property without their consent are not generally acceptable and publication can only be justified when in the public interest.

Note: Private property is defined as any private residence, together with its garden and outbuildings, but excluding any adjacent fields or parkland. In addition, hotel bedrooms (but not other areas in

designed to be acceptable in the context of a system of self-regulation. The Code applies in the spirit as well as in the letter.

It is the responsibility of editors to co-operate as swiftly as possible in PCC enquiries.

Any publication which is criticised by the PCC under one of the following clauses is duty bound to print the adjudication which follows in full and with due prominence.

a hotel) and those parts of a hospital or nursing home where patients are treated or accommodated.

5 Listening Devices

Unless justified by public interest, journalists should not obtain or publish material obtained by using clandestine listening devices or by intercepting private telephone conversations.

6 Hospitals

i) Journalists or photographers making enquiries at hospitals or similar institutions should identify themselves to a responsible official and obtain permission before entering non-public areas.
ii) The restrictions on intruding into privacy are particularly relevant

to enquiries about individuals in hospitals or similar institutions.

7 Misrepresentation

i) Journalists should not generally obtain or seek to obtain information or pictures through misrepresentation or subterfuge.
ii) Unless in the public interest, documents or photographs should be removed only with the express consent of the owner.
iii) Subterfuge can be justified only in the public interest and only when material cannot be obtained by any other means.

8 Harassment

i) Journalists should neither obtain nor seek to obtain information or pictures through intimidation or harassment.
ii) Unless their enquiries are in the public interest, journalists should not photograph individuals on private property without their consent; should not persist in telephoning or questioning individuals after having been asked to desist; should not remain on their property after having been asked to leave and should not follow them.
iii) It is the responsibility of editors to ensure that these requirements are carried out.

9 Payments for articles

Payment or offers of payment for stories, pictures or information, should not be made directly or through agents to witnesses or potential witnesses in current or criminal proceedings or to people engaged in crime or to their associate – which includes family, friends, neighbours and colleagues – except where the material concerned ought to be published in the public interest and the payment is necessary for this to be done.

10 Intrusion into grief or shock

In cases involving personal grief or shock, enquiries should be carried out and approaches made with sympathy and discretion.

11 Innocent relatives and friends

Unless it is contrary to the public's right to know, the press should generally avoid identifying relatives or friends of persons convicted or accused of crime.

12 Interviewing or photographing children

i) Journalists should not normally interview or photograph children under the age of 16 on subjects involving the personal welfare of the child, in the absence of or without the consent of a parent or other adult who is responsible for the children.
ii) Children should not be approached or photographed while at school without the permission of the school authorities.

13 Children in sex cases

1) The press should not, even where the law does not prohibit it, identify children under the age of 16 who are involved in cases concerning sexual offences, whether as victims, or as witnesses or defendants.
2) In any press report of a case involving a sexual offence against a child–

i) The adult should be identified.
ii) The term "incest" where applicable should not be used.
iii) The offence should be described as "serious offences against young children" or similar appropriate wording.
iv) The child should not be identified.
v) Care should be taken that nothing in the report implies the relationship between the accused and the child.

14 Victims of crime

The press should not identify victims of sexual assault or publish material likely to contribute to such identification unless, by law, they are free to do so.

15 Discrimination

i) The press should avoid prejudicial or prejorative

reference to a person's race, colour, religion, sex or sexual orientation or to any physical or mental illness or handicap.
ii) It should avoid publishing details of a person's race, colour, religion, sex or sexual orientation, unless these are directly relevant to the story.

16 Financial journalism

i) Even where the law does not prohibit it, journalists should not use for their own profit, financial information they receive in advance of its general publication, nor should they pass such information to others.
ii) They should not write about shares or securities in whose performance they know that they or their close families have a significant financial interest, without disclosing the interest to the editor or financial editor.
iii) They should not buy or sell, either directly or through nominees or agents, shares or securities about which they have written recently or about which they intend to write in the near future.

17 Confidential sources

Journalists have a moral obligation to protect confidential sources of information.

18 The public interest

Clauses 4,5,7,8 and 9 create exceptions which may be covered by invoking the public interest. For the purposes of this code that is most easily defined as:
i) Detecting or exposing crime or a serious misdemeanour.
ii) Protecting public health and safety.
iii) Preventing the public from being misled by some statement or action of an individual or organisation.

In any cases raising issues beyond these three definitions the Press Complaints Commission will require a full explanation by the editor of the publication involved, seeking to demonstrate how the public interest was served.

Media Institutions and Production **201**

INSTITUTIONAL DETERMINANTS: EXTERNAL REGULATIONS

The media operate relatively freely in countries like Britain, compared to those under more repressive regimes such as China. Nevertheless, there are a plethora of laws and regulations which act as constraints on media production. Most of these emanate from the state, and are kept in reserve for when the media step out of line. We need to distinguish between general laws which apply to all the media, and more specific regulations relevant to individual media institutions.

Political Controls

The government rarely intervenes directly to censor the media, as this would be perceived as anti-democratic. It reserves that right for national emergencies or crises such as wartime. For example, in 1939 Winston Churchill banned the *Daily Worker*, a communist newspaper, as it was seen as a threat to a united war effort.

More recently, during the Falklands and Gulf Wars, the Ministry of Defence (MoD) vetted all news reports. This frequently led to censorship in the case of reporting the Falklands War, whereas in the Gulf War the MoD guidelines generally produced self-censorship in reports (Figure 6.5).

The Official Secrets Act, passed originally in 1911 and updated in 1988, allows the media to be prosecuted for disclosing information about the security services, defence and the conduct of international relations. It is no defence to claim any leak of information is in the public interest. In the 1980s, a number of famous prosecutions occurred under the act, including that of the journalist Duncan Campbell, whose *Secret Society* television series for the BBC contained an episode on Britain's satellite spy system (called Zircon) which was banned. The affair included MI5 visiting a BBC office in Glasgow in a dawn raid. The Official Secrets Act is criticised by many as being a means by which the state hides its actions from proper public accountability.

Equally controversial is the Prevention of Terrorism Act. Journalists who make contact with 'terrorist' or illegal organisations risk prosecution. In 1988, it was extended in the form of a specific ban on the broadcasting of the voices of any representative of proscribed Northern Ireland organisations and their political offshoots. It is still possible to report the words of such representatives but only if dubbed or with subtitles. Broadcasters have largely adhered to the spirits of the law, thus seriously curtailing opportunities for organisations like the IRA to put their point of view on television and radio.

6.5 *The Guardian*, 29 January 1991.
© The Guardian

MoD guidelines for the Gulf War

Fourteen categories (covering 32 subjects) of information cannot be published or broadcast without talking to the Ministry of Defence. These include:

- Numbers of troops, ships, aircraft and other equipment: specific locations of British or Allied military units; future military plans.

- Photographs showing locations of military forces. Photographs of wounded soldiers.

- Information about casualties should not be broadcast until next of kin contacted.

- Specific information on British ships and planes which have been hit.

- Information on how intelligence is collected.

Not the full story . . .

First World War (1914–18)

Strict censorship began in August 1914. A government-appointed officer, Colonel Sir Ernest Swinton, wrote 'eye-witness' reports for the press, but they gave few deatils.

Newspaper proprietors Lord Northcliffe and Lord Beaverbrook were among those working closely with the government.

Second World War (1939–45)

The Ministry of Information employed, at one stage, 999 people to turn 'news' into an anti-German crusade. No British soldier could be named. The true extent of Japan's attack on Pearl Harbor was hidden until after 1945.

Vietnam War (1954–75)

The first television war: American journalists reported for the first time without direct censorship from the army. The US military issued general guidelines which journalists were expected to follow, but media criticism, especially of the 1968 Tet Offensive, helped turn American public opinion against the war.

Falklands War (1982)

Twenty-nine carefully selected British reporters were kept under strict Ministry of Defence control. Reporters, who had to agree to censorship, were told what was happening after the event. Some reports had to pass through three stages of vetting before they could be released.

Anti-monopoly Controls

Fears of excessive concentration of media ownership should be allayed by the existence of legislation designed to maintain fair competition in the market place. Broadcasters, in particular, have been subject to strict control, preventing any one company owning more than one ITV franchise or owning both a national newspaper and television station. However, these controls are continually being eroded. Rupert Murdoch's takeover of national newspapers (he owned five national titles in 1993) and his monopolisation of British satellite television have been allowed to proceed without resistance from the Monopolies Commission.

Moral Standards

In 1990, the Obscene Publications Act was extended to include all the media. It is designed to uphold standards of taste and decency. Any material thought liable to 'deprave and corrupt' audiences is subject to prosecution. In the case of pornographic videos and magazines, this may be relatively straightforward, but it is frequently difficult to achieve any consensus on what is likely to 'deprave and corrupt'. This raises issues concerning not only what qualifies as obscene, but also how it can be demonstrated that audiences will be corrupted.

Libel

There have been numerous well-publicised cases of individuals being awarded damages against media organisations found guilty of issuing unjustified or harmful statements about the individual in question. The satirical magazine *Private Eye* is perhaps the most frequent offender as a result of its willingness to criticise and make fun of the rich and powerful. The problem is that it is the rich and powerful who are most able to take advantage of the protection offered by the libel law, through their ability to pay the huge court costs which such cases often incur. Robert Maxwell's success in not being exposed before his death as a corrupt businessman was certainly aided by the frequency with which he threatened his accusers with legal proceedings.

Each area of the media is also subject to more specific forms of control, either by separate legislation or by regulatory bodies.

- *Cinema/video.* The British Board of Film Classification issues certificates for all cinema and video releases, applying the categories U, PG, 12, 15 and 18, plus UC for video, meaning it is particularly suitable for children. Controls are stricter for video because of the possibility of young children viewing films rented by adults or older children.
- *Newspapers.* The Press Complaints Commission (see Figure 6.5) exists primarily to consider complaints made by the public about the accuracy and standards of reporting in newspapers. It also issues guidelines for responsible behaviour and monitors how well the press adheres to these guidelines. There has been criticism of the ineffectiveness of the Commission and regular calls for stronger legal provision to prevent what is seen by some as excessive behaviour by some newspapers (e.g. publishing private telephone calls allegedly involving members of the royal family).
- *Broadcasting.* Television and radio are subject to the strongest controls of any media, for technological and political reasons (see Chapter 2). The BBC's licence is renewed every ten years, and the licence fee set by the government, which also appoints the board of governors. Their role is to ensure that the BBC fulfils its obligations as laid down by law, and

if necessary to intervene if individual programmes are deemed to exceed the BBC's remit, e.g. the banning of *Real Lives* (see p. 125).

Non-BBC television services, including ITV, Channel Four, cable and satellite, are licensed and regulated by the Independent Television Commission (ITC). A similar role for radio is played by the Radio Authority. Both the ITC and the Radio Authority publish codes to which licensees must adhere, covering programmes, advertising and sponsorship. Viewers or listeners may complain to either body, which, if feeling the complaint to be justified, may take action, such as requesting a broadcast apology.

The public can also complain to two further bodies, the Broadcasting Standards Council, whose role is to consider complaints about violence, sex, taste and decency, and the Broadcasting Complaints Commission, which deals with accusations of unfair treatment or invasion of privacy. Both organisations can insist their findings are published.

- *Advertising.* The Advertising Standards Authority (ASA) tries to ensure that advertisers live up to their much-quoted ideal of producing adverts that are 'honest, decent, legal and true'. They issue codes covering matters like cigarette advertising, monitor the flow of adverts being produced and respond to public complaints – sometimes by demanding the change or removal of an advert. Such requests are normally heeded, but this was not the case in 1992, when Benetton ignored the ASA. In a campaign which had depended on images of an increasingly provocative nature, Benetton caused most offence when they used a picture of a man suffering from AIDS at the moment of his death. Many people complained that it was immoral to use such an image within a commercial context, in this case promoting a brand name of clothing.

INDEPENDENT PRODUCTION

What is Independent Production?

To be independent implies autonomy and freedom from external constraints. In the context of media production, it is most often seen as meaning not under the direct control of a larger organisation, be that commercial or governmental. As such, independence carries a positive status, and may even be invoked in order to lay claim to being more trustworthy or authentic. *The Independent* newspaper's advertising campaign used the phrase 'It is ... are you?' when the paper was launched in 1986. This was designed to draw attention to both the absence of a corporate owner, such as Murdoch's News International Corporation which owns *The Times*, and its editorial policy of political neutrality.

However, complete independence in media production is virtually impossible, as the support or co-operation of other organisations in the cycle of productions and distribution is necessary if any kind of 'mass' audience is to be reached. What is more, there is no agreed criteria by which any media organisation can be labelled independent. 'Independent television' most often refers to the ITV companies holding the regional franchises, many of which are large media corporations, whereas 'independent video' is normally associated with small-scale, grassroots production, often involving voluntary labour. Nevertheless, there are some principles to which most independent media production conforms, to varying degrees:

- A *democratic/collectivist process of production*. This may take the form of a workers' co-operative, an absence of hierarchy, participative decision making etc. Often audiences may be actively involved at both a consultative and productive level, e.g. fanzines.
- A *targeting of minority audiences*. Audiences perceived as being ignored by mainstream media include local, ethnic, political and subcultural groups. Such groups tend to be marginalised in terms of power and influence in society and may lack economic clout (and hence media profitability).
- A *commitment to innovation or experimentation in form and/or content* – so-called alternative media. This 'radicalism' can be manifested in experimental design and rule breaking within media conventions, as well as in a campaigning, political mode of address, which challenges the status quo, e.g. environmental action.

All three elements can be seen as being in contrast to mainstream or dominant media production practice, i.e. that which is widely accepted and recognised as 'the norm', and which is most available for audiences to consume. Only when independent production 'takes off' in popularity does it come to the attention of the wider public, e.g. the adult comic *Viz*. Most of the time, it is produced and distributed haphazardly or within a narrow social channel, access to which must be actively sought by audiences, e.g. through mail order or specialist group meetings.

From the radical press of the nineteenth century, through workers' film societies of the 1930s, to the 'underground' hippie press of the 1960s and up to the 1980s/1990s pirate radio stations, there has been a thriving tradition of independent production. The dynamics of such movements can be examined more closely by considering specific examples.

Football Fanzines

Fanzines can be traced back to the 1940s when, in the USA, specialist magazines were distributed to fans of various cults like science fiction. The contemporary essence of fanzines is that they are produced by and for fans. Prior to the recent boom in football fanzines, music fanzines flourished in the late 1970s and early 1980s in the wake of the punk/new wave movement. It was estimated that in the 1988–9 season, approximately one million copies of football fanzines were sold, although most individual magazines averaged between 200 and 1,000 circulation (Leicester University research). A few of the less parochial titles, such as *When Saturday Comes*, have gained access to high-street newsagents. What, then, is their appeal?

A key factor is that they provide a forum for the views of fans hitherto ignored, especially by those running the game, who are often perceived as being 'out of touch' and bent on ruining the traditional experience of supporters standing on the terraces. The official view of the club is usually expressed

6.6 *Hammer*, Official Matchday magazine, 14 January 1992

No. 30 £1

Over Land and Sea

WEST HAM'S NO.1 FANZINE

The objective West Ham fanzine that is finding it very hard to be objective lately!

GOING DOWN
GOING DOWN
GOING DOWN!!!

West Ham United Football Club
AGAIN
The laughing stock of English Football

PAGE 4 **JANUARY 1992**

VIEWPOINT
THE EDITOR SAYS

WEST HAM UNITED?
DON'T MAKE ME LAUGH!!

The time has now arrived to stop playing games here at Upton Park, and I am not talking about football, it's a good job that I'm not considering the utterly disgraceful scenes that we have witnessed of late! The games that must be stopped are the ones currently being played by the board.

I don't feel that this present unrest will ever die down while the present board of directors remain in power of our stagnant, rotting excuse for a football club.

West Ham United Football Club are in a state of turmoil that is like no other ever witnessed before. We are used to having a football team capable of achieving things and we are used to the team never delivering things, this is something synonymous with being a West Ham supporter.

We have had plenty of players here who are absolutely pathetic and basically unskilled, some however, try their hardest to achieve success for us. We all know that not everyone is a natural born star, and we don't expect them all to be, but at best we have respect for those that give us their all.

Unfortunately we do, at the moment, have a team that *can* play a bit but won't and that is what really pisses me off more than any other. At the moment, with only a few exceptions, we have a team that are a bloody disgrace, a right load of bottlers. If I was in charge I would drop most of them and bring in the kids, I'm absolutely certain that they would be more comitted and show more pride. I won't waste any more time going on about what we already know, as it only gets me at it, thinking about what should be happening.

I would say one thing though and that is aimed at Billy Bonds. You know that you need new players but the board won't give you any money, tell them to poke their job then.

6.7 *Over Land and Sea,* January 1992

Compare the official West Ham programme with the fanzine as representations of the club and its relationship to the fans.

via the club programme, which voices very different sentiments to those expressed in fanzines (Figures 6.6 and 6.7).

Another attractive ingredient for the fans is the 'inside' humour, which draws on folklore, gossip and affectionate lampooning of players and rival fans. Fanzines for unfashionable and poorly supported clubs generate a participative camaraderie and sense of collective identity despite, or because of, the employment of basic, sometimes primitive, production techniques (Figure 6.8).

Independent Film and Video

Whereas fanzines can be produced at minimal c⁓st with low-tech facilities, film production requires consid⸺ ⸺ ⸺ital investment. Added to that are problems of d⸺ exhibition not faced by the major product⸺ which have automatic access to cinema ch⸺ when there is vertical integration).

The fact that independent film and vide⸺ at all is largely due to some kind of subsi⸺ the past, this has been from state-suppor⸺

Arts Council or the British Film Institute, but increasingly it has been television which has provided the key investment for independent British films. Channel Four's backing was vital for the stream of 1980s' productions such as *My Beautiful Laundrette* and *A Letter to Brezhnev*. The BBC has followed suit with films such as *Truly Madly Deeply*, a sort of British version of *Ghost*. While reflecting aspects of British culture not found in the Hollywood-dominated contemporary cinema, most of these films employed a narrative form and cinematic style which were very conventional, albeit on a modest scale compared to Hollywood. This is not surprising, since the primary motivation in making these films was commercial, i.e. to avoid excessive costs and, if possible, make a profit.

More radical independent cinema has emerged from film and video workshops, often rooted in local communities or interest groups eager to provide an alternative voice to that of mainstream cinema and television. Sometimes it has been possible for such productions to gain exposure via a loose-knit network of independent film distributors and exhibitors. With the increasing use of video as a means of communication, this has become less of a problem. For example, *The Miners*

Campaign Tapes, produce during the coal strike of 1984–5 and representing the miners' perspective, were viewed nationally and internationally due to the flexibility of the video format.

Workshops have tended to focus on documentary forms of film making as a means of projecting their own social and political concerns. Furthermore, it is relatively cheap compared to fictional film making. A good example of a workshop incorporating many elements found in such organisations is that of Red Flannel, a women's film and video workshop based in south Wales and funded by Channel Four, the Welsh Arts Council and the South East Arts Association. They see themselves giving a voice to the women of the Welsh Valleys, hitherto largely neglected. An example of their work was *Mam* (1988), a historical documentary about working-class women and their role in the valley communities (Figure 6.9).

6.9 *Mam*, Red Flannel Films, 1988

HOW WE MADE THE FILM

The core of the film rests on the interviews we did with women in the Valleys. We met many of them through the screening groups we had set up in the Valleys. Out of these groups there also emerged a core of women who were interested in working with us on the film and acting as consultants. They formed a production group which saw the film through to its final stages. As well as the contacts made from the screening groups we also visited Old People's homes in the Valleys.

We then found a lot of our archive material from the BFI, the BBC film library, St Fagans, the Miner's library, Swansea and local libraries and museums. We also spoke to women historians like Dee Beddoe and Angela John and spent a lot of time talking to as many women as we could find, as well as employing a Welsh speaking feminist historian who found a lot of interesting material in the Welsh language.

'Mam' was very much a Red Flannel joint effort, all members of Red Flannel worked on its research and we had regular meetings where all our information was brought together and knocked into shape.

By the end of the research period we had a pretty thorough understanding of womens role in the developing history of the Valleys, but we wanted women themselves to tell the story, through their own memories and experiences.

From the very many women we spoke to during the research period we finally chose our film interviewees. We chose on the basis of firstly personality, women who could speak articulately and engagingly about

the past, secondly we needed a good age range so that the film could cover a long period in time. Lastly, it was important that their personal stories reflected what was the common experience.

The script was developed through the following process:

- Screening and discussions on questions raised under 'background'

- Formation of production group

- Sound interviews

- Archive research: feature films, documentary, stills

- Background reading: historical, sociological, economic, literature

- Choosing material for dramatisation and documentary development

- Creating basic structure of film

- Drama improvisations

- Shaping of documentary material into cohesive sequences

- Final scripting

The production group carried on working with us during the editing of the film, so that our decisions could be informed by their opinions.

Red Flannel feel that because of the long term involvement of Valleys women during the making of 'Mam', via screenings, discussions and within the production group, that the final result is a truer representation of their lifes, than a film made under normal mainstream constraints would allow.

The Life Cycle of Independents

Given the precariousness of most independen insecure funding, small audiences and fragile s surprising that longevity is not easily achiev than not, an independent will wither or col supportive component is removed, such as grant or an inspirational and creative memb tion. However, there are occasions when independents flourish and 'break through' into the mainstream market. A spectacular case is that of *Viz*, a comic originally distributed in a few local Newcastle pubs, but eventually achieving a one-million circulation. With growth and commercial success frequently come takeover bids by major organisations, or else the independent itself becomes a company with diversifying interests to sustain its growth. For example, *Viz* publishers have begun to launch new leisure magazine titles, including gardening. Finally, some independents manage to maintain economic viability while retaining the core principles which stimulated their original conception, an outstanding example being *Private Eye*, the satirical magazine which has survived three decades of litigation.

INSTITUTIONAL CASE STUDY: *THE MUSIC INDUSTRY*

Majors versus Indies: A Historical Overview

'To be totally ruthless about it, our job is to see the trends coming on the street, steal them, and sell them back to them' (Garfield, 1986). This comment, made by a record company executive in the mid-1980s, might be said to epitomise the dynamic tension that exists between popular music as a culturally creative activity and as a form of cultural commodity marketed by industrial corporations. This tension has been mirrored to some extent in the contrasting roles of major and independent record companies (majors and indies) ever since pop music, or rock and roll, first became big business in the 1950s.

As an emergent musical style (based fundamentally on black rhythm and blues), rock and roll was launched on independent record labels in the USA. Small companies like Sun Records (whose roster included Elvis Presley) were willing and able to support new music for which there was initially a local, then a national, and finally an international market. The major record companies, after first ignoring what was perceived as a 'passing fad', eventually responded by signing up many of the new stars, like Presley (who switched from Sun to RCA in 1956), as well as supplying their own much less authentic versions in a bid to halt their declining market share, based mainly on older-established musical styles. Whereas prior to rock and roll in the early 1950s the top eight major companies enjoyed an average 95 per cent share of the singles market, by the early 1960s this had fallen to less than 50 per cent. Having stabilised during the 1960s era of pop and rock, the majors eventually regained a dominant market share of over 80 per cent by 1973. Peterson and Berger (1975) have indentified this pattern as a *cyclic* phenomenon; whereby the 'degree of diversity in musical forms is inversely related to the degree of market concentration'. In other words, when the major companies are in a dominant market situation it is because there is little variety of musical choice, but this is only temporary, as new musical styles burst on to the scene to be taken up by the indies and, much later on, by the majors. This could be seen as a process of generational renewal, whereby each new wave of teenagers rebels against the perceived conformity of the existing musical styles.

Soon after Peterson and Berger published their thesis, the cycle they described seem to be back in full swing, when punk and new wave made a significant impact during 1976–9. Once again, independent labels, like Rough Trade and Chrysalis in Britain, played a key role. However, the cyclic model, although containing some legitimacy as a historical description, provides an over-simplistic view of the relationship between majors and indies, which is much less valid today. Even in the 1960s, for Britain many of the new beat and rhythm-and-blues groups, such as the Beatles and the Rolling Stones, were signed to majors from the start of their careers, while in the USA, some of the major labels like CBS were quite willing to 'experiment' with new acts during the hippie or counterculture period of the late 1960s. In actuality, there has always been an element of co-operation as well as competition between majors and indies in the music industry. Few indies have the resources to manufacture and distribute records, tapes etc. other than on a localised scale, and so they have usually depended on the majors to gain access to a national or international market. Meanwhile, the majors have frequently relied on the indies as a source of new talent, a sort of 'research and development' role.

Majors versus Indies: the 1990s

In previous decades the music market tended to be dominated by relatively few musical forms (e.g. the early 1970s was characterised by 'teenybop' singles and 'progressive' rock albums), but in recent years there has been a growing fragmentation. This is reflected in the diversity of charts published which monitor sales. Apart from the traditional top 40, there are charts for dance, indy, reggae, metal and other forms of music. Consequently, it is much more difficult to control the market, as many of these musical styles are quite specialised, thus allowing independent labels with the requisite knowledge and reputation to carve out a niche in the market. This is not entirely new, as illustrated by the case of Atlantic (soul music) in the 1960s and Island (reggae music) in the 1970s. Some indies may even become a showcase for a local area's new talent, as Factory Records did for Manchester in the late 1980s.

Keith Negus (1992) argues that instead of seeing majors and indies as separate and oppositional organisations, it is more appropriate to distinguish between major and minor companies:

> Majors increasingly split into semi-autonomous working groups and label divisions, and minor companies connected to these by complex patterns of ownership, investment, licensing, formal and informal and sometimes deliberately obscured relationships. This has resulted in complex and confusing, continually shifting corporate constellations which are difficult to plot, as deals expire, new relationships are negotiated, new acquisitions made and joint ventures embarked upon. At the end of 1990 the trade magazine *Music Week* reported that 82 different labels were operating 'under the banner' of the Polygram group in the UK alone. Which companies are owned, part owned or licensed becomes difficult to ascertain. If it can be done, what it means in terms of working practices becomes equally harder to infer, as the distinctions between an inside and outside, and between centre and margins, has given way to a web of mutually dependent work groupings radiating out from multiple centres.
>
> These organisational webs, of units within a company and connections to smaller companies, enable entertainment corporations to gain access to material and artists, and to operate a coordinating, monitoring and surveillance, operation rather than just centralised control. The corporation can still shape the nature of these webs through the use and distribution of investment. But it is a tight–loose approach, rather than a rigidly hierarchical form of organisation; tight enough to ensure a degree of predictability and stability in dealing with collaborators, but loose enough to manoeuvre, redirect or even reverse company activity.
>
> *Negus (1992)*

Music Week comes to similar conclusions:

> When the PJ Harvey album Rid Of Me, their first release on Island Records, entered the national chart at number three in May its success consolidated the group's position as one of the best new acts in Britain.
>
> The chart position marked a vital breakthrough for Polly Harvey and her band. But it also had a wider significance

for it was a prime example of just how much independent and major labels are now working together to develop new artists.

Nevertheless it still raised questions about the relationship between the two sectors. Like how much do the majors need independent acumen to help them develop new acts? And how much do independent labels need major muscle to secure commercial success both at home and abroad? And furthermore, what can the smaller labels do to protect their interest in the bands they discover and nurture?

In the case of PJ Harvey, of course, Island was involved almost from the beginning. An Island scout had seen the group's sixth gig and preliminary talks with the band had already taken place before the release of their debut Too Pure single, Dress. And, when they ultimately signed to Island early in 1992, it was agreed that their first album, Dry, should appear on Too Pure, with whom the band had a longstanding verbal agreement.

The advantages of such an arrangement were immediately obvious. Secure in the knowledge that they had a longterm future with one of the country's most respected major labels, Harvey and her band were still able to grow their music organically, free of many of the commercial pressures that might have applied had they signed immediately to a major.

Island Records stood to benefit too. Too Pure's fully independent status meant that Harvey's profile could be developed modestly and inexpensively through the independent charts and a music press that is perceived to be biased in favour of the independent artist.

Music Week, *24 July 1993*

---

activity **6.3** Compare the top 40 singles/album charts with the independent charts (e.g. in *New Musical Express* or *Music Week*), and identify the musical acts and styles with which the independent labels are achieving chart success.

One issue which does reflect a divergence of musical policy and investment strategy between majors and the minors, or indies, is the attitude towards the format for recorded music (Figure 6.10). There is no doubt the rise of the CD has been to the benefit of the major companies. It has several advantages. First, as music companies have increasingly been prone to vertical integration (e.g. Sony–CBS), the sales of CD hard-

6.10 BPI Yearbook, 1993

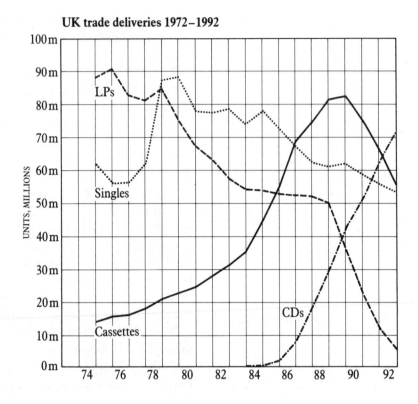

UK trade deliveries 1972–1992

ware (the player) and software (the disc) have been mutually stimulating. Having purchased a CD player, new owners need to acquire a CD collection in order to justify the investment. Secondly, purchasers of CDs tend to be older and more affluent. Such an audience has a more conservative musical taste and is thus attracted to the artists who are well established (invariably tied to major companies). Indeed, reissuing 'old' music on CDs has been a prominent commercial ploy, resulting in up to 40 per cent of weekly album sales being based on back catalogues. Finally, profit margins on CDs are appreciably higher than on cassette tape or vinyl, a fact which has generated considerable criticism, not least from hard-up music lovers (Figure 6.11).

As the album and the CD have grown in strength so has the power of the major companies. The 'big five' (CBS, WEA, EMI, Polygram and BMG) share an estimated 65–70 per cent of the European recorded music market and well over a third of the world market. All five companies are part of entertainment conglomerates embracing electronics, music, film, video etc., and so their music acts are often marketed in many forms, including CD, audio and video cassette, and various merchandising deals. In terms of global impact, it could be

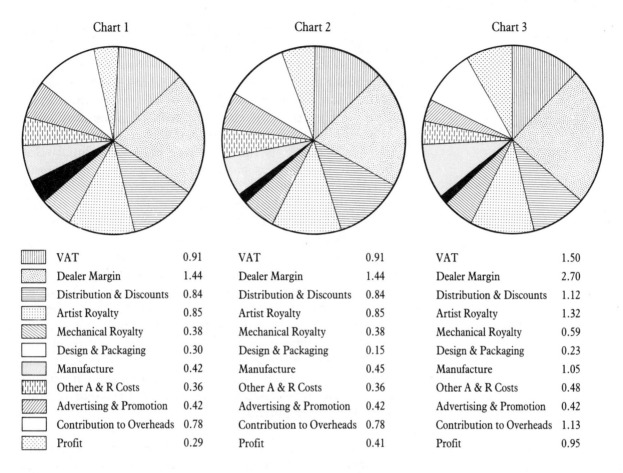

	Chart 1			Chart 2			Chart 3	
	VAT	0.91		VAT	0.91		VAT	1.50
	Dealer Margin	1.44		Dealer Margin	1.44		Dealer Margin	2.70
	Distribution & Discounts	0.84		Distribution & Discounts	0.84		Distribution & Discounts	1.12
	Artist Royalty	0.85		Artist Royalty	0.85		Artist Royalty	1.32
	Mechanical Royalty	0.38		Mechanical Royalty	0.38		Mechanical Royalty	0.59
	Design & Packaging	0.30		Design & Packaging	0.15		Design & Packaging	0.23
	Manufacture	0.42		Manufacture	0.45		Manufacture	1.05
	Other A & R Costs	0.36		Other A & R Costs	0.36		Other A & R Costs	0.48
	Advertising & Promotion	0.42		Advertising & Promotion	0.42		Advertising & Promotion	0.42
	Contribution to Overheads	0.78		Contribution to Overheads	0.78		Contribution to Overheads	1.13
	Profit	0.29		Profit	0.41		Profit	0.95

6.11 Chart 1: Price breakdown for £6.99 LP; price breakdown for £6.99 cassette; price breakdown for £11.49 CD. BPI Yearbook, 1993

argued that contemporary pop stars such as Madonna and Michael Jackson have superseded Hollywood film stars (not withstanding the fact that such artists often have a parallel film career).

Meanwhile, the single is in decline and vinyl has been effectively reduced to a marginalised role as either a cheap and flexible option for independent (especially dance) music or else a collector's item. The major companies argue that this is a consequence of consumer preference. Others see it as an outcome largely dictated by corporate power and self-interest. While the majors may have prevailed over the format of recorded music, the control of audience taste has, and continues to be, less certain.

Mediating the Market

Approximately 80 per cent of all recorded music released on to the market fails to make a profit. For example, of the 10,800 new albums issued in Britain in 1990, only 317 made it into the top 40. Given this poor rate of success, together with the considerable fixed costs in terms of pressing plant, recording studios etc., it is not surprising that much effort is directed towards stimulating consumer demand for the music in the search for the best-selling album or smash single which will offset the majority of failures.

Between those making the music and those purchasing the end product there exists a range of *gatekeepers* – filters sifting out the likely hits from the flow of excess production. Keith Negus (1992) prefers the concept of *cultural intermediary*, since it engages with the fact that music, unlike conventional industrial manufacturing, is a product with symbolic cultural value which affects how it is perceived by producers, distributors and consumers alike. The 'intermediaries' are those who help to shape the three key decisions identified by Simon Frith (1983) – 'who records, what is recorded, and which records reach the public'.

Of course, the music itself is not the whole 'product'. Performers add cultural meaning and value depending on their perceived image. For those with 'star' appeal, the actual music may be of secondary significance to the audience. Furthermore, music is often embedded within distinct subcultures which facilitate processes of identification and group solidarity among participants, especially in adolescent and teenage groups. Therefore, the analysis of music mediators which follows is necessarily contingent on the kinds of artist involved and their potential market niche.

In the record company, at the front line of discovering and developing musical talent is the *A and R* (artists and repertoire) representative, whose responsibilities include: signing artists (perhaps 'poaching' them from other companies); examining the company catalogues for potential hits; developing the musical policy and direction of a company's record labels. Negus (1992) describes A and R culture as predominantly white, male and college educated (dating from the late 1960s/early 1970s). Consequently, there tends to be a conservative ethos in musical policy among the well-established, mainstream record labels – the rock-music aesthetic still being preferred at the expense of new styles, which are often viewed with suspicion or hostility.

When a band or performer has been signed to a record company, the *producer* plays a key role in organising and co-ordinating the actual recording of the music. Achieving 'the right sound' often involves skilful engineering during the mixing or post-production stage. Some producers' reputations have exceeded the artists' in being able to create a recognisable sound, e.g. Phil Spector in the 1960s ('the wall of sound'), Georgio Moroder in the 1970s (disco) and Phil Oakenfeld in the 1980s (remixing tracks to enhance the dance element). New technology, in the form of synthesisers, samplers, drum machines etc. linked to a computer, has made possible DIY music production for a modest outlay, undermining the necessity of employing expensive studios owned by the major companies. The success of KLF in the early 1990s is testimony to the possibilities of utilising such new technology creatively in music production.

Working in conjunction with the A and R team is the *marketing* department, which usually has a 'product manager' overseeing the packaging of an artist. This requires giving close attention to the appropriate image of the artist in relation to his or her target audience. In extreme cases, it may be possible to contrive totally an identity or image for a musical act that has been synthetically created by the company. Perhaps the best-known example is the Monkees, a group created and marketed as an attempt to imitate the success of the Beatles in the 1960s. The group were brought together by the company, Calpix, and provided with a television series along with the requisite songs and session musicians. Pop music is as much image as music, and given the competitive nature of the business, the vital elements much sought after are 'uniqueness' and 'authenticity'. These qualities are frequently cited by fans to justify their support for particular artists. To claim that audiences are manipulated or duped by skilful marketing alone is to underestimate the critical scrutiny applied by the majority of such audiences to the music, performances, interviews, lifestyle etc. of the artists. That is not to deny the existence of some degree of artifice and fantasy, especially within the traditional core of adolescent and pre-adolescent female fans, whose loyalty and identification is notoriously fickle. One of the greatest challenges, both in terms of music and image management, is making the transition from the teenage to the adult market. George Michael achieved this very successfully following the break-up of Wham! Less successful was Kylie Minogue, who attempted to replace the wholesome image sustained by her role in *Neighbours* with a more voluptuous and knowing performance in her post-*Neighbours* music career. Marketing images is further explored below in the discussion of the press, television and video.

Apart from producing and marketing, the other key function for a record company is to ensure effective distribution of the music. Larger record companies employ a *strike force* whose aim is to ensure good visibility for the company's output in the high-street retailers, the shops from which the charts are compiled. Various strategies may be applied to persuade shops to co-operate, such as issuing glossy packages, point-of-sale displays, joint advertising etc. As with record companies, the trend for music retailers is horizontal integration, so that in

Britain the multiple stores like W. H. Smith, Our Price and HMV have emerged as the dominant outlets for music distribution and consumption. In some cases, record companies are able to guarantee outlets for their music via vertical integration, two examples in Britain being EMI–HMV and Virgin–Virgin. In contrast to the multiples and their flagship megastores are the specialist independent record shops, which focus on specific musical styles as well as catering for the beleaguered lovers of vinyl. Such shops often generate the initial sales for new music ignored by the conservative multiples until, and if, such music gains a chart entry (Table 6.3).

Table 6.3 Number of shops selling records/tapes/CDs

	Nov 1984	Mar 1986	Feb 1987	Mar 1988	Jun 1989	Mar 1990	Sep 1991	Aug 1992
Specialist chains								
HMV	37	54	59	58	59	73	80	84
Our Price	93	127	179	203	270	283	336	335
Virgin	37	57	88	100	9	9	11	13
Multiples								
W.H. Smith	260	262	263	277	282	302	313	336
Woolworths	896	832	824	803	801	800	811	781
Menzies	110	109	117	112	163	158	178	170
Boots	275	274	260	263	265	264	255	251
Other multiples	316	321	346	319	346	375	347	319
Independent specialists								
Large	375	333	401	437	330	175	152	126
Medium	673	752	778	792	641	339	366	347
Small	1159	929	846	763	821	857	666	648
Others	800	800	800	800	800	800	800	800
Total	5031	4850	4961	4927	4787	4435	4315	4210

Definitions of specialists: large (1,000 + units per week); medium (500–1,000 units per week; small (100–500 units per week); others (an estimate of all others shops selling less than 100 units per week)

Source: Gallup

There is little doubt that the record company plays a significant role in determining the outcome to the questions of who records and what is recorded. Most companies negotiate contracts with artists that cede rights over the end product – what is released, when it is released, how it is promoted etc. – to the company on their terms (excepting those artists whose popularity strengthens their bargaining position).

The answer to the third question as to what music reaches the public is more at the mercy of other mediators.

The relationship between the music press and the music business is on the whole, symbiotic. Most music journalists are dependent on the rest of the industry for news, interviews, access etc., while the companies and artists are keen to gain as much favourable publicity as possible. Indeed, it is not unusual for careers to cross over in both directions, e.g. Neil Tennant of Pet Shop Boys began as a writer for *Smash Hits*. It is generally acknowledged that critical reviews are not particularly influential in damaging sales, but that very positive reviews are helpful in the drive to 'break' new acts – in helping to stimulate a 'buzz' around an act.

In recent years, the range of music press has broadened to encompass the growth in musical diversity and audience taste. The longstanding teenage 'pop' magazines like *Smash Hits* act as quasi-consumer guides for a mainly female teen audience (although this role has become subsumed by the more general magazines like *Just Seventeen*). The attitude is unashamedly one of being a fan, unlike that of the weekly music 'newspapers' targeting an older, more musically knowledgeable (and usually male) readership, such as *New Musical Express*. Like its main rival, *Melody Maker*, *NME*'s identity and musical policy have undergone various shifts over the decades, but of late have focused on the independent or college-based music scene with only a limited interest in dance, hip-hop, metal etc. To cater for these more specialised audiences there are contemporary titles such as *Kerrang!* and *Hip Hop Connection*, readership of which implies a commitment and knowledge well beyond the causal consumer. An even more partisan and dedicated audience can be found in the purchasers of the numerous music fanzines whose original inspiration can be traced back to the punk movement of the late 1970s. The cut-and-paste style and irreverence of such titles as *Sniffin Glue* can still be found in current examples, but others have taken advantage of desk-top publishing to achieve a professional finish indistinguishable from that found in titles in the high-street newsagents. Finally, there is the new wave of glossy, more adult-oriented music magazines which are as much about past as present music. The brand leader is Q magazine, whose rise mirrors that of the CD at whose owners it is targeted. Much space is devoted to re-releases and charting the career of artists who rose to fame in the 1960s and 1970s, (e.g. Eric Clapton, Dire Straits).

The agenda set by Q magazine is also paralleled in the broadsheet daily newspapers, each of which has at least one (usually male) pop music critic whose taste and selection reflects the age, education and class of the readers. Very different in approach is the tabloid press, whose rising interest in pop music (*The Sun* having established its first pop column, 'Bizarre', in 1982) ties in with the growth in entertainment news values of such papers. Journalists on the tabloids are more interested in the private lives of the artists than the music, and so their publicity value is certainly double edged, as many, like Boy George, have found to their cost. Whatever the attitude of newspapers and magazines, the target for record companies and artists is maximum public exposure to coincide with the release of an album or single, and, via the company's own press officer and marketing department, considerable resources are directed to that goal.

activity 6.4

Survey the range of music-based magazines available in the main high-street newsagents. From an examination of the front covers, musical content, adverts, price and design, build up a descriptive profile of the music styles represented and the likely target readership of the magazines.

Your conclusions can be validated by writing to the magazines and requesting a 'media pack', which includes synopsis of the readership profile, circulation and editorial policy.

Given the fact that pop music is essentially aural in nature, and that most consumers like to hear a sample of music before buying it, it is not unreasonable to identify radio as the key form of mediation between artist and audience. Following scandals of bribery (or 'payola') in the American music industry in the early years of rock and roll, mainstream radio has been at pains to demonstrate its independence in the selection of what is played over the airwaves. Most radio stations in Britain use the *playlist* as a means of choosing which music is played most frequently. For Britain's most popular radio station, Radio 1, there exist two playlists. The twenty tracks selected for the 'A' list are guaranteed fifteen plays per week, and the 'B' list ten plays. In recognition of the much greater volume of albums sold than of singles, there is also an album list where six new album tracks receive a minimum of four plays per week. Records on the playlist account for approximately 50 per cent of Radio 1's daytime output.

In choosing tracks for playlists, the perceived needs of the station's audience are uppermost in the radio producers' minds. The Radio 1 playlist panel of disc jockeys and producers is anticipating the taste of those aged between 11 and 15, who account for the biggest proportion of singles buyers. On independent local radio (ILR), a similar, if even more cautious, policy exists in compiling playlists. It is rare for an unknown artist to be selected for a playlist until the release enters the charts. Gallup, the company that compiles the charts, suggests (1993) that the majority of top 75 singles arrive in the charts without being originally playlisted. The purpose of the playlist is to help sustain sales of music once a chart position has been obtained.

For ILR, playlisted music is increasingly the only means of airplay for new releases. Its desire to maximise the audience for advertisers' benefit has led to the widespread practice of adhering to a musical format based on a mix of past and present hits selected by computer so that each song differs from the last in terms of tempo, mood and origin, but that none of the music is likely to alienate the target audience. Many stations split their frequencies in order to differentiate between music by generation – the AM service usually providing a more easy-listening format (often called 'gold') for older listeners. The formatting of radio services is a trend emanating from the USA, which has developed the system to a fine art:

USA radio formatting

There are over 10,000 radio stations in the US, and in a bid to achieve a distinctive audience profile which might be attractive to advertisers, stations have increasingly adopted specialised formats, the most prominent of which are listed below.

Adult Contemporary (AC) is America's most popular radio format and aims for the 25 to 54-year-old group, advertisers' most desired group, by playing less abrasive contemporary hits. This means no hard rock, no raucous upbeat dance tunes, no pre-rock, no supper club singers. There are at least five main subspecies: **Full service** stations are descendents of the huge MOR mainstays of the past and play soft hits with emphasis on news, talk and personalities; **gold intensive** stations play 80 to 90 per cent oldies with tiny current playlists of the safest hits; **life** encompasses everything from love songs to easy listening and aims for the upper end of the AC age bracket; **music intensive** have playlists of 20 or 30 records and are the most aggressive about playing new artists and crossovers; **adult alternative** stations feature an AC base with emphasis on other types of music such as jazz or soft rock.

Album Oriented Rock (AOR) grew out of progressive rock radio in the late Sixties and had a broader musical scope in the past. Nowadays it seldom strays from white rock, rarely playing more than one track from an LP during a two month period. Presentations still try to preserve the 'rock and roll outlaw' attitude of the format's early years, though the music is now safe and predictable. The last remnants of AOR's free-form roots are the dozens of college stations which are increasingly important in exposing new music.

Contemporary Hit Radio (CHR) is the descendent of Top 40, which by the Eighties had a shopworn image. CHR made a comeback in 1983–85, bucking the narrowcast trend by picking up hits from Urban and AOR stations.

Classical has a long and lucrative history, with sufficient population to support its minority appeal. Listeners are few, but their economic standing is an ad agency's dream.

Comedy formats have been attempted at various junctures, most recently in Washington DC and suburban Los Angeles. They've never prospered. A constant comedy diet doesn't seem to have the appeal of comedy extracts interspersed with other elements.

Contemporary Christian Radio is a relatively recent development arising from a growing Christian music industry. Some stations are like other Adult Contemporary stations ('Christians need traffic reports too'); others maintain a more religious atmosphere.

Country is one of the oldest formats and, in total number of stations, the largest. Loyalty is to artists rather than the latest record. Country remains a heavily oldies-based format, but rarely reaches back before 1970.

Easy Listening Radio is an umbrella term encompassing nostalgia, big band, and other non-rock material. Though easy listening ratings are excellent, it means an older (45 plus), less-profitable audience to ad agencies.

Gold is a blanket term for a format playing exclusively post-1955 oldies, pioneered by WCBS in New York 20 years ago. In the last couple of years a second gold rush has materialised (the first came in the wake of 'American Graffiti' in the mid-Seventies). The biggest oldies phenomenon remains 'classic rock', concentrating on the 1967–75 heydey of progressive rock; loads of Cream, Doors and so on.

Gospel is divided into black and white stations, both concentrated in the South and serving constituencies too small to register in the ratings.

Hispanic stations specialising in modern and traditional Latin forms of music are bound to increase in importance as the nation's Hispanic population rises.

Jazz is rarely found as a full-time format. Similar to classical in attracting upscale, loyal listeners, but doesn't have the same prestigious image.

New Age music – instrumental atmospheric records largely popularised by the Windham Hill label and characterised by unbelievers as 'aural wallpaper' – has been a quiet industry phenomenon. Most stations also include jazz, AC or soft AOR programming.

News stations have found a successful AM only niche. It's cheaper to play records than maintain a big news staff, so news stations aren't feasible outside big markets.

Quiet Storm is named after the Quiet Storm programme on WHUR in Washington in the mid-Seventies which played softer R and B ballads and mellow jazz. Increasingly popular.

Religious refers to religious talk programming, often 'dollar a holler' air time purchased from stations by exposure-seeking evangelists.

Sports radio received its first exclusive station last year – WFAN in New York, broadcasting sports talk shows and play-by-play events.

Talk stations consist mostly of call-in shows, with instructional programmes as ballast. Expensive to produce and therefore limited to major markets.

Urban Contemporary is a synonym for black radio but, with more and more white artists in traditionally black musical domains, it is a more accurate term. Urban stations have made great strides in the ratings. Economic prosperity has not kept pace, however, as ad agencies persist in viewing Urban Listeners as denizens of the underclass.

From 'Facing The Music' by Simon Frith.
© 1988 by Simon Frith. Reprinted by permission of
Pantheon Books, a division of Randon House, Inc.

- To what extent are these formats reproduced on British radio?
- Are there any notable formats which have been overlooked?
- What do you consider to be the advantages and disadvantages of such a system in comparison with contemporary British radio?

It seems likely Britain will follow this pattern as more stations are granted licences. Already, many local incremental stations are dedicated to specific musical styles, e.g. Kiss (dance), Jazz and WNK (various forms of black music). Minority music tastes ignored by ILR and daytime Radio 1 are only likely to be acknowledged by those disc jockeys still allowed freedom to make a personal choice of music for broadcasting, e.g. on evening Radio 1 or on pirate radio. Programmes or services containing a diverse range of musical styles in their output will be increasingly rare; examples are offered by Radio 1 under the BBC's public service remit. The more specialist music channels appear on radio (like Virgin, which targets the older, 25–45 year-old, Q-reading audience), the more Radio 1's audience share and future survival will be under threat.

Television exposure is much sought after by companies and artists as a means of enhancing audience awareness and hence sales. Until Channel Four pioneered youth programmes based on music, from *The Tube* to *The Word*, BBC's *Top of the Pops* (*TOTP*) was the main television showcase for pop music. While being consistently criticised for its musical conservatism and exclusive concern with the singles chart, its impact on sales is undeniable. A 1988 Gallup survey estimated that a single's sales were likely to be boosted by between 50 and 100 per cent overnight as a result of a *TOTP* performance. The only television opportunities to exceed this are those supplied by the annual BRIT awards (which have a similar effect to that of the Oscars on film audiences) and occasional live charity concerts, the most famous being Live Aid in 1985. Such events can significantly stimulate an artist's international sales.

At the heart of many television music performances is the *pop video*. Its potential as a promotional tool was first fully realised when Queen's 1975 video for their song *Bohemian Rhapsody*, broadcast on *TOTP*, played a vital role in sustaining the song for nine weeks at number 1 in the singles chart. The 1980s saw a huge expansion of pop videos, with some television programmes like *The Chart Show* relying almost exclusively on video clips. The rising costs of making the videos, plus a desire to gain international penetration, has meant that the pop video has favoured the established, better-known artists for whom making the video is more likely to be a safe investment. Furthermore, there has been a recent decline in the use of pop videos by mainstream television, due partly to the effect of transmission charges of between £500 and £800 per minute being levied on television companies from 1985 in a bid to recoup some of the high production costs, which can vary between a few thousand pounds and $2 million (for Michael Jackson's 1987 video *Thriller*).

Aside from terrestrial television, the main outlet for pop videos has been MTV. Launched in 1981 on American cable television, its rapid global growth has meant its impact on young audiences cannot be ignored (though this is less true in Britain, where satellite/cable access is still limited). In some respects, it resembles top 40 commercial music radio, with its emphasis on a conservative playlist of singles and albums, mixing past and present hits but on a worldwide basis.

Likewise, videos that do not fit the normal parameters of style (e.g. fast editing) and content (e.g. avoidance of overt sex and violence) are unlikely to be playlisted. The extent to which the pop video has foregrounded image at the expense of music is debatable. It seems apparent that artists able to produce more imaginative or compelling videos, e.g. Madonna, do gain an advantage, not least in boosting sales of the videos themselves (especially when they have been subject to censor-

6.12 Goodwin, 1993: *Dancing in the Distraction Factory*, Routledge. The cycle illustrates the role of music videos in generating consumption of records, CDs and tapes, which in turn supply revenue for more videos

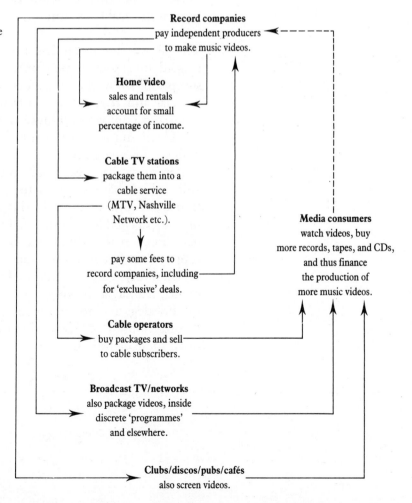

Record companies
pay independent producers
to make music videos.

Home video
sales and rentals
account for small
percentage of income.

Cable TV stations
package them into a
cable service
(MTV, Nashville
Network etc.).

pay some fees to
record companies, including
for 'exclusive' deals.

Cable operators
buy packages and sell
to cable subscribers.

Broadcast TV/networks
also package videos, inside
discrete 'programmes'
and elsewhere.

Media consumers
watch videos, buy
more records, tapes, and CDs,
and thus finance
the production of
more music videos.

Clubs/discos/pubs/cafés
also screen videos.

ship on television, like Madonna's *Justify My Love*). However, it is questionable how much close attention they receive. It has been suggested that, for most of the audience, pop videos (especially on MTV) are used as background entertainment, rather like radio. None the less, it seems likely that in future audiovisual CDs will become a prominent format for consuming music (Figure 6.12).

The pop video as a generic form overlaps with television advertising through the use of fast edits, special effects, unusual camera angles etc. Indeed, it is a form of advertising in itself. Meanwhile, television adverts have been increasingly prone to apply music soundtracks drawn from the past. The Levi 501 jeans campaign is a notable example. Its resurrection of 'golden oldies' has led to a succession of chart successes for songs like *I Heard it Through the Grapevine*, *When a Man Loves a Woman* etc. This has led to accusations of commercial values corrupting the original meaning and power of the songs themselves. (An extreme example is Dunlop Tyres' use of the Velvet Underground, icons of 1960s underground pop culture, as musical background.)

The above discussion has focused on the most salient and trusted means by which music is chosen for audience consumption. All of the mediators are subject to the normal commercial and regulatory constraints which work in favour of the major companies. However, there is an alternative 'system' by which music can flourish from the grassroots through to mainstream recognition.

Pop music has always had an undercurrent of subcultures or cults which have surfaced to gain more widespread recognition from time to time. In the 1960s it was folk 'protest' and hippie psychedelic music; in the 1970s, Northern Soul and gay disco; in the 1980s, hip-hop and rap etc. The structural support for such music subcultures, particularly in recent years, revolves around the interplay between a few key ingredients, namely a thriving club or club scene, pirate radio, DIY or bootleg record production, fanzines and independent record shops. The case study in Figure 6.13 includes examples of all these elements.

6.13 © *New Statesman & Society*, 17 June 1988

Thriving by night

A combination of black DJs, illicit bootleggers and pirate radio entrepreneurs have established an alternative entertainment sphere. Cynthia Rose traces the emergence of an unofficial enterprise culture.

"Recently," Jazzie B is saying, "I've been following this Jesse Jackson business in America. I was shocked that he's gettin' votes from white states – and I was thinkin' to myself, Oh *damn!* Maybe the time has *come!* It's kinda wound me up. And now, in what I do, I'm really adoptin' a more professional attitude."

What does Jazzie do? He's the DJ head of Funki Dredd Productions, and the founder of north London's 16-strong Soul II Soul crew. Started five years ago by Jazzie and an old school friend Philip 'Daddae' Harvey, Soul II Soul run a sound system, a weekly club (Centre of the World, every Sunday night in Old Street), and a shop: the Soul II Soul Basement Store at 162 Camden High Street. Soul II Soul is also the name on a Ten Records' release entitled "Fair Play", which entered May's pop charts at number 65. Jazzie B is a Renaissance dude – but the Renaissance of which he's a part has changed London itself.

During the past half-decade, Jazzie's milieu – DJs, nightclub aficionados, hustlers of vinyl and the men behind pirate radio – have made social history of a singular sort. They have established a completely alternative entertainment sphere; one which is powered by black aesthetics.

Jazzie's part of this new environment started to shape itself early in 1986, via the magnet of illicit warehouse parties. These were the result of young white entrepreneurs (like the Family Funktion team) working in tandem with black crews like Soul II Soul or Shake & Fingerpop, under black DJs such as Jazzie and Norman Jay.

"Family Funktion were middle-class white guys," notes DJ Trevor Nelson, a staffer at pirate radio KISS-FM, and known as "Madhatter" for his affiliation to Madhatters sound system. "They were trendies; who knew a lot of people, all at college, all with a lot of money. With them and Soul II Soul, it was two complete opposites coming together – and pulling 3,000 people illegally."

"White guys invented the warehouse," says Nelson. "They had the know-how regarding the legalities. And they made sure it was never busted, which black kids could never have done. Put a white guy on the door and everything could be cool. You could make a couple of grand off an illegal affair – and half the police force's sons would be there."

Warehouse parties made big money and set bigger precedents. But more than this, they succeeded in integrating young London in a fashion which made the GLC or Rock Against Racism seem quaint. "Warehouses brought the cultures together, black kids and white kids," says Madhatter Trevor. "There were always soul boys and soul girls, who always came together. But their cultures were words apart. Now they're still together, though. Which is absolutely brilliant."

What warehouses initiated, pirate radio helps maintain. On London's 30 odd illegal stations, black musics provide the majority format (soul, hip-hop, jazz, reggae, house, and the 1970s soul called "rare groove"). And some of the stations have ambitious set-ups: like LWR (once "London Weekend Radio", now "London-Wide Radio"), a five-year-old, single-propietor enterprise which broadcasts 24 hours a day, seven days a week. Or KISS-FM, the two-year-old weekender which trades on a roster of "name" DJs from the burgeoning nightclub scene.

Drawing on personal knowledge and on family record collections which can span three generations, such DJs easily one-up the playlist-crippled commercial broadcasters. And their clear connections to and love for black music have generated a whole new market for soul in Greater London. The clearest symbol of this may be seen in Soho. There, where six record retailers have flourished for some years (Tower Records, Groove Records, Daddy Kool, Hitman Records, Virgin's Megastore and HMV Records), three more have chosen this moment to move in. They are Beak Street's Red Records (where Madhatter and KISS-FM's Lloyd Brown can be found), Black Market Records (the brainchild of two more DJs, Steve Jervier and Rene Gelston), and Bluebird Records.

Black Londoners who work for the pirates take pride in exercising an expertise excluded from the capital's entertainment mainstream. LWR jock Steve Edwards: "British legal radio is too controlled, too conservative. And its DJs are so complacent! We're not afraid to play *our* music. You know, you've got a collection – you blow the dust off a few things. You *think* about it. It takes me two hours to put together a show. I don't just throw things on the turntable. I've always wondered why the legal stations don't utilise the skills of pirate DJs – because, at the end of the day – it *works*."

Indeed it does. The pirates use street news and gossip as well as music to provide a complement to the club scene. They've also discovered how to support themselves – with advertising for venues, gigs, shops and new record releases. (Several also run clubs and record fairs themselves.) Through plugs and airplay for each other's every project, the pirate DJs control the entire marketplace they inhabit.

Within those precincts, Lloyd "Daddy Bug" Brown of Red Records is known as the "cut-out king", a former independent wholesaler who has recycled many a "rare groove". "The pirates have created a whole thing for themselves," says Daddy Bug. "It goes like this: it's cheap to advertise on a pirate. But you get whatever it is plugged every hour, 24 hours a day. If you got something to offer, you know, that is gonna *work*."

Thus far, what talent mainstream entertainment has poached from the pirates has been white (radio's Gilles Peterson, *Night Network*'s Tim Westwood). But, from Radio London's *Nite FM* through BBC2's *Def II*, they have forced alterations in attitudes and responses. And airplay over establishment waves is often contingent on pirate success. Jazzie B's "Fair Play", for instance, was heard in clubs and on the pirates almost two months before it "appeared". (It was then "silenced" for a fortnight, to starve the marketplace.) "It can be an absolute pain," grins Madhatter Trevor Nelson. "Now the kids will come into your store asking for things before they've even been *pressed* – because some pirate has had a cassette. And they won't believe you when you say it's not out yet. After all – they've heard it!"

"The national radio boys," he adds, "now wait for us to make these records safe. Face it, they wouldn't know a good house track from a bad one." In financial terms, the "safe" record – this week's "boom cut" or certified hit – has never been more desirable. Sometimes it's a rare groove: a soul cut whose physical scarcity enhances its marketplace value. Other times, the pirates hype rap music, hip-hop hits or the neo-disco known as house. Each of these genres has played its part in London's recent deluge of DIY record production, aka bootlegging. Many pirate DJs also lend their knowledgable ears to sampling, a digital collage which spikes new records with audible references from other hits.

Almost everyone dabbles, at least, in bootlegs. And more than curiosity drives them – "booties" can bring up to £30,000 per pressing. "It's all to do with information," explains Daddy Bug. "Knowing what tune will sell. Once you get the information, anybody can do it." ("If you don't put something on vinyl," argues another

pirate DJ, "You ain't got no CV – you got no proof of what you do.")

Like hustling "rare grooves" or throwing a warehouse jam, this unofficial industry provides a foot in the door for black British business talent. "As black people in Britain," says Trevor Nelson wryly, "there's not a lot we are responsible for – apart from controlling our own hair products. All we've got in the general mind is we're good athletes, we can sing and dance, and so on. What upsets most of us is, if that's all we get, why can't we *control* it? That's why most guys are into blatantly bootleggin' records – they just feel blatantly left out."

And that is where a figure like Jazzie B comes in. Jazzie is determined that Soul II Soul should, in the words of one pirate ad, stand firm for the culture. "Black people in this city can't hide from the political thing," he contends. "Our living, our existence in this society, is really political. And I've made the assumption that I've got to anchor something here. To produce something from Britain that will be looked on as positive."

Touring as the Soul II Soul sound system has taught Jazzie B the kind of clout Anglo style is able to command abroad. But he considers respect at home a more important priority. "I want to see more young business people, more people doing what we're doing here in the shop. I want to see more of us in the charts, more of us in the media's eye.

"I know I'm black, right? I know I'm from the ghetto. I don't want to be reading that anymore. I want my nephews and my nieces, my friend's children and my godchildren to be readin' in the papers about this person doing *good*. And have it give them something to really think about."

It's unsurprising Jazzie B should feel ambivalence about the media. Truly interracial and composed of

the young and the officially marginal, London's entertainment underground is rarely represented in the media. It supports its own cottage industries – booties, clubs, mixes, pirate radio and boutiques. From fanzines through to semi-slick mags such as *Soul Underground* or *Straight No Chaser*, it has started to foster a leisure press of its own. But the single mainstream commentator to comprehend its size and importance has been comic Lenny Henry. His pirate DJ character "Delbert Wilkins" benefits from primary-source smarts: Henry is the Chairman of pirate KISS-FM, which claims an audience of 200,000.

Home with CDs and VCRs (or languishing in the Groucho Club) by one am, other establishment pundits remain ignorant of that new London which thrives by night. Regardless of them, however, it operates seven days a week. "People who aren't a part of it," smiles Madhatter Trevor, "can't imagine the size this whole scene has grown to. Maybe they should just stand round Cambridge Circus between one and three am. They'd see hundreds of people go by, all eating dodgy takeaways, hustling to get the night bus. They're all under 20, all dressed the same. And they're black and white, and Chinese and Greek and Indian."

Its movers and shakers know this cosmopolitan scene faces stiff challenges. For one thing, among the competitive pirates, violence has increased. A faster-growing hazard, perhaps, is drug use on the circuit. And blind self-interest can rear its head in any sphere. Even so, men like Jazzie B feel it brings a specific hope. "There's definitely a generation out there now," says Jazzie, "which knows what 'multiracial' means. You're talking about youth of all kinds. All we need now is to stick together."

activity **6.5**	Try and identify a current example of music culture which is based wholly or partly on an 'alternative' system of support, as described in Figure 6.13. You should consider the role of the following: independent record labels, clubs, fanzines and specialist music papers, pirate or incremental radio, DIY record and tape production, and independent record shops.

INSTITUTIONAL CASE STUDY: *LOCAL NEWSPAPERS*

Studies of the media tend to focus on national or mutinational texts and institutions, but for many people one of the most immediate and 'close-to-life' examples of media consumption is the local newspaper that reflects the news, events and values of their particular community. Local newspapers serve a function that neither local radio, usually based upon national music charts or golden oldies, nor local television, with its limited local slots sandwiched between the network output, can easily provide.

Ownership and Control

In 1988, *Benn's Directory* registered 797 weekly paid-for local newspapers, 931 free local newspapers, 70 daily local newspapers (including 11 daily morning provincial newspapers) and 3 Sunday local newspapers in England alone. Many of these newspapers had circulations in excess of 100,000 and had over 80 per cent penetration in their local areas.

Despite this, however, the number of local weekly newspapers declined by 40 per cent between 1921 and 1983. Franklin and Murphy (1991) have examined some of the recent developments in the local newspaper market, and their research suggests that there is a change taking place in the nature of local newspapers, most significantly in the structure of ownership and economic organisation of the local press. They identify an increasing concentration of ownership of local press by a small number of large media groups, which seem intent on expanding their horizontal integration by taking over competitors and creating regional monopolies.

Some of the largest groups identified by Franklin and Murphy are Thompson Regional Newspapers (part of the Canadian company International Thompson), Reed Regional Newspapers (part of Reed International), Associated Newspapers, EMAP, who also publish business and consumer magazines, United Newspapers (who also own 31 per cent of

Yellow Advertiser free newspaper group, as well as Express Newspapers), Westminster Press (part of the Pearson Longman group), and the American company Ingersoll Corporation. Between them they own over half the value of the UK local press market. Other large groups include *The Guardian* and *Manchester Evening News*, and Lonrho (Table 6.4). The local press is attractive to these groups because of its high advertising revenues. For example, in 1987, the local and regional press attracted 36 per cent of all the money spent on press advertising and 22 per cent of the national advertising revenue for all media.

Table 6.4 Top 20 publishers of local and regional newspapers in the UK (by circulation/distribution)

	Paid-for daily newspapers*			Paid-for weekly newspapers†			Free weekly newspapers†			Total: paid-for and free		
	No. of titles	Circulation per issue		No.of titles	Circulation per issue		No. of titles	Distribution per issue		No. of titles	Circulation/distribution per week	
		'000	%		'000	%		'000	%		'000	%
TRN	11	929,882	16.0	18	538,525	7.2	37	2,347,001	7.1	66	8,464,818	11.3
of which: TVN	*1*	*25,719*	*0.4*	*1*	*13,079*	*0.2*	*2*	*132,607*	*0.4*	*4*	*300,000*	*0.4*
Northcliffe Newspapers	13	808,130	13.9	15	312,329	4.2	32	1,657,955	5.0	60	6,819,064	9.1
UPN	6	473,638	8.2	22	402,347	5.4	39	2,223,925	6.8	67	5,468,100	7.3
Reed	4	153,564	2.6	15	324,497	4.3	61	3,885,933	11.8	80	5,131,814	6.8
Westminster Press	8	427,016	7.4	19	382,473	5.1	35	1,796,406	5.5	62	4,740,975	6.3
Trinity‡	4	308,662	5.3	35	568,412	7.6	29	1,415,627	4.3	68	3,836,011	5.1
Midland Independent	3	319,632	5.5	2	149,535	2.0	24	1,519,718	4.6	29	3,587,045	4.8
GMEN	*1*	*221,479*	*3.8*	*9*	*190,071*	*2.5*	*20*	*1,296,173*	*3.9*	*30*	*2,815,118*	*3.7*
Midland News Association	2	317,855	5.5	4	42,929	0.6	18	646,092	2.0	24	2,596,151	3.5
Eastern Countries Newspapers	4	207,376	3.6	12	138,141	1.8	25	1,155,661	3.5	41	2,538,058	3.4
EMAP	3	114,474	2.0	36	534,122	7.1	31	1,253,196	3.8	70	2,474,162	3.3
Portsmouth & Sunderland Newspapers	4	195,482	3.4	7	106,624	1.4	15	792,412	2.4	26	2,071,928	2.8
Southern Newspapers	3	140,489	2.4	9	145,457	1.9	20	1,055,442	3.2	32	2,043,833	2.7
Bristol United Press	2	169,146	2.9	2	49,479	0.7	5	382,555	1.2	9	1,446,910	1.9
Johnston Press	–	–	–	27	405,769	5.4	25	976,731	3.0	52	1,382,500	1.8
Tindle Newspaper Group	2	98,467	1.7	10	116,414	1.6	21	658,748	2.0	33	1,365,964	1.8
Yellow Advertiser Newspaper Group	–	–	–	4	43,687	0.6	19	1,004,521	3.1	23	1,048,208	1.4
Yattendon Investment Trust	1	64,432	1.1	6	94,410	1.3	19	497,493	1.5	26	978,495	1.3
Southnews	–	–	–	9	147,131	2.0	17	741,044	2.3	26	888,175	1.2
The Adscene Group	–	–	–	7	77,241	1.0	9	573,425	1.7	16	650,666	0.9
Sub-total: largest 20 publishers (as above)	71	4,949,724	85.3	268	4,769,593	63.6	501	25,880,058	78.8	840	60,347,995	80.3
Others	16	854,648	14.7	199	2,724,190	36.4	154	6,981,538	21.2	369	14,833,616	19.7
Known total: all local and regional newspapers	87	5,804,372	100.0	467	7,493,783	100.0‡	655	32,861,596	100.0‡	1,209	75,181,611	100.0‡

*Does not include the *Evening Standard*, an evening daily newspaper serving, primarily, the Greater London region (with an average circulation of 488,131 (January to June 1993).

†Includes local and regional Sunday newspapers. Also includes newspapers published more than once a week (but not daily) in different editions, but excludes newspapers published less frequently than once a week.

‡Figures do not sum to 100 due to rounding.

‡Includes data for Argus Newspapers (after deducting certain titles subsequently sold to Southnews) and Joseph Woodland & Sons Ltd.

Source: MMC, based on data from PressAd Services' data bank (as at 18 November 1993)

One of the main growth areas for local newspapers during the 1980s was the free sheet, rising from 169 titles in 1978 to over a thousand by 1988. These local newspapers were distributed free, often directly into people's homes, and were partly the result of advances in new printing technology and low staffing overheads as well as the expansion in advertising revenue. One of the earliest and best-known of the free-sheet groups was Eddie Shah's Messenger group, based in Stockport. Although primarily vehicles for advertising and containing little editorial or journalistic content, these free sheets did present serious competition for many established weekly 'paid-for' newspapers. Many of the free-sheet companies were bought up by existing local newspaper groups, or else the latter launched their own free sheet in direct competition, having the advantage of an established editorial and printing network. Some of the larger local newspaper groups, like Westminster Press and Reed Regional Newspapers, often published both 'paid-fors' and free sheets in the same area. The ILR Red Rose group also launched their own free local newspapers. However, since the economic recession of the early 1990s, many of these free sheets have had to close down due to a decline in advertising revenue.

As part of the concentration of ownership of the local press, Franklin and Murphy identify an increasing homogenisation of local newspapers, where small independent companies have been bought out by larger groups that want to eliminate competition, reduce costs and streamline production. For many newspapers this has resulted in a loss of 'local' identity, and many 'local' newspapers, like those of the Portsmouth and Sunderland Newspaper group, are now printed at regional centres away from their communities, and are often only one in a series of 'local' newspapers whose only difference is their front and back pages, while the articles and features on the inside may often be identical.

The consequences of this homogenisation can easily be seen by looking at the 'alternative' or independent local press that has tried over the years to establish various titles as voices for alternative views in society, often youthful and/or left wing, such as the *Manchester Free Press*, *Leeds Other Paper*, *East End News*, *Northern Star* or *New Manchester Review*. Only a few of these titles have survived, usually by focusing on listings and 'lifestyle' rather than maintaining a radically alternative editorial line, one of the best-known being London's *Time Out*. This success, as various commentators have noted (Franklin and Murphy, 1991; Whitaker, 1984), is generally at the expense of any radicalism, and rather than extending choice and variety those 'alternative' newspapers that have survived have been absorbed into the mainstream values, attitudes and styles of big-business newspaper production and ownership.

Local newspapers traditionally used to be the entry point into the industry, where young cub reporters served their apprenticeship, their ambition being to move on to the national press of Fleet Street, or, more hopefully, into local radio and/or television and then perhaps on to national news. This traditional route was overseen by the National Council for the Training of Journalists, originally set up in 1952. Today many of the larger newspaper groups operate their own training schemes, and learning to become a journalist is today less about the acquisition of knowledge and more about gaining competencies. Beharrell (1993) points to this change in the training of journalists as one of the reasons for the change in style and content of local news reporting: 'For how a person has been equipped to deal with media situations, and how a media industry prepares its practitioners, will determine individual and group reactions to media situations both commonplace (and therefore predictable) and out of the ordinary.' Beharrell suggests that the modern reporter, trained in a climate of 'commercial reality', will rely upon previous successes in the types of story that appeal to both the editor and readers. Stories become shorter in length, less detailed or informed, and instead simpler and more emotional. Local newspapers have tended to become more populist in character, relying on a 'house (or group) style' that consists of a diet of human interest stories and moral panics, a style that is no longer the result of a professional ideology of balance and impartiality but rather a campaigning sensationalism that is aimed at increasing sales.

For many people the local newspaper is likely to be the single most important source of news within their area, especially as the local newspaper may reach over 80 per cent of households and be kept around the house for several days, rather than being thrown away the next day as usually happens to daily newspapers. Local newspapers have an important relationship with the communities that they serve, recording the 'organized output of symbolic events, decisions and official accounts produced by a local establishment in sectors of the state, business and the formal voluntary sector' (Franklin and Murphy, 1991). A report on the sources of 865 stories in fourteen British local newspapers, accounting for over 67 per cent of all news stories, revealed five main sources of news: local and regional government, voluntary organisations, the courts, the police and business (Table 6.5). Franklin and Murphy (1991) suggest that this reliance upon these limited sources means that the local press tends to reinforce the *status quo* and celebrate the values of a stable, well-ordered and, as much as possible, conflict-free community.

Table 6.5 Local press: sources of news

Source	Total	Percentage
Courts	105	12.0
Coroner	10	1.0
Police	98	11.5
Other emergency services (fire, ambulance)	11	1.5
Council (and regional authorities)	199	23.0
Business	73	8.5
Government	32	3.5
MPs	11	1.5
Schools/colleges	33	4.0
Clubs/voluntary sector	107	12.5
Charitable appeals	36	4.0
Political parties/pressure groups	13	1.5
Churches	25	3.0
Public protest	14	1.5
Investigations	9	1.0
Other	89	10.5
Total	865	100.5

Sources: Glossop Chronicle, Bury Times, Westmorland Gazette, Cumberland and Westmorland Herald, Burnley Express, Rochdale Observer, Rossendale Free Press, North Wales Weekly News, Wigan Observer, Lochaber News, Oban Times, Warrington Star, Stockport Express Advertiser, Lothian Courier

---

activity **6.6**

Look through a copy of your local newspaper and identify the main sources of news. How many of the stories will have been sent in and how many are the result of investigation or research by a journalist from the newspaper? How does your newspaper compare with Table 6.5?

The Newbury Weekly News

A local 'paid-for' weekly newspaper that has served its local community since 1867 is the *Newbury Weekly News*. This is a broadsheet that was started during the explosion of small newspapers that resulted from the abolition of the various taxes (stamp duty, paper tax and advertising duty – see Chapter 2) on newspapers in the 1850s and 1860s. This meant that both the cost of production and the cover price of newspapers fell. For the first time a legal, mass readership was possible, and legitimate newspapers like the *Newbury Weekly News* became an economic possibility. Originally, it contained only a small amount of local news and syndicated material from

London-based newspapers. As the size and prosperity of Newbury grew so the demand for local news and information on trade and agriculture developed. Today, very little of the newspaper's content is from sources outside of the newspaper itself.

Ownership of the *Newbury Weekly News* is through a private company, among whose shareholders are members of families who have controlled the newspaper since it started. The company also produces a weekly free sheet, the *Advertiser*, and monthly and quarterly supplements aimed at the local business and leisure sectors.

Table 6.6

	Newbury	GB average
Households 1989	12,929	–
Population 1989	34,706	–
Social class	%	%
I Professional	6.4	3.8
II Intermediate	20.6	16.5
III N Skilled Non-manual	9.9	9.0
III M Skilled manual	23.1	21.3
IV Semi-skilled	7.4	10.7
V Unskilled	2.7	3.5
Economically Inactive	27.9	33.2
Employment	%	%
Agriculture	0.9	2.3
Energy/water	2.6	3.1
Manufacturing	21.4	27.1
Dist/catering	23.7	19.2
Transport	6.7	6.5
Construction	8.5	7.0
Other services	38.2	34.1
Car ownership	%	%
Any car	71.8	60.5
1 car	50.7	45.1
2 cars	18.3	13.2
3+ cars	3.0	2.3
Home tenure	%	%
Owned	62.0	55.7
Council rented	25.4	31.2
Other rented	11.7	12.8
Other markets	%	%
Self-employed	9.1	9.4
Apprentices/trainees	3.0	3.5
Households with 2+ economically active	42.6	40.3

Source: Newsbury Weekly News

One of the advantages of being independent, the company claims, is that any decisions concerning the running of the *Newbury Weekly News* are made by a management team consisting of local people, living within the community the newspaper serves, who should therefore be able to keep in touch with the conditions and feelings of the community. Editorial decisions are internal, and unlike the editors of local newspapers that are members of large groups, the *Newbury Weekly News*'s editor does not have to worry about outside or group interests, although the editor will still have commercial, and circulation, pressures to consider.

The *Newbury Weekly News* claims its readership to be 'everyone who lives locally'. A survey it commissioned in 1989 suggested the paper reached about 72 per cent of adults in the area and up to 80 per cent in Newbury itself. In 1993 the circulation was 29,500, a reduction from its 1987 peak of about 32,000. The number of copies printed each week varies throughout the year. August, when families are on holiday, will mean less sales, whereas local events for which the *Newbury Weekly News* produces a supplement, such as the annual agricultural show, will mean extra copies being printed and sold. The paper is mainly distributed through newsagents, and a substantial number of readers have their copy delivered to their door.

As there is no immediate competition there is no overt 'segmentation' of readership, and specific groups are not targeted in terms of age, socio-economic grouping or gender but simply defined by locality; if you live in the Newbury area you are a potential reader of the *Newbury Weekly News* (Table 6.6).

activity 6.7

Try to establish a reader profile for your local newspaper. What categories are used and what does it tell you about:

1 the local community?
2 the newspaper that serves it?

Competition for the *Newbury Weekly News* is limited, and one of the clues to its apparent success is its unique role as the only truly local medium for a fairly specific geographical area. Newbury and its surrounding villages exist on the edge of various other regions, southern, western, London or south Midlands, but none seems to offer the specific local service of the *Newbury Weekly News*. Other local newspapers, daily and weekly, that are available come from towns several miles away, such as Reading, Swindon or Basingstoke, and are part of larger newspaper groups and therefore very different in character. These papers reflect the news and needs of their larger, more urban, communities.

It is unlikely that any new newspaper will appear to challenge the hegemony of the *Newbury Weekly News*; the last competitor was seen off at the turn of the century. The Royal Commission on the Press in 1977 found that out of a sample of 24 local weekly newspapers launched since 1961, only one was established in direct competition with an existing local weekly (Curran and Seaton, 1991). There is no alternative or community press borne on the back of supposedly cheaper technology to challenge the *Newbury Weekly News*, and the local council does not produce its own PR-minded municipal free papers, as Franklin and Murphy (1991) suggest may occur in some urban areas.

6.14 *(and opposite)* *Newbury Weekly News*, 15, 22 June 1961

An ILR station, Radio 210, is available in Newbury. Based in Reading, it is part of the GWR regional network and has some local programming, but generally offers chart or 'golden oldie' music. In 1992 the BBC opened a local radio station, Radio Berkshire, but it offers a limited local service and aims to cover the whole county. Both local radio services suffered budget and staff reductions during the early 1990s.

The most recent challenge to the *Newbury Weekly News* came when the commercial television franchise changed in January 1993. Meridian took over from TVS and set up a local TV studio in Newbury, which, since January 1993, has had its own local news programme on ITV at 6.30 every evening. This has presented some competition to the *Newbury Weekly News*, mainly because it has the immediacy of a daily programme and the attraction of pictures over print.

The distinct geographical nature of the *Newbury Weekly News*'s catchment area makes it suitable for a community or

'incremental' radio station. It is likely to be some time before the local economy is strong enough to support such an initiative, and any group interested in offering such a service will probably need to include the paper and its news-gathering network as part of any bid to the Radio Authority.

The traditional nature of the paper and its readers is perhaps reflected in the debate about its page size. When most newspapers are moving to tabloid, letters to the *Newbury Weekly News* indicate a strong support among its readers for it to retain its traditional broadsheet format. The *Advertiser*, its freesheet sister, is tabloid and has a higher distribution. It is particularly popular in the neighbouring town of Thatcham with its higher concentration of new housing and 'non-professional' households.

Despite various small adjustments to the type face and masthead, the only major change that readers might have been aware of was the move of news on to the front page in 1961 (Figure 6.14). Although the *Newbury Weekly News* was one of the last newspapers to take classified advertising off the front page, it has been quick to take advantage of new technology. The old hot metal process was replaced in 1974 with web offset and photosetting, and in 1984 new Solna printers were bought from Sweden. These new machines mean that the paper can be produced at the rate of 20,000 copies per hour, and they can handle a maximum of 32 broadsheets or 64 tabloid pages in one run. Perhaps because of its fairly strong union chapel (branch), the introduction of this new technology was carefully negotiated and avoided any of the redundancies or strife associated with similar moves in larger newspapers. No staff at the *Newbury Weekly News* have been made redundant, and only in 1990, when Danish Thorsted conveyors inserting equipment and automated stackers were introduced, did the number of casual staff employed diminish.

The *Newbury Weekly News* is unusual in having its own presses, but this gives it the advantage of longer deadlines and greater flexibility to produce one-offs such as the edition recording the 1993 by-election result that was produced overnight (Figure 6.15). The presses are also a source of income, as they print two other weekly newspapers.

In 1989 the news room went 'electric'. All copy is now handled in a computerised operation via pcs and computer design screens.

Advertising provides the *Newbury Weekly News* with about 80 per cent of its revenue. Without this source of income the cover price would be around £1.50 per copy, rather than the 30p charged in 1993. Most of the advertising comes from local businesses and so the economic health of the paper is

6.15 *Newbury Weekly News*, 7 May 1993

bound up with that of the town's businesses. During the late 1980s when Newbury was a 'boom' town, there would be up to a dozen pages advertising job vacancies; in 1993 the 'Situations Vacant' adverts covered about two and a half pages. There has been a similar decline in advertising for house and car sales, as well as in the amount of advertising taken out by local shops and businesses. It is therefore important that the *Newbury Weekly News* retains a good relationship with its advertisers, and to this end the newspaper and its management try to play a leading role in the local business community.

Like all newspapers, the *Newbury Weekly News* has a department responsible for attracting advertising to the paper. Although the advertising and editorial departments are separate (a fact that the editor emphasises), there has to be some co-operation, particularly for advertisement feature pages or

6.16 *Newbury Weekly News*, 9 September 1993

supplements that may contain a combination of advertising and specially written supporting editorial copy (Figure 6.16). Sometimes the editorial copy for these feature pages is bought in from agencies that offer specialist material on such topics as weddings, DIY, gardening or holidays, or else regular *Newbury Weekly News* reporters are engaged to write suitable copy.

Advertising is part of the service a local newspaper offers. The balance between adverts and editorial needs to be finely judged: if the newspaper contains too much advertising, readers become dissatisfied; too little, and the newspaper loses money or has to raise its cover price. The *Newbury Weekly News* tried to keep that balance at about 65 per cent advertising to 35 per cent editorial. As the advertising pays for the editorial, the amount of advertising revenue available will affect the size of the paper. At its height in the late 1980s, editions of the paper could have up to 72 pages, but in the early 1990s they fell to around 44 pages each. There is also a risk in becoming too small, as the newspaper may start to lose readers if it is not considered good value.

Editorially the *Newbury Weekly News* tries to reflect the community that it serves – a conservative one, despite in 1993 not electing a Conservative MP for the first time in nearly seventy years. Contrary to some local perceptions, Newbury is still a prosperous, middle-class town, rated one of the four wealthiest districts in the country in a survey carried out in 1993 by the School of Advanced Urban Studies at Bristol University. Although claiming to be impartial, the *Newbury Weekly News* echoes these local values and ambiguities, and its pages frequently reflect the issues that concern the more established or prosperous members of the community. Letters

Table 6.7 A survey of 32 letters published in one issue, 1.7.93

Subject matter	Number
Thanks or congratulations	10
Bloodsports (3 for, 2 against)	5
Road safety/traffic	5
Gardens/neatness	3
Religion	1
Health/caring	2
AWE safety fear	1
Council spending	1
Politicians	1
Size of Newbury Weekly News	1
Spoilsports	1
Planning	1

AWE, Atomic Weapons Research Establishment (Aldermaston)
Source: Beharrell, M. (1993)

to the editor can take up two or three pages and usually include contributions from local councillors, political activists and other local 'notables'. Beharrell (1993) notes that although the letters pages tend to reflect the concerns of the more vociferous members of the community, these are often local variations of national issues such as the health service, public spending or road safety. The other significant features of the letters pages are public expressions of gratitude for help or information, or congratulations for successes, public or private (Table 6.7 and Figure 6.17).

6.17 Letters taken from the *Newbury Weekly News*

Treasures of the parish

THANKS to Mrs Bromfield for her kind remarks about Shaw Church and the welcome she was accorded as she witnessed the unusual and moving nuptials of members of The Sealed Knot. I hope that Pikesman Kerr and his new wife, Mistress Rita, are unscathed after the battles of the weekend at Wash Common.

Their wedding was one of a number of distinctive events here at St. Mary's; readers no doubt were able to participate vicariously in Mr and Mrs O'Dell's wedding a week or two before. May I invite them to attend in person this coming Sunday afternoon a "Songs of Praise for Harvest" when favourite hymns of a seasonal nature will be interspersed with reminiscences by local people. Perhaps there is another Mrs Bromfield who needs to discover the treasures of Shaw cum Donnington?

Special thanks to Andy

A VERY big thank you to all members of our branch without them the Newbury Show would not have been such a success, for the branch. Also a big thank you to all the people who came and supported us over the two days. We made a total of over £1,913 during the days of the show. I would also like to thank Andy for putting up and taking down the stalls. Thanks Andy.

Thanks for a holiday

MAY I, through your paper, thank the Thatcham branch of the British Legion, for a wonderful holiday at Weston-Super-Mare. I understand this is the first one from the Thatcham branch.

Also, thank you to the Volunteer Bureau, for transporting me down there and back, and with such care and consideration.

Thanks to Sealed Knot

MAY I take this opportunity of thanking, via your newspaper, all those willing volunteers in the Sealed Knot who so kindly gave up their valuable time to give us all an insight in what life was like over 300 years ago.

We took three classes of junior children, aged between seven and 11, to the 'encampment' site set up at Skinners Green. They were held enthralled by Sealed Knot members who explained the diary of the battle, showed them how guns worked and demonstrated many aspects of life during the times of the Civil War. The high spot for many children was being drilled as a 'lancer' or a 'musketeer'. The whole experience of bringing history to life lasted two hours and was something that the children will remember for many years to come.

A good sign of a successful trip – no-one asked to go to the toilet or asked when we were going back to school!

Many thanks indeed Sealed Knot, keep up the good work.

activity **6.8**

Carry out a content analysis of the letters page of several editions of your local newspaper. What are the most common types of letter and who writes in most frequently? Does your local newspaper edit or in any way control the letters it publishes? How does your local newspaper compare with the *Newbury Weekly News* and the letters pages of other types of newspaper?

Franklin and Murphy (1991) note that one of the functions of the local press is to respond to national news events in a local way, reflecting the local dimension. After the massacre in Hungerford in 1987, the *Newbury Weekly News* tried to deal with the incident as a local matter with personal dimensions, rather than in the more lurid and sensational way the national tabloids approached it. The *Newbury Weekly News* claims to have received only one complaint about its treatment of the story, whereas reporters from the national newspapers supposedly alienated many of the local population in their hunt for 'good' copy.

The other national story that has been local to the *Newbury Weekly News* is the Women's Peace Camps at Greenham Common. Research carried out by Beharrell (1993) found that, perhaps contrary to expectations, the paper during its ten-year reporting of the Peace Camps was generally impartial and balanced in its treatment of the camps and, despite much strong local hostility, tried to see both sides. This, Beharrell suggests, reflects the aims of the newspaper's non-conformist founders to 'refrain from advocating the views of any party or sect but rather give an opportunity for all sides to be heard without ourselves being committed to any' (Stokes, 1992), as well as an increasingly old-fashioned journalistic 'professional ideology' that values balance and impartiality.

Beharrell contrasts the *Newbury Weekly News*'s treatment of the Greenham Peace Camps with the treatment given to New Age travellers in Birmingham, where the local newspaper, the *Birmingham Evening Mail* (part of the Ingersoll group), launched a campaign to 'Keep this scum out', and called on the police to 'hound 'em'. In contrast, the tone of the *Newbury Weekly News* seems aimed at the more 'educated' middle-class reader. The paragraphs are up to three times the length of other tabloid local newspapers, the language is generally more restrained, and sentences are longer than in most popular newspapers.

News stories at the *Newbury Weekly News* come mainly

from its own reporters, but up to 40 per cent of the editorial can originate from other sources, such as the network of local correspondents in surrounding villages, members of the public, or more PR-minded businesses and organisations. The paper's pages reflect the concerns of its mainly middle-class readership, what Franklin and Murphy (1991) call the 'rituals of the community': weddings, Christmas concerts in local schools and churches, exam and degree results, and, of course, births, deaths and engagements. A regular feature on the letters pages is 'Old memories revived', with newspaper cuttings going back 125 years, helping to reinforce a sense of history for both the newspaper and the community. There is also a junior weekly news section and a monthly woman's page.

The deadline is 7 p.m. on Wednesday for publication on Thursday, market day in Newbury. The majority of pages in the first section of the paper, including the front page and sports pages, are finished between 2 p.m. and 7 p.m., and births, marriages and deaths are accepted up to 4 p.m. Other features may have been prepared some time in advance.

A typical story may come about because someone phones in to ask why the police are redirecting traffic at the local roundabout. A reporter will telephone the police station and discover that a lorry has shed its load on a busy roundabout. If the incident is sufficiently interesting, a photographer is sent out and the reporter may also attend to investigate the story. The reporter may then phone copy back to the newsroom from the scene, or return to the office and write up the story using a pc. Laptop computers are also available for working away from the office.

The reporter will then print the story out and pass it on to the 'copy-taster', usually the news editor or chief reporter. The copy-taster, who initially checks for inaccuracies and whether the story has fulfilled its news potential, sorts and classifies incoming stories and decides if and how the story will be used. Whether the story will appear in the paper depends upon various criteria: what is its news value? Was anyone injured? Does it make a good picture? Have other similar accidents happened recently? (Traffic in Newbuy is a current issue as a result of the go-ahead, despite much local opposition, for a new by-pass.) How does this incident relate to the wider by-pass story? Is it a way of updating a long-running but rather 'dry' story? How much space should it be given?

If the story passes copy-tasting, the report moves into the subbing department, where it is again judged on news value as well as being checked for grammar, balance, legality and accu-

Long delays as lorry sheds part of its load

AN item which quite literally fell off the back of a lorry caused serious traffic delays on Thursday lunchtime.

A heavy goods vehicle carrying girders through the town lost part of its load as it drove under the A34 and on to the Robin Hood roundabout. The construction completely blocked one lane and the other was soon blocked too as recovery crews used a crane to winch the heavy welded assembly from the road.

Queues quickly built up through Newbury town centre and back along the A4 towards Newbury College. Delays were also caused on all other roads leading on to the busy roundabout.

● Our picture shows recovery crews using a crane to lift the lost load off the road and clearing the route for traffic.

6.18 *Newbury Weekly News*

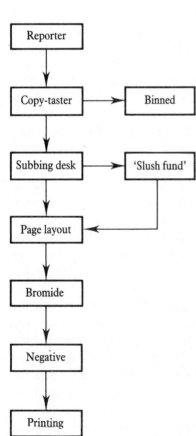

6.19 Flow chart showing progress of news copy

racy, and given a headline, a possible page number and a type face. All of this is done on screen. For a relatively minor story the copy may be kept in a 'slush fund', from which articles are used to complete pages as necessary. Major articles, news items and features are generally allocated pages straight away. The final report of the accident may only be one or two paragraphs long or may be part of a longer feature (Figure 6.18).

As the deadline approaches, decisions are made and the copy is put into place electronically. Unlike larger newspapers, the *Newbury Weekly News* does not have a formal editorial meeting to decide the main stories, but instead relies upon informal discussions between the editor, deputy editor and news editor. The editorial page is designed and made up on screen, checked and then passed on, with pictures and advertisements added, again electronically, to be made into a bromide (a type of high-definition, emulsified photocopy) which will be converted into a negative and form the basis of the printing plate (Figure 6.19).

The *Newbury Weekly News* is apparently a successful newspaper because it reflects a large proportion of the community that it serves and that provides it with its market. It is a traditional newspaper, with perhaps slightly old-fashioned values, that assumes its readers are well informed and want to know both sides of a story. Like the town it serves, it has an air of 'quiet respectability' (Beharrell, 1993). It is the type of newspaper that Franklin and Murphy (1991) see as becoming increasingly rare in England, although still strong in America, where the locally owned newspaper offers a focus for the community's particular sense of itself, defined in terms of the local economy, the local political system and local social relationships. It is the type of newspaper that tries to combine high moral and journalistic standards with a vested interest in maintaining the status quo and the comfortable 'middle-England' background of many of its readers and the community itself.

The lack of a real rival to the *Newbury Weekly News* means, at the moment, that it is unlikely to be bought out by a larger group trying to eliminate competition, and so as long as the community stays the same, or as long as the paper can change as the community changes, it should survive.

activity **6.9**

1 Draw up a profile of your own local newspaper, looking at such issues as who owns it, what type of reader it is aimed at, what other local media are in competition with it, what proportion of its revenue comes from advertising, and how that might affect the content of the newspaper and the types of story it contains. How successful is your local newspaper and what are its criteria for success?
2 Compare your local newspaper with another contrasting example, e.g. rural with urban or independent with one that is part of a large group. Look at such areas as news values, style, political bias and content.

FURTHER READING

Fountain, N. 1988: *Underground: The London Alternative Press 1966–1974*. Comedia.
Frith, S. 1983: *Sound Effects*. Constable.
Frith, S. and Goodwin, A. (Eds) 1990: *On Record*. Routledge.
Garfield, S. 1986: *Expensive Habits: The Dark Side of the Music Industry*. Faber and Faber.
Gillett, C. 1983: *The Sound of the City*. Souvenir.
Goodhart, D. and Wintour, C. 1986: *Eddy Shah and the Newspaper Revolution*. Coronet.
Kerr, P. (Ed) 1986: *The Hollywood Film Industry*. Routledge.
Negus, K. 1992: *Producing Pop*. Edward Arnold.
Schlesinger, P. 1987: *Putting Reality Together*. Methuen.

7 | *Media Practice*

Practice and theory cannot be separated: their relationship is both complementary and integrated. Chapter 3 deals with how meaning is created through the use of certain codes, forms and conventions. This chapter shows how creating a practical piece of work will not only help illustrate in a very direct way the ideological implications of many of the choices, decisions and constraints that 'professional' producers experience, but also provide direct experience of the manipulation of the media language that 'professional' producers work to and that we, the audience, respond to. Practical exercises are important because they clearly show that the output of different media operates in clear social and economic contexts and is the result of men's and women's own actions.

Creating media texts raises questions about the criteria by which 'professionals' interpret 'reality' and how it is represented back to us and other audiences. Practice helps, too, to illustrate the effect the notion of 'audience' has as a determining factor in both the shape and content of a production. It also provides an opportunity to experience directly the constraints, decisions and structures involved in the media's products and to understand the effect these can have on the shape and outcome of the process itself.

There are some dangers associated with practical work, and perhaps the main one is thinking of what is produced in mainstream media as being 'professional', the one and only way of constructing media images and the model which all other work is compared with. This attitude can mean that what is produced outside of the mainstream is dismissed as amateur and inferior. Although the level of technology may be inferior, many of the processes and problems will nevertheless be very similar or even identical. The value of individual or non-professional practical work is that it is not working to long-established institutional patterns or constraints but allows for the exploration of different ways of presenting ideas and images, and can attempt to subvert or challenge this 'professional' notion of there being only one correct way.

Another danger that many first-time producers experience is the expectation that the final product should look like the 'real thing' and be of the same standard as if produced by mainstream media. Practical work is an exciting, intense, challenging and rewarding process; an end product is a bonus. A realistic 'product' tends to be emphasised by professionals and others, who are sometimes keen to maintain ideas of 'standards' and 'expertise' as a means of maintaining an exclusivity and mystique associated with their own status and with creating media texts. There are in fact many instances where the opposite is the case and the 'professional' is keen to emulate the success of the 'amateur', particularly in the area of youth programmes on television or in magazines, where the 'off-the-street' style of scratch videos or fanzines has an immediacy that the mainstream can only copy and try to incorporate into its own output.

The value of practical work is that this professional aura can be demystified, examined and then challenged. It is important to remember that practical work is not an end in itself but a means to an end. It is not about acquiring a series of purely disembodied practical skills – the 'technicist trap'; its purpose is both to produce a practical piece of work and to illuminate the practices of the media as outlined in this book. Creating practical exercises is more than simply learning 'how to do it'; it is an opportunity to construct individual pieces of work and in the process to explore, experiment with and challenge some of the mainstream ways of working. It involves 'deconstructing' what others put together and learning to present alternatives – first learn the rules and then break them.

This chapter deals with the processes of production and in particular will look at the three main stages involved in creating a piece of media work: pre-production, including planning and research; production, including interviewing; and post-production, which includes editing and evaluating the work created and reviewing the knowledge gained.

PRE-PRODUCTION

Pre-production is perhaps the most time-consuming of the three stages and involves the processes of planning and research. Most productions start with an idea, an interest, a point of view or a feeling that someone wants to explore. As this idea develops, both the aims of the production and the sense of audience should become clearer. Whatever the medium and technologies being used, however long or short the production, all successful productions have to be clearly thought out and should have a thoroughly researched and planned structure. Depending upon the medium used, and how ambitious the finished production is, this planning and preparation can take up to 50 per cent of the available time. The following questions will need to be considered:

- What are the aims of this production?
- Who is its target audience?
- Which medium is most appropriate for it?
- What resources are available for it?

The Aims

All media texts aim to produce some kind of meaning, whether it be explicitly informative or educational, or more open or entertaining. This may be a clear and unambiguous message, like 'Tomorrow will be sunny in the south', or it may be more abstract and open-ended, trying perhaps to convey an emotion or feeling, or simply hoping to elicit a response. As Chapters 3 and 4 demonstrate, media texts and their meaning can sometimes be confusing, misinterpreted or even redundant, and there can be many different criteria used in trying to evaluate the end product. For most productions, however, a well-developed sense of purpose and a clear set of aims have to be defined at some stage.

A common danger is that of being too ambitious in deciding upon the aims of a production, particularly if there are limited resources. It is probably unrealistic, for example, if using video for the first time, to try and tell the audience about the role and influence of the motor car in late twentieth-century industrialised society. It would probably be a very interesting programme, or series of programmes, but what are the resources necessary to make it, and are they available?

A clearly defined set of aims will also help measure the success or otherwise of a production and can be an important part of the review and evaluation process. It is therefore often useful to ask the question, 'At the end of watching/reading/listening to this piece of work the target audience should . . . what?'

- Understand the seriousness of the local traffic problem?
- Know what the local council's plans are?
- Understand the objections being raised by the local conservation groups?
- Know how to get their opinion heard?

The Target Audience

For most productions, whether student or 'professional', however long or short, an audience is envisaged, as it helps focus the style and content of the work. For *Time* magazine the audience may be millions of readers throughout the world, for Classic FM it may be three or four million listeners in Britain who enjoy classical music, and for the *Newbury Weekly News* (see Chapter 6) it may only be a few thousand living in West Berkshire who share a common interest in local events and personalities.

When clarifying ideas about a target audience it is important to try and be as specific as possible. Is the audience a specific group of people? If so, how can they be categorised? Do they belong to certain age groups, ethnic groups, or socio-economic grades? What else do they have in common – perhaps their interest in the media? Perhaps they all come from the same locality? Do they have similar hobbies and interests? It is also important to be realistic when defining an audience. Unmarried males over the age of 50 who live beside the sea and are interested in volleyball do probably exist, but it could be very difficult to reach a significant number.

activity **7.1**

Using the information in Chapter 5 produce a clearly defined 'profile' of a target audience for a particular text, preferably one that you have produced yourself. Try using the following categories: age; sex; social grade; location; interests/hobbies. Is there any other information or category that could be useful?

Remember: *when in doubt, keep it simple.*

The Most Appropriate Medium

A production often starts with the idea of 'doing something on video' or 'writing a piece for radio'. However, it should only be after answering questions about aims, target audience and resources that the most appropriate medium is decided upon. The aims of the production will influence the medium because some topics are more suited to certain media than others. For instance, if the topic is very visual then a visual medium would seem to be most appropriate. If the aim is to transmit a lot of facts and figures then a printed medium may be more successful than an audio one. If the production focuses on music then video or radio will probably work better than printed material. If the aim is to inform through the use of different points of view or experts, then radio or a printed medium may be more suitable than a visual one consisting mainly of 'talking heads'.

The target audience will influence the decision about the most appropriate medium, as certain groups of people have different attention spans and preferences as to how they receive information, are persuaded or are entertained. Different audiences consume the media in different social contexts, and whereas some groups are more willing to sit and read, perhaps privately, others prefer a visual or more active medium that they can share. (Chapter 5 looks in more detail at how different groups consume different media.)

One way of challenging or subverting existing conventions is to use a medium not usually considered appropriate for a particular audience, genre of programme or type of message.

---

activity **7.2**

Choose a production in one particular medium – say, radio – and then consider how it would be modified to fit another medium – say, print or television.

Resources

Chapter 6 illustrates how media texts have certain common factors that determine their shape, size and content. All productions have to work to a budget, often decided by someone other than the person putting the production together. Often these budgets limit the time, the equipment and the personnel available, and they may affect the production values. This can include the technologies and expertise that might be used. If high-tech equipment with lots of special effects is available there is a strong temptation to use it irrespective of the time or cost. A decision is made, perhaps unconsciously, to use special effects as a substitute for content, running the danger that what is being said is seen to be less important than how it is being said. With most media becoming increasingly dependent upon new technological hardware, it is easy to become awed or infatuated with new pieces of equipment that seem to do the same old tasks better, faster and more easily. Technical competence is not, however, the only criterion for success, and often the old, tried and tested methods can be more successful in producing the desired end result without the necessity of having to master new and unfamiliar technology in a short space of time.

activity **7.3**

Explore how developments in television technology have influenced the 'look' of programmes. Compare current television output with the output of 1950s and early 1960s, looking in particular at the use of graphics and computer-generated special effects, and the number of angles of cameras being used. Sports programmes are a particularly interesting genre to look at, especially high-profile events like the Olympic Games or world championships.

It is useful to make a list of all the equipment that is needed for a particular production:

- Estimate how much time is available and how it is going to be allocated. A time-scale for all the different jobs, working back from the final deadline, is very useful.
- Make a plan of action, listing all the research to be done, letters to be written, telephone calls to be made, interviews to be arranged etc., and put beside each activity the name of the person who will be responsible for making sure that it is completed on time.
- Be realistic. How much money is there to spend? A rough costing needs to be worked out. Include expenses incurred while undertaking research, such as travelling expenses or photocopying, as well as the cost of any extra materials that may have to be purchased. Copyright is often overlooked, but it may also have to be paid for and can be very expensive, particularly for well-known pieces of music or film.

Figure 7.1 shows two forms that will help in planning resources and scheduling shooting.

Research

Good research should mean that the production almost writes itself. The difficulty comes when the information has to be transferred into sound and/or vision or print. There are many different sources of information, depending upon the choice of topic. The most obvious sources are libraries, particularly the reference sections, newspaper cuttings, trade magazines and computer databases. Hard data can be difficult to present in an appealing way, particularly in audio where, without the visual back-up, it is often hard for the audience to absorb the information being given. 'Visual' research can include looking for suitable archive footage either in film libraries, which can be expensive, or among in-house stock. Commercial videos and other student work can also be a source of difficult or elusive shots. Computer graphics software, slides and black-and-

PROJECT

REQUIRED RESOURCES

PLANNER   PROJECT

START _____ TARGET _____ FINISH _____

PURPOSE _____

_____

_____

_____

IDEA/SUMMARY _____

_____

_____

_____

_____

_____

PLAN Main steps   Time required

RESEARCH _____

PRE-PROD _____

POST-PROD _____

_____

_____

_____

PERSONS Contacts, services graphics etc. . .   PHONE

EQUIPMENT _____

BUDGET Expenses _____

7.1a and (*opposite*) 7.1b Project planner
and shooting schedule

white agency shots can be useful, but always check copyright. It can also help to look at other work within the same genre, or aimed at the same audience, or trying to serve the same function. It is important always to be critical of the information that is researched and be wary of any implicit or explicit bias that it may contain.

Keeping a record of the production process can be useful, especially if it is not just a factual, diary-type record of the choices and decisions made in the construction of a production, but rather a record that can be the basis for explaining what choices were available and why certain decisions and modifications were made. This record can be an important reminder when reviewing and evaluating a production and can help to highlight the critically informed ideas and intentions that should underlie any successful production.

SHOOTING SCHEDULE

PERSONNEL:

DATE:	EQUIPMENT:
LOCATION:	
CALL:	REMARKS: Cameras, contingency plans etc.
TO FILM:	
WRAP:	DEADLINE:
DATE:	EQUIPMENT:
LOCATION:	
CALL:	REMARKS: Cameras, contingency plans etc.
TO FILM:	
WRAP:	DEADLINE:

As the production develops, this record should include how the target audience, aims and resources all affected the shape and content of the production. How was the production researched, what sources of information were used, and how easy or difficult was it to gain access to these sources? How was the material evaluated or modified to suit the requirements of the medium, the target audience and the aims of the production? How did the resources, such as time and equipment, affect the shape and content of the production? What problems were experienced, how were they overcome, and how did they affect the development, final content and shape of the production?

PRODUCTION

Every production has a certain style, and this will depend upon a number of factors. If the audience aimed at is a youth one then the style usually borrows from current musical trends and includes fairly rapid editing, fast-moving visuals, graphics, loud sound-track, special effects and a variety of messages all being broadcast simultaneously. This style has become a well-known genre and it is common to try and emulate it. However, what looks easy and 'rough' is often difficult to do successfully with limited resources. It can be more worth-while, and offer a greater chance of success, to try for a more original style that is within the means of both the creator and the resources.

If the production has an older audience as its target then a more sedate style is often considered appropriate; for example, a loud pop-music background is usually considered not to work well with this type of audience.

All media texts have some kind of narrative and should have a structure that is appropriate for the purpose. Both producers and audiences have ideas and expectations, sometimes articulated, often just assumed, as to what a particular production is about, where it should start from and how it should develop and finish. This will depend up such factors as whether or not the programme is part of a series, whether the characters or narrative are already familiar, or whether it is a one-off that has to create its characters' identities quickly and have a self-contained narrative within a given time-slot.

In Chapter 3 the significance of the title sequence was discussed. Most radio and television programmes are 'top-and-tailed', usually through the use of a theme tune, text or graphics. An effective start is sometimes made by using a sound or visual montage that not only introduces some of the main issues of the production but also hopefully attracts the audience's attention. Most successful productions vary their pace and content, perhaps by following a 'talking-head' segment with some action shots, or a piece of music with some speech. Each segment should lead naturally into the next.

Commercial radio stations often work to a common hourly format (Figure 7.2).

7.2 Hourly programming on a typical commercial station

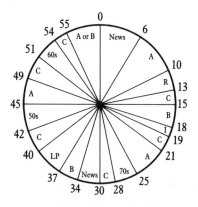

Key

A Hit record from charts

B New release

C Commercial break

I Information

R Recent record

| activity 7.4 | Choose a radio or television programme and deconstruct its different segments. How many are there? How long are they? How are they linked? Is there a pattern? |

7.3 McRoberts, Macmillan, 1987

KATOOMBA, 4 April. – Local police and volunteer searchers this morning rescued four school boys trapped overnight on a mountain ledge. One of the boys fell late Tuesday afternoon.
FACTS A friend climbed down to him, while another went for help. Darkness, however, fell before police were told.

BACK-GROUND The boys were taking part in a survival course run as part of their school Physical Education programme.

FACTS When lifted to safety the boys were examined by a police doctor. They were unharmed apart from minor abrasions.

QUOTE 'I feel fine,' said one of the boys. 'I wasn't scared, just cold.'

FACTS The boys' parents were informed of the accident late last night.

BACK-GROUND The school has only just started this course

Printed material frequently has an 'inverted pyramid' structure (Figure 7.3), setting out a story with the five Ws (who, what, when, where and why) in the first paragraph, subsequent paragraphs being a mixture of additional information and background. Paragraph three or four usually contains a quotation. One advantage of writing a feature this way is that the end of the article should contain the least useful information and can therefore be most easily cut if there is a shortage of space.

| activity 7.5 | Read the following information and write a newspaper story, following the 'pyramid' guidelines:

Fire brigade Fire began at 7.05. am today in Laing's Hotel, The Parade, Seamouth. Believed started in kitchen |

storeroom and spread rapidly by adjacent lift shaft to all three floors. Woman and man badly burned. Brought out by firemen.

Police Four people taken to Axebridge Royal Infirmary by ambulances. Flames began to break through roof.

Ambulance 1 took chef Alan Edwards, of 6, Langsett Road, Seamouth. Second contained hotel owner Alan Laing and wife, and a guest, Miss Irene Smollett of Exton.

Hospital Miss Smollett and Mr Laing dead on arrival. Chef badly burned on face and hands: admitted. Wife treated for shock.

Hotel receptionist, Karen Broughton, said
'Alan was preparing breakfast when he discovered the fire. He was burned trying to fight it. He told me, and I roused the Laings and we ran round the hotel warning the other staff and 17 guests. Everyone seemed to get out safely but when Mr Laing held a roll-call Miss Smollett was missing. He ran into the hotel. It was well alight by then. Then the fire brigade arrived.'

Chief fire officer, David Granville, said
'My men found Mr Laing and a woman huddled at one of the top floor corridor. We got them out just before the roof collapsed. There was no hope of saving the building. Its age and the draught from the lift shaft meant it was certain to be destroyed once the fire had a good hold.'

From your own knowledge and office files
Hotel built 1842. The Laing family have owned it for 53 years. Lived with wife, Anne, in hotel. Aged 63, wife 58. No children.

Media Techniques. Newspaper and Radio Journalism.
© London Institute.

Although, as Chapter 5 discussed, we often consume the media while paying very little direct attention, any successful production should engage the audience so that they want to carry on watching, listening or reading. This can often mean a compromise between something that is short, sharp and limited in content and a production that is long, thorough but boring.

Some productions make a claim of being spontaneous, and some, like *Zoo TV* or *The Big Breakfast* on Channel Four, or the *Chris Tarrant Breakfast Show* on Capital Radio, claim to be wacky and anarchic in their apparent lack of planning and rehearsal. Almost all radio and television shows, however, have a well-prepared script, and even 'reality TV' programmes like these, as part of 'mainstream' broadcasting, will have well-prepared playlists and a tightly controlled time schedule.

Although script writing and storyboarding can be seen as part of the pre-production stage, they have been included in the production section because they are the next step after the research and planning.

Guidelines for Preparing a Script

- Decide what is to be said.
- List the points in a logical order.
- Make sure that the opening is both interesting and informative.
- Try to visualise the individual listener or viewer. Remember that often we watch/listen or read alone or in small, intimate gatherings (often with our close family), so the production should have that same intimate feeling.
- Try out what is to be said by speaking the text aloud, then write it down if it sounds 'natural'. Some people have better speaking voices than others and it is important to make sure that the best voices are used.
- Try to write in short sentences or phrases but keep the language 'natural'. Some people immediately start to talk in an artificial, convoluted and rather pompous way when being recorded. This will usually detract from what is actually being said.
- If someone else is going to speak the text then make sure that they can understand it. Use clear punctuation and paragraphs and have the script typed with double spaces.
- Allow for rehearsals.

---

activity **7.6**

Plan and produce a seven-minute radio feature where each segment is no longer than ninety seconds. The feature should include both an introduction and an 'outro', as well as a variety of different presenters.

Television pictures are increasingly providing a common language or 'grammar', where every shot has a certain meaning and, when placed in sequence, will build up a story or message that can be understood by people from many different cultures – a kind of visual esperanto. As audiences become more tele-literate and increasingly share the same, usually American, production values, this style and language become more and more prevalent, so that we all come to share an understanding of what a close-up or an establishing shot mean and when it is appropriate to use them.

---

activity 7.7	While watching some television programmes, note how the 'grammar' is used, for instance by cutting from the outside of a building to a group of people talking indoors so that we assume that it is the same building. Try to find other examples.

Guidelines for Preparing a Storyboard

- Decide what is to be shown.
- List the visuals in a logical order.
- Create a 'picture' of what will be in each shot.
- Describe the type of shot, e.g. long shot, close-up etc.
- If possible give a rough idea of the length of each shot.
- Explain what sound is going on at the same time, e.g. music, speech etc.
- If someone else is involved in the shooting then make sure that they can also understand the storyboard.

See Figure 3.11 in Chapter 3 for an example of a storyboard.

---

activity 7.8	*Either* plan and produce a storyboard for a video lasting no longer than three minutes. The video should aim to tell a story or create an atmosphere using only pictures – no sound or dialogue.
	Or create a storyboard that shows the way 'real time' is condensed. What stages have been left out or shortened? How is this shortening of time indicated? How is one shot bridged with the next?

When both sound and vision have been planned and detailed on scripts and storyboard, they should be married together in a shooting script. Although this is a long and complex process, it is important for everyone to understand exactly what is required of them and how their part fits into the overall production. See Table 7.1(a) and (b) for two examples of shooting scripts.

Two or three different voices can be used for voice-overs, perhaps varying between male and female, as one person's voice can quickly become monotonous. A commentary is often made to sound more realistic by using background noise, or 'actuality', to give a sense of realism and of 'being there'.

Table 7.1(a) Cartier Bresson

SHOT NO	CAM	VISION	SOUND
1	5	black – 10 secs	Clock & Black mute – 10 secs
			/cue grams after 5 secs/
2	3	MIX to cap 1 (Cartier Bresson)	FADE UP GRAMS
3	2	MIX presenter /CUE HIM/ (MS)	FADE DOWN GRAMS / FADE UP STUDIO
			Good evening – This is the first of a series of programmes about the life and work of Cartier Bresson. Perhaps one of the greatest photographers the world will ever know.
4	1	CUT CU camera	With this camera, the Leica, he has taken many hundreds of photographs.
5	2	CUT presenter (MS)	Much of his success can be attributed to the simplification of his equipment and technique. Since the very beginning of his career he has worked with Leica cameras.
6	1	CUT cap 2	In this photograph we can see him using a Leica M3 camera. The 750,000th Leica to be manufactured. Altogether he has three of these cameras:– one for black and white work, one for colour and one for emergencies.
7	2	MIX presenter MS	When he is out and about on the hunt for pictures he carries only a single body and lens. He hides it under his coat and only brings it out when the moment comes to shoot.
8	1	MIX CU presenter	The phantomlike way in which he works is echoed in the finished print –
9	2	CUT cap 3	For rarely are the subjects seen staring into the lens.

Table 7.1(b)

THEALE COLLEGE MEDIA STUDIES   SHOOTING SCRIPT
LOCATION: THEALE COLLEGE (various locations)

DATE	SHOT	ACTION	DIALOGUE/ (FX)
14.2	1	Opening sequence college logo	Graphics/Music If you are thinking of improving your future prospects look to Theale College Fade to natural/V.O: as per script
	2 (tape 1)	MS Girl student sitting on grass with sketch pad	We are the major centre for further education in Berkshire MIX
	3 (tape 2)	CU overshoulder shot of sketch pad	There are exciting opportunities for everyone here – with a wide range of academic and vocational courses MIX
	4 (tape 1)	MS tutor + pupil in mech. wksp. Pull back to WA	CUT
	5 (tape 1)	CU tutor hand indicating read-out on monitor	Designed to cover a broad spectrum of tastes, abilities and needs FLIP
	6 (tape 2)	LS kitchen, tutor walking towards camera – follow action to table	We offer courses as varied as technology and computing, business studies and catering to social care and the performing arts CUT
	7 (tape 2)	CU tutor	We also offer literally hundreds of adult studies courses MIX
	8 (tape 1)	LS motor veh. wksp students + car/pan right to show tutor	Some courses are run for pleasure while others meet the requirements of local employers and higher education institutes. MIX
	9 (tape 2)	MS students in goggles working on car/tilt to show welding.	

activity **7.9**

Look at a television programme and analyse one particular section. Watch it to see how it has been constructed. Try to note every shot, giving its type and duration. Note also the use of any graphics or cutaways. Look particularly for the ways that sound and pictures are linked. Working back, now transcribe the commentary and reconstruct the script, giving commentary, camera shots and other relevant information.

In an attempt at creating a sense of realism, documentaries often require the filming process to be as discreet at possible, frequently using the fly-on-the-wall approach discussed in Chapter 3. One method is to use a participant observer – someone who becomes one of the group or social situation under observation. These methods, although increasingly popular, have moral implications, particularly for individual privacy, and raise questions about the role of investigative journalism, particularly as technology improves and the recording equipment becomes smaller, more discreet and more sophisticated.

Interviews

Interviews can play a large part in both the research and the production stages, particularly if the aim of a production is to inform or persuade. As edited parts of interviews are often included in the final programme, interviews are important not only as a means of acquiring information but also because they may affect the content, shape and style of a production. 'Every scrap of information that reaches the airwaves stems from an interview of some sort – a chat at a bar to get some background, an informal phone call to clear up some details, or a recording for transmission' (Boyd, 1988).

If a production is dealing with an issue of law and order – for example, drinking and driving or drug abuse – then the people most often interviewed are representatives of the police or related professions. This is because they are relatively easy to contact, and usually have a spokesperson whose job it is to deal with the public and answer questions. They are often considered the 'experts' in matters of law and order, who mediate between 'us', society, and 'them', the criminal. It may well be in their own interest to gain media exposure, as they often have a point of view, some information or an appeal for information that they want to publicise. This dependence upon a quick and easy sound-bite is often much more convenient than trying to obtain an interview with someone who represents the opposite or an 'anti-establishment' view. Not many people are willing to admit publicly that they drink and drive or take illegal drugs, although it may be possible to get an interview with someone who has 'reformed'. This unwillingness to 'confess' in public may be circumvented by offering someone anonymity, perhaps by appearing with the face blacked out or the voice distorted, but this is increasingly difficult to do without looking either clichéd or humorous.

Interviews are usually arranged well in advance, as most people are unwilling or unable to stop what they are doing and immediately answer questions in any meaningful or useful way. Interviewees sometimes ask to see the questions in advance too, as they want time to prepare their answers. Some interviewers feel that this loses the spontaneity and excitement of an interview, but, although it may be considered cheating, it is common practice, especially if the interviewee is important to the content or style of the programme. Increasingly some people, particularly politicians and those in authority, also ask to see the finished, edited product, and can even ask for a right of veto if they feel that they have been misrepresented. Most professionals would regard this as unacceptable, although in some cases producers do agree and then state in the programme that this has occurred. It is usual, however, to send a copy of the finished product to anyone who has helped in its construction.

To draft a set of questions, it is helpful first to make a list of the points that need to be covered. Good questions are simple and direct. The interviewer should be prepared to deviate from the prepared questions if other relevant issues come up. Wherever an interview takes place it should allow both the interviewer and the person being interviewed to relax, as it is usually when people are relaxed that they start to talk more volubly and naturally. Body language is a good indication of how people are feeling. People being interviewed often prefer to conduct the interview on familiar territory where they feel in control. If an interview is being recorded for use in a production, it is important to have an environment that does not have any disturbing background noises, such as roadworks or police-car sirens. These may not be noticeable in the excitement of carrying out the actual interview, but can be very obvious and distracting when reviewing the material, and although sometimes they can be removed at the editing stage there can be problems with continuity.

activity **7.10**	Try out some of the interviewing exercises that illustrate the effect of body language; for instance, conducting an interview sitting back to back where there is no eye contact, or across a desk with a physical barrier between the two people, or in unfamiliar surroundings.

Guidelines for an Interview

- Check equipment, particularly the sound levels, as there may only be one opportunity to carry out a particular interview.
- Be prepared. Think about the type of interview and have a clear idea of its purpose. Will the person being interviewed be sympathetic and co-operative, or reticent and unwilling to impart the relevant information?
- Introduce yourself, say who you are, and state the purpose of the interview and its context.
- Ask 'open' questions – those that start with 'What', 'Where', 'Why', 'When', 'How' or 'Who'.
- Structure the questions, possibly around the past, the present and the future. 'What did you do before...?' 'What are you doing now...?' 'What are your plans for the future...?'
- Recap the main points and check dates and the spellings of names of people and places.
- Ask a 'bucket' question along the lines of 'Is there anything else you would like to say?'. This allows the interviewee to drop in anything not covered so far.
- Close the gate. There was a famous reporter who during his career got a number of exclusives, and one of them concerned a vital witness in a notorious case. This witness, a woman, would not talk to any reporters, although hordes of them laid siege to her in her house. This reporter, like everyone else, got no reply when he called. However, he left a visiting card with a note saying that he would very much appreciate a chance to talk to the lady, and he promised that the interview would be on her terms. Later that day the woman rang him, saying that she did not want to talk to the entire press, so would he come that afternoon for an exclusive interview.

    Years later when they met again the woman asked the reporter if he knew why she had picked him rather than any of the others. 'Was it my little note on the back of the visiting card?', he asked. 'No,' she replied, 'lots of them tried that one ... but you were the only one who closed my garden gate properly on the way out.'

The lesson is that a little care and consideration can pay big dividends.

Most interviews on television are carried out with one camera, and the cutaways (where the interviewer asks the questions) and noddies (where the interviewer nods in agreement) are filmed later. A more complicated way of conducting interviews on video without having to use cutaways is to use two cameras.

activity **7.11**

Think up a scenario for an interview and ask someone to play the part of the interviewee. Try to conduct the interview as realistically as possible, with either pen and notebook, or audio or video equipment. Discuss the interview afterwards and assess to what extent the interviewee was reassured and put at his or her ease. Are there any other ways the interviewer's 'bedside manner' could have been improved?

Crossing the Line

When an interview is being recorded, whether with one or two cameras, it is important that the impression of two people talking to each other is achieved. This is done by setting up the cameras in such a way that they do not cross an invisible line but both stay on the same side of this line. The effect is

7.4 The positioning of cameras

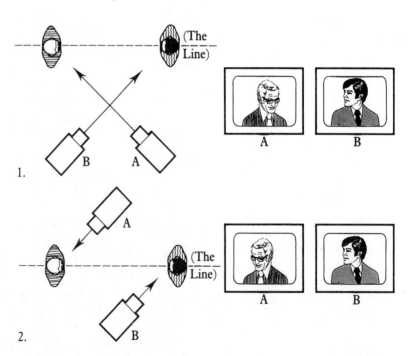

that of one person looking to the left talking to the other who is looking to the right. In Figure 7.4, cutting between cameras A and B on the same side of the line would be acceptable and give the impression of the two speakers facing each other as in a conversation. If however, one camera crosses the line, the speakers no longer look as if they are talking to each other and this might confuse the audience, or at least be aesthetically unpleasing.

Vox Pops

Vox Pop ('the voice of the people') is a common and popular convention in most media. Producers like it because it is fairly easy and cheap to produce and is popular with audiences, who like it because it is usually humorous as well as appearing to let 'the man or woman in the street' air his or her point of view. In television or radio the vox pop is usually a series of short reactions or comments from members of the public about a given topic, often recorded in the local high street or shopping centre to give a sense of immediacy.

The reporter is rarely heard asking the question, except perhaps at the very beginning. On the finished excerpt the public's answers are strung together to give a variety of voices but perhaps a common view point. On television this device is frequently used to add some humour or as a more light-hearted alternative to 'talking heads'. In print it is presented as a series of interviews carried out 'on the streets' or under the banner 'What our readers say'.

POST-PRODUCTION

The post-production stage, although the last, is possibly the most valuable, because it contains two important operations: the editing or putting together of all the work, and an evaluation of how successful the whole exercise has been, which includes a review of what has been learnt about the process of creating media products.

Editing

Audio and video editing is necessary because, although some programmes may broadcast events or interviews 'live', generally very little of the raw material that has been filmed or recorded is tidy enough to be seen or read by its audience without going through some sort of editing process. Editing can be time-consuming, taking longer than the actual production stage, but for many people it is also the most enjoyable and exciting part, as it is at this stage that the individual producer can have the greatest effect.

Editing has four main functions: to make sure that the production is the required length; to remove unwanted material or mistakes; to alter, if necessary, the way or sequence that events have been portrayed; and finally, and perhaps most importantly, to establish the particular style and character of a production. There is still time to change ideas, and the editing stage offers the opportunity to experiment with different combinations of media or sequences. Each combination will work in a slightly different way and each version will create a slightly different meaning.

activity **7.12**   Look at the section on narrative in Chapter 3 and then, using a series of pictures taken either from your own sources or from the family album in Figure 3.12, try to rearrange them to produce different atmospheres, moods or 'meanings'.

The producer often has an 'ideal' version of the final production that may be carefully planned and written down in detail on paper or may just exist in the mind's eye. Sometimes this ideal vision works, sometimes it is unachievable, and the editing stage is often a process of experimentation and trial and error to see what works aesthetically. Frequently because of time and money constraints the editing stage often ends in some sort of compromise between what is desirable and what is realistically achievable.

Depending upon the medium that is being used, there will be different editing methods. For newspaper or magazine writing it is at the subeditor stage that the copy is checked for correct spellings, grammar and length and, where necessary, that any headlines, captions or visuals are added. Different layouts of the material are tried out, in particular to balance visuals and text. This process can be carried out by 'cut-and-paste' methods but is increasingly being done on a computer screen, using desk-top packages such as Aldus Pagemaker. For audio and film it is also often a case of 'cut and paste', using a slicing kit and a razor blade (Figure 7.5). For video the process is electronic and can mean simply copying from machine to machine or (more complex) using an edit suite (Figure 7.6).

Whatever the editing process for video and audio, it is useful to prepare an 'off-line' or paper edit where all the editing points are worked out beforehand on paper. This limits the amount of time needed sitting at an editing suite, but requires thorough logging of all the shot material.

In video where two or more media are being used, they are edited to complement each other and to hide breaks or cuts. One effective example aims to avoid 'parallel edits' by using a

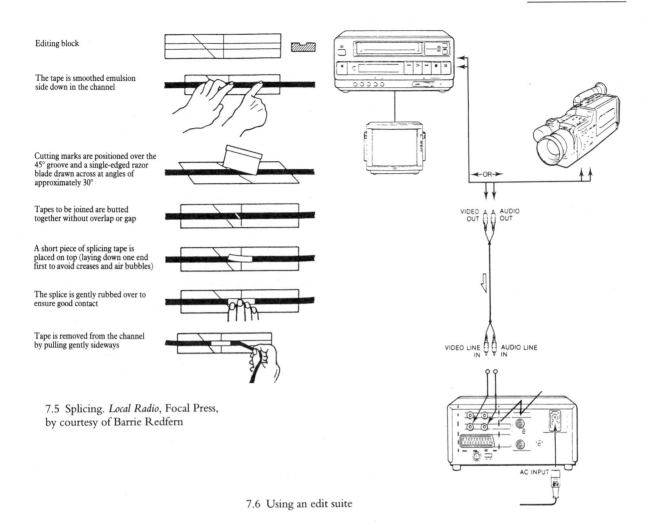

Editing block

The tape is smoothed emulsion side down in the channel

Cutting marks are positioned over the 45° groove and a single-edged razor blade drawn across at angles of approximately 30°

Tapes to be joined are butted together without overlap or gap

A short piece of splicing tape is placed on top (laying down one end first to avoid creases and air bubbles)

The splice is gently rubbed over to ensure good contact

Tape is removed from the channel by pulling gently sideways

7.5 Splicing. *Local Radio*, Focal Press, by courtesy of Barrie Redfern

7.6 Using an edit suite

voice-over or other audio such as music to carry on across a change of visual image. This has the effect of keeping a sense of continuity and, as mentioned in Chapter 3, the American soap *Dallas* was very successful in using this technique.

Evaluation

There are many criteria for success or effectiveness in creating media productions. For the mainstream 'professional' producer these are often external or institutional and can be related to commercial and critical acclaim, ratings, and coming within budget. For others, the criteria for success are often more subjective, reflective and often largely personal – although still dependent to some extent on the opinion of others, such as peer group, teachers or audience.

The process of review and evaluation should allow the opportunity to stand back, reflect, and ask critical questions of the product, its producers and the processes of its production. The review also presents an opportunity to re-examine decisions made earlier about the audience, the aims and the style and content of the production, and to see if, in retrospect, these were correct. It is an opportunity, too, to assess the extent to which the existing codes and conventions of mainstream media may have been assimilated, copied or challenged.

For many productions, one of the most simple criteria for success is whether the *audience* liked it or not. Although not all productions are aimed at a specific audience or their pleasure, most productions, whatever their size or length, do have some kind of target audience in mind. The evaluation is an opportunity to consider whether that particular target audience was the correct one for that particular production and whether the aims and objectives of the production have been realised.

This can involve looking at how the audience was identified; for instance, was it an established and recognisable audience or was it a new configuration created specifically for the production? There may have been some difficulty in assessing what a new audience wanted, particularly if the production was aimed not at meeting an existing need but at creating a new one, which is why many mainstream producers find the concept of 'genre' useful. (See Chapter 3.) It is helpful to consider how the target audience and their perceptions, needs and patterns of media consumption might have affected the shape and content of the production and the audience's response to it. What assumptions were made about the audience's feelings, prejudices, and levels of prior knowledge and understanding, and how did this affect the way the message was presented or received?

activity **7.13**

Look at Chapter 4 and consider what assumptions were made during your production process about the way certain groups or ideas should be handled, and how these groups were or were not stereotyped, or how stereotyping was avoided.

Remember that a finished product is a bonus and that it is in the processes that the learning takes place. However, if there is a finished product it should be given to a sample of the target audience. Consider whether the audience had any preconceived ideas about whether the production would (or should) look (or not look) like the 'real thing' and how this might have affected their expectations and responses.

An evaluation should show to what extent a production achieved its aims and whether anything else, perhaps unexpected or unplanned, came across and could perhaps be something of a bonus. Although not a primary concern, it may be useful to consider the technical quality to the extent that it may have affected the audience's responses by being, in their opinion, either impressive and 'professional' or perhaps 'amateur' and of poor quality. It is also important to consider the producer's own reactions, as not all productions are necessarily audience-led.

The whole *process* of planning, preparing and production can be looked at to see what particular aspects, in both the audience's and the producer's opinion, were successful or unsuccessful, what seemed to work or did not work, what could be changed or kept in future exercises. Did the production attract and hold the audience's attention? Was balance an objective, and if so how far was it achieved? How did the producer's own social standpoint affect the content? Were there any particular problems in carrying out the interviews?

Most productions develop organically and their shape changes during the production process, and adjustments are often made to the notional target audience and/or aims. Were there any major problems, and if so how were they overcome? How did decisions about the conditions of production, budget and the use of technologies affect the final form and content of the production?

Most productions are a collective enterprise, involving group or team work. It is useful therefore to consider how well everyone worked together and how tasks and roles were negotiated and allocated. If there was any conflict, what were the main causes and how was it resolved? Was there, for instance, a bias that meant males volunteered for the hardware and the apparently more technically difficult tasks, and the females tended to be left with other roles, such as presenting?

The process of creating media texts, whether large or small, individually or as part of a team, is usually an exciting and challenging experience. It should offer insight into how individuals work as well as how 'professionals' and media institutions operate. The experience should provide a greater understanding of the choices, decisions and constraints that shape the form and content of media texts and that are discussed in other sections of this book.

activity **7.14**

1 Compare and contrast the way advertisements on radio stations such as Classic FM and a local independent chart station are shaped and presented for their different audiences.

2 Take the front page of either a broadsheet or tabloid news-paper and 'reverse' it — rewrite the stories for the different readers, reselect and prioritise the stories, and redesign the page layout.

3 Using a piece of video recorded without sound, add contrasting types of musical soundtrack. Note how the different pieces of music affect the 'meaning' of the visuals. A similar exercise can be done by putting different voice-overs to a piece of news footage, to highlight how the 'meaning' can be altered.

4 Choose a television or radio series and outline the main stages in its production, with special consideration of the main kinds of pressure and constraint that the producers work under.

FURTHER READING

Boyd, A. 1988: *Broadcast Journalism*. Heinemann.

Evans, H. 1986: *Pictures on a Page*. Heinemann.

Hedgecoe, J. 1991: *On Video*. Hamlyn.

Hodgson, F. 1987: *Modern Newspaper Editing and Production*. Heinemann.

Kaye, M. and Popperwell, A. 1992: *Making Radio*. Broadside Books.

Millersen, G. 1989: *Video Production Handbook*. Focal Press.

Quilliam, S. and Grove-Stephensan, I. 1990: *Into Print*. BBC.

Stafford, R. 1993: *Hands On*. BFI.

Watts, H. 1984: *On Camera*. BBC.

Watts, H. 1992: *Directing on Camera*. Aavo.

USEFUL RESEARCH SOURCES

British Rate and Data (BRAD). Maclean Hunter Ltd.

Chater, K. 1989: *The Television Researcher's Guide*. BBC TV Training.

Cooke, L. 1984: *Media Studies Bibliography*. BFI.

Goodwin, A. 1987: *TV Studies Bibliography*. BFI.

Peak, S. (Ed): *Guardian Media Book*. Fourth Estate.

Willings Press Guide, Vol. 1. Reed Information Services.

Changing Media
Worlds

8

The key theme in this final chapter is change, and two main areas of study dominate the agenda. Each in turn deals with a specific series of questions about the changing nature of the media, in a changing, fluid and often unstable world. The first focus for study encourages you to assess some of the ways in which *new media technologies* are being harnessed and developed in the current phase. How they are destabilising or impacting on older and established forms of media production and consumption, and the extent to which, as is often claimed, they offer the potential for new and diverse kinds of cultural relationships to emerge, are central questions here.

The second focus of the chapter entails the analysis of world-wide media networks and the consequent emergence of what we should understand as international or *global culture*. This is a process which has deep historical roots but which many commentators have suggested has accelerated rapidly from the 1960s onwards. In part, this can be accounted for in terms of the development and potentials of certain 'new' media channels and communication technologies – notably satellite forms of extra-terrestrial broadcasting – and their abilities to cross national and international boundaries. However, it is not only at the global level that new media technologies are credited with the powers to effect radical forms of change in our social and cultural environments. The two areas contain some of the key dilemmas and debates involved in media policy in the current phase. Changes in British media policy have in part been stimulated by the dynamics of new media technologies, but, as we shall suggest, there are other issues at stake here too.

NEW TECHNOLOGIES FOR NEW TIMES?

We are living in a period which has frequently been characterised as a 'communications revolution', a cycle of profound
and accelerating social and cultural change often attributed to
the impact of new media technologies. These technologies
continue to play an important part in restructuring and
changing certain aspects of the production, distribution and
reception of 'old' media. Cable and satellite forms of broadcasting, video recorders, computers, word processors and digital disc technologies have all in recent years been developed
and marketed, adding to the media saturation of modern life.
Collectively, they have contributed to an important series of
changes in many homes and domestic environments. These
private spaces are increasingly 'multiscreen', 'multichannel',
'wired' or 'cabled' households, where the computer game and
the CD personal stereo operate alongside more established
media machines and forms (Figure 8.1).

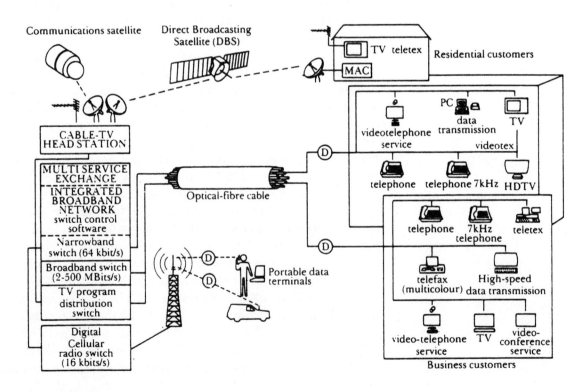

8.1 *Telecommunications in the 21st cen-
tury*. Report of the Committee on
Financing the BBC (Peacock, 1986),
Cmnd 9824, p. 105

activity 8.1	Map changes in media technologies and forms in your own household in recent years. Start with the most recent and work back. It may be useful to involve other, older members of the household in this activity and to develop a generational map. The data in Figure 8.2 may be useful. See also Activity 5.7 in Chapter 5.

8.2 Photograph: Jarrod Cripps

As well as having important consequences for private, leisure or 'non-work' time, the development and expansion of these technologies have also had important implications for public institutions and affairs – in the workplace, the college or the supermarket, for instance. In the face of these changes, it is important to bear in mind that all media – the press, cinema, radio and television broadcasting – have relied on the development and regulation of 'new' media technologies. The printing press, the film projector, gramophone, 'wireless' and 'television' have all, at one time, been regarded as rather strange, new, unfamiliar, 'one-way' machines for social and political communication. For many writers, these 'new' machines have been defined as causal historical agents, capable of bringing about 'revolutionary' forms of social and political change. The media, because of their public and private visibility and presence, have often operated to condense anxieties and debates about more general forms of change in the modern period (Figure 8.3).

8.3 Spectrum, Winter 1992, ITC

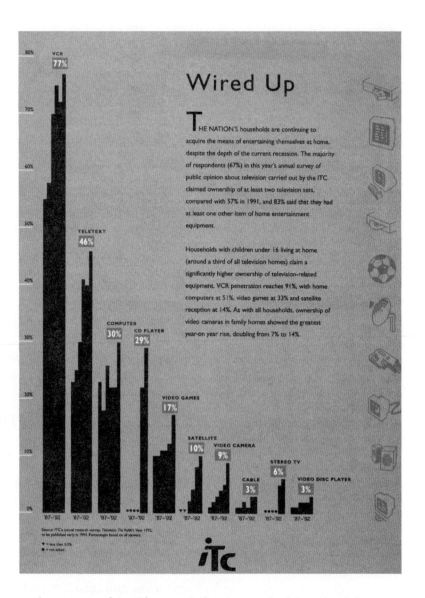

As suggested in Chapter 2, however, the history of the various media concerns the ways in which these 'machines' have been socially and commercially organised for the provision of information, entertainment and culture. This emphasis on the commercial or political forces which constrain or condition the social realisation of the technologies is an important counter to technological determinism. Such determinism is an oversimplified view that exaggerates the power of technologies themselves to cause 'effects' directly, without sufficient understanding of the variety of factors which may govern the technologies' social applications and use (see Williams, 1990).

Recent debates about changing media technologies have focused on a series of general themes. These have been subject to optimistic and pessimistic forms of assessment and debate.

Computerisation lies at the heart of many recent developments. The increasingly sophisticated systems for information storage, management and distribution have transformed many of the processes and practices involved in media production and consumption. Developments in what have become known as information technologies have been central in the redesign of news rooms, for example – for both press and broadcast production. At a general level, it is the convergence of these technologies within modern telecommunications industries that is responsible for a greatly increased speed and scale of information interchange. This shift in scale concerns not only the amount of information but also, via satellite links, world-wide networks. Cable systems, based on fibre-optic technologies, provide additional extensions to networks at local, regional or national levels. Furthermore, the goals of these kinds of development are ever-more integrated systems which are capable of handling and linking up many types of information: written and spoken languages, still and moving visual images, data of all kinds. Previously discrete media are merging into new and hybrid, multimedia forms, including, for example, the worlds of virtual reality.

Within these developments, much has been made of the interactive qualities of new media technologies. If older systems tended to the 'one-way' form of communication, new media, it is claimed, allow for plurality and interactivity. Examples tend to concern changes in television. VCTV (viewer controlled cable television) in the United States, for instance, allows viewers to create their own schedules. Some cable viewers in Britain were recently offered sports programmes where they could choose channels with either different camera angles, replays or computer-generated information as accompaniments to their viewing of the live coverage. In October 1993, QVC, an American company, in conjunction with SKY television became the first channel to offer 24-hour-a-day, all-year-round satellite shopping facilities. The channel will pioneer the round-the-clock selling of a wide range of domestic, consumer and electrical goods to consumers 'at home', linked by phone and credit card. Home shopping, home banking and other on-screen computer and video services and games are further examples of the ways in which the interactive potentials of new technologies are being developed and mobilised. In addition, interactivity allows for rapid viewer response: the computer keyboard linked to the screen enables views to 'answer back', whether this is in the form of votes in a televised talent contest or of registering their opinions on matters of political or current affairs.

Interactivity, combined with increased channels for new

information and entertainment services, gives rise to one of the most hotly debated issues, that of greater or expanded forms of consumer choice. For many writers, new media technologies have brought about the possibilities for much greater, more complex forms of choice and 'menu'. At one level, new technologies have had important consequences for the costs involved in many forms of media production and allowed for expansion to take place in new media markets. At another, viewers, listeners and readers may now exercise choice across new, increasingly segmentalised or specialised 'narrowcast' channels and services, as for example in the case of sports, movie, home 'lifestyle' or children's channels etc. Recent developments in cable services provide some useful examples. About half a million homes now receive broad-band cable services in Britain. As well as the four terrestrial channels and a wide mix of channels relayed from satellite, subscribers also have access to a menu of services provided exclusively by cable operators. The main source of income for most channels is on a pay-per-view basis plus advertising, or in some cases sponsorship. The types of programme service on offer include the following:

- *Asia Vision*. This channel provides a wide range of pro-grammes targeted at the Asian community. Programmes are produced in a range of languages, including Hindi, Urdu, Punjabi, Bengali, Gujarati and English, and are mostly replayed from the Indian subcontinent. Films are included in the service and many of these originate from the 'Indian Hollywood', Bombay. The channel was launched in 1986, and is available in 29 cable areas to approximately 80,000 households.
- *The Box*. This is a 24-hour, interactive video and music channel targeted at 16–34-year-olds. The viewer can dial in to request video plays. The channel was launched in 1992 and is now available in 30 cable areas to about 30,000 homes.
- *Identity Television*. This is the only channel to date which is aimed at Afro-Caribbean viewers in the UK. Many of the programmes are derived from the USA and cover a wide range of entertainment, drama, music and documentary formats. The channel was launched in 1993 and is available on the London Interconnect network to approximately 160,000 households.
- *The Landscape Channel*. This combines music with film images of natural landscapes from around the world. These are designed to produce a relaxing, atmospheric format. The channel was launched in 1988, and is available to about 350,000 homes.

- *The Learning Channel.* This provides a daytime educational service for families and students. Most of the programming is acquired from independent UK producers and distributors. Launched in 1992, it is available in 350,000 homes.
- *The Parliamentary Channel.* This provides continuous, live coverage of the daily proceedings in the House of Commons, with edited summaries and highlights from the House of Lords. Established in early 1992, the channel may be extended to cover Select Committees and the European Parliament. It is available in 54 cable areas with a reach of around 450,000 homes.
- *Super Channel.* This is a pan-European entertainment channel offering a broad mix of programming, including news, sports, variety, drama and films. It transmits in English 24 hours a day and is distributed to cable operators across Europe from London via satellite. The service was launched in 1987, and in the UK it is available in 60 cable areas with access to about 480,000 households.
- *Vision Broadcasting.* This is a non-profit-making, Christian channel, aimed at children and families. A three-hour tape is sent to cable operators on a weekly basis and the programmes are usually shown on Sundays. Launched in 1980, it is available in some 15 cable areas to about 180,000 homes.
- *Performance – the Arts Channel.* This channel offers viewers four kinds of material, often filmed performances of opera, dance, classical concerts or recitals, and jazz or blues music. The majority of the material is acquired from distributors across Europe. The channel was launched in 1992 and is available in 29 cable areas with a reach of about 275,000 homes.

These are some of the cable services available to viewers who are connected to cable systems. Other channels would include dedicated news channels, for example Euronews; home movie, film and video channels; and channels such as the Children's Channel. Further services available include a range of local channels produced by individual operators, minority-language programming, and foreign-language channels picked up from European satellites.

activity **8.2**

Research the development and availability of cable services in your own area. *The Cable and Telecom Year Book* is a good source for reference. *Spectrum,* the quarterly magazine of the Independent Television Commission, also contains useful articles on the expansion of cable services in the UK.

There are two issues which need to be considered in this context. First, to what extent do satellite, cable and video forms provide genuine diversity as opposed to a repackaging of old formats – 'more of the same'? This issue has been fore-grounded in virtually all recent discussions of the changing nature of television in Britain. Secondly, we need to note related arguments concerning access to these new forms and services. Rather than operating as public services, open to all, the great majority of new information and entertainment channels require private investment or subscription. Individual spending power has become a key factor in determining whether one can or cannot afford to participate in the new media services (Table 8.1). Consumer 'choice' can be exercised, but at a price. This has been a key issue in the recent debates surrounding the future of public service broadcasting in Britain, discussed in Chapter 2.

Table 8.1 Ownership of communications equipment among households in different income groups (1989)

Household weekly income (£)	Percentage owning		
	Phone	Video	Home computer
46–60	64.3	13.9	0.8
81–100	73.9	25.9	6.2
126–150	83.9	42.6	6.9
151–175	83.9	55.4	11.2
176–200	87.2	65.5	14.1
226–250	96.2	75.4	25.8
276–325	96.2	80.5	29.4
376–450	98.6	85.2	33.1
Over 550	99.7	77.7	34.3
All households	86.2	56.6	16.6

Source: Family Expenditure Survey 1989.

In summary, the debates on the development of new media technologies in the 1980s and 1990s are extensive, and more complicated and interwoven than they might appear at first sight. Advertisements for new media and their services have tended to stress the ways in which they 'liberate' viewers and consumers and offer whole ranges of new and exciting possibilities. The theme of consumer freedom or sovereignty has also been central in the policies of 'deregulation' which have accompanied and underpinned their growth. All the 'old' media – press, cinema, radio and television – now face considerable challenges as they compete in changing markets and circumstances. The changes in media production – for instance, desk top publishing (DTP), or the portable video camera – as well as in the forms of what is produced and consumed are of considerable significance in any current analysis. As Curran and Seaton (1991) have argued, the major debates in this area take place between the 'neophiliacs', who welcome the new media technologies in optimistic terms, and the 'cultural pessimists', who view these developments with considerable disquiet and scepticism. The two, contrasting positions may be summarised as follows:

New media technologies
TV based: video, cable, satellite, HDTV etc.
Print: DTP, printing, distribution, CD text systems
Music: synthesiser, video, CD

Effects?

Neophiliacs	**Cultural pessimists**
A Choice?	
1 Many more channels, 'Communacopia'	1 Market forces (esp. with deregulation) → squeezing out minority tastes (unless rich consumers) → 'Wall to Wall *Dallas*'
2 Narrowing and segmentation	2 Rental costs → exclusion of poor and powerless
3 Experimentation and innovation (esp. with deregulation)	3 Costs of production → more imports, cheaper productions
B Democracy?	
1 More imformation and services available to consumers	1 Increased control by media barons and multinational companies
2 Interactive uses (e.g. voting)	2 Loss of public-service principles and public sphere
3 DIY and community production → autonomy	3 Increasingly privatised culture, reliance on advertising revenue
C Demand?	
1 Technological determinism	1 Failure or low take-up of some new technologies
2 IT 'revolution', the 'wired' society	2 Video growth and decline of terrestrial, public-service TV viewing (displacement)
3 Growth of private commercial culture	3 Quality of existing services eroded

<table>
<tr><td>

activity **8.3**

</td><td>

I List some of the ways in which new media systems – satellite, cable and video – have changed the use of television in the home. Carry out some research interviews with people who subscribe to these services. What have been some of the main reasons for investing in them?

2 How have new media technologies changed conventional forms of media production? Have any alternative forms emerged as a result? You might focus on the camcorder, desk-top publishing or new musical technologies.

3 What kinds of 'interactivity' do new systems make available?

4 Discuss the recent popularity of computer and video games. How are they changing patterns of leisure inside and outside the home?

</td></tr>
</table>

EVERYWHERE AND NOWHERE: GLOBAL CULTURE

One recurrent theme in recent writing about the media, notably television, has concerned the need for students and researchers to recognise the importance and growth of worldwide media networks. No longer can, or should, the study of the media be locked into an inward-looking, ethnocentric focus, fixed solely on the characteristics and dynamics of the domestic, particular, national situation.

Despite the fact that media institutions in Britain continue to be guided in a number of decisive ways by a framework of ideas and organisational considerations in which the 'imagined community' of the 'British nation' – 'British' identity, experience, history, heritage and so on – continues to occupy a central place, changes in the last thirty years or so have altered things considerably. The British cultural economy of the 1990s, more than ever before, is part of a wider set of global cultural relations. This encompasses both economic and cultural flows of import and export, in businesses and cultural commodities, in media hardware and software.

Some evidence for this changing state of affairs can be found very readily in everyday forms of media consumption. British terrestrial forms of television, for example, regularly feature a mix of films and programmes which have been produced in other national locations around the world, originally for other audiences. Films from America, India, France and Canada are scheduled side by side with TV series and co-productions from the USA and Australia, and live or recorded sports coverage from Japan, New Zealand and Germany. The amount and typical content of imported programming has varied historically. Recent developments in satellite and/or cable TV channels have added to these amounts of imported material (Figure 8.4).

8.4 The *Financial Times*, 6 October 1993

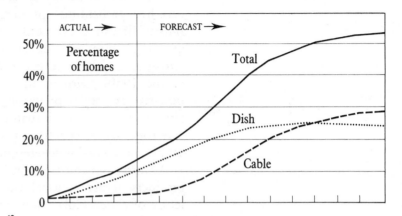

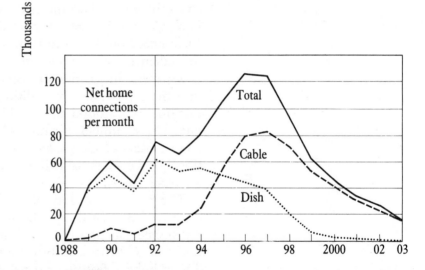

activity **8.4**

Analyse the 'terrestial' TV schedules for one week according to the percentages of 'home' and imported programmes shown. Break down imports into their national origins. Compare the patterns which emerge with a similar analysis of satellite TV schedules for the same week. What kinds of programme are imported? What conclusions might be drawn from this data overall?

In British cinemas, the pattern of American dominance over the production of films appearing on British screens was established well before the Second World War. This pattern is still repeated, with some variations, and not just in current multiscreen cinemas; it also reappears in the video rental store and on some satellite 'movie' channels – MTV is an interesting case. Film stars and television personalities, stars of music and sport are mediated and merchandised to world-wide audiences, often in media spectaculars which involve simultaneous, live, global link-ups, performances or appeals. In terms of music, British charts and music radio also give access to a growing number of international forms, styles and 'crossovers'. The emergence of the category of 'world music' in the 1980s, with its mission to introduce western ears to non-western styles of music, to provide a platform for many voices, and to allow instruments and traditions to communicate together irrespective of national boundaries, has been one visible, noteworthy development here.

Advertising campaigns and imagery have accompanied their products across national boundaries to the extent that the icons of Coca–Cola, Benetton, Del Monte, Marlboro, Levi and others have become truly world-wide signs, part of the new 'global language'. 'Personalities' from Michael Jackson to Madonna, from Bono to Jason Donovan, have been mediated to audiences on a world-wide basis. The contents of many newspapers, magazines and other print media are also tuned into these processes. In addition to relaying news and information from around the world, they may be centrally produced for a number of national editions (*Cosmopolitan, Reader's Digest, National Geographic*) or increasingly aimed at international or pan–national markets (*Time, Newsweek, The European, Financial Times*).

The process and duty of mediating accounts of the 'world out there' into British public and private life has been a long-established function of the British media and their relation to domestic audiences. In broadcast news segments on radio and TV, in holiday feature or travel documentary programmes, we are effortlessly transported or moved around the world in live or recorded time.

activity **8.5**

Monitor or map this process in one evening's television viewing. Where does television take you?

For many recent commentators, these and other aspects of modern culture are understood as part and parcel of this shift into postmodern conditions, whereby older forms of national identity and their historical 'securities' and divisions are being replaced, challenged or dislocated by new, multiple allegiances derived from a diversity of local and global movements and imagery. As we noted in Chapter 1, this is a version of ideas popularised by Marshall McLuhan in the 1960s, concerning the effects of television and computerised media technologies and communication systems on the world and their abilities to establish a 'global village'. In the 'global village', differences of time and space or geographical or national location are eroded as a result of the 'instantaneous' nature of modern media and world communications. In this vision, as the speed, extent and complexity of communication systems accelerate, the world 'shrinks' and the media synchronise us into a randomised 'world time'. They also enable us to tune into a globally derived 'cocktail' or mix of places, events, personalities and locations. The mediation of these two dimensions – of time and of space – is crucial in the construction of social identity at both public and private levels. A great deal of postmodern analysis has echoed McLuhan's arguments on these themes. We have become, it is argued, dislocated and resynchronised into a new kind of simulated and decentralised world. There are now few limits or boundaries, it is suggested, in this new 'hyperspace' world with its excess of information and entertainment. (See Morley, 1991, for a useful discussion.)

In the face of these arguments and claims, it is important to recognise that globalisation is a process which has encompassed two linked levels of relationship. First of all, we need to recognise that a great deal of this process lies behind the growth in channels and technologies of images and information, whether on screen or on the page. Several writers have argued that internationalisation is a normal part of the commercial development of media markets in the twentieth century. The logic of this process has seen the emergence of multinational conglomerates, media companies with extensive networks of interests operating across national boundaries. One example is Rupert Murdoch's News International Corporation:

> It includes major press and publishing interests in the USA, UK and Australia, as well as America's fourth largest television network, Fox, and a controlling interest in Britain's direct satellite broadcasting service, British Sky Broadcasting. Other important examples include Sony of Japan which owns CBS records and Columbia Pictures, and the Bertelsmann company of Germany, which controls RCA records and Doubleday books as well as a major domestic chain of newspapers and magazines.
>
> *Murdock and Golding (1991), p. 23*

In the British context, internationalisation encompasses both the ways in which British companies have invested in operations outside the UK (Thorn–EMI, for example) and the ways in which American, other European or Japanese companies have bought into British media concerns – the domestic market (USA or Canadian interests in UK cable TV, for example). Multinational conglomerates are geared to operate in and to develop world-wide cultural markets for information and entertainment facilities. Their activities concern the production and distribution of cultural commodities, not just for domestic national consumption, but for readers, listeners and viewers who inhabit a range of diverse national and international territories.

If the first level of analysis here concerns the growth and development of world-wide multimedia conglomerates, their structures and transnational operations, the second, linked level concerns the consequences of their growth and operation, the cultural flows of commodities – packaged programmes, films, images etc. – and their reception by audiences in diverse situations world-wide. At the heart of current debates about globalisation are a number of key issues which relate to important differences in the interpretation of the increase in international forms and patterns of media operation.

For some writers, globalisation is a process which results in 'sameness' or homogeneity on an increasingly world-wide basis. As Hebdige has suggested in this context: 'The implication here is that we'll soon be able to watch *Dallas* or eat a Big Mac in any part of the inhabited world' (1989, p. 51). Put crudely, world culture and media have become relay stations for the most powerful multinational corporations and their forms of popular, profitable culture.

For others, these considerations of similarity or convergence have to confront the diversity of world culture and the fragmentation of audiences, both within and across national boundaries. Emphasis on the power of the multinational media conglomerates and their products is counterbalanced by an emphasis on the potential and actual diversities of their creative reception or use and cultural impact. In order to develop this further, we need to step back from discussions of globalisation, and set them in the context of related studies and analyses of media or cultural imperialism. 'We' also need to remember the particular national point of view and part of the globe from which these issues are addressed.

Table 8.2
Satellite dishes in Europe

Austria	345,000
Belgium	30,000
Bulgaria	1,000
Croatia	3,000
Czechoslovakia	60,000
Denmark	80,000
Estonia	25,000
Finland	5,000
France	225,000
Germany	120,000
Greece	2,000
Hungary	150,000
Ireland	20,000
Italy	4,000
Luxembourg	200
Netherlands	200,000
Norway	60,000
Poland	10,000
Portugal	30,000
Slovenia	2,000
Spain	35,000
Sweden	120,000
Switzerland	12,000
Turkey	220,000
United Kingdom	2,500,000

Source: International Broadcasting and Audience Research Library, June 1992

activity **8.6**	Analyse the data in Tables 8.2 and 8.3 on ownership of TV, VCR, radio and satellite facilities world-wide. Compare the number of sets per head of population in different areas. What conclusions might be drawn from this data?

Table 8.3 World radio and television receivers, 1991

(all figures approximate)	Population ('000s)	Radio						Television				Number of VCRs ('000s)
		Number of radio sets (excluding wired receivers) ('000s)						Number of TV receivers ('000s)				
	1991	1955	1965	1975	1985	1991	1965	1975	1985	1991	1991
World Figures	5,337,000	237,000	529,000	1,010,000	1,650,000	2,148,000	177,000	398,000	737,000	1,052,000	233,000
Europe											
Western Europe	851,000	65,310	116,500	186,600	297,800	575,000	49,400	103,400	162,900	366,800	79,700
USSR and Eastern Europe		20,260	59,700	92,600	164,300		24,000	87,000	130,100		
Arab World (inc. North Africa)	283,000	2,200	12,300	29,300	58,100	75,200	1,250	6,000	19,500	38,100	11,100
Africa											
South Africa	38,000	875	2,600	4,800	10,000	12,000	–	500	3,000	4,000	800
Other countries	453,000	360	4,800	18,500	42,600	61,300	100	600	7,900	14,300	2,300
South Asia and Far East											
Chinese P.R.	1,154,000	1,000	6,000	35,000	120,000	290,000	70	750	56,000	150,000	3,000
India	859,000	1,000	4,800	24,000	50,000	75,000	2	300	2,300	40,000	3,000
Japan	125,000	12,000	27,000	87,000	100,000	120,000	18,000	42,000	70,000	75,000	26,000
Other countries	823,000	1,800	13,300	49,700	111,600	129,200	700	8,950	31,000	64,900	14,400
North America and Caribbean											
USA	252,000	111,000	230,000	380,000	500,000	560,000	68,000	110,000	175,000	185,000	68,000
Canada	26,000	5,500	14,000	23,000	32,000	42,000	5,000	9,500	14,000	15,500	6,000
Caribbean	11,000	190	860	4,000	5,600	6,400	100	1,200	2,000	2,500	400
Latin America	432,000	12,600	29,400	62,800	133,500	171,100	7,400	22,600	54,900	86,200	13,300
Australasia and other ocean territories	29,000	2,760	7,800	13,000	24,700	30,600	3,200	5,000	8,600	9,800	4,700

Source: International Broadcasting and Audience Research Library, June 1992

One of the conclusions which might result from such an analysis is that access to the means of reception varies widely from country to country. For example, in Mali, West Africa, it has been calculated that there are seven radio sets and two TV sets per hundred population. This stands in stark contrast to the United Kingdom, where there are 148 radio sets and 72 TV sets per hundred population. Furthermore, although pat–

terns of ownership of television sets, video cassette recorders and radios world-wide may be a significant indicator of the relative availability of the hardware necessary for media reception, they tell us little about the ways in which these media may be used in context; equally they reveal little about the related questions of content – what is broadcast or available to watch or listen to within different international or national territories.

activity **8.7**

Compare the structure and range of media sectors in Britain with those in any other countries that you can get access to. Make use of other material – TV and radio schedules etc. from other countries (Figures 8.7 and 8.8). Refer to the further reading list at the end of the chapter for some useful sources.

8.5 Photograph: Jarrod Cripps

8.6a and (*opposite*) b The *Financial Times*, 6 October 1993

Percentage of hours broadcast

		Domestically produced		Imported	Method of funding
UK	BBC	90		10	Mainly licence fee
US	PBS	85		15	Voluntary donation and govt grant
Japan	NHK (terrestrial)	84		16	Mainly licence fee
Germany	ARD	80		20	Mixed licence fee and advertising
Germany	ZDF	80		20	Mixed licence fee and advertising
Italy	RAI (average)	80		20	Mixed licence fee and advertising
Netherlands	NOS	65		35	Mixed licence fee and advertising
Australia	ABC	53		47	Government grant
France	FR3	50		50	Mixed licence fee and advertising
New Zealand	TVNZ	27		73	Mainly advertising

Percentage of hours watched at prime time

Country	Public	Private
New Zealand	88	12
Sweden	77	23
Netherlands	54	46
Italy	49	51
Germany	47	53
UK	44	56
Franco Canada	42	58
France	40	60
Anglo Canada	19	81
Australia	18	82
Japan	9	91
US	3	97

Note: Figures for Sweden, Canada and the US are for average rather than prime time viewing. Public service audience share for Japan includes commercial stations, although their audience share is negligible.

TV today

12noon: Bugs Bunny Show.
12.25pm: Police Academy 5: Assignment Miami
1.50: Great Experiments
This programme shows how scientific experiments have proved to be milestones on technology developments and have helped shape the way we live today.
2.15: Dream Machine
Modern man would be lost without the computer. This series charts its origins, development and impact in a user-friendly way that make sense even to the most scientifically illiterate.
3.05: Banana Joe
Movie starring Bud Spencer as Banana Joe.
4.35: My Two Dads
5: MASH
5.25: Hollywood Wives
7pm: Local News
7.15: ITN news
7.40: Beyond 2000
8.25: May To December
Anton Rogers and Lesley Dunlop star in this comedy about an affable Scottish solicitor in his mid-fifties, romancing an attractive gym mistress half his age.
8.55: Hill Street Blues
9.45: Local News
10pm: CBS news
10.20: BBC news
10.35: Wiseguy
11.25: Closedown (for West only)
11.25: Porridge (For Suva only)
When a lack lustre show business soccer team play the inmates of Slade Prison, habitual prisoner Norman Stanley and his young cellmate Lennie Godber find themselves unexpectedly free and Fletcher's main problem is how to break into jail.
11.55: Closedown (Suva only)

TV tomorrow

12noon: Count Duckula
12.25pm: WKRP In Cincinnati
Comedy in a radio station.
12.45: Highway To Heaven
A contemporary series starring Michael Landon as a probationary angel sent to earth. Along the way he teams up with an ex-cop and they travel the country helping and bringing people together.
1.30: Carpenters Motors One World Of Sport
A sporting bonanza featuring top overseas sporting events. Today we have a Five Nations match between France and England and the second part of *More than a Game* documentary.
4pm: Running On Empty
5.55: Sunday choir
7pm: Local news
7.15: ITN news
7.40: The Cosby Show
8.35: Supertots
Can training children in sports from an early age produce super-athletes? A Californian coach, Marv Marinovich, believes it does. He has developed a highly successful training technique which he perfected by using his own children as guinea pigs. With the aid of a strict diet, a routine of physical exercise and a host of scientists, he has turned his 21-year-old son Todd into one of the hottest properties in American football with a career that could make him a millionaire.
9.05: Trainer
9.50: Local news
10.05: CBS news
10.25: BBC news
10.45: Equal Justice
11.30: Porridge (for West viewers only)
12midnight: Closedown (for West only)
12.20: Closedown (for Suva only)

QTV

5.00 p.m.	SIMPSONS: *"Burns Verkaufen De Kraftwerk"*. The nuclear power plant where Homer works is sold to a German company; Homer falls into a state of depression after he is the only one at the plant to lose his job. Stars: Dan Castellaneta, Julie Havner.
5.30	NEIGHBOURS: Lou is concerned by Lauren's strange behaviour. Doug jumps at a delivery job opportunity, paying thousand dollars a trip and Annalise catches Jeffrey in a compromising position at Lindy's flat. Starring Julie Mullins, Rebecca Ritters and Terence Donovan. (G)
6.00	EYEWITNESS NEWS: (G)
7.00	HINCH: Derryn Hinch presents a hard-hitting half hour of top quality current affairs. (G)
7.30	HEALTHY WEALTHY & WISE: (G)

ABC

5.00 p.m.	THE AFTERNOON SHOW WITH MICHAEL TUNN: (G)
5.02	THE BABYSITTERS' CLUB: *"Dawn's Dream Boy"*. (G)
5.30	PRESS GANG: (Rpt)
6.00	THE GOODIES: (G) (Rpt)
6.30	TVTV: News and reviews of television programs. (G)
7.00	ABC NEWS: (G)
7.30	THE 7.30 REPORT: (G)
8.00	A YEAR IN PROVENCE: "Bread Winner". The village baker's bread is very bad today – what is wrong? His wife has left him – and it's up to the Mayles to reunite them. Cast: John Thaw, Lindsay Duncan. (G)
8.28	NEWS UP-DATE: (G)
8.30	FOUR CORNERS: (S)

EMTV

5.00 p.m.	MAGILLA GORILLA: Children's Cartoon. (G)
5.28	EMTV TOK SAVE: (G)
5.29	EMTV NEWS BREAK: (G)
5.30	HOME AND AWAY: Half-hour teenage drama (G)
6.00	NATIONAL EMTV NEWS: (G)
6.30	A CURRENT AFFAIR: (G)
7.00	SALE OF THE CENTURY: Australia's richest and most popular quiz show. Hosted by Glenn Ridge. (G)
7.30	LOTTO DRAW: (G)
7.32	CHM SUPERSOUND NEW RELEASE: (G)
7.35	NEIGHBOURS: Henry comes up with a double interesting wedding idea for the other two engaged couples. (G)

ATI

5.00 p.m.	PALACE OF DREAMS: (G)
5.55	CONSUMING PASSION: (G)
6.00	NEWS HEADLINES: (G)
6.05	PLAY SCHOOL: (G)
6.30	SWAP SHOW: (G)
7.00	MR SQUIGGLE: (G)
7.30	PLAY SCHOOL: (G)
8.05	EARTH WATCH: (G)
8.30	INFANT MATCHES: (G)
9.05	WATCH! YOUR LANGUAGE (G)
9.30	AUSTRALIA NEWS: (G)
9.35	OPEN LEARNING – OUT OF EMPIRE: (G)
10.05	QUESTION OF SURVIVAL: (G)
10.30	NEWS HEADLINES: (G)

8.8 Extracts from schedules in the *Post Courier*, Papua New Guinea, 18 October 1993

Modernisation and Development

Historically, the data in Table 8.2 does provide some index of the international growth and spread of TV, radio and VCR in the last thirty-five years or so. It is important to bear in mind the broad historical perspective, and recognise that the international growth and spread of organised systems of mass communication and broadcasting in the modern period has been part of broader political and economic processes of industrialisation and commercialisation.

8.9 Photograph: Jarrod Cripps

Some historians and other writers suggest that the growth and diffusion of mass media did not just follow more general patterns of industrialisation and trade, but played an essential and active part in the overall process of 'modernisation'. Early studies often emphasised the function and impact of media in what was perceived as a broad and world-wide development process. The media – newspapers, films, radio and TV – were identified as key agencies for changing the attitudes and values of populations experiencing phases of world-wide industrialisation. In particular, 'developing nations' – often newly independent from colonial rule – were the basis for studies in the 1950s and 1960s which sought to assess the ways in which the media might be used to change traditional ways and beliefs; for example, by means of education or advertising campaigns and programmes. From this perspective, it is important to note that the media tended to be regarded as benign agencies capable of engineering positive social and cultural change, and assisting in the pursuit of greater industrial, technical, economic or social 'development'. Two key factors tended to be absent from this view: the power of the 'developed' nations, and the increasing dependency of 'developing' economies and nation states. These ideas have, however, formed the basis for more recent studies of international media relationships, and a series of debates concerning media or cultural imperialism.

MEDIA IMPERIALISM

Fundamental to this view of international media relations is the general argument that capitalist, western media have played an important role in the domination and control of the cultures of many developing and Third World nations. Far from any benign or neutral process of 'modernisation' occurring, western, especially American, communication systems and their values have 'invaded' and have established forms of world-wide control and influence in the production and supply of information and entertainment. This process is seen as historically systematic and linked to the more general economic and political processes of first colonial, and then imperial, developments in the twentieth century. 'Imperialism' in this sense refers to the ways in which certain industrialised nation states have emerged as 'world powers', by extending their forms of control and rule over other political, economic and cultural communities and nations for the purposes of commercial advantage, military security, political or ideological 'mission' etc. Whereas colonialism is viewed as an early stage in this process, predominantly concerned with economic advantage and exploitation, imperialism results from wider and more complex forms of dominance, directed towards empire building, at the global level. Imperialism is the systematic production of massive disparities in wealth, power and influence, on a world-wide scale. Dominant, 'First World' (a term usually referring to North America, Western Europe, Japan and Australia) economies are able to control supply and demand on world markets, and poorer countries are encouraged to import First World goods and commodities in exchange for raw materials or cheap labour.

Our concern here lies with the cultural aspects of these processes. Studies of international media flows and relations have consistently pointed to what Varis (1974), in the context of TV, has called 'one-way traffic', from the relatively restricted centres of advanced commercial states, via multinational corporations, to world markets, especially the 'developing' market of the 'Third World' (South America, Asia, Africa) and 'Second World' (the now ex-Soviet bloc and China). This traffic, it is argued, introduces the values and commodities of consumer capitalism. Media networks become vehicles for the world-wide dissemination of language, identity, aspirations and values congruent with the dominant ideologies of western capitalism.

An early focus for work of this type was the Hollywood dominance of world film industries, although more recent studies have focused on later 'waves' of television, video (Alvarado, 1988), satellite, advertising, news and music (Malm and Wallis, 1984). In a study first published in 1969, entitled *Mass Communication and American Empire*, Schiller argued that American TV exports represented part of an imperialist policy

8.10 Photograph: Jarrod Cripps

to subjugate the world – world domination is the aim. Importantly, this type of analysis noted that the process did not solely concern the programmes, films, adverts and so on; it also embraced the changing technologies of production and reception, the practice of production, and the whole profiles – tastes, aspirations, fashions and lifestyles – of goods and values cultivated or 'transmitted' by these commodities. For writers like Schiller, the media play an important part in a general process of cultural imperialism. In this view, traditional and indigenous cultures world-wide are 'penetrated' and transformed by American cultural influences, which act to 'spearhead' forms of global American consumerism. For developing nations, it is a major problem to try to retain or preserve cultural autonomy in the face of external, often American, influence. From this point of view, satellite broadcasting, with its abilities to cross national boundaries, has simply enabled this process to occur more rapidly and completely. Satellite forms of delivery threaten what Mattelart *et al.* (1984) have referred to as the 'audiovisual space' or cultural autonomy of many nations, with significant consequences for their cultural identity.

From the mid 1970s, these themes of cultural dependency and the global communications power of developed nations have been regularly debated and criticised under the auspices of UNESCO (United Nations Educational, Scientific and

Cultural Organisation), which has dealt with a series of demands for a New World Information Order, which would seek to redress the imbalance between information-rich and information-poor countries and nation states. Such proclamations, however, appear to have little material impact on subsequent developments.

In recent years, the debate about media imperialism has developed in a number of ways (see the further reading list at the end of the chapter). At the heart of these developments has been a reassessment of some of the evidence cited in favour of its operation. This has largely concerned television. One of the best guides to the general patterns of television distribution and flow world-wide has been provided by Varis (1984), in a long-term study sponsored by UNESCO which reported on amounts of imported programming in some sixty-nine countries between 1973 and 1983. (Alvarado (1988) provides a study of international flows in video.) The patterns indicated here suggest that, overall, imported programmes average about one third or more of total programming. The USA imports relatively little – between 2 and 5 per cent. Canada is a major importer of American-originated programmes (30 per cent), and Western European systems also import about this amount. Many Latin American stations have 50 per cent or more of their schedules occupied by American output, and this pattern is repeated in many African, Asian, Pacific and other Third World sectors (Table 8.4).

The study showed that some 20 per cent of programming in the former Soviet Union was imported. At a global level, most of the programme material imported originates from the USA, and to a lesser extent from Western Europe, Japan and Australia. It is important to note that these flows are mainly of a recreational kind: light entertainment, movies and sports programmes. These programmes can be bought in packages at a fraction of the price it would cost to produce 'home-grown' versions, and therefore the economic logic for purchasing them to fill schedules world-wide is clear and compelling. For example, a recent discussion of Zimbabwe TV notes:

> ZTV can only afford to produce about twelve hours of indigenous drama a year, albeit incredibly cheaply with the actors also doing day jobs and providing their own costumes. Drama series like *Ziva Kawakaba* (*Know Your Roots*) are very popular with the majority black audience, but the advertisers know that they are going to get better value for money from imported programmes that appeal to the more affluent white or middle-class black audiences. And ZTV know that they can acquire an episode of *Miami*

Vice, say, for the special 'Third World' rate of $500 – a fraction of the already minimal budget of an episode of *Ziva Kawakaba*.

Dowmunt (1993), pp. 6–7

Table 8.4

Country	Television station	Ownership	Programming	Approx. population
Antigua	ABS TV	Government	60% canned American programmes 40% local information, news and govt. news	79,000
	CTV	Private	Cable. 24-hour broadcast of American programmes	
Bahamas	ZNS	Government	Several local programmes including news and govt. information Many US programmes	226,000
	Cable	Private	All US programmes	

In addition, because of the proximity of the Bahamas to the US, it is possible to pick up programmes from Florida quite easily, with a good antenna.

Barbados	CBC Cable	Government Private	Local and foreign programming All American programmes	250,000
Belize	Cable	Private	All American programmes	170,000
Dominica	Cable (Martin TV Co)	Private	All foreign programmes	83,000
Grenada	GTV	Government	All foreign programmes	95,000
Jamaica	JBC	Government	Many local and regional programmes. Approx. 40% foreign programmes	2.4 million
Montserrat	Cable	Private	All foreign programmes	12,000
St Kitts/Nevis	ZIZ	Government	Govt. information and news locally Mainly foreign programmes	45,000
	TBN	Private	American-owned religious station No local input	
	Cable	Private	All foreign programmes	
St Lucia	Cable	Private	All foreign programmes	138,000
St Vincent	SV TV	Private	Mainly foreign programmes	110,000
Trinidad and Tobago	TTT	Government	About 30% local programming	1.2 million

Source: Index on Censorship 7/1990

More work is needed on these patterns in the age of video, satellite and multichannel forms of delivery. We should also note that a significant dimension to this debate concerns not just popular programme formats like *Dallas* but also the mediation of news and other forms of information; for example, with the multinational operation of MTV or the Cable News Network (CNN). The international operations of major western news agencies, and their abilities to set the global news agenda, have been the focus for a series of critical studies in this context (see Gurevitch, 1991).

Assessing Imperialism

For some writers, the model of 'one-way flow' oversimplifies what is in fact a more complex set of interrelationships, with significant internal patterns and groupings occurring within different continental, linguistic and geographical regions. However, the main challenge to the media imperialism thesis in recent years has emerged in the form of a questioning of the limits to the evidence provided. In short, does the evidence of amounts of imported programming add up to the 'imperialist effect'? As one writer has observed:

> There is an assumption that American T.V. imports do have an impact whenever and wherever they are shown, but actual investigation of this seldom occurs. Much of the evidence that is offered is merely anecdotal or circumstantial. Observations of New Guinean tribesmen clustered around a set in the sweltering jungle watching *Bonanza* or of Algerian nomads watching *Dallas* in the heat of the desert are often offered as sufficient proof.
>
> *Lealand (1984), pp. 6–7*

What is centrally at stake here is the way in which media audiences in a diversity of national and other cultural locations make sense of and relate to imported programming. We have seen that those who support the ideas of media imperialism assume that American films and programmes 'blot out' authentic and original forms of indigenous culture, and replace them with the ideologies and values of American consumer capitalism. However, little actual evidence has been presented about the precise nature of the forms of reception or decoding which are in play in the world-wide situations confronted with such imported material. Some recent developments in this context are worth noting.

By the mid-1980s, many cultural critics and writers agreed with the then French Minister for Culture, Jack Lang, when he attacked the American soap opera *Dallas* as 'the symbol of American cultural imperialism'. Set in a world of Texan oil families and their private and public feuds and conflicts, the soap opera had enjoyed massive international popularity in over a hundred countries world-wide (see Ang, 1985; Silj, 1988). One study which set out to explore how *Dallas* was made sense of in a diversity of cultural and global locations was carried out by Katz and Liebes (1990). They studied a large number of groups, many of whom were newcomers to Israeli society from a diversity of ethnic and cultural contexts. They viewed the different audience groups that formed the basis for their study as active, and as capable of negotiating a range of diverse positions with regard to the serial, its stories and characters, and its relevance to their own lives. The study offers some evidence for the need to reassess this aspect of the imperialism thesis. Audiences on the 'receiving end' of American cultural products like *Dallas* emerge as active agents, more complex, critical or resistant and certainly less predictable in their cultural responses than has been assumed. Certainly, as Tomlinson in his recent assessment points out, 'We clearly cannot assume that simply watching *Dallas* makes people want to be rich' (1991, p. 49). The detailed study of the uses made of television in diverse national and ethnic locations has recently been developed in a series of studies by Lull (1988). For discussion of some of these themes, see Chapter 5.

One final question has been posed in recent work. This first emerges in an account given by Penacchioni (1984) of some observations of television viewing she made in northeast Brazil. One of the situations she describes concerns a group of country people laughing at a communally watched, televised Charlie Chaplin film. Penacchioni noted that she and they appeared to be laughing at the same things, but that this is by no means necessarily the case. Western media researchers, she suggests, face formidable problems of understanding and interpretation. They and their research subjects, people in Third World settings, may appear to 'laugh at the same things' – the tramp character in Chaplin's films – but within very different or irreconcilable frames of reference. Ultimately, her study does pose some important questions about the assumptions often made about Third World audiences by western researchers and their methods.

The study also highlights some important issues about the 'universal' nature of the appeal and meanings of images like Chaplin or even J.R. Ewing in *Dallas*. Tracey (1985) provides an interesting polemic in this context when he suggests that the world-wide appeal of American popular culture has, in part, to be explained not by its imposition, but in understanding how it taps into certain universal feelings, 'common chords', which transcend national cultures and differences of lived identity. As Tomlinson notes, however, this kind of argument comes dangerously close to ignoring the power of western media systems to saturate developing cultural economies with certain types of material: 'One reason why Chaplin's humour can be plausibly seen as universal is that it is universally present' (1991, p. 53).

To recap, this section has suggested that there is considerable evidence available which points to a global concentration of power over media production and distribution in western nations and states. Ongoing debates about the dynamics of media imperialism may need to address more directly questions of how the international audiences for the films, programmes, music, videos and so on make use of and interpret these cultural products. In so doing, they also need to deal with the arguments and ideas contained in recent accounts of 'globalisation'. Both of these issues are centrally linked with the emergence of more complex, new, multichannel media technologies, satellite, cable and video being perhaps the prime examples of the moment. Media studies has to move with these changes if it is to remain relevant and viable as a means of systematically confronting, challenging or changing the media environments of new times.

FURTHER READING

Curran, J. and Seaton, J. 1991: *Power without Responsibility.* Routledge.

Dowmunt, T. (Ed). 1993: *Channels of Resistance.* BFI/C4.

Hayward, P. and Wollen, T. (Eds). 1993: *Future Visions: New Technologies of the Screen.* BFI.

Morley, D. 1991: 'Where the Global Meets the Local: Notes from the Sitting Room'. *Screen.* Vol. 32 No. 1.

Murdock, G. and Golding, P. 1991: 'Culture, Communications, and Political Economy' in J. Curran and M. Gurevitch (Eds). *Mass Media and Society.* Edward Arnold.

Ostergaard, B. (Ed). 1992: *The Media in Western Europe.* Sage.

Reeves, G. 1993: *Communications and the 'Third World'.* Routledge.

Sreberny-Mohammadi, A. 1991: 'The Global and the Local in International Communications' in J. Curran and M. Gurevitch (Eds). *Mass Media and Society.* Edward Arnold.

Tomlinson, J. 1991: *Cultural Imperialism.* Pinter.

Williams, R. 1990: *Television: Technology and Cultural Form.* Routledge.

Bibliography

Allen, R. 1987: *Channels of Discourse*. Methuen.

Alvarado, M. 1988: *Video Worldwide*. John Libbey.

Alvarado, M., Gutch, R. and Wollen, T. 1987: *Learning the Media*. Macmillan.

Ang, I. 1985: *Watching Dallas – Soap Opera and the Melodramatic Imagination*. Methuen.

Anwar, M. and Shang, A. 1982: *Television in a Multi-Racial Society: A Research Report*. Commission for Racial Equality.

Armes, R. 1978: *A Critical History of British Cinema*. Oxford University Press.

Armes, R. 1988: *On Video*. Routledge.

Baehr, H. and Dyer, G. (Eds). 1987: *Boxed In: Women and Television*. Pandora.

Bandura, A. and Walters, R. 1963: *Social Learning and Personality Development*. Holt Rinehart and Winston.

Barker, M. 1989: *Comics, Ideology, Power and the Critics*. Manchester University Press.

Barnard S. 1989: *On the Radio*. Open University Press.

Barnes, J. 1976: *The Beginnings of Cinema in Britain*. David & Charles.

Barnett, S. 1988: *The Listener Speaks*. Broadcasting Research Unit.

Barr, C. 1986: *All Our Yesterdays*. BFI.

Barthes, R. 1973: *Mythologies*. Paladin.

Barthes, R. 1975: *S/Z*. Cape.

Barthes, R. 1977: *Image-Music-Text*. Fontana.

Barwise, P. and Ehrenberg, A. 1988: *Television and its Audience*. Sage.

BBC 1992: *Extending Choice*: The BBC's Role in the New Broadcasting Age. BBC Publications.

BBC International Broadcasting Audience Research. 1993: World Radio and Television Receivers, London, BBC.

Beharrell, M. 1993: *Protest, Press and Prejudice: RAF Greenham Common 1982–92*. Institute of Education, University of London.

Berger, A. 1991: *Media Research Techniques*. Sage.

Berger, J. 1972: *Ways of Seeing*. Penguin.

Blanchard, S. and Morley, D. (Eds) 1983: *What's This Channel Four? An Alternative Report*. Comedia.

Blumler, J. and Katz, E. (Eds) 1974: *The Uses of Mass Communication*. Sage.

Boyce, G. *et al* (Eds) 1978: *Newspaper History: From the 17th Century to the Present Day*. Constable.

Boyd, A. 1988: *Broadcast Journalism*. Heinemann.

Briggs, A. 1979: *The History of Broadcasting in the UK*. Vols 1–4. Oxford University Press.

Briggs, S. 1981: *Those Radio Times*. Weidenfeld & Nicolson.

British Rate and Data (BRAD). Maclean Hunter Ltd.

Brunt, R. 1992: 'A Divine Gift to Inspire' in D. Strinati and S. Wagg (Eds), *Popular Media Culture*. Routledge.

Buckingham, D. 1987: *Public Secrets: EastEnders and its Audience*. BFI.

Burns, T. 1977: *The BBC: Public Institution and Private World*. Macmillan.

Burton, G. 1990: *More than Meets the Eye*. Edward Arnold.

Carr, E.H. 1961: *What is History?*. Macmillan.

Carter, M.D. 1971: *An Introduction to Mass Communications*. Macmillan.

Cater, N. 1985: *Ten 8*, no. 19.

Chanan, M. 1980: *The Dream that Kicks: The Pre-History and Early Years of Cinema in Britain*. Routledge and Kegan Paul.

Channel Four. 1991: *This is Channel Four*. C4.

Chater, K. 1989: *The Television Researcher's Guide*. BBC TV Training.

Chippendale, P. and Horrie, C. 1990: *Stick it Up Your Punter – The Rise and Fall of the Sun*. Heinemann.

Clarke, M. 1987: *Teaching Popular Television*. Heinemann.

Collett, P. 1986: 'The Viewers Viewed'. *The Listener*. 22 May.

Communications Research Group (Aston University). 1990: *Television Advertising and Sex Role Stereotyping*. Broadcasting Standards Council.

Constantine, S. 1986: *Buy and Build: The Advertising Posters of the Empire Marketing Board*. HMSO.

Cook, J. (Ed) 1982: 'Television Sitcom'. BFI Dossier No. 17. BFI.

Cook, P. (Ed) 1985: *The Cinema Book*. BFI.

Cooke, L. 1984: *Media Studies Bibliography*. BFI.

Corner, J. (Ed) 1991: *Popular Television in Britain*. BFI.

Cranfield, G.A. 1978: *The Press and Society*. Longman.

Crisell, A. 1986: *Understanding Radio*. Methuen.

Cumberbatch, G. et al. 1990: *Television Advertising and Sex Role Stereotyping*. Broadcasting Standards Council.

Curran, J. and Porter, V. (Eds) 1983: *British Cinema History*. Weidenfeld & Nicolson.

Curran, J. and Seaton, J. 1991: *Power without Responsibility*. Routledge.

Curran, J., Gurevitch, M. and Woollacott, J. (Eds) 1977: *Mass Communication and Society*. Edward Arnold.

Curtis, L. 1984: *Ireland: The Propaganda War*. Pluto Press.

Daniels, T. and Gerson, J. 1990: *The Colour Black*. BFI.

Davis, A. 1988: *Magazine Journalism Today*. Heinemann.

Donzelot, J. 1980: *The Policing of Families*. Hutchinson.

Dowmunt, T. (Ed) 1993: *Channels of Resistance*. BFI/C4.

Dutton, B. 1986: *The Media*. Longman.

Dutton, B. 1989: *Media Studies: An Introduction*. Longman.
Dyer, G. 1982: *Advertising as Communication*. Methuen.
Dyer, R. 1977: 'Entertainment and Utopia'. *Movie*. Vol. 24.
Eco, U. 1981: *The Role of the Reader*. Hutchinson.
Ellis, J. 1982: *Visible Fictions: Cinema, Television, Video*. Routledge.
Evans, H. 1986: *Pictures on a Page*. Heinemann.
Ferguson, M. 1983: *Forever Feminine: Women's Magazines and the Cult of Femininity*. Heinemann.
Fiske, J. 1982: *Introduction to Communication Studies*. Methuen.
Fiske, J. 1987: *Television Culture*. Routledge.
Fiske, J. and Hartley, J. 1978: *Reading Television*. Methuen.
Fountain, N. 1988: *Underground: The London Alternative Press 1966–1974*. Comedia.
Franklin, B. 1994: *Packaging Politics*. Edward Arnold.
Franklin, B. and Murphy, D. 1991: *What News? The Market, Politics and the Local Press*. Routledge.
Frith, S. 1983: *Sound Effects*. Constable.
Frith, S. and Goodwin, A. (Eds) 1990: *On Record*. Routledge.
Gallup Chart Services. 1993: *The UK Music Charts*.
Gamman, L. and Marshment, M. (Eds) 1988: *The Female Gaze: Women as Viewers of Popular Culture*. The Women's Press.
Garfield, S. 1986: *Expensive Habits: The Dark Side of the Music Industry*. Faber and Faber.
Garnham, N. 1973: *Structures of Television*. BFI Television Monograph No. 1. BFI.
Geraghty, C. 1991: *Women and Soap Opera*. Polity Press.
Gerbner, G. and Gross, L. 1976: 'Living with Television: The Violence Profile'. *Journal of Communication*. Vol. 28 No. 3.
Gillett, C. 1983: *The Sound of the City*. Souvenir.
Glasgow University Media Group. 1976: *Bad News*. Routledge.
Glasgow University Media Group. 1985: *War and Peace News*. Open University Press.
Goldie, G. 1977: *Facing the Nation: Television and Politics, 1936–76*. Bodley Head.
Golding, P. 1974: *The Mass Media*. Longman.
Goodhart, D. and Wintour, C. 1986: *Eddy Shah and the Newspaper Revolution*. Coronet.
Goodwin, A. 1987: *TV Studies Bibliography*. BFI.
Goodwin, A. 1993: *Dancing in the Distraction Factory*. Routledge.
Goodwin, A. and Whannel, G. (Eds) 1992: *Understanding Television*. Routledge.
Gordon, P. and Rosenberg, D. 1989: *Daily Racism*. Runnymede Trust.
Gray, A. 1992: *Video Playtime*. Routledge.
Griffiths, T. 1976: *Comedians*. Faber and Faber.
Gurevitch, M. 1991: 'The Globalisation of Electronic Journalism', in J. Curran and M. Gurevitch (Eds), *Mass Media and Society*. Edward Arnold.
Hall, S. 1980: *Culture, Media, Language*. Hutchinson.
Halloran, J. 1970: *The Effects of Television*. Panther.
Harris, R. 1983: *Gotcha: The Media, the Government and the Falklands Crisis*. Faber and Faber.

Harrison, S. 1974: *Poor Men's Guardians*. Lawrence and Wishart.

Hartley, J. 1982: *Understanding News*. Methuen.

Hartley, J., Goulden, H. and O'Sullivan, T. 1985: *Making Sense of the Media*. Comedia.

Hayward, P. and Wollen, T. (Eds) 1993: *Future Visions: New Technologies of the Screen*. BFI.

Hebdige, D. 1989: 'After the Masses'. *Marxism Today*, January.

Hedgecoe, J. 1991: *On Video*. Hamlyn.

Hetherington, A. 1985: *News, Newspapers and Television*. Macmillan.

HMSO 1966: *Sound and Television Broadcasting in Britain*. HMSO.

HMSO 1992: *Social Trends 22*. HMSO.

Hobson, D. 1982: *Crossroads: The Drama of a Soap Opera*. Methuen.

Hobson, D. 1985: 'Ladies' Men'. *The Listener*. 25 April.

Hodge, B. and Tripp, D. 1986: *Children and Television*. Polity Press.

Hodgson, F. 1984: *Modern Newspaper Practice*. Heinemann.

Hodgson, F. 1987: *Modern Newspaper Editing and Production*. Heinemann.

Hoggart, R. 1957: *The Uses of Literacy*. Pelican.

Hood, S. 1980: *On Television*. Pluto Press.

Izod, J. 1989: *Reading the Screen*. Longman.

James, L. 1976: *Print and the People 1819–1851*. Penguin.

Johnson, R. 1986: 'The story so far and further transformations?' in D. Punter (Ed), *Introduction to Contemporary Cultural Studies*. Longman.

Katz, E. and Liebes, T. 1986: 'Mutual Aid in the Decoding of Dallas' in P. Drummond and R. Paterson (Eds), *Television in Transition*. BFI.

Katz, E. and Liebes, T. 1990: *The Export of Meaning*. Oxford University Press.

Kaye, M. and Popperwell, A. 1992: *Making Radio*. Broadside Books.

Kerr, P. (Ed) 1986: *The Hollywood Film Industry*. Routledge.

Kingsley, H. and Tibballs, G. 1989: *Box of Delights*. Macmillan.

Knightley, P. 1978: *The First Casualty*. Quartet.

Lazarsfeld, P., Berelson, B. and Gaudet, H. 1944: *The People's Choice*. Duell, Sloan and Pearce.

Lealand, G. 1984: *American Television Programmes on British Screens*. Broadcasting Research Unit.

Lee, A.J. 1976: *The Origins of the Popular Press 1855–1914*. Croom Helm.

Levy, E. 1990: 'Social Attributes of American Movie Stars'. *Media Culture and Society*. Vol. 12 No. 2.

Lewis, J. 1991: *The Ideological Octopus*. Routledge.

Lewis, P. and Booth, J. 1989: *The Invisible Medium*. Macmillan.

Local Radio Workshop. 1983: *Capital: Local Radio and Private Profit*. Comedia.

Lull, J. (Ed) 1988: *World Families Watch Television*. Sage.

Lusted, D. (Ed) 1991: *The Media Studies Book*. Routledge.

Madge, J. 1989: *Beyond the BBC*. Macmillan.

Malm, K. and Wallis, R. 1984: *Big Sounds from Small Peoples*. Constable.

Masterman, L. 1984: *Television Mythologies; Stars, Shows and Signs*. Comedia.

Mattelart, A., Delcourt, X. and Mattelart, M. 1984: *International Image Markets*. Comedia.

McIntyre, I. 1993: *The Expense of Glory: A Life of John Reith*. HarperCollins.

McLuhan, M. 1964: *Understanding Media*. Routledge and Kegan Paul.

McMahon, B. and Quinn, R. 1986: *Real Images*. Macmillan.

McMahon, B. and Quinn, R. 1988: *Exploring Images*. Macmillan.

McNair, B. 1993: *News and Journalism in the UK*. Routledge.

McQuail, D. 1975: *Communication*. Longman.

McQuail, D. 1987: *Mass Communication Theory: An Introduction*. Sage.

Media Monitoring Unit. 1990: *Broadcasting and Political Bias*. Hampden Trust.

McRoberts, R. 1987: *Media Workshops*. Vol. 1, *Words*. Macmillan.

Messenger Davies, M. 1989: *Television is Good for Kids*. Hilary Shipman.

Metz, C. 1974: *Film Language*. Oxford University Press.

Miller, W. 1992: 'I Am What I Read'. *The Listener*. 24 April.

Millersen, G. 1989: *Video Production Handbook*. Focal Press.

Monaco, J. 1977: *How to Read a Film: The Art, Technology, Language, History and Theory of Film and Media*. Oxford University Press.

Moores, S. 1993: *Interpreting Audiences*. Sage.

Morgan, J. and Welton, P. 1986: *See What I Mean*. Edward Arnold.

Morley, D. 1980: *The Nationwide Audience*. BFI.

Morley, D. 1986: *Family Television*. Comedia.

Morley, D. 1991: 'Where the Global meets the Local: Notes from the Sitting Room'. *Screen*. Vol. 32 No. 1.

Morley, D. 1992: *Television Audiences and Cultural Studies*. Routledge.

Morley, D. and Whitaker, B. (Eds) 1983: *The Press, Radio and Television*. Comedia.

Mulvey, L. 1975: 'Visual Pleasure and Narrative Cinema'. *Screen*. Vol. 16 No. 3.

Murdock, G. 1974: 'The Politics of Culture' in D. Holly (Ed), *Education or Domination*. Arrow Books.

Murdock, G. and Golding, P. 1991: 'Culture, Communications and Political Economy' in J. Curran and M. Gurevitch (Eds), *Mass Media and Society*. Edward Arnold.

Negrine, R. 1989: *Politics and the Mass Media in Britain*. Routledge.

Negus, K. 1992: *Producing Pop*. Edward Arnold.

Norman, B. 1984: *Here's Looking at You*. BBC.

Orwell, G. 1949: *1984*. Secker and Warburg.

Ostergaard, B. (Ed) 1992: *The Media in Western Europe*. Sage.

O'Sullivan, T., Hartley, J., Saunders, D., Montgomery, M. and Fiske, J. 1994: *Key Concepts in Communication and Cultural Studies*. Routledge.

Packard, V.I. 1957: *The Hidden Persuaders*. Longman.

Partridge, S. 1982: *Not the BBC/IBA – The Case for Community Radio*. Comedia/Minorities Press Group.

Paulu, B. 1981: *Television and Radio in the UK*. Macmillan.

Peacock, A. 1986: HMSO, *Report of the Committee on Financing the BBC*. Cmnd 9824. HMSO.

Peak, S. (Ed): *Guardian Media Book*. Fourth Estate.

Pennachionni, I. 1984: 'The Reception of Television in North East Brazil'. *Media Culture and Society*. Vol. 6 No. 4.

Perkins, T. 1979: 'Rethinking Stereotypes' in M. Barrett, P. Corrigan, A. Kuhn and V. Wolff (Eds), *Ideology and Cultural Production*. Croom Helm.

Petersen, R.A. and Berger, D.G. 1975: 'Cycles in Symbolic Presentation: The Case of Popular Music'. *American Sociological Review*. Vol. 40.

Peterson, R.C. and Thurstone L. 1933: *Motion Pictures and Social Attitudes*. Macmillan.

Pines, J. (Ed) 1992: *Black and White in Colour*. BFI.

Posener, J. 1982: *Spray it Loud*. Pandora.

Power, M. and Sheridan, G. (Eds) 1984: 'Labour Daily? – Ins and Outs of a New Labour Daily and Other Media Alternatives'. Campaign for Press and Broadcasting Freedom.

Propp, V. 1968: *Morphology of the Folk Tale*. University of Texas Press.

Quilliam, S. and Grove-Stephansan, I. 1990: *Into Print*. BBC.

Reeves, G. 1993: *Communications and the 'Third World'*. Routledge.

Reith, J. 1949: *Into the Wind*. Hodder and Stoughton.

Robertson, J.C. 1989: *The Hidden Cinema: British Film Censorship 1913–1972*. Routledge.

Rosen, M. and Widgery, D. 1991: *The Chatto Book of Dissent*. Chatto & Windus.

Sales, R. 1986: 'An Introduction to Broadcasting History' in D. Punter (Ed), *An Introduction to Contemporary Cultural Studies*. Longman.

Scannell, P. 1987: 'The State and Society: Broadcasting Rituals'. OU D209.

Scannell, P. 1987: *The Making of Britain: Mass Media, Mass Democracy*. C4.

Scannell, P. and Cardiff, D. 1991: *A Social History of British Broadcasting*. Vol. 1. Blackwell.

Scannell, P. and Cardiff, D. 1991: 'Popular Culture: Radio in WW2'. OU U203.

Schiller, H. 1969: *Mass Communication and American Empire*. Kelley.

Schlesinger, P. 1987: *Putting Reality Together – BBC News*. Methuen.

Schlesinger, P. 1991: *Media State and Nation*. Sage.

Schlesinger, P. et al. 1992: *Women Viewing Violence*. BFI.

Seymour-Ure, C. 1991: *The British Press and Broadcasting Since 1945*. Blackwell.

Silj, A. (Ed) 1988: *East of Dallas*. BFI.

Smith, J. 1990: *Misogynies*. Faber and Faber.

Snagge, J. and Barsley, M. 1972: *Those Vintage Years of Radio*. Pitman.

Sontag, S. 1977: *On Photography*. Penguin.

Sreberny-Mohammadi, A. 1991: 'The Global and the Local in International Communications' in J. Curran and M. Gurevitch (Eds), *Mass Media and Society*. Edward Arnold.

Stafford, R. 1993: *Hands On*. BFI.

Stead, P. 1989: *Film and the Working Class*. Routledge.

Stokes, P. 1992: *No Apology Needed: The Story of the N.W.N*. Blacket Turner.

Strinati, D. and Wagg, S. (Eds) 1992: *Come On Down: Popular Media*

Culture in Post War Britain. Routledge.

Tasker, Y. 1993: *Spectacular Bodies: Gender, Genre and the Action Cinema*. Routledge.

Taylor, A.J.P. 1965: *English History 1914–45*. Clarendon Press.

Taylor, J. 1991: *War Photography*. Comedia.

Taylor, P. 1992: *Propaganda and Persuasion in the Gulf War*. Manchester University Press.

Thompson, E.P. 1968: *The Making of the English Working Class*. Penguin.

Thompson, J.B. 1988: 'Mass Communication and Modern Culture: Contribution to a Critical Theory of Ideology'. *Sociology*. Vol. 22 No. 3.

Todorov, T. 1973: *The Fantastic: Towards a Structural Approach*. Case Western Reserve University Press.

Tomlinson, J. 1991: *Cultural Imperialism*. Pinter.

Tracey, M. 1985: 'The Poisoned Chalice? International Television and the Idea of Dominance'. *Daedalus*. Vol. 114 No. 4.

Trowler, P. 1989: *Investigating the Media*. Tavistock.

Tunstall, J. 1983: *The Media in Britain*. Constable.

Turkle, S. 1984: *The Second Self: Computers and The Human Spirit*. Granada.

Varis, T. 1974: 'Global Traffic in Television'. *Journal of Communication*. Vol. 24.

Varis, T. 1984: 'The International Flow of Television Programmes'. *Journal of Communication*. Vol. 34 No. 1.

Walker, A. 1986: *Hollywood England*. Harrap.

Ward, K. 1989: *Mass Communications and the Modern World*. Macmillan.

Watson, J. and Hill, A. 1993: *A Dictionary of Communication and Media Studies*. Edward Arnold.

Watts, H. 1984: *On Camera*. BBC.

Watts, H. 1992: *Directing on Camera*. Aavo.

Wenden, D.J. 1974: *The Birth of the Movies*. Dutton.

Whitaker, B. (Ed) 1984: *News Ltd: Why You Can't Read All About It*. Comedia.

Williams, R. 1965: *The Long Revolution*. Pelican.

Williams, R. 1966: *Communications*. Chatto & Windus.

Williams, R. 1974: *Television, Technology and Cultural Form*. First edn, Fontana. Second edn, Routledge 1990.

Williams, R. 1976: *Keywords: A Vocabulary of Culture and Society*. Fontana.

Williams, R. 1990: *Television: Technology and Cultural Form*. Routledge.

Williamson, J. 1978: *Decoding Advertisements: Ideology and Meaning in Advertising*. Marion Boyars.

Willings Press Guide. Vol. 1. Reed Information Services.

Winn, M. 1977: *The Plug-in Drug*. Penguin.

Winship, J. 1987: *Inside Women's Magazines*. Pandora.

Index

'A' Level Media Studies ix
A & R 216
Abba 121
Abyss, The 139
Access 278
Adams, Bryan 190
Advertising
  analysis 90–2
  drugs 155
  Gillette 139
  Levi jeans 90, 190, 226, 282
  myth 115
  new media 278
  revenue 194–5, 237, 240
  regulation 204
  stereotypes 13
Advertising Standards Authority (ASA) 204
Aldus Pagemaker 266
Alien 97, 100, 139, 187
Allen, R 158–9
Alternative local press 231
Alternative media 205, 226
Alvarado, M 290, 292
Anchorage 82, 163
Ang, I 168, 178, 295
Annan Report 65
Another Country 140
Apocalypse Now 101
Archers, The 77
Arena 137
Armes, R 44
Arts Channel, performance 277
Arts Council 208
Asian Leader 149
Asian Vision 276
Askey, Arthur 54
Associated Newspapers 229
Atlantic Records 212
Auden, W H 107
Audience
  gender 130, 169
  identification 137, 158
  positioning 157
  profile 164, 194, 268
  research 164
  targeting 72, 160, 194, 248, 249
Auteurs 196

Baby Boom 102
Back To The Future 100, 103
Bad News 122–3
Bad Timing 92

Bandung File 149
Bandura, A 152
Bandwagon 54
Bangles, The 121
Barker, M 127, 158, 176
Barthes, R 81, 115
Basic Instinct 140
Batman 90, 167, 187, 188
Battle of Britain 116
BBC 25–75, 121, 123, 125, 149, 152, 160, 198, 201, 203, 224
BBC Charter 1996 72
BBC Radio Berkshire 237
BBC2 65
Beano 176
Beatles, The 211, 217
Beatty, Warren 193
Beaverbrook, Lord 34
Beharrel, M 232, 244
Behind the Beat 149
Benetton 204, 282
Benns Directory 229
Benny, Jack 55
Berelson, B 154
Berger D 211
Beverly Hills Cop 145
Bias 122
Bill, The 104
Big Breakfast, The 256
Big Sleep, The 93
Biography and media 26
Birmingham Evening Mail 242
Birt, John 52, 73
Bite 136
Black and White Minstrel Show, The 142
Black Dwarf 39
Blazing Saddles 104
Blue Velvet 100
Blumler, J 155–6
BMG 214
Body Language 262
Bohemian Rhapsody 224
Bogart, Humphrey 131
Bonanza 294
Bond, James 92, 100
Bono 282
Born on the 4th July 101
Bowie, David 137
Box, The 276
Boyd, A 261
Brass Tacks 124
Bread 105

Breakfast television 160
Breakfast With Frost 65
Brit Awards, The 224
British Board of Film Classification 151, 203
British Film Institute (BFI) 208
Britten, Benjamin 107
Broadcasting Act (1981) 65
Broadcasting Act (1990) 66, 69, 124
Broadcasting Audience Research Board (BARB) 166
Broadcasting Complaints Commission 204
Broadcasting – historical development 49–75
Broadcasting in the 1990s 67
Broadcasting Research Unit (BRU) 67
Broadcasting Standards Council 204
Bronson, Charles 131
Brookside 95, 105
Brunt, R 118
BSB 64
BSkyB 64, 191, 193, 283
BTEC Media ix
Buckingham, D 168
Bush, George 125

Cable TV 272, 275–7, 281, 283
Cagney and Lacey 139
Calpix Records 217
Campbell, Duncan 201
Capital Radio 256
Candid Camera 108
Cardiff, D 51
Carlton Television 69
Carr, E H 26
Carter, M 27
Cathy Come Home 61
Caxton, William 25
CBS 192, 211, 213, 214, 283
CD personal stereo 272
Censorship and war coverage 121, 125, 201
Central Office of Information (COI) 86
Central Television 69
Centre for Contemporary Cultural Studies 162
Chanan, M 15, 25, 44
Chandler, Raymond 93
Channel Four 26, 65, 121, 140, 149, 160, 194, 204, 208, 209, 224, 256
Chaplin, Charlie 295
Character functions 100
Chart Show, The 224

Children's Channel 277
Children, TV consumption 5
Children, media effects 152, 154
Child's Play 3 151
Chippendale, P 162, 198
Chris Tarrant's Breakfast Show 256
Chrysalis Records 211
Churchill, Winston 201
Cinema (*see also* Hollywood)
   attendance 7, 25, 48
   censorship 203
   history and development 44–9, 281
   independent 207–8
   primary medium 179
   representation of race 145
   spectators 157–8
Cinematographic Act (1909) 47
Cinema verité 107
Citizen Kane 92, 97
Clapton, Eric 219
Clarke, M 101
Classic FM 70, 193, 249, 269
Closed texts 82
Close Encounters 100
CNN 294
Cobbett, William 37
Coca Cola 282
Codes 84, 157, 163, 196
   action 97
   enigma 97
   narrative (*see also* Narrative) 92–100
   symbolic 84, 88
   technical 84, 87
   visual 80–90
   written 84, 87
Collett, P 180, 182
Collins, Joan 176
Columbia 188, 283
Comedians 128
Comics and subversion 176
Commission for Racial Equality
   (CRE) 109–10
Commodities, media 8
Communications revolution 272
Community radio 149
Compact discs 213–14, 219, 226
Company 136
Computers 183, 272, 275, 278
Computer games 272
Conglomerates 188, 190, 283–4
Connotative meanings 81
Content analysis 108, 133, 242
Consciousness industries 16
Consumer choice 278
Consumer durables 8
Consumer society 17
Consumer sovereignty 278
Conventions 90, 157, 163, 196, 250
Copytaster 243
Coronation Street 139, 147, 156
Cosby Show, The 147, 177, 178
Cosmopolitan 136, 138, 282
Cranfield, G 32
Crisell, A 179
Crocodile Dundee 103
Cropping 82
Crossing the line 264
Crossroads 174
Culloden 108
Cultivation analysis 166
Culture, and media 19–21
Cultural capital 169
Cultural competence 168
Cultural imperialism 178
Cultural intermediary 216
Cultural pessimists 279

Cumberbatch, G 133
Curran, J 40, 43, 51, 76, 191, 198, 236, 279
Curtis, L 125

Daily Courant, The 25, 36
Daily Express 198
Daily Herald 195
Daily Mail 79, 191, 195
Daily Mirror 162, 195, 198
Daily Telegraph, The 43, 134, 195
Daily Star 191
Daily Worker 201
Dallas 105, 106, 168, 178, 267, 279, 284,
   294–5
Day, Robin 59–60
Dambusters, The 116
Darling Buds of May, The 193
Davis, Bette 139
Death on the Rock 67, 125
Decoding *see* Encoding
Def Jam 149
Defiant Ones, The 145
Del Monte 282
Demand and supply in media
   development 31–6
Denotative meanings 81
Dependency, media dependency 16
Deregulation 278
Dern, Laura 189
Desert Hearts 140
Desktop Publishing 219, 272
Desmonds 149
Destructive, The 39
Die Hard 92
Different World, A 147
Digital technologies 272
Dimbleby, Richard 59–60
Dire Straits 219
Dixon of Dock Green 61
D.O.A. 92
Documentary 105, 107
Docudrama 105
Donovan, Jason 282
Donzelot, J 22
Do the Right Thing 145
Dowmunt, T 293
Dressed to Kill 140
Dumb Blonde 129
Dyer, R 156, 169, 174
Dynasty 176

EastEnders 105, 147, 168
East End News 231
Eastwood, Clint 102
Eco, U 168
Editing, audio, video, print 265–6
Effects Research 151–2
Eldorado 72, 198
Electronic newsroom 237
Ellis, J 102, 180
EMAP 229
EMI 214, 218, 284
Empire Marketing Board 85
Encoding, decoding 76–80, 162, 168, 179
English, David 191
Equilibrium, disequilibrium (in narrative) 99
E.T. 100
Ethnography 167
EuroNews 277
European, The 282
Evans, Harold 191
Everything I Do, I Do For You 190
Everywoman 140
Extending Choice (BBC) 73

Factory Records 212

Falklands War 51, 105, 116, 119, 201
Family Pride 149
Family, The 107
Family photograph albums 96
Family Viewing 159, 181
Fanzines 193, 206
   football 206
   music 206, 226
Farewell My Lovely 93
Fatal Attraction 140, 187
Faulty Towers 142
Feminism 130, 134, 140, 177
Femme fatale 140
Ferguson, M 111, 138
Ferris Beuller's Day Off 158
Fibre Optic systems 275
Fiji Times, The 287
Film (*see* cinema)
   cooperative production 196
   production costs 193
Film noir 135
Financial Times 194, 282
Fiske, J 92, 106, 177
Flow, radio and television 90, 103, 179–80
Fly on the wall 107–8
Ford, John 102
For Women 136
Fosters, The 147
Fox 283
Franklin, B 17, 229, 242, 244
Freesheet 230
Frith, S 216, 223

Gallup 221, 224
Gamesmaster 137
Game Shows 103
Garfield, S 210
Garnett, Alf 142
Garnham, N 51
Gatekeeper 216
Gaudet, B 154
Gauntlet, The 39
Gay
   audiences 136, 176
   disco 226
   representations of 140, 176
GCSE Media Studies ix
Gender
   audiences 130, 169
   narrative 101
   representations of 130, 134, 135, 137,
      176
   technology 183
   television viewing 182
General Strike (1926) 51
Genre 101–4, 250, 268
Gentlemen's Quarterly (GQ) 137
George, Boy 137, 220
Geraghty, C 101, 147, 173–4
Gerbner, G 166
Ghost 208
Ghostwatch 152
Glasgow University Media Group 111,
   122–4
Global culture 90, 271, 280–96
Global village 13, 283
Globalisation 188
GMTV 69
GNVQ Media Studies ix
Godfather, The 101
Goldblum, Jeff 189
Golding, P 31, 35, 283
Gone With The Wind 141
Good, The Bad and The Ugly, The 102
Gordon, D 142
Gordon, Noele 174

Gordy, Berry 149
Gorgon, The 39
GPO Film Unit 107
Graef, Roger 107
Gray, A 169, 183
Greene, Hugh 61
Gremlins 100
Grierson, John 107
Griffiths, Trevor 128
Gross, L 166
Guardian, The ix, 230
Gulf War 51, 116, 119, 125, 201
Gulf Between Us, The 121
Gurevitch, M 294

Haley, Bill 141
Hall, S 162–3
Halloran, J 155
Hand That Rocks The Cradle, The 140
Hard News 134
Hardy, Oliver 158
Hartley, J 24
Harvey, P J 212
Hawn, Goldie 129
Hebdige, D 284
Hegemonic model 114, 162, 163, 178, 193
Hepburn, Katherine 139
Hetherington, A 122–4
Hidden Agenda 105
Hidden Persuaders, The 151
Highway 73
Hill Street Blues 147
Hip Hop Connection 219
History, media development 25–75
Hitchcock, Alfred 196
HMV 218
Hobson, D 135, 174
Hodge, B 176
Hoffman, Dustin 131, 139, 193
Hoggart, R 61
Hollywood 140, 141, 145, 147, 151, 158, 187, 198, 208, 215, 290
Home and Away 105, 130
Hood, S 17
Hope, B 55
Horrie, C 162, 198
House Party 145
Houston, Whitney 190
Hussein, Saddam 121, 125
Hypodermic needle effect 152

IBA 63
I Heard It Through The Grapevine 226
I Will Always Love You 190
Identity and the media 12–13
Identity Television 276
Ideological effects 127, 154–5, 162–3, 178, 191–2
Ideology 114, 118, 126, 169, 246
    gender 130
    race 140
Illustrated London News 43
ILR 26, 63, 194, 220, 224, 237
Impartiality and broadcasting 122, 124
Implication, extrication 168
Independent cinema 207–8
Independent local press 213
Independent, The 90, 204
Independent on Sunday, The 190
Independent media production 148, 149, 204, 207
Independent record companies 210, 211, 226
Independent television 58
Information society 17

Ingersoll Corporation 230
INR 70
In Sickness and in Health 142
Inspector Morse 104
Institution 186
Interactivity 275
Intertextuality 90, 167, 177
Interviews 261
Interview guidelines 263
In the Heat of the Night 145
Integration, vertical and horizontal 187
Invention and media development 35
Invisible Sun 125
IRA 125, 201
Ishtar 193
Island Records 149, 212–3
It Ain't Half Hot Mum 142
ITA 58
ITC 67, 204
ITN 59, 123
ITV 194, 204, 205
I've Heard The Mermaids Singing 140

Jackson, Michael 137, 176, 215, 225, 282
Jaws 105
Jazz FM 224
Jazz Singer, The 141
Jeffersons, The 147
John Bull 42
John, Elton 121
Jolson, Al 141
Jurassic Park 105, 189–90
Just Seventeen 137, 139, 219
Justify My Love 226

Katz, E 155–6, 178, 295
Kerrang! 219
Kiss FM 224
KLF 217
Kramer vs Kramer 139
Kuffs 158

Lamb, Larry 191
Landscape Channel, The 276
Lang, Jack 294
Laurel, Stan 158
Lazarsfeld, P 154
Lealand, G 294
Learning Channel, The 277
Lee, Spike 143, 147
Leeds Other Paper 231
Legal controls 34
Lesbian
    audiences 176
    representations of 140, 176
Letters to the Editor 240–1
Letter to Brezhnev 208
Levy, E 131
Lewis, Jerry 131
Lewis, J 177–8
Libel 203
Liebes, T 178, 295
Literacy 33, 43
Live Aid 144, 224
Lloyds Weekly News 43
Loach, Ken 105
Local newspapers
    circulations 230
    sources of news 233
Lonhro 191, 198, 230
Look Who's Talking 102
Love Story 105, 171
Lull, J 182–3
Lumiere, Louis & Auguste 44

Lusted, D 129
Lynch, Bet 139
Lynch, David 100, 196

Madonna 135, 176, 215, 225–6, 282
Magazines
    modes of address 161, 180
    women's 161
Malcolm X 143
Mam 209
Manchester Evening News 230
Manchester Free Press 231
Marketing 217
Marlboro 282
Marley, Bob 149
Marx, K and ideology 114–5, 178, 191
Mass communication 13–16, 20, 22–4
Mass manipulation 151–2
Matsushita 69, 188
Mattelart, A 291
Maxwell, Robert 195, 198, 203
MCA 188
McDonald, Trevor 147
McLuhan, Marshall 13, 283
McKenzie, Kelvin 196, 198
McQuail, D 13, 14
Media consumption 10
Media commodities 8, 15
Media diary 2
Media events 17
Media generations 26, 273
Media, historical development 25–75
Media imperialism 289–96
Media Monitoring Unit 123
Media policy 271
Media practice and production 246–70
Media saturation x, 1–17
Mediation 12–13, 18–19, 77
Melody Maker 219
Men *see* Gender
Meridian TV 237
Messenger Davies, M 153
Metz, C 46
Miami Vice 292
Michael, George 217
Mind Your Language 142
Miners Campaign Tapes 208–9
Miners/Coal strike (1984–5) 123
Miller, W 154
Minogue, Kylie 217
Minority broadcasting 65–6
Mirren, Helen 139
Mirrors, media mirrors 16
Mizz 137
Mode of address 93, 158, 205
Modernisation 288–90
Mona Lisa 101
Monkees, The 217
Monroe, Marilyn 129
Moral panics 19, 151, 232
Moroder, Georgio 216
Morley, D 167, 168, 176, 182, 283
Ms 139
MTV 180, 225, 282, 294
Multimarketing 188
Multiset (multichannel, multiscreen) homes 8, 272, 274
Mulvey, L 134, 158
Murdoch, Rupert 34, 68, 162, 188, 191, 198, 202, 205, 283
Murdock, G 20, 283
Murphy, D 229, 242, 244
Murphy, Eddie 145, 177
Music industry 210–26
Music press 219
Music Week 212–3

My Beautiful Launderette 101, 208
Myth 115

Narration 93
Narrative 92–100, 153
  cinema 158
  character functions 100
  classical narrative structure 137
  gender 101, 175, 177
  time 93
Narrator 93–7
Narrowcasting 72, 195
National Geographic 282
Nation, representations of 160, 280
National broadcasting 49
National Council for the Training of
  Journalists (NCTJ) 232
National Curriculum x
National Viewers and Listeners Association
  (NVALA) 71
Nationwide 168
Negrine, R 17
Negus, K 212, 216
Neighbours 105, 217
Neil, Andrew 191
Neophiliacs 279
New Manchester Review 231
New Musical Express 219
Newbury Weekly News, The 233–45, 249
New print technologies 237
New World Information Order 291
News and race 142
News At Ten 73, 106
News Chronicle 195
News Corporation 188, 205
News International 64, 283
News of the World 43
Newspapers
  advertising revenue 194–5
  circulations 11, 39, 230
  editors 191, 196, 240
  history 36–43
  local 229
  modes of address 161–2, 180
  ownership 202
  politics 154, 195
  pop music coverage 219–20
  readerships 10
  regulation 202, 203
  and the royal family 119
News value 243
Newsweek 282
Nicholson, Jack 168
Night Mail 107
Nightmare on Elm Street 102, 187
999 108
1984 18
Northcliffe 34
Northern Ireland and media coverage 105,
  125, 201
Northern Star, The 231

Oakenfold, Paul 216
Obscene Publications Act (1990) 202
Observer, The 191, 198
Official Secrets Act 122, 201
Old Devils, The 97
Olympic Games 15, 251
Open questions 263
Open texts 82
Open Your Heart 135
Opinion Leaders 154
Oral history 48
Orwell, George 18
O'Sullivan, T 187
Our Price 218

Out 140
Outlaw Josey Wales, The 100
Ownership 64, 71, 187, 191–2, 202, 229,
  296

Packard, V 151
Paine, Tom 37
Pallas 119
Panorama 121
Parliamentary Channel, The 277
Patten, John ix
Payne studies 152
Pay per view 276
Pearson Longman Group 230
Peeping Tom 135
Penacchioni, I 295
Penny Magazine, The 41
Penny Politician, The 39
Peoples Choice, The 154
Period drama 105
Perkins, T 126–7
Peterloo Massacre 39
Peterson, R A 211
Pet Shop Boys 219
Photographs 81
Photography 45
Pierce, C 81
Pilkington Committee (1962) 65
Pirate Ratio 62, 205, 226
Playboy 177
Playlist, radio 220
Plug in Drug 151
Plums, The 57
Pluralist model 119, 178, 193
Point of view 93
Poitier, Sidney 145
Police Academy 102
Police series 104
Police Story 104
Police, The 107
Political controls 201
Political economy 191
Political Handkerchief, The 39
Political impact of media 17
Political persuasion 154
Political Touchwood, The 39
Polygram Records 212, 214
Polysemy 82, 157, 163, 176, 178
Poor Man's Guardian, The 38, 39
Popular Culture 22
Porcupine, The 39
Pornography, and censorship 203
Pop videos 135–6
Post Courier, The (PNG) 288
Postmodern conditions 282
Post-production 265
Pre-production 248
Press Complaints Commission (PCC) 203
Preferred meaning/reading 82, 163, 169
Presley, Elvis 141, 210
Primary medium 179
Primary, Secondary and Tertiary media
  consumption/involvement 2–3
Prime Suspect 139
Prisoner in Cell Block H 176
Private Eye 203, 210
Private sphere 22
Professional
  autonomy 193, 196
  codes 142, 232
  routines 162, 232
Professionalism 196, 246–7
Project planner 252
Propaganda 119, 151
Propp, V 100
Pryor, Richard 145

Psycho 135
Public Service Broadcasting 19, 160, 278
Public sphere 22

Q Magazine 219, 224
Quantum Leap 96
Queen 224
Quiz Shows 103
QVC, Home Shopping Channel 275

Race, representations of 140–2, 145, 176
Radical press 36–43, 78, 205
Radio Authority 67, 71, 204, 238
Radio
  formats 160, 220–3
  flow 179
  listening 7, 63
  phone-ins 160
  regulation 204
  as a secondary medium 2–3, 179
Radio Caroline 62
Radio Luxembourg 54
Radio Normandie 54
Radio 1 62, 160, 220, 224
Radio Times 10, 49, 50
Rambo 92
Rape, representations of 134
RCA 210
Readers Digest 282
Readerships
  magazines 11
  newspapers 10
Real Lives 51, 125, 204
Realism 104, 153, 177
Rebel Without A Cause 101
Received Pronounciation (RP) 160
Reception Theory 157–8, 168, 179
Record Companies and music
  production 216
Red Flannel 209
Red Rose Group 231
Reed Regional Newspapers 229
Regional press 230
Regulation 193, 198
Reith, John 49, 52
Representations
  gender 176
  nation 115, 160
  race and ethnicity 140–2, 145, 176
  royal family 117–8, 160
Research, production research 251
Resolution 92
Rhetoric 159, 163
Right to Reply 65
Rising Damp 142
Robin Hood, Prince of Thieves 190
Roche, Mazo de la 86–7
Rocky 102, 193
Rocky Horror Show, The 104
Rolling Stones, The 211
Rosenberg, P 142
Ross, Diana 149
Rough Guide series 144
Rough Trade 211
Rowland, Tiny 191, 198
Royal Commission on the Press (1977) 236

Saturday Night's Alright for Fighting 121
Satellite television 15, 64, 149, 191, 193,
  202, 225, 271–2, 281, 284, 291
Saussure, F de 81
Scannell, P 51, 61
Schiller, H 290
Schlesinger, P 134
Screen 157, 164
Script preparation 257

Searchers, The 101–2
Seaton, J 40, 43, 51, 191, 236, 279
Secondary medium 2–3, 179
Secret Society 51, 201
Segmentation 235
Selective exposure, perception 154
Semiology 157
Semiotics 80, 92
Seven Year Itch 129
Seymour-Ure, C 17
S4C 65
Shaft 145
Shah, Eddie 231
Shooting schedule 253
Signs 80
Silj, A 295
Situated culture 12–13, 81, 104
Situation comedies 104, 142, 177, 194
Sky 64–65, 275
Smash Hits 219
Smith, J 134
Smith, W.H. 218
Sniffin Glue 219
Soap opera 95, 105, 111, 130, 139, 147,
    168, 173–5, 180, 194, 198
Social concern and the media 18–19
Society for the Diffusion of Useful
    Knowledge 41
Songs of Praise 77
Sontag, S 95
Sony 69, 188, 213, 283
Spectators 157
Spector, Phil 216
Spectrum 277
Spielberg Steven 100, 189
Spitting Image 119
Stallone, Sylvester 193
Stars, film and media 131, 187, 215, 216
Star Trek 96, 102
Starsky and Hutch 139
Steptoe and Son 61
Stereotypes 14, 126, 142, 147
    dumb bonde 129
    gender 134–5, 154
    race and ethnicity 141–2, 147, 154
Stone, Sharon 140
Storyboards 258
Stranger Among Us, A 140
Streisand, Barbra 131
Structuralism 157
Suez 51
Sun Records 210
Sun, The 9, 116, 121, 134, 154, 162, 164,
    191, 194, 195, 196, 198, 220
Sunday Times, The 68, 90, 191
Sunrise Radio 149
Super Channel 277
Superman 102
Supply and demand in media
    development 15–16, 31–6
Suture 157
Swanson, G 129
Sylvania Waters 107
Synergy 190

Talking heads 250, 254
Tamla Motown Records 149
Tanner, Elsie 139
Target groups 14, 72, 248, 249
Taylor, A J P 48
Technology
    media development 34

media and gender 185
media and technologies 14, 246
new media 271–80
new musical 216
new print 237
Technological determinism 35, 274
'Technicist trap' 247
Telenovellas 183
Telephone ownership 278
Television
    domestic medium 180–2
    gender representation 130, 134–5
    grammar 257
    modes of address 159
    politics 122
    regulation of 71, 186, 204
    sex role stereotypes 132
    representations of race 147
    ratings 3–6, 166
    uses and gratifications 155–6
    viewing 3–6
Television is Good For Your Kids 153
Telstar 26
Tennant, Neil 219
Terminator, The 139
Terminator 2 187
Terrorism 125
Tertiary medium 2–3, 179
Thames Television 125
Thatcher, Margaret 69, 125, 191
That Was The Week That Was 61
Third World, representations of 144
Thompson J B 13–15
Thompson Regional Papers 229
Threads 105
Three Men and a Baby 102
Thriller 177, 225
Time 176, 249, 282
Time and the media 3–8, 283
Time Out 231
Time Warner 69
Times, The 25, 28–31, 37, 164, 191, 205
Title sequences 96, 254
Today 192
Tomlinson, J 295
Too Pure Records 213
Top of the Pops 125, 224
Trafalgar 27
Trelford, Donald 191
Tripp, D 176
True Crimes 108
Truly, Madly, Deeply 208
Tube, The 224
Tumbledown 105
Tunstall, J 2, 48, 179
Turkle, S 183
TV-AM 67
TV Times 10
Twin Peaks 104
Two-step flow 154
2.4 Children 104
24 Hours 145
2000 AD 137

UK Gold 65
Ulysses 93
UNESCO 291
United Newspapers 229
Universal 188, 189
Unstamped press 37, 78
Uses and gratifications survey 156–7,
    178

Varis, T 290, 292
VCTV 275
Velvet Underground, The 226
Video 143, 180, 183
    cassette recorders 8, 183, 272
    games 183
    hiring of pre-recorded tapes 9
    ownership 278
    nasties 18, 151
    pop 177, 224–5
    world wide VCR's 285
Video diaries 108
Video Recordings Act 151
Vietnam War 119
Vision Broadcasting 277
Virgin Records 218, 224
Virgin 1215 70–1
Viz 193, 205, 210
Voice, The 149
Voice overs 258
Vox Pops 265
Voyeurism 134–5

Waiting for God 104
Walk Like an Egyptian 121
Walters, R 152
War and Peace 93
War of the Worlds 152
Waterloo 121
Watson, Paul 107
Wayne, John 102, 131
WEA Records 214
Weekly Journal, The 149
Welles, Orson 152, 196
We Speak for Ourselves 55
Wham 217
When a Man Loves a Woman 226
When Saturday Comes 206
White Dwarf, The 39
Who Bombed Birmingham 105
Williams, R 22, 35, 61, 179, 180, 274
Williamson, J 115
'Windows on the world' 16
Winfrey, Oprah 147
Winn, M 151
Winship, J 139, 161
WNK 149, 224
Women *see* Gender
Women's fiction 173
Women's magazines 137
Women and narrative 101
Womens Peace Camp, Greenham
    Common 242
Wonder, Stevie 149
Word, The 224
Word processors 272
World In Action 122, 124
World music 282
World Radio Receivers 285
World TV Receivers 285
World VCR's 285
World War Two 18, 54, 61, 86, 116,
    281
Working Man's Friend, The 39

Young Ones, The 105
You've Been Framed 108

Z Cars 61
Zimbabwe TV 292
Zoo TV 256